Nova Doctrina Vetusque

American University Studies

Series VII
Theology and Religion

Vol. 207

PETER LANG
New York • Washington, D.C./Baltimore • Boston
Bern • Frankfurt am Main • Berlin • Vienna • Paris

Nova Doctrina Vetusque

Essays on Early
Christianity in Honor
of Fredric W. Schlatter, S.J.

Edited by
Douglas Kries
and Catherine Brown Tkacz

PETER LANG
New York • Washington, D.C./Baltimore • Boston
Bern • Frankfurt am Main • Berlin • Vienna • Paris

Library of Congress Cataloging-in-Publication Data

Nova doctrina vetusque: essays on early Christianity in honor
of Fredric W. Schlatter, S.J. / edited by Douglas Kries and Catherine Brown Tkacz.
p. cm. — (American university studies. VII, Theology and religion; vol. 207)
Includes bibliographical references and index.
1. Church history—Primitive and early church, ca. 30–600. 2. Church history—
Middle Ages, 600–1500. I. Schlatter, Fredric W. II. Kries, Douglas.
III. Tkacz, Catherine Brown. IV. Series: American university studies.
Series VII, Theology and religion; vol. 207.
BR162.2.N68   270.1—dc21   98-26795
ISBN 0-8204-4136-8
ISSN 0740-0446

Die Deutsche Bibliothek-CIP-Einheitsaufnahme

Nova doctrina vetusque: essays on early Christianity in honor
of Fredric W. Schlatter, S.J. / ed. by Douglas Kries and Catherine Brown Tkacz.
–New York; Washington, D.C./Baltimore; Boston; Bern;
Frankfurt am Main; Berlin; Vienna; Paris: Lang.
(American university studies: Ser. 7, Theology and religion; Vol. 207)
ISBN 0-8204-4136-8

The paper in this book meets the guidelines for permanence and durability
of the Committee on Production Guidelines for Book Longevity
of the Council of Library Resources.

Printed in the United States of America.

. . . neque enim nova tantum contenti debemus esse doctrina, sed et ueterem excolere et nostro iungere comitatui, si tamen sacro cultu fuerit erudita.

We must not be content with the new doctrine alone, but also refine and unite with our own community the old, if within that sacred worship there was erudite doctrine.

St. Jerome
In Ezechielem 13.44.22–31

TABLE OF CONTENTS

ACKNOWLEDGMENTS

Many people have contributed generously to this project: The three photographs by John Travlos appearing in Professor Kleinbauer's essay were originally published in *Bildlexikon zur Topographie des antiken Attika* (1988). They are republished here by permission of Ernst Wasmuth Verlag, Tübingen. The photograph by Alison Frantz is published by permission of the Photographic Archives at the American School of Classical Studies at Athens. The text of the volume was skillfully composed by Sandy Hank, of Faculty Services at Gonzaga University. Patrick Ford, S.J, and Michael W. Tkacz, both of Gonzaga University, have graciously supported the project, as have Robert C. Carriker and the William L. Davis, S.J., Lectureship at Gonzaga University.

ABBREVIATIONS

AASS   *Acta Sanctorum*

AC   *Antike und Christentum*

CCG   Corpus Christianorum Series Graeca

CCL   Corpus Christianorum Series Latina

CSEL   Corpus Scriptorum Ecclesiasticorum Latinorum

DACL   *Dictionnaire d'archéologie chrétienne et de liturgie*

FC   Fathers of the Church

GCS   Die griechischen christlichen Schriftsteller

IG   *Inscriptiones graecae*

IGLS   *Inscriptions grecques et latines de la Syrie*

IGSK   *Inschriften griechischer Städte aus Kleinasien*

NPNF   Nicene and Post-Nicene Fathers of the Church

ODB   *Oxford Dictionary of Byzantium*

OLD   *Oxford Latin Dictionary*

PG   Patrologiae Cursus Completus Series Graeca

PL   Patrologiae Cursus Completus Series Latina

RAC   *Reallexicon für Antike und Christentum*

REA   *Realencyclopädie der klassischen Altertumswissenschaft*

SC   Sources chrétiennes

INTRODUCTION

Nova doctrina vetusque, the new teaching and the old, are doubly relevant to this volume of essays. The phrase can readily be taken to refer to Early Christian studies generally, the broad subject of this collection. From the vantage point of the end of the second millennium, the patristic era is old, and what we do today to understand and interpret it is new. The phrase is also, however, used by St. Jerome in his commentary on the Book of Ezekiel in a passage that Fredric W. Schlatter, S.J., the scholar whom this volume honors, has recently brought to our attention as containing "an astonishing statement expressing Jerome's willingness to see the wisdom of Hellenism absorbed into the teaching of the Church." Jerome, he has pointed out, asks us to respect both *nova doctrina* and *vetus doctrina*, both "the wisdom contained in the law and the prophets" and the wisdom of Hellenism "refined and clarified by Christianity."[1] The essays here gathered to honor Professor Schlatter treat the patristic era and its influence in later culture and are offered by colleagues, former students, fellow members of the Society of Jesus, and those whose work has proceeded along paths kindred to Fr. Schlatter's own research.

The sixteen essays in the volume are, for the most part, ordered chronologically according to the first work substantively treated in each essay. The first three essays, however, treat topics that extend to many centuries. The collection begins with Rev. Prof. W. H. C. Frend's magisterial analysis of the development of the archaeology of Early Christianity, which he views as an evolution "From Confessional Propaganda to International Scholarship." The breadth of coverage is chronological, confessional, and geographic, spanning its "uneasy" beginnings with the empress Helena ca. 326/27 to the present and including discoveries of orthodox, Montanist, Donatist, Monophysite, Manichaean, and Gnostic material. Finds from places as wide-flung as Water Newton, England and Chinese Turkestan are treated.

The second essay, by Robert F. Taft, S.J., is concerned with the eucharistic symbols pertaining to unity. The exhaustive study especially explores the origin and development of the ancient practices of the "eulogy," or the sending of a piece of eucharistic bread to bishops of neighboring churches; the *fermentum*, or distribution of the Eucharist from the pope's Mass to the presbyters of the Roman *tituli;* and the commingling of the particle of consecrated bread into the eucharistic wine. Fr. Taft considers the evidence as it is found in sources as early as Ignatius of Antioch and as late as Theodore of Mopsuestia. He argues that these liturgical customs have their origin as early as the second century, and he traces their development into the seventh century.

The third study that stretches across many centuries is that of Daniel J. Nodes, who considers the thought of Origen of Alexandria (ca. 185–ca. 254), its revival by Renaissance Humanists in 1481–1510, and also the reception of that revival by twentieth-century historians. Just as Fr. Schlatter has argued that St. Jerome has influenced Early Christian art in the form of the apse mosaic at Santa Pudenziana, so Dr. Nodes supports theories of Origen's influence on several works of fifteenth-century Florentine art, including Lorenzo Ghiberti's "Gates of Paradise," the gilded east doors of the Baptistery, and works by Botticelli in the Sistine Chapel.

The volume then turns to essays focussing on a particular figure or movement in Early Christianity. Although Eusebius of Caesarea (ca. 260–339/40) has been especially kind to subsequent historians because of his practice of citing his own historiographic sources, there are a few passages in his *Historia Ecclesiastica*—seven, to be exact—in which he uncharacteristically does not tell us whom he is following. These "Seven Unidentified Sources" are considered by Andrew J. Carriker, who considers the arguments regarding the various authors that have been suggested as sources for Eusebius' discussions of Pilate's suicide, the famine in the reign of Claudius, Nero's depravity, the exile of Flavia Domitilla, St. John's sojourn at Ephesus, the Jewish War of 115–117, and the rain miracle of 172. He himself contributes the suggestion that Cassius Dio was the bishop's source for *Historia Ecclesiastica* 3.20.8 and that Hegesippus furnished the information at 3.18.4.

The dynamic christocentric exegesis of St. Athanasius (298/99–373), archbishop of Antioch from 328, is demonstrated in Charles Kannengiesser's analysis of "Lady Wisdom's Final Call: The Patristic Recovery of Proverbs 8." Distinctive as the only leader of the Alexandrian church who wrote no biblical commentaries and who proceeded with no Origenist allegory, Athanasius produced what, in fact, constituted the patristic era's most extended "commentary" on Proverbs 8 in his second *Oration against the Arians* (completed in 339). For two decades Arius and his followers had focused on this scriptural passage, taking it literally as implying that the second person of the Trinity was in some sense created. The archbishop counters their interpretation with a creative reading of this passage that is consistent with the context of scripture generally. Professor Kannengiesser also engages this fourth-century exegete with contemporary biblical critics.

The Vulgate version of the Bible, on which St. Jerome labored from 382–406, is the subject of two essays in the present collection. The first treats "Seeking Classical Allusions in the Vulgate" and is part of the ongoing work in the new field of literary studies of the Vulgate. Fittingly is this research included here, for Fr. Schlatter has been an insightful and encouraging supporter of this new field for several years. Building on the discovery that when translating the Bible St. Jerome drew on diction from a passage with relevant parallels in Ovid's *Metamorphoses* to construct a classical allusion, the essay explores which texts by which classical authors it may be likely that Jerome drew on in his biblical translations, and for which biblical books. The forty-six classical authors Jerome quotes in his original compositions, including his biblical commentaries and prefaces to his biblical translations, his growing facility with Hebrew, as analyzed by Benjamin Kedar-Kopfstein, and his own comments about classical allusions in Christian texts are considered.

It is an honor indeed to include Edward A. Synan's learned excursus on "The Vulgarity of the Vulgate," an essay which is one of the final pieces of scholarship completed before his untimely death in the summer of 1997. Noted for his erudition and wit, Fr. Synan graciously chaired, at the Twenty-First International Conference on Patristic, Medieval and Renaissance Studies at Villanova University, the session on "Literary Studies in the Vulgate" in which were presented both this contribution to the present collection and the previous essay by Catherine Brown Tkacz. He begins with the Council of Trent's designation of the "Vulgate" text of the Bible as *vetus et vulgata editio* and proceeds to the origins of that translation in the patristic era. He also examines the exchanges among SS. Jerome, Damasus, and Augustine (especially his Letter 71 to Jerome in 403) concerning appropriate scholarly and pastoral ways of handling the biblical texts.

The volume then turns its attention to Augustine, who is treated in four essays. First, Anne P. Carriker addresses directly "Augustine's Frankness in His Dispute with Jerome over the Interpretation of Galatians 2:11–14," a dispute Fr. Synan touched on in passing. The issue in Galatians is Judaizing Christians, for at Antioch Peter had acted counter to the Council of Jerusalem by withdrawing from a Gentile table, an action for which Paul criticized him. After Jerome had followed Origen in interpreting the disagreement between Peter and Paul as staged, Augustine wrote to Jerome out of concern that this view implied that Scripture could contain lies. Carriker sensitively analyzes the debate, grounding it thoroughly both in the writings of the principals and also in modern scholarship, concluding that Augustine's own behavior in this issue is a microcosm of Augustine's thought on the passage from Galatians and his larger understanding of the propriety of frankness in human friendship.

In a particularly apt hommage to one who is a learned teacher, Douglas Kries brings to bear the rigorous attention to the text that is so prized by Fr. Schlatter in an investigation of Augustine's *De magistro*. Taking seriously the dialogic genre as distinct from other forms of philosophical expression, as well as Ernest Fortin's call to consider the "zetetic" qualities of Augustine's dialogues, Dr. Kries is especially concerned with the *De magistro*'s allusions. He finds the tripartite structure of this unique discussion with Adeodatus to be punctuated by two seemingly casual allusions—one to Virgil and one to Daniel—that were in fact selected carefully to point to the Christian transformation of classical poetics, and indeed to point quietly to Augustine's own role in expressing the new Christian poetics.

Augustine's definition of sacrifice in the *City of God* is the subject of the essay by Roland Teske, S.J. By appealing to the distinction between the proper, pregnant, and typological senses of "true," Fr. Teske shows that Augustine's definition did not exclude visible sacrifices, whether of the Old Testament or of the New, from being true sacrifices, though the bishop did place the emphasis in his definition upon the interior act of mercy. The essay contends that this emphasis upon the interior or spiritual sacrifice was motivated, at least in part, by Augustine's desire to make the Christian doctrine of sacrifice as acceptable as possible to the spiritual ideals of non-Christian platonists whom he hoped to convert to Christ. One is reminded of the implicit pastoral concern for Jews shown by St. Jerome, whose respect for the *Hebraica veritas* and for Jewish objections to the Septuagint translation of the Hebrew Bible was a considerable impetus in his undertaking the monumental task of retranslating the Old Testament directly from the Hebrew. Both of these Fathers evinced a concern to remove obstacles to conversion.

Fittingly, this volume also contributes to the study of women in the early Church, for Fr. Schlatter actively supported Gonzaga University's lecture series on "Women in the Early Church." That series was the origin of two of the essays in the present collection. (See also "women" in the index.) In the volume's final essay on Augustine, Katherin A. Rogers explores "Augustine on the Nature and Role of Women," drawing widely on writings from the whole of his career as well as from his own actions. She argues that the evidence shows that, counter to what several feminists have claimed, Augustine cannot reasonably be accused of "misogynism." For instance, he held that women are capable of virtue, intellectual work, and—most important—salvation, and that each spouse in a marriage has an equal claim on the other's sexual companionship. Dr. Rogers also argues that Augustine countered the prevailing cultural norms of the Roman Empire, holding that adultery was equally wrong in a man and in a woman and in asserting that the victims of rape are themselves innocent. In such acts as his esteeming Monica as one who attained the highest intellectual and spiritual experience humanly possible, Dr. Rogers adduces evidence that the practices of this Church Father were quite consistent with his theoretical understanding of women.

"Fathers," of course, is a generic noun, including both men and women. For instance, the Byzantine feast of the Sunday of the Fathers of the Old Testament before Christmas includes Susanna, the heroine of the book of Daniel, and the *Apothegmata patrum* includes accounts of women as well as men. Among the women deemed midwives of wisdom by Mary Forman, O.S.B., are St. Mary of Egypt, who is venerated universally in the Church calendar, in the West on April 2, but with greater prominence in the East, with the Fifth Sunday of Great Lent being the Sunday of Mary of Egypt.[2] Dr. Forman also discusses Sarah, Theodora, and Syncletica (whose wisdom is recorded in the *Apophthegmata patrum)*, as well as Mary (superior of a women's community in the Thebaid in Upper Egypt), Paula (one of the women for whom Jerome wrote several of his commentaries, including the one on the Letter to the Galatians), Melania the Elder, Melania the Younger (383–439), Egeria (4th-c.), and St. Macrina the Younger (ca.330–379), the eldest sister of Gregory of Nyssa, likened by him to a second Socrates. The Early Christian term for such women was *ammas*, meaning "spiritual mothers," and they were focal in the spiritual growth of many individuals in ways that Forman shows influenced the course of western monasticism.

Whereas Professor Frend's essay gives an overview of the archaeology of the Early Christian era, W. Eugene Kleinbauer engages in detail a cutting-edge issue in this field, addressing the nature ("Christian or Secular?") of the tetraconch in the so-called Library of Hadrian at Athens (late 4th-c.–ca. 460). Modern scholarly consensus has leaned toward identifying it as the first public church building in Late Antique Athens, especially since the discovery in 1980 of a forecourt or atrium at the tetraconch's west end. Professor Kleinbauer adduces a wide range of textual evidence and data derived from architectural comparanda to argue that, to the contrary, the building was probably built for a secular purpose, perhaps as *kaisereion* or as a lecture hall for the Neoplatonists, or as Athen's new *bouleuterion.* Tantalizing as it would be to accept the building as Christian, the ambiguity of the epigraphic and historical evidence (regarding putative patronage by the prefect Herculius or the Empress Eudocia, and the smallness of the early fifth-century Christian community in Athens), the lack of all Christian remains (especially a baptistery) within the fabric of the original building, and the fact that at this time the double-shell tetraconch was used for secular as well as Christian buildings, all argue against such a conclusion.

The Vandal persecution of orthodox Catholics under Geiseric and Huneric is recorded by eyewitness Victor of Vita in the *Historia persecutionis Africanae provinciae* (ca. 489), and William Edmund Fahey shows that this highly circumstantial and detailed account is constructed with an alert and pastoral rhetorical sense. "History, Community, and Suffering" are brought together by Victor as he provides role models and resonant emblems to comfort and inspire the Africans to remain steadfast, encouraging them to understand their sufferings as a participation in the suffering of Christ. Victor draws numerous examples of individual persecuted and martyred Catholics from all social classes and ages, from city and country, naming and recounting the experiences of men, women, and children. The Arians' rejection of the Trinitarian baptismal formula is consistently undercut by Victor at the dictional level, in his nuanced selection of imagery (as when he compares Geiseric to Pharaoh), and memorably in his recurring use of the motif of the baptismal garment. For instance, when Dionysia—a woman whose story is recounted both in its own right and also in a manner making her a Christ-like spokesman for the Church—has been stripped and beaten for her faith, she speaks of retaining one's wedding garment, i.e. the baptismal robe.

Joseph W. Day offers an initial step "Toward a Pragmatics of Archaic and Paleochristian Greek Inscriptions." Curses, epitaphs, acclamations, and liturgical texts are among the genres he takes into consideration. The study looks at the intentionality of the composer, the experience of the reader, and the role of inscriptions as performative utterances. Particularly of interest is Dr. Day's discussion of inscriptions based on the Trisagion, for he demonstrates that this ancient liturgical troparion, sung during the Little Entrance when the Word of God is brought in procession from the sanctuary to the people, was often inscribed on the entrances of churches and other structures in the fourth through seventh centuries. As a result, when believers enter a structure, see the inscription and form the words either aloud or in their mind, they are, by walking, bodily recreating an important moment of the liturgy. The perception is as tantalizing as the recognition that when the standing congregation sings the Ode of Daniel 3, the hymn of the Three Young Men, they are, in posture and song, recreating the actions that occurred in the original miracle. In an appendix Dr. Day identifies over fifty Early Christian inscriptions based on the Trisagion, inscribed on entrances, other architectural features, liturgical equipment, graves, ostraka, and so forth.

"Eastern Monasticism in South Italy" is treated by Anthony P. Via, S.J., and while his focus is the tenth and eleventh centuries, he begins with evidence of the Byzantine monasticism of the "new Thebaide" of Calabria of the seventh century. A rich collation of primary sources, including *vitae*, *euchologia*, and *typika* yields evidence not only about the development and technical terminology of the monasteries, but also about their libraries, economic life, and involvement in world affairs, including relations between Byzantium and the West. The essay examines in particular the lives of SS. Elias of Enna (823–903), Elias Speliotes (ca. 860–960), Nilus of Rossano (910–1004), and Luke, bishop of Isola Capo Rizzuto (d. 1114).

In concluding, it is appropriate to mention the many achievements of this volume's honoree. Fr. Schlatter entered the Society of Jesus in 1943 and was ordained to the priesthood in 1956. He has taught classical languages and history at Gonzaga University for over forty years, earning several teaching awards while introducing countless students to the mysteries of Latin, Greek, and ancient history. He held the chair of the Powers Professor of Humanities at Gonzaga from 1983 to 1997. During his tenure as Powers Professor, his research was especially focussed on an intriguing and influential text once erroneously associated with John Chrysostom, the *Opus imperfectum in Matthaeum*, and also on the oldest extant mosaic in Rome, the apse mosaic of Santa Pudenziana. His most recent project has been a study of Gerard Manley Hopkins's work on Homer. More than anything else, it has been an intense devotion to the study of Christianity in late antiquity that has marked Fr. Schlatter's work, and it is therefore particularly appropriate to honor him with a volume of essays on that period of the Church's history.

NOTES

1. F. W. Schlatter, S. J., "The Two Women in the Mosaic of Santa Pudenziana," *Journal of Early Christian Studies* 3.1 (1995):20.

2. Robert F. Taft, S. J., "Lent," *ODB* 2:1205; Karl Holl, *Gesammelte Aufsätze zur Kirchengeschichte*, 2: *Der Osten* (Tübingen, 1928) 155–203. There were also at least twenty-five Byzantine hymns celebrating S. Mary of Egypt; Henrica Follieri, *Initia hymnorum ecclesiae graecae*, 5 vols., Studi e Testi 215 bis (Città del Vaticano, 1966), 5:218.

From Confessional Propaganda to International Scholarship: The Archaeology of Early Christianity

W. H. C. Frend
Gonville and Caius College, Cambridge

The literary legacy of early Christianity is immense. Generations of scholars have pored over the works of the Church Fathers published in double columns in the stately volumes of Migne's Patrologia Latina and Patrologia Greco–Latina. Still the mysteries remain. What anonymous moralist hides behind the pseudo–Cyprianic "On the Twelve Abuses of the Age" or the poet who wrote 400 lines of verse to Flavius Felix on the "Resurrection of the Dead"?[1] Are the Latin sermons fathered on John Chrysostom in reality a North African Donatist collection?[2] Topics for research will not be exhausted, but during the last hundred years, the church historian and doctrinal scholar has had an additional tool to aid his quest, namely the results of archaeological research. This has become increasingly international and ecumenical, shedding ever more light on the progress of the Church's mission in the early centuries, and on the influence and beliefs of the non–orthodox traditions on its history.

The story of the archaeology of early Christianity begins, uneasily, with the empress Helena, Constantine's mother. Soon after the Council of Nicaea in May–July 325, probably in 326/27, the empress was in Jerusalem, doubtless as part of her son's aim to convert the pagan city of Aelia Capitolina into a beacon of Christianity. The Church historian Eusebius of Caesarea, however, records the discovery of "that monument of His [i.e., Christ's] most holy Passion [probably fragments of the "True Cross"] buried beneath the ground," before he mentions Helena's visit to Jerusalem.[3] In fact, crediting the empress with the discovery of the "True Cross" through excavation appears only at the end of the fourth century, while the healing cures associated with the event become more miraculous in the accounts given by the fifth-century writers, Socrates and Sozomen.[4]

Helena's efforts had two contrasting results. On the one hand, they added archaeological method to the various means open to Christians to establish the truth of Biblical events. On the other, they linked these discoveries with the miraculous and with the acquisition of relics of the saints. From Late Antiquity through the European Middle Ages trade in the latter flourished. Few large towns were without their holy relics to ensure the saint's protection against capture by an enemy or the onset of plague. The prevailing bias moreover was against scientific research as "curiosity," that is, seeking knowledge beyond the bounds sanctioned by the Church, and this condemned archaeology for centuries to be the handmaid of superstition.

The Renaissance altered this situation radically. Archaeology, including Christian archaeology, is its child. The Roman catacombs had long attracted pilgrims. There were Itineraries to guide them and indicate routes to be followed if a pilgrim wished to venerate a particular tomb. In the fifteenth century, however, scholars began to explore the catacombs for their own sake. Thus, in 1475 Pomponius Leto and his companion in the Roman Academy explored what proved to be the catacomb of St. Callistus on the Appian Way. Unfortunately, irreverence got the better of them. They left their signatures on some of the frescos, and dedicated their work to "Pope Pomponius." Charged with impiety, they were lucky to escape punishment.[5]

It was not until a century later, and then through an accident, that research relating to the catacombs was undertaken once more. On May 31, 1578 a workman digging in a vineyard near the Via Salaria Nuova north of the city was too vigorous. His spade disappeared into a hole. Efforts to retrieve it showed that the hole was no ordinary one, but a passage in the catacomb of Praetextatus. Popular excitement was intense, and after a short interval the exploration of the "underground city," as Baronius called it, began in earnest.[6] The early explorations will always be associated with the name of a young Maltese member of the Orotarian Order, Antonio Bosio (1573–1629), who began his explorations in 1595 at the early age of 22. Year by year, Bosio explored and mapped the more accessible catacombs, copying frescos as he came on them and leaving in draft four large volumes embodying his results under the title of *Roma sotteranea*, to be published after his death. He deserves the title given to him of "Columbus of the Catacombs."[7]

Unfortunately, the seventeenth century was not the time for impartial scholarly research on the history and role in the life of the Church of the catacombs, and their art. Bosio died when the Thirty Years War was at its height, and even after it ended with the Peace of Westphalia in 1648, there was no religious harmony between Protestants and Catholics. The second half of the seventeenth century witnessed the attempt of Louis XIV of France to subjugate Europe in the interests of Catholic France, while the Revocation of the Edict of Nantes in 1685 showed what he thought of Protestants in France itself. One by–product of this renewed counter–Reformation was an enormous export of relics from the Roman catacombs. Bosio had opened up some of the best known and most accessible galleries. His successors were anxious to identify the burials not as those of ordinary Roman Christians but specifically as martyrs. The palm–branch symbol on a number of the earlier, third–century funerary tablets was interpreted to signify martyrdom, while the small ampoule once filled with red liquid, either Eucharistic wine or balsam, found with some burials was seen as martyr's blood. Land in Germany, such as the Upper Palatinate, regained for Catholicism during the Thirty Years War provided a ready market for such relics. Skeletons were dismembered and provided with convincing names of saints, including "St. Anonymous."[8] Little wonder, that the scholarly Benedictine, Jean Mabillon (1638–1707), to whom the study of early Church history owes much, cast doubt on the authenticity of relics arriving in France from the Roman catacombs.[9]

In the next century a new set of circumstances restored a more scholarly interest in Christian antiquities. By 1700 it had become clear that the highwatermark of Turkish expansion into central Europe had been reached. In the ensuing equilibrium between the Turks and the Christian Powers trade with the Ottoman dominions particularly on the part of Britain and France increased. "Factories," or trading–posts, were established in the Ottoman dominions, not least in Algeria and the Levant. Consuls and members of trade missions found themselves at liberty to travel with relative freedom in the Mediterranean territories of the Ottoman Empire. For the first time for over a thousand years the stark skeletons of once prosperous Roman and Greco–Roman cities were revealed to western travelers. All were struck by the wealth of Classical and early Christian remains that they encountered. Thomas Shaw and James Bruce, both British Consuls in Algiers, record finding "heaps of ruins" and "remains of large cities completely deserted" in Algeria and Tunisia.[10] The Frenchman Jean Peyssonnel described Suffetula (Sbeitla) which he visited in 1724 as a city that "had not been destroyed but simply fallen into ruins."[11] The fact was that from the mid–seventh century onwards the successive waves of Arab invaders were nomads who shunned the remains of the Byzantine cities and destroyed the settled villages together with their Christian inhabitants. The result was that the remains of churches as well as temples and other public buildings stood much as they had when they were abandoned. A vast potential field of exploration of the remains of early Christianity had been opened up to balance the prevailing concentration on the Roman catacombs and the religious propaganda connected with them.

Such was the position at the end of the eighteenth century, before the Enlightenment and the French Revolution destroyed the clerical monopoly on early Christian studies in Continental Europe. The importance of Napoleon in furthering this process can hardly be over–estimated.[12] The general himself had shown an interest in scientific scholarship before he led the Revolutionary armies to victory in north Italy in 1796–97. His expedition to Egypt, designed to secure French control of the Mediterranean against the British was accompanied by scholars, who had the prime task of studying and recording the enormous wealth of Pharaonic remains awaiting decipherment. If the accidental discovery of the Rosetta stone in July 1799 was to provide the key to the latter task, the capture of Aswan in May of the same year opened the way to the first European exploration of Nubia and the discovery of the Christian civilization that had flourished there for a thousand years, from 500 to 1500 A.D.

Napoleon's army was trapped after Nelson's victory in the battle of the Nile in 1798 and eventually forced to capitulate to General Abercromby in August 1801.

The Rosetta stone found its way to the British Museum, where its decipherment, combined with the studies in hieroglyphic script and the Coptic language by Jean–François Champollion (d. 1832), opened up new possibilities for the study of the Old Testament, in particular the Exodus narrative and the fraught relations between Egypt and Israel.

North Africa, however, was to experience the most lasting influence of Napoleon's idea of conquest combined with scholarly mission. The journeys of Shaw and Bruce had prepared the French officers who landed near Algiers in June 1830 as part of Charles X's punitive expedition, for the vista of antiquities that would confront them. Moreover, ready to encourage the Napoleonic tradition of conquest and scholarship was Marshal Soult (1769–1851), one of the emperor's marshals who was Chef de Cabinet first under Charles X and then under his successor, Louis–Philippe (1830–1848). In one letter to the Permanent Secretary of the Académie des Inscriptions et Belle–Lettres in 1833, he urged that "the occupation of the Regency of Algiers by our troops should not be without results for science." There was "double interest of arms and civilisation that could offer a good understanding of the geography of Mauretania under ancient civilisation and the history of Roman colonisation in that country."[13] One fortunate response to this opinion was the arrival of Adrien Berbrugger (1801–1869) in Algiers as secretary to General Clauzel.

Though French officers had discovered the ruins of an early Christian church at Rusguniae (Cape Matifou) in September 1852, the direction of the first generation of French scholars in Algeria was lay, and oriented towards Classical antiquities. Berbrugger's own researches extended from Neolithic to early Islamic. He was determined that remains, such as the Severan triumphal arch at Djemila (Cuicul) should not be transported back to Paris, but early Christianity was incidental. Nonetheless, the *Revue Africaine* that he founded in 1856 had scope for articles reporting early Christian churches such as at Caesarea.[14] The wealth of discoveries awaiting research was revealed by Christian mosaics at Djemila and Castellium Tingitanum (Orléansville).[15] In the 1850s and 1860s, it was furthered by the discoveries of the first Christian churches in southern Numidia (eastern Algeria) by officers of the Bureau Arabe. This had been established at Tebessa (Theveste) after the capture of that center by General Négrier in 1842 and its officers were often to prove keen archaeologists.[16]

Berbrugger died suddenly at Algiers in July 1869.[17] Two years before, however, an appointment had been made to the newly created Archbishopric of Carthage that was to affect the progress of Christian archaeology in North Africa profoundly. Though the spirit of the Algerian policy of both Louis–Philippe and Napoleon III (1852–1870) had been lay–oriented, there had always been influential voices stressing the onetime Christian heritage of North Africa, the land of Cyprian and Augustine, and the duty of the colonial power to revive that heritage. In 1817, Antonio Morcelli (1737–1821) had written a complete gazeteer of known information about the geography of North African bishoprics and about the individual bishops and where possible their sees. Fifty years later the arrival of Archbishop (later Cardinal) Charles Lavigerie enabled that information to be put to use.[18]

Lavigerie landed in Algiers in the early summer of 1867 as the leader of a well–organized Church, with bishops in Oran and Constantine and a network of parishes throughout northern and central Algeria.[19] Keenly interested in archaeology himself, one of his first instructions to his clergy, in December 1867, was that they should register all archaeological and historical discoveries in their parishes relating to the early Church in North Africa.[20] His aim was not only to restore the heritage of Augustine in Algeria but to extend that heritage accompanied by French rule to Tunisia and across the Sahara to central Africa. He was an ecclesiastical Cecil Rhodes in the service of France. Months before the occupation of Tunisia by the French in May 1881, he wrote a long memorandum to the Permanent Secretary (Secrétaire permanente) of the Académie des Inscriptions et Belles Lettres emphasizing that French–led archaeology in Tunisia was a matter of national honor.[21] He had already purchased nine hectares of land on the Byrsa at Carthage on which to found a college and placed Père A. L. Delattre (1850–1932) of the Missionaires d'Alger in charge of excavations, which he hoped would lead to the creation of a Musée National at Carthage. With the same aim he established a shrine in the amphitheatre of Carthage in honor of the martyrs Perpetua and Felicitas (d. March 203). The Cathedral of St. Louis which he dedicated on Ascension Day 1890 was intended to stamp Carthage as the Primatial See of Christian (Roman Catholic) Africa as it had been in the days of Cyprian and Augustine.

Lavigerie died in November 1892. By that time his contemporary G. B. de Rossi had taken up Bosio's mantle as explorer and excavator of the Roman catacombs. There he had shown how sound scholarship was compatible with complete loyalty to the Roman See. De Rossi (1822–1894) was the greatest of the nineteenth–century Roman archaeologists, and though his loyalty to the Papacy was rewarded by Pius IX's permission for his publications to bear the Vatican imprint he set an example of objective scholarship in catacomb research.[22] Inspired in 1848 by his discovery of an inscription reading (Cor) Nelius Martyr used in a stairway forming part of a vineyard store, he identified the Cemetery of the Popes (part of the great Praetextatus catacomb) and dated its origins plausibly to the period of relative toleration under the emperor Alexander Severus (222–235).[23] He rid catacomb archaeology of the mythological, including the view that some Christian catacombs dated from the sub–Apostolic period (70–120 A.D.) He showed, too, that, far from being mainly poor and needy, most of the Christians of Rome must have had the resources to belong to well–organized burial societies. Christianity's gradual penetration of the Roman upper classes and with that, Christian funerary art, did not begin before the early third century. As a scholar he summed up his work in three huge volumes of *Roma sotteranea* (1864–1877), in the *Bulletino di archaeologia cristiana* (founded 1863) to inform the learned world of the progress of catacomb research, and the *Inscriptiones cristianae Vobis Romae veteres* (1857–1915). He was also one of the earliest popularizers. He held the attention of audiences in the catacombs on anniversary days, when he would describe in exact detail and vivid gesture where martyrs, such as Pope Xystus II and his deacons, had perished.[24] The assembly at Split in August 1894, a few weeks before his death, of the First Congress of Christian Archaeology was a lasting memorial to a great scholar.

As in the eighteenth century, what was threatening to become a monopoly for Roman Catholic scholarship was ended by discoveries in other parts of the Mediterranean. Down to the 1870s travel in the interior of Asia Minor was hazardous. Roads were practically non–existent and the local population suspicious of foreigners. After the Congress of Berlin in 1878 the situation began to improve as Western companies established themselves with the object of bettering communications by road and rail and modernizing the ramshackle Turkish Empire. Among those who took advantage of the new set of circumstances was William Ramsay (1851–1939), a native of Aberdeen but in 1880 a graduate student at Oxford. Ramsay hoped that travel through the Pauline cities recorded in Acts of the Apostles would enable him to vindicate the truth of Acts and prove St. Luke's claim to be a "great historian."[25]

Though he was less successful in this particular project than he had hoped, he made major pioneering discoveries relating to early Christian and Jewish society in Asia Minor. These were mainly the result of his discovery and decipherment of inscriptions on hitherto unexplored urban sites in the interior, especially Classical Phrygia. What turned out to be his most significant single find came early. In 1881, working among the ruins of Greco–Roman towns in the valley of the River Glaukos (a tributary of the Maeander in Phrygia), Ramsay came upon a funerary inscription of a certain Alexander, son of Antonius, dating precisely to A.D. 216. The first lines of the inscription, however, read, "I, a citizen of a distinguished (*eklektes*) city made this time while I was still alive ..." Back at Oxford, Ramsay's researches showed that this line corresponded with the first line of a funerary inscription whose text was recorded in the *Acta Abercii*, which gave an account of the life of the anti–Montanist Bishop of Hieropolis, Avircius Marcellus who lived ca. 180.[26] Two years later, Ramsay returned to the same area with an American colleague C. S. Sterrett and found re–used in a bath–house south of the site of Hieropolis three fragments of the funerary inscription set up by Avircius Marcellus himself during his own lifetime. Looking like an ordinary late–second–century pagan altar, the inscription included words such as *icthun* (fish), "golden," and *Euphraten* (the River Euphrates), and the description of the owner as "a citizen of a distinguished [or elect] city" and "servant of the shepherd." This proved the owner was Avircius Marcellus of the *Acta Abercii* and demonstrated the veiled Christianity of its confession. Ramsay had found the earliest known Christian inscription, and with its emphasis on "all being gathered together" in the unity of liturgy and belief, it was also an anti–Montanist statement made at the height of the

Montanist crisis.[27] Little wonder that Ramsay's discovery resulted in heated controversy between those, mainly French Roman Catholic scholars, who accepted Ramsay's view that this was a Christian inscription and German scholars, led by Adolf von Harnack, who did not. Ramsay's view ultimately prevailed and he was glad to present his discovery to the Lateran Museum.[28]

Meantime, in North Africa itself archaeological scholarship was beginning to prevail over propaganda. In 1893 and 1894, Stéphane Gsell and Henri Graillot undertook journeys through southern Numidia between the Aurès mountains and the salt lakes to the north that bisected the Numidian high plain.[29] They traversed a land once densely populated by romanized Berbers dwelling in villages made prosperous through the wealth of olive plantations, and in the fourth and later centuries profoundly Christian. But the Christianity was not orthodox. French scholars have tended to fight shy of admitting the strength of the Donatist Church in North Africa, but here was the evidence on the ground. Few sites which the explorers surveyed were without recognizable evidence of ruined churches, and in some were inscribed stones bearing either the tell–tale Donatist watch–word *Deo Laudes* (Praise to God) or some other words that betrayed their Donatist allegiance.[30] The archaeology of the early Church was beginning to make one of its most important contributions towards understanding early Christianity in revealing something of the ideas and strength of non–orthodox traditions.

Apart from the strongly ideological approach of Orazio Marucchi and Josef Wilpert who continued de Rossi's exploration of the Roman catacombs, the archaeology of early Christian in the twenty years before the First World War reflected the secular interests of the rival Great Powers. This was the classic age of Imperialism, when the European Powers sought to outdo each other commercially as well as to imprint their influence on the cultural life of less advanced countries. While Ramsay and his younger colleagues continued to make further discoveries, including Montanist inscriptions in Asia Minor,[31] French, German and Austro–Hungarian scholars worked on prime sites on the coast excavating impressive Classical buildings in the ruins of Classical cities. In this race to find the most sensational monuments with which to stock national museums the archaeology of late Antiquity took second place. Early Christian and Byzantine levels were too often neglected and destroyed in the scramble to reach the more exciting remains of Classical civilization buried beneath.

In two new areas of exploration, however, the archaeology of early Christianity benefited. Central Asia, the vast area between India and China and its ancient Silk Route, where in the nineteenth century Great Britain and Russia had jockeyed for influence, became a target for explorers from western Europe. The Turfan oasis, capital of the Turkish semi–nomadic tribe of the Uigurs from the seventh century A.D. into the Middle Ages, was a magnet that drew rival teams from the Great Powers. Thus, Grünwedel and Lecoq for Germany (four expeditions), Pelliot and Chavannes representing France, and Sir Aurel Stein for the Indian government all visited the site and found there not only Buddhist remains as would be expected, but the first Manichaean manuscripts ever discovered. Further east, in Chinese Turkestan, Aurel Stein visited the ancient temple library that had been safeguarded in a cave at Tun–Huang and there found more Manichaean manuscripts showing how Mani, the founder of this third–century Christian sect truly had worldwide ambitions, to spread his religion from China to the Atlantic Ocean.[32]

The explorers of the Turfan oasis had represented their countries and their divergent aims and interests. In the Nile valley there was greater collaboration between British, French and American scholars. The establishment of the Anglo–Egyptian Condominium over Sudan at the end of 1898 invited research into the vanished Nubian Christian civilization. This had flourished for a thousand years, between A.D. 500 and 1500, and had left standing remains of churches and monasteries in settlements along the banks of the Nile. Building the (first) Aswan dam gave an added urgency to the work. Between 1899–1914 expeditions under Somer Clarke's direction collaborated with those under Reisner and C. S. Mileham representing the United States in exploring, planning, and carrying out limited excavations on some of the most important sites in Nubia, including Faras and Qasr Ibrim.[33] What was to prove to be the remains of the magnificent Monophysite civilization linking the Churches of Ethiopia and Coptic Egypt began to be revealed in these years.

The First World War ended forever the predominance of the Great Powers of Europe in world affairs. From now on, the United States would be a major player in archaeological exploration as in the economic and cultural life of the world. This was to be demonstrated on a major excavation that revealed one of the most important early Christian remains to date. The site of Dura Europos on the Euphrates was first found by a detachment of British soldiers establishing a fortified position against Arab insurgents in 1920. Soon afterwards, however, the frontier between Iraq and Syria was moved upstream leaving Dura on the Syrian side. The result was ten seasons of joint work between Yale University and the Académie des Inscriptions et Belles–Lettres, resulting among other discoveries in the finding of remains of a church built ca. 232, the earliest known Christian building. It was a house–church, forming part of a dwelling built up against the city wall, with an assembly hall and baptistery decorated with frescos and holding a congregation of about seventy. It showed Christianity like Mithraism as minority newcomer among the oriental religions that dominated the life of the town.[34]

Collaborative archaeology was henceforth to be the rule, involving international teams working together to preserve so far as possible archaeological heritage in the face of urban sprawl and new methods of agriculture and huge public works, such as the Egyptian High Dam, all the result of the explosion of world–population. In the 1970s "Save Nubia" was succeeded by "Save Carthage," in both of which teams drawn from a wide variety of countries in Europe and America worked with scholars from the host nations to save what could be saved of the remains of early civilizations threatened with destruction. Confessional considerations were banished to the past.

In Nubia in 1963–65, the cathedral and splendid frescos of Faras were discovered by the Polish expedition led by Professor Kazimierz Michałowski.[35] At Qasr Ibrim J. M. Plumley and the writer recovered remains of the only stone–built cathedral in Nubia, and literary evidence in the form of leather scrolls proving the survival of Christianity at least to the last quarter of the fifteenth century.[36] They also found texts from a Monophysite Eucharistic liturgy with fragments of hymns to the Virgin Mary.[37] These were among the harvest of discoveries relating to the history of Christianity in the Nile valley salvaged through international scholarship.

All the time, methods of work have been improving. Air photography, better understanding of stratigraphy and pottery types, and carbon dating were succeeding the wasteful "déblayage" (clearance) methods and concentration on individual large buildings of previous generations. This has also applied to the study of the Roman catacombs as elsewhere. In 1922 Pope Pius XI (formerly the scholarly Cardinal Ratti) instituted a Pontifical Institute of Christian Archaeology, designed as a center of teaching and research for students, and using the most up–to–date methods of excavation and research.[38] The result was a greatly improved quality of research and publication of catacomb archaeology. The discovery and excellently researched catacomb on the Via Latina, a "fourth-century picture gallery" containing pagan as well as Christian motives, was accompanied by a useful re–examination of earlier discoveries.[39]

The excavations under St. Peter's have proved a test of method and impartial scholarship.[40] The discovery of the "Red Wall" forming part of the exterior of a second–century pagan mausoleum, but containing a shrine (*Aedicula*) identifiable with the "trophy" set up in honor of the Apostles Peter and Paul recorded by the Roman presbyter, Gaius in ca. 200[41] was a surprise. It showed, however, that by ca. 160, the date of the wall's construction, this particular area beneath the High Altar of St. Peter's was associated with the Apostles.[42] This, however, was nearly a century after their reputed death at the hands of the emperor Nero in 64. What had happened in between? We do not know. That there was a fervent cult, possibly in honor of Peter, at the same spot between 290–320 does not help prove its origin. Whether greater attention to pottery finds and stratigraphy during the excavations from 1940–1949 might have led to more definite results remains a matter for speculation.[43] All that can be said is that Constantine built the first St. Peter's basilica over the spot that for a century and a half Roman Christians associated with the burial place first of both Peter and Paul, and later, by the early fourth century, of Peter alone.[44]

Roman Britain, finally, provides some contrasts to these problems. If at Rome Bishop Gilbert Burnet was unwise enough to dismiss the murals in the Roman catacombs as "of Gothic date," research into the origins of Christianity in Britain had always sought scholarly objectivity.[45] William Camden's *Britannia* published in 1607 after more than twenty years' research aimed "to restore Britain to antiquity and antiquity to Britain" and "to recover certainty which either the carelessness of writers or the credulity of readers have bereaved us."[46] The huge folio volumes assembled every scrap of literary and epigraphic evidence, such as an inscription in honor of Magnus Maximus and Flavius Victor (384–388) from Boulogne, relating to Roman Britain and Anglo–Saxon England. Camden may have believed that the Britons were descended from the Trojans, but his was an essay in impartial scholarship at a time when this was lacking on the Continent. Today, Christianity in Roman Britain is still characterized by outstanding individual finds rather than firm information about its organization and clergy. The existence of wealthy communities is however shown by the Water Newton chalice, paten and other altar utensils.[47] Christian villa owners are proved by the bust of Christ on a mosaic at Hinton St. Mary (Dorset) and the wall plaster from Luddington (Kent), hoards of precious metal objects have been found at Mildenhall and Hoxne (Suffolk) and the adherence of some members of the poorer classes to Christianity is attested by the lead candlestand with its crude figures from Lode (Cambs),[48] but no coherent picture of progressive evangelization emerges. It looks as though Christianity never became the dominant religion in Britain as it did in the last quarter of the fourth century on the Continent.

There, the harvest of material remains which allows such a conclusion to be reached has been great. The mission and spread of Christianity from the mid–third century onwards is the main contribution which archaeology had made to the study of the early Church. The second, hardly less important, is the emergence of the non–orthodox traditions from the shadows imposed upon them by orthodox theologians and emperors. Gnostics, Manichees, Montanists, Donatists and Monophysites now speak for themselves, archaeology filling out the meagre literary remains left by their representatives. While orthodoxy retains a pride of place, the totality of the early Christian experience can no longer be understood without the remains of dissenting interpretations of the faith being fully taken into account.

And for the future? The great expansion of archaeological research, especially on early Christian and Byzantine sites, witnessed at the 14th Congress of Christian Archaeology at Split/Poreč in September 1994, is likely to continue. Many threatened sites will be excavated or preserved. At the same time, areas such as central Algeria, once open to research on the Donatist movement, may remain closed indefinitely until there is a change in the political climate of Algeria. Much will depend, too, on the accurate recording of chance finds made by metal detectors. Can detectorists be transformed from greedy collectors to allies of scholarship? Looking ahead, one of the most hopeful developments is the continued discovery of new documentary evidence, such as the Divjak collection of Augustine's letters and memoranda, and the co–ordination of literary with archaeological research. The latter still needs integration into the university Faculties of Theology and Ancient History. In this connection Fr. F. W. Schlatter's interpretation of the apse mosaic in the church of Santa Pudenziana at Rome with the aid of a detailed study of Jerome's *Commentary on Ezekiel 40–43* provides an excellent example of the direction of future work.[49] It is in recognition of the importance of this and other similar examples of Schlatter's contributions to scholarship that this essay is presented to him.

NOTES

1. Published in Cyprian's *Opera Omnia*, Pt. 3, ed. William Hartel (Vienna, 1871), 152–73 and 308–26.

2. PL Supplementum 4:669–740. I owe the suggestion of a Donatist origin to Fr. Professor F. J. Leroy of Lumbumbashi University, Zaire: *Homily* 18 is Donatist and *Homily* 28 almost certainly is so also.

3. Eusebius, *Vita Constantini* 3.30 and 34 in *Eusebius Werke* 1, ed. I. A. Heikel, GCS 7 (Leipzig, 1902), 90 and 95. See J. W. Drijvers, *Helena Augusta: Waarheid en Legende* (Groningen, 1989), Pt. 1.

4. Socrates, *Historia Ecclesiastica* 1.17; Sozomen, *Historia Ecclesiastica*, ed. J. Bidez and G. C. Hansen, GCS 50 (Berlin, 1960), 2.1.4–9.

5. See J. Stevenson, *The Catacombs* (London, 1978), 47–48. Pomponius and his friends also entered the catacombs of Praetextatus and of Peter and Marcellinus.

6. Stevenson, *Catacombs* 48.

7. For Bosio's career, see H. Leclercq, "Bosio" *DACL* 2.1:1083–93.

8. Trevor Johnson, "Holy Fabrications: The Catacomb Saints and the Counter–Reformation in Bavaria," *Journal of Ecclesiastical History* 47.2 (April 1996):274–97. For "St. Anonymous," see p. 281.

9. For Jean Mabillon, see David Knowles, "Jean Mabillon," chap. 10, in *The Historian and Character* (Cambridge, 1963), 230.

10. Thomas Shaw, *Travels and Observations Relating to Several Parts of Barbary and the Levant* (Oxford, 1738), 85; James Bruce, *Travels to Discover the Sources of the Nile* (Edinburgh, 1790), 1:viii–xi.

11. See N. Duval, "La solution d'une enigme: les voyageurs Peyssonnel et Guinemez à Sbeitla en 1724," *Bulletin de la Société nationale des antiquaires de France* (1965):94–135, esp. 101.

12. For a short summary of French archaeology's debt to Napoleon, see the writer's *The Archaeology of Early Christianity: A History* (Minneapolis, 1996), chap. 4 ("Archaeology").

13. Ibid, chap. 5, p. 56 where a key passage of the letter is quoted.

14. Described by Berbrugger in *Revue Africaine* 1 (1856–57):119ff ("Julia Caesarea, Inscriptions chrétiennes").

15. See Paul–Albert Février, *Approches du Maghreb romain* (Edisud, 1989), 1:37–38.

16. Such as Colonel Carbuccia (d. 1854 on his way to the Crimea). See the article by N. Duval and M. Janon, "Le dossier d'églises d'Henchir Guessarian," *Mélanges de l'Ecole française de Rome* 97 (1985):1079–1112.

17. An appreciation of his role as an archaeologist in Algeria is given by Georges Marçais, *Revue Africaine* 100 (1956):8.

18. Published in two volumes as *Africa Christiana* (Brixiae, 1816–17). Morcelli made a powerful plea for the reconquest of North Africa for Christianity from "the Saracens."

19. See Louis Baunard, *Le Cardinal Lavigerie*, 2 vols. (Paris, 1920).

20. Baunard, *Cardinal Lavigerie*, 1:185–86. Even before, he had reminded the clergy of the past glories of the Church in North Africa (164).

21. "De l'Utilité d'une mission archéologique permanente à Carthage."

22. Leclercq's account of de Rossi's career in *DACL* 15.1:18–99 is lengthy and fulsome, but with a bibliography of his work that could be used as a starting point for the study of this remarkable scholar. De Rossi records his researches in the July number of his *Bulletino di archeologia cristiana* (1864) and in *Roma sotteranea* 1:250 and 287ff. This latter work was dedicated to Pope Pius IX.

23. De Rossi, *Roma sotteranea* 1:198–99.

24. Cited from Leclercq, *DACL* 15.1:25; see also Louis Duchesne in his tribute to de Rossi in *Revue de Paris* (1894):720.

25. W. H. Ramsay, *St. Paul, the Traveller and the Roman Citizen* (London, 1896), 14.

26. Ramsay described his discovery briefly in the *Bulletin de correspondence Hellenique* (1882):518–19, and in "The Tale of Saint Abercius," *Journal of Hellenic Studies* 3 (1882):339–52, he demonstrated the link between this inscription and the *Acta Abercii*.

27. An English translation of the relevant passage of the *Acta Abercii* is given in J. Stevenson and W. H. C. Frend, *A New Eusebius* (London, 1987), 110–12, while Ramsay records his discovery in *Cities and Bishoprics of Phrygia* (Oxford, 1897), 2:722–29.

28. For a short account of the course of the controversy in the 1890s see Frend, *Archaeology*, 96–99. The fragments of the inscription are illustrated (with acknowledgement to Vatican Museums) on the plate facing p. 77.

29. See S. Gsell and H. Graillot, "Ruines romaines au nord de l'Aurès," *Mélanges de l'Ecole française à Rome* 13 (1893):461–541 and 14(1894):17–86, and their "Ruines romaines au nord des Monts de Batna," ibid., 501–609.

30. Donatist inscriptions recovered very largely from these expeditions are discussed by Paul Monceaux, *Histoire littéraire de l'Afrique chrétienne* 4 (Paris, 1912), 437–84.

31. The first "Christians for Christians" inscriptions had been found by the French explorers, Le Bas and Waddington, in the Tembris Valley in northern Phrygia in the 1840s. Ramsay found others, and published them in the *Expositor* (1888):251–55. It was left to his successor in the field, W. M. Calder, to identify them as Montanist in his "Philadelphia and Montanism," *Bulletin of the John Rylands Library* 7 (1923):309–55. I do not accept revisionary queries as to the religious identity of these inscriptions.

32. See N. C. Lieu, *Manichaeism in the Later Roman Empire and Mediaeval China: A Historical Survey* (Manchester, 1984), 7 and 191–93, 201–9.

33. See Somers Clarke, *Christian Antiquities in the Nile Valley* (Oxford, 1912). The discoveries by him and other scholars are discussed by the writer in *Archaeology*, 144–55.

34. See C. Hopkins, "The Christian Church" (chap. 7) in *Preliminary Report on the Fifth Season's Work at Dura Europos* (New Haven, 1934); P. Baur, "The Paintings in the Christian Chapel" (chap. 8) in ibid.; and M. Rostoutzev, *The Art of Dura Europos* (Oxford, 1938).

35. K. Michałowski, *Faras: Die Kathedrale aus dem Wüstensand* (Cologne/Zürich/Einsiedeln, 1967). Plates 3 and 4 show a magnificent fresco depicting the Archangel Michael with the Three Youths in the Fiery Furnace.

36. For the scrolls dated to 1372 found on the body of Bishop Timotheos, see J.M. Plumley, "The Scrolls of Bishop Timotheos: Two Documents from Mediaeval Nubia," *Texts from Excavations* 1 (Oxford, 1975). For the fifteenth–century leather scrolls, see Frend, "The Qasr Ibrim expedition, Dec. 1963–Feb. 1964," *Akten des vii. internationalen Kongresses für christliche Archaeologie* (Vatican, 1969), 561–68. The latest scroll was dated 1464.

37. Published in the *Jahrbuch für Antike und Christentum* 30 (1987) and 35 (1992).

38. "Motu Proprio del S. Padre Pio XI," *Rivista di archeologia cristiana* 3 (1926):7–19.

39. See A. Ferrua, "Le pitture della Nuova Catacomba di Via Latina," *Monumenti di antichità cristiana*, 2nd Ser., 8 (Vatican City, 1960) and see J. M. C. Toynbee's review in *Journal of Roman Studies* 52 (1962):356–57.

40. The best summary is still that of J. M. C. Toynbee and J. Ward Perkins, *The Shrine of St. Peter and the Vatican Excavations* (London, 1956). For Margharita Guarducci's subsequent claims, see her article "Vatican" in *Encyclopedia of the Early Church* (New York, 1992) 2:862.

41. Eusebius, *Historia Ecclesiastica* 2.25:6–7.

42. Toynbee and Ward Perkins, *Shrine of St. Peter*, 144ff.

43. See the writer's *Archaeology of Early Christianity*, 270–71.

44. Discussed by the writer, *Archaeology of Early Christianity*, 273–74.

45. Cited from Stevenson, *Catacombs* 52.

46. William Camden, *Britannia*, Eng. tr. from the Latin by Edmund Gibson, Bishop of London, 4th ed. (1772). Preface.

47. See K. S. Painter, *The Water Newton Christian Silver* (London, 1977).

48. J. M. C. Toynbee, "A New Roman Mosaic Found in Dorset," *Journal of Roman Studies* 54 (1964):7–14; E. W. Meates, *The Lullingstone Roman Villa* (London, 1955), chap. 10; K. S. Painter, "The Mildenhall Treasure: A Reconsideration," *British Museum Quarterly* 37.4–5 (1955):154ff.; C. Johns and R. Bland, "The Hoxne Late–Roman Treasure," *Britannia* 25 (1994):165–73; and A. J. Rank and W. H. C. Frend, "A Decorated Lead Object from Lode," *Antiquaries Journal* 72 (1992):168–70.

49. F. W. Schlatter, "A Mosaic Interpretation of Jerome, *In Hiezechielem*," *Vigiliae Christianae* 49.1 (1995):64–81.

One Bread, One Body:
Ritual Symbols of Ecclesial Communion
in the Patristic Period

Robert F. Taft, S.J.
Pontifical Oriental Institute, Rome

A popular American hymn by John Foley, S.J., still extols the ancient Pauline principle of eucharistic unity, both symbolic and actual:

> One bread, one body, one Lord of all,
> one cup of blessing which we bless.
> And we, though many, throughout the earth,
> we are one body in this one Lord.

Amidst the plethora of chalices and ciboria full of individual hosts that grace Roman Catholic altars today, this is little more than wishful thinking.[1]

In the patristic period of Late Antiquity, however, the situation was quite different, as the Church struggled to maintain the unity of its ecclesial communion symbols in imaginative ways. Several separate but related "unities" and the respective rituals symbolizing them were involved in this effort:

1. *The unity of the eucharistic bread.* The symbolic unity of the Body of Christ was maintained by consecrating, if possible, only one eucharistic loaf, to be broken and distributed to all as a sign of our unity with one another in the one body of Christ, following the teaching of 1 Cor. 10:16–17: "The cup of blessing which we bless, is it not a communion in the blood of Christ? The bread which we break, is it not a communion in the body of Christ? Because there is one loaf, we who are many are one body, for we all partake of the same loaf." This provided the *raison d'être* and symbolism of the rite known as the fraction.

2. *The unity of the eucharistic community.* One congregation, one altar, one eucharist was the universal rule symbolizing this unity in the early centuries of the Church. Our modern practice of holding several Sunday eucharists in a single parish church on the same day would have been anathema to the Fathers of the Church.

3. *The unity of the eucharistic Body and Blood of Christ,* That the consecrated
    eucharistic species are the one and inseparable Body and Blood of the living,
    Risen Christ was (and continues to be) symbolized in the eucharist by the
    "commixture" or "commingling." This "union (ἕνωσις)," as later Byzantine
    sources call it, consists in "uniting" Christ's eucharistic Body to his Blood by
    breaking off a particle of the consecrated bread at the fraction, and dropping
    it into the chalice of consecrated wine.
4. *The unity and unicity of the once-and-for-all sacrifice of Christ.* The one
    indivisible oblation of the cross, unrepeatable though re-presented again and
    again sacramentally in every sacrifice of the eucharist, in the patristic period
    was represented symbolically in several ways, some of them related to the
    commixture rite, most of them now lost except to historical memory.

These practices, all but one (3) long-forgotten, and their relation to the commixture
(3) and to the unity of the eucharistic community (2), comprise the object of this
study.

I. Unity Rituals

In any discussion of the origins of the various Late Antique eucharistic unity
symbols, such as "uniting" the consecrated bread and wine by the commingling or
some similar rite preparatory to communion, one must distinguish several distinct
but possibly related ritual actions:

1. The *eulogies,* the ancient custom of sending a piece of the consecrated
    eucharistic bread to bishops of neighboring local churches as a sign of
    communion with them.
2. The *fermentum,* a Late-Antique Roman usage in which a piece of the
    previously consecrated eucharistic bread (the "fermentum") from the pope's
    mass was sent on Sundays as communion to the presbyters of the Roman *tituli,*
    where originally no mass was held. Later, when mass came to be celebrated
    also at the *tituli,* it seems, the fermentum continued to be sent around and put
    into the consecrated chalice as a symbol of ecclesial communion and of the
    oneness of the eucharistic banquet.
3. The Roman *sancta,* derived from the fermentum. At the papal mass the pope
    added to the consecrated chalice a particle of presanctified eucharistic bread
    (the "sancta") from the reserved sacrament, as sign of the oneness and
    continuity of the eucharist from mass to mass.[2] There may be many masses;
    there is but one saving sacrifice of Christ, one eucharist.
4. *Consecration "by contact,"* via pouring some of the Precious Blood into
    vessels of unconsecrated wine for the communion of the faithful from the cup,
    or by placing a particle of the consecrated bread in the chalice of
    unconsecrated wine, as at Byzantine Liturgy of the Presanctified Gifts.[3]

5. The *commixture, or commingling,* which consists in dropping a particle of the consecrated bread into the Precious Blood.
6. The *intinction,* or dipping of the Sacred Body into the Precious Blood and then removing it.
7. The *consignation* or "signing" of the Sacred Body with the Precious Blood, usually by using the intincted portion (6) to trace the sign of the cross on the rest of the consecrated bread.

The last four (4–7) of these ritual elements are the only ones still in use today. Of these, the more sober Roman, Byzantine, and Armenian rites know only the commingling (5), except when the eucharistic species are prepared for reservation by consignation of the host with the Precious Blood (7). The elaborate rites of intinction and consignation so highly developed in the Ethiopian and in the three Syrian traditions,[4] are later ritual elaborations of the commixture and not directly related to our present topic. But the no longer extant eulogies (1), fermentum (2), and sancta (3), though now in desuetude, provide the backdrop for understanding the context and debate concerning the origins and meaning of the commixture (5).

II. The Background

As G. Dix has pointed out, our concept of liturgy as a *public* service is post-Constantinian. The early liturgy, especially in times of persecution, was "a highly *private* activity" from which all outsiders were "rigidly excluded." This does not mean that liturgy was an *individual* affair. "Christian worship was intensely corporate, but it was not 'public.'"[5] Because it was corporate,

> It was at the *ecclesia*—in 'the church'—alone that a christian could fulfil his personal 'liturgy', that divinely-given personal part in *the* corporate act of the church, the eucharist which expressed before God the vital being of the church and each of its members. The greatest emphasis was always laid upon the duty of being present at this, for which no group-meeting could be a substitute.[6]

Since Paul's First Letter to the Corinthians, our earliest extant witness to the Lord's Supper and its liturgical continuation, the Christian eucharist has been a sign of our unity with one another in the one body of Christ. It was precisely against the divisive Corinthian abuse of each one eating his or her own meal separately that Paul argues:

> For in the first place, when you assemble as a church, I hear there are divisions among you... When you meet together it is not the Lord's supper that you eat. For in eating, each one goes ahead with his own meal... Anyone who eats and drinks without discerning the body eats and drinks judgement upon himself... So then, my brethren, when you come together to eat, wait for one another... (1 Cor. 11:18–21, 29, 33).

The same insistence continues into the next generation. St. Ignatius of Antioch at the beginning of the second century is the classic witness:

> Take care, then, to use one eucharist, for there is one flesh of our Lord Jesus Christ, and one cup of union in his blood, one altar just as there is one bishop together with the presbytery and the deacons, my fellow servants... (*Phil.* 4; cf. 6:2).
>
> All of you to a man...come together in one faith in Jesus Christ...to show obedience to the bishop and presbytery with undivided mind, breaking one bread... (*Eph.* 20:2; cf. 5:1–3).

But it was not just the inner unity of each separate liturgy that was the issue, as we tend to conceive it today. The liturgy itself and its ministry in each local church had to be *materially* one. Consequently, there could be but one liturgy per local church, as Ignatius of Antioch repeatedly insists:

> Shun schisms as the source of troubles. Let all follow the bishop as Jesus Christ followed the Father, and the priests as you would the apostles. Revere the deacons as you would the command of God. Apart from the bishop, let no one perform any of the functions that pertain to the Church. Let that eucharist be held valid which is offered by the bishop or by one to whom the bishop has committed this charge. Wherever the bishop appears, there let the people be; as wherever Jesus Christ is, there is the Catholic Church. It is not lawful to baptize or give communion without the bishop's consent. But whatever has his approval is pleasing to God. In this way, whatever you do will be safe and valid (*Smyrn.* 8).[7]
>
> Strive to do all things in harmony with God, with the bishop presiding in the place of God, the presbyters in place of the council of the apostles and the deacons...entrusted with the ministry of Jesus Christ... Love one another at all times in Jesus Christ. Let there be nothing among you that could divide you, but be united with the bishop and those presiding... Just as the Lord did nothing by himself or through the apostles without the Father, being one with him, so neither should you undertake anything without the bishop or presbyteral council. Do not try to make anything private appear reasonable to you, but let there be in common one prayer, one supplication, one mind, one hope in love, in the blameless joy that is Jesus Christ, above whom there is nothing. Come together all of you as to one temple of God and to one altar, to one Jesus Christ, who came forth from the Father in whom he is, and to whom he has returned (*Magn.* 6–7).[8]

Other subapostolic documents—*Didache* XIV, 2 (ca. 50–70 AD),[9] *1 Clement* 34:7[10] from the last decade of the same century, the slightly later *Ep. of Barnabas* 4:10[11]—reflect the same concern, as, indeed, do the sources of East and West right up until the end of Late Antiquity.[12] Eusebius (ca. 263–339), citing in his *Church History* X, 4:68 his famous panegyric at the inauguration of the new cathedral at Tyre ca. 317 AD, calls the one altar in Tyre the "only-begotten" (μονογενὲς θυσιαστήριον), like the one Christ whose altar it is.[13]

Indeed, "to set up altar against altar" will become a topos in Greek and Latin literature for dividing the Church. In 341 AD, canon 5 of the Synod of Antioch condemns priests or deacons who set up an altar (θυσιαστήριον ἔστησε) apart from their bishop, and later, ca. 400 AD, the *Canons of the Apostles* 31, enacts measures against priests who dare to do the same (θυσιαστήριον ἔτερον πήξει).[14]

Similarly, in North Africa Cyprian of Carthage († ca. 258), *Ep. 43*, 5, uses the same symbol of church/eucharistic unity:

Deus unus est et Christus unus et una ecclesia et cathedra una super Petrum Domini uoce fundata. Aliud altare constitui aut sacerdotium nouum fieri praeter unum altare et unum sacerdotium non potest. Quisque alibi colligerit spargit.[15]	There is one God and one Christ and one Church and one episcopal throne founded on Peter by the voice of the Lord. Another altar cannot be set up or a new priesthood established. Whoever would congregate elsewhere scatters.

And in *Ep. 72, 2*, Cyprian reproaches the Novatians that "against the one divine altar they tried to offer false and sacrilegious sacrifices separately (...contra altare unum adque diuinum sacrificia foris falsa ac sacrilega offerre conati sint)."[16]

Augustine (354–430), *In Ep. Iohannis ad Parthos, tract.* III, 7, uses the same argument against the Donatists. Applying to them John 2:19—"they went out from us, but were not of us"—he says:

...ergo nec illi a nobis exierunt, nec nos ab ipsis. Si ergo non a nobis exivimus, in unitate sumus: si in unitate sumus, quid faciunt in hac civitate duo altaria?[17]	...hence they did not go out from us, nor we from them. If, therefore, we did not divide, we are united; but if we are united, what are two altars doing in this city?

In short, two eucharists in Hippo as in Carthage meant a divided church, a charge Augustine repeats in *Contra Cresconium* II, 1.2 against the Donatist Cresconius, "...qui altare contra altare in eadem ciuitate primus erexit, magnum scandalum factum est..."[18] And Pope Leo I (440–461), in his *Ep. 9, 2*, to Dioscorus of Alexandria in 444/5, admits more than one eucharist in a city only when the cathedral basilica cannot hold the entire congregation.[19]

Such strict principles were feasible only in the demographic context of early Christianity, largely an urban phenomenon centered in the cities of the Roman Empire.[20] The basic unit, the "parish," a cross between today's parish and diocese, designated the local urban congregation, not the territory it covered. It had one *domus ecclesiae* or meeting house, and the pastor was the bishop, not a presbyter.[21] Presbyters and deacons assisted the bishop, but originally he alone baptized, confirmed, preached, reconciled penitents, and presided over the eucharist.[22] Presbyters "concelebrated"[23] with him, but had no absolute, independent authorization to preside at the eucharist or administer the sacramental mysteries on their own unless delegated to do so by the bishop.[24]

Initially such a system caused no special problems. Except in the largest cities like Rome, the number of clergy in a town was quite small. At the outbreak of the presecution of Diocletian in 303, in Roman North Africa, Cirta (Constantine in Algeria) had a bishop, four presbyters, three deacons, four subdeacons, seven readers, and some sextons. A century later, Hippo under Augustine (†430) is thought to have had two presbyters, half a dozen deacons, and one subdeacon.[25] This is like the pre-Nicene situation envisaged in the letters of Ignatius of Antioch already cited. In the later *Apostolic Tradition* (ca. 215), the bishop is still the center of just about everything, and great stress is put on services in the local congregation, celebrated by the bishop, assisted by the deacons, and surrounded by his presbyterate and people—an image of the Church in microcosm.[26]

But as the Church spread beyond the cities of the eastern Mediterranean litoral to the interior, and in the West into the countryside of the *pagani* between the towns, this system broke down and presbyters, whom bishops were forced by necessity to commission with the pastoral care of these satellite communities, were conceded certain powers once reserved to the bishop, most notably the right to preside at the eucharistic synaxis. Under the pressure of the growing number of converts, a similar breakdown of the old one-eucharist-per-city system would occur later in urban areas too.

> ...This insistence on a single eucharistic assembly of the whole church, bishop, presbyters, deacons and laity together...always remained the ideal, until it was finally lost to sight in the later middle ages. But the growth of numbers and the size of the great cities early made it impossible to fulfil it in practice; and Ignatius already recognises that the bishop may have to delegate his 'special liturgy' to others at minor eucharistic assemblies: 'Let that be accounted a valid eucharist which is either under the bishop or under one whom the bishop has assigned this.' [*Smyr.* 8:1] The last church to abandon the tradition of a single eucharist under the bishop as at least an ideal was the church of the city of Rome. There the Pope's 'stational mass' at which he was assisted by representatives of the whole clergy and laity of the city continued as the central eucharistic observance right down to the fourteenth c., and did not wholly die out until 1870. Of course there were other celebrations simultaneously in the 'Titles' or parish churches. But for centuries it was the custom at Rome to dispatch to each of these by an acolyte the *fermentum*, a fragment from the Breads consecrated by the Pope at 'the' eucharist, in token that each of these was still in Ignatius' phrase, 'under the bishop', as the 'liturgy' of the presbyters to whom 'the bishop had assigned' it.[27]

This is the ideological framework for the customs we must now examine.

III. The Eulogies

The Greek term εὐλογία, transliterated directly into Latin as "eulogia," literally "blessings," has had a bewildering variety of meanings in Christian usage East and West.[28] The following list is indicative rather than exhaustive:

1. Initially, and in some sources for centuries thereafter,[29] eulogia commonly designated the consecrated eucharistic species,[30] a usage probably derived from τὸ ποτήριον τῆς εὐλογίας of 1 Cor. 10:16[31] and found thereafter in Christian literature from the early 3rd-century apocryphal Acts of Thomas on.[32]

2. But by the 3rd century, eulogia has also come to mean blessed but unconsecrated bread[33] (in some but not all cases the leftover bread offered at the eucharist but not consecrated[34]).

3. Unconsecrated blessed bread given or sent to other Christians as a sign of Christian fellowship,[35] to ward off evil,[36] in commemoration of the departed,[37] as a blessing,[38] etc.

4. Fruits or other victuals distributed, as in Egeria's *Journal,* after eucharistic communion (3.7) or to participants at other church services (15.6), or even apart from the liturgy, as a sign of hospitality to guests (11.1, 21.3), especially in monastic circles.[39]

5. Victuals distributed to the needy, and, indeed, any gift at all.

6. As a synonym for the small loaves (ἄρτος, προσφορά), prepared for use in the eucharist.[40]

7. Blessed bread distributed at the end of the eucharist, a custom once common in East[41] and West[42] (the French "pain bénit"), and still reflected in Armenian and Byzantine usage in the blessed bread or "antidoron" distributed at the end of the Divine Liturgy,[43] and, formerly in Byzantine monastic usage at the end of the Typika office,[44] originally a presanctified monastic communion rite for aliturgical days.[45]

8. A holy object sanctified by contact with a saint's relics.[46]

9. In Byzantine usage, any dispensation or permission from a bishop or religious superior, within or outside the context of the liturgy, usually requested with the formula "Bless, master (εὐλόγησον, δέσποτα)."

Our interest here will focus on the liturgical use of the term "eulogies" to designate bread offered, blessed—and sometimes but not always consecrated—at the eucharist. From the bread the faithful offered for the eucharistic sacrifice, only as much as was needed for communion was consecrated. The rest, though not consecrated, was considered blessed by the very fact of its having been offered for the eucharist. This leftover bread was distributed after the service in a variety of ways, depending on the epoch and locale: to the clergy as part of their upkeep, to monks, to the communicants, to the non-communicants as antidoron. As for the bread consecrated at the eucharist, it was distributed in communion at the service, to be consumed there, brought to those absent, or taken home for communicating during the week. What remained of the consecrated species was consumed forthwith or, if necessary, destroyed.[47]

There is substantial evidence that both types of eulogies, consecrated or merely blessed, were once sent to those unable to attend the service. We know that in

Antiquity the faithful took the consecrated eucharistic species—doubtless only the consecrated bread—home with them from the one Sunday synaxis for communion on weekdays,[48] when there was normally no liturgy except in special circumstances.[49] They even carried the eucharist about with them on trips, as a sacred object, the way one would carry a relic or an icon in later times.[50] Communion was also brought to members of the local community unable to attend the eucharistic service.[51] These absent members were not only the infirm. In those days churches and their liturgies were mostly urban, travel difficult, transportation slow or non-existent, and many Christians in the countryside, which in most areas did not begin to have resident clergy until the 4th c., lived too far away from the church to be present at every Sunday synaxis.[52] Furthermore, there were the persecutions, and communion had to be brought, doubtless clandestinely, to the Christians who languished in prison.[53]

The unconsecrated eulogia served the same symbolic purpose. Paulinus of Nola (355–431), writing of the eulogia he and his wife Therasia sent to Sulpicius Severus from their retreat at the sanctuary of St. Felix in Cimitele near Nola in Campania in 409–410, clearly distinguishes it from the eucharist:

Panem Campanum de cellula nostra tibi pro eulogia misimus...tu licet uberioribus micis a domini mensa iam saturatus sis, dignare a peccatoribus acceptum in nomine domini panem in eulogiam uertere.[54]	From our cell we have sent you bread from Campania as eulogia...even though you are already nourished by richer morsels from the Lord's table, deign to turn into an eulogia the bread received from sinners in the name of the Lord.

These usages were a sign of everyone's communion with one another in the one body of the Lord, both eucharistic and mystical. That, in fact, is what the eucharist was all about, from our earliest evidence in 1 Cor. 10:16–17 up through the Apostolic Fathers,[55] until the decline in communion from the 4th c., and the later multiplication of private chapels and eucharists, effectively destroyed the primitive meaning.[56] But these usages were a sign of the communion of members *within* the local eucharistic community, the Church writ small.

More germane to our investigation is the custom of sending the consecrated eucharistic eulogies to the bishop of a distant congregation as a sign of the universal church communion *among* local eucharistic communities throughout the Great Church. We see this emerge for the first time in the 2nd century, during the famous paschal controversy. The story has come down to us in a letter of Irenaeus to Pope Victor I (ca. 189–198/9) preserved in Eusebius, *Church History* V, 23–24. Irenaeus is attempting to persuade the pope not to excommunicate local churches that insisted on following their ancient Quartodeciman paschal usage of celebrating the Pasch on 14 Nisan, date of the Jewish Passover. He argues that Victor's predecessors, though themselves not Quartodecimans, remained in peaceful communion with those who were: "...The presbyter before you, who did not observe it, sent the eucharist to those parishes that did observe it (τοῖς ἀπὸ τῶν παροικιῶν τηροῦσιν ἔπεμπον εὐχαριστίαν⁵⁷)." Here of course παροικία does not mean "parish" in our modern sense of a diocesan pastoral subdivision. It means, rather, what we would call a diocese or eparchy, an ecclesiastical circumscription under the jurisdication of a bishop, an episcopal see.⁵⁸ This is clear from Irenaeus' references in the same letter to Pope Victor's attempt to excommunicate "the parishes of all Asia," and to the Quartodecimans who came to Rome "from the parishes in which it [sc., the Quartodeciman Pasch] was observed."⁵⁹

This Christian custom had pagan and non-eucharistic Christian parallels.⁶⁰ Pagans also sent a μέρις or portion of their sacrifice to the absent as a sign of sharing in the oblation, and Christians held agape meals, and repasts in honor of the martyrs, "...calling one another together and sending portions (μερίδας) to those nearby and banqueting in all the churches and celebrating 'with psalms and hymns and spiritual songs' (Col. 3:16, cf. Eph. 5:19)—...ἀλλήλους συγκαλοῦντες καὶ πέμποντες μερίδας τοῖς πλησίον καὶ κατὰ πᾶσαν ἐκκλησίαν εὐωχούμενοι καὶ πανηγυρίζοντες ψαλμοῖς καὶ ὕμνοις καὶ ᾠδαῖς πνευματικαῖς"—as we read in The Martyrdom of the Ten Holy Martyrs in Crete in the City of Gortina 10, a document from around the end of the 4th c. describing events during the persecution of Decius in 249–251 AD.⁶¹

How far back the usage of sending the eucharist abroad goes we do not know. Irenaeus lists Pope Victor's predecessors back to Xystus (Sixtus) I (ca. 116–ca. 125 AD), with whom Dix thinks the usage may have originated,⁶² but that is just guesswork. Speculation, too, are the theories regarding who sent the eulogies to whom.⁶³ It is unlikely that they were sent any great distance. The usage was probably restricted to neighboring churches and, once intermediate church unities had developed, to the churches within the same metropolitanate or ecclesiastical province. The metropolitan had the right to preside over the ordination of his suffragan bishops, and the eulogies were undoubtedly an ongoing symbol of their communion and interdependence.

F.J. Dölger sees in St. Filastrius († ca. 397), bishop of Brescia, Diversarum hereseon liber 49, 5, evidence that the custom had by then fallen into disuse. Filastrius reports the rumor that the Montanists mixed the blood of a child with the Easter sacrifice, then sent a portion of it to their adherents everywhere: "Dicunt enim eos de infantis sanguine in pascha miscere in suum sacrificium, suisque ita ubique emittere perniciosis et falsis satellitibus."⁶⁴ This story most likely reflects a misunderstanding of the by then defunct custom of sending out the eucharistic eulogies as a sign of communion at Easter.⁶⁵

The paschal context of both this and the Quartodeciman account, as well as the Synod of Laodicea (ca. 360–390 AD), suggests that sending the eulogies was restricted to paschaltide. Canon 14 of Laodicea explicitly forbids the custom of sending the eucharistic eulogies around to other "parishes"—i.e., dioceses—at Easter: "That at the feast of Easter the sacred gifts no longer be sent to foreign dioceses as eulogies (περὶ τοῦ μὴ τὰ ἅγια εἰς λόγον εὐλογιῶν κατὰ τὴν ἑορτὴν τοῦ πάσχα, εἰς ἑτέρας παροικίας διαπέμπεσθαι)."[66] The prohibition, obviously, is aimed at the custom of sending around the eucharist. Easter is mentioned only because that is when this was usually done. Thereafter, it becomes the *unconsecrated* eulogies that are usually sent as a sign of communion, though remnants of the older custom continue to crop up again in later sources.[67]

Note that none of these witnesses to the paschal eulogies indicate what the local church did with the portion it received. Doubtless it was consumed; how is not said. In the light of what we shall see about Roman developments with the fermentum one might hypothesize that it was dropped into the consecrated chalice during mass, but that would be sheer inference for this early period.

IV. The Fermentum

Though the eulogia tradition broke down at a relatively early date in the East, an analogous custom, the fermentum, had grown up meanwhile within the local church of Rome. *Pace* the persistent mythology to the contrary, sober Rome was far more conservative and attached to ancient ways than the East. So it was Rome that devised a compromise solution to preserve at least a semblance of that unity without which the eucharist could no longer mean what it was meant to.[68] Faced with the problem of providing pastoral care for a growing Christian population, Rome opted, at least initially, for an intermediate solution without abandoning the principle that the entire community was under the direct pastoral care of the bishop, and that his eucharist—everybody's eucharist—was the only one. A network of titular churches or *tituli*, eventually fixed at twenty-five in number, was established to care for the neighborhood Christians.

Each *titulus* or "title" was staffed by five or six presbyters assisted by clerics in minor orders.

> But the duties of these clergy were confined at first to preparing the people living in the streets near the church for baptism and looking after those undergoing public penance. The pope took not only all baptisms, but also all masses, celebrating at each church in turn, and the consecrated elements were carried by acolytes to each of the titular churches and here administered to the people by the priests. Some historians think that this system of the one mass for the whole city lasted in Rome till the opening of the fifth century. At any rate masses celebrated in city churches by the priests attached to these churches were a late development.[69]

These are the only sacramental ministries mentioned in the *Liber pontificalis* 31, for the twenty-five *tituli* set up in Rome by Pope Marcellus (308–309):

Hic fecit cymiterium Novellae, via Salaria, et XXV titulos in urbe Roma constituit, quasi diocesis, propter baptismum et paenitentiam multorum qui convertebantur ex paganis et propter sepulturas martyrum.[70]

He made the cemetery of Novella[71] on the Via Salaria, and erected in the city of Rome twenty-five "tituli," like dioceses,[72] for the baptism and penance of the multitude of pagans who were converting, and for the burial of the martyrs.

The text dates only from between 530–687, but its omission of any mention of the eucharist is significant.[73] For Nautin the reason is indubitably the fermentum, Rome's compromise solution to the dilemma of eucharistic unity and the growing pastoral need for mutiple eucharists.[74]

Though the *Liber pontificalis* 33 attributes the usage to Pope Miltiades (311–314), and refers to it again in §40 apropos of Pope Siricius (384–399),[75] these texts (like most of the rest of this document) have been challenged.[76] So Innocent I (401–417) provides the earliest unimpeachable evidence for the fermentum. Bishop Decentius of Gubbio had written the pope with a series of questions, one of which concerned the fermentum. Should he do what the pope does, and send the fermentum to all the parish churches of his jurisdiction? In his reply, *Ep. 25,* 8, dated 19 March 416, Innocent patiently explains that the two situations are not the same. Gubbio is a small Umbrian hill town with one cathedral and a number of rural parish churches in the surrounding countryside. Rome is an urban center with all its *tituli* within the city itself.

De fermento vero quod die dominica per titulos mittimus, superflue nos consulere voluisti, cum omnes ecclesiae nostrae intra civitatem sint constitutae. Quarum presbiteri, quia die ipsa propter plebem sibi creditam nobiscum convenire non possunt, idcirco fermentum a nobis confectum per acolitos accipiunt, ut se a nostra communione maxime illa die non iudicent separatos. Quod per parrochias fieri debere non puto quia nec longe portanda sunt sacramenta nec nos per cimeteria diversa constitutis presbiteris destinamus et presbiteri eorum conficiendorum ius habeant atque licentiam.[77]

As for the fermentum which we send out to the *tituli* on Sunday, you wished to consult us on it to no purpose, since all our churches are established within the city. Since their presbyters cannot come together with us on that day because of the people confided to their care, they receive from the acolytes the fermentum consecrated by us, so that they might not feel themselves separated from our communion especially on that day. But I do not think this should be done throughout the outlying dioceses,[78] because the sacraments should not be carried far, and because we ourselves do not send it to the presbyters established in the various cemeteries, but the presbyters [there] have the right and the faculty to confect them [the sacraments] themselves.

Recent research on this topic by P. Nautin indicates that contrary to what was once thought,[79] the Sunday synaxis in the *tituli* was originally only a Liturgy of the Word for the catechumens, and the fermentum was communion for the presbyters presiding over these non-eucharistic services, not a particle of the pope's eucharist to be added to theirs, as it will later become.[80] This seems clear from the letter of Innocent I. He says that the fermentum is not sent to the outlying dioceses because of the distance, nor does it need to be sent to the cemetery chapels *extra muros* not just because of the distance,[81] *but because the cemetery presbyters were empowered to say mass themselves.* From this I would infer that the urban *tituli* presbyters were not.

Though Innocent I is our first clear witness to the fermentum, it surely existed long before his time. According to Eusebius, *Church History* VI, 43:11, in 253 the clergy of Rome already comprised forty-six presbyters, seven deacons, seven subdeacons, and ninety-four minor clerics.[82] They must have been engaged in a ministry similar to that Innocent describes, since it is hardly imaginable that Roman presbyters had acquired less rather than more eucharistic authority between 253 and 416 AD.

Just how the urban Roman presbyters actually consumed the fermentum they received cannot be demonstrated, though it is presumed they placed it in the chalice of wine, which was considered to be consecrated by this contact with the Body of Christ.[83] Eventually the Roman *tituli* system breaks down and the local urban communities acquire the right to hold their own mass. But a relic of the earlier usage was preserved. On festive occasions the fermentum was still sent round, no longer to allow the presbyters to participate in the bishop's eucharist, the unique Sunday eucharist of the local church, but as a sign that their eucharist and his were one. In this case, on feasts when the fermentum was sent, it was added to the consecrated chalice during the manual acts, as we see in the 8th c. *Ordines Romani II*, 6 and *XXX B,* 64–65.[84]

V. The Sancta

It is at this juncture that an analogous rite, the "sancta," surely derived from the fermentum, first appears at the papal mass in the *Ordines Romani.* If the pope is presiding at the eucharist, he cannot, of course, send himself the fermentum. Instead, he puts into the chalice a piece of the sancta or presanctified eucharistic bread reserved in the tabernacle ("in conditatio") from a previous mass.[85] This is done at the same moment of the service when the fermentum was added at non-papal masses. Since the pope selects just a small portion of the reserved sacrament for this purpose, and leaves the rest in the tabernacle,[86] one cannot see in this usage a practical rite for renewing the reserved species and consuming the old. It must have been purely symbolic, and presumably derived from the fermentum.

We see this usage at the turn of the 7/8th c. in *Ordo Romanus I,*[87] as well as in several later sources.[88] According to the earliest document, *Ordo I*, the manual acts of the solemn papal mass unfolded as follows (the numbers in brackets refer to Andrieu's edition):

1. At the *"Pax domini sit semper vobiscum"* the pope puts the sancta into the consecrated chalice [95].
2. After the kiss of peace, fraction, comminution, and *"Agnus dei..."* [96–106] the pope communicates from the host, saving a particle of his portion which he *also puts into the consecrated chalice,* saying the traditional Roman commixture formula: *"Fiat commixitio et consecratio corporis et sanguinis domini nostri Iesu Christi accipientibus nobis in vitam aeternam. Amen"* [107].
3. Some of the precious blood from this chalice is poured into the communion cup (*sciffus, scyphus,* from the Greek σκύφος) of *unconsecrated* wine [108].
4. After the clergy have received the host from the hand of the pope [108–9], an assisting bishop administers to them the chalice [110].
5. Then the archdeacon takes the chalice, pours its contents into the communion cups (*sciffi*), from which the faithful receive the precious blood by means of a straw (*pugillaris*) [111], while the subdeacon removes the empty chalice to the sacristy [112].[89]

There are fully *four separate commixtures* described here:

1. Of the presanctified (sancta) with the consecrated wine.
2. Of the particle from the pope's host with the same.
3. Of a portion of the consecrated wine holding 1–2 (the sancta plus the particle) with the unconsecrated wine in the *sciffus.*
4. Of what is left of the consecrated wine with the *sciffus* again, after the communion of the dignitaries.

These four commixtures represent three distinct rites:

1. The fermentum/sancta.
2. The commixture *tout court.*
3. The consecration-by-contact of the wine in the *sciffus* for the people's communion in the cup.

This complicated usage did not survive the Roman Rite's transalpine crossing to the Carolingian Empire. The fermentum/sancta rite is suppressed in such Frankish adaptations of *Ordo Romanus I* as the *Ordo of St. Amand* (= *Ordo IV,* 56–66), where the commixture follows the *"Pax domini sit semper vobiscum"* and fraction, as in later usage.[90] We see this already by the end of the 8th c. in *Ordo II,* 6 as well as *III,* 3, *IX,* 46,[91] and that is where it has remained in the Missals of Pius V and Paul VI.[92]

VI. Toward the Origins of the Commixture

Much has been written about the relation of all this to the commingling of the Roman Mass, and its possible origins in the paschal eulogies. De Jong, who has perhaps had more to say on the topic than anyone, sums up contemporary thinking on the links in all this:

> Fermentum [is] the particle of the Eucharistic Bread sent by the Bishop of Rome to the bishops of other churches as a symbol of unity and intercommunion. According to Eusebius this custom was already known to Irenaeus as a longstanding tradition.[93] In the 4th c. the Council of Laodicea forbade sending the Eucharist abroad. In Rome, however, at the time of Innocent I (402–417), acolytes brought the fermentum to the priests of the titular churches every Sunday. This too was a symbol of unity between the bishop and his priests. For the same reason, the officiating priest, who represented the pope at the stational Mass, also received the fermentum. When this custom finally fell into disuse, every priest nonetheless continued to drop a particle of the consecrated Host into the chalice at the Commingling, but the Host was the one consecrated in the same Mass.[94]

In my view, however, although the similarities among these various usages are undeniable, there is no convincing evidence for any genetic link between fermentum and commixture, the only rite that interests us here. Since the commixture proper, performed by putting a particle of the host into the chalice of the Precious Blood, is found in documents that also have the fermentum/sancta rite, it would be temerarious to conclude without further evidence (which is wanting), that the commixture is derived from the fermentum. And if it were, then *why is there also a commixture where there is already the fermentum*? Of course such argumentation is never ironclad, since in fact all sorts of inconsistencies, unnecessary duplications, and general mixups occur in later liturgical texts once people have forgotten—or no longer care—what things originally meant.

What of "consecration by contact"? Could this be at the root of the commixture? De Jong first thought so.[95] He argued especially from the rubrics of *Ordo Romanus IV,* 74–75, 83, which explicitly call for both the Precious Blood plus the intincted particle put into it at the commixture to be poured together into the communion cups of unconsecrated wine.[96] But there was no need of a commixture for this: contact with the consecrated wine alone would have sufficed to consecrate the wine in the *sciffus*.[97] Furthermore, as Jungmann objected, how does one explain that the consecrated particle was dropped into the *consecrated wine,* as we saw above in *Ordo I,* 107?[98] So there is no convincing reason to assert that the commixture had to antedate the Roman practice of consecrating the communion cups by contact. Besides, we have no earlier evidence for that practice than *Ordo I.*

Could the Roman custom have come from Syria? Initially de Jong rejected the possibility proposed by Jungmann and Haberstroh that an earlier, purely symbolic commixture of Syrian origin could have influenced the Roman Mass.[99] This could not have occurred, de Jong argued, before the influx of Orientals to the West at the end of the 7th c., when the *Agnus Dei* was introduced into the Roman Mass from Syria.[100] But I find it hard to grasp the point of this argument. There is in fact no Roman evidence for the commixture before the end of the 7th c., when it first appears in *Ordo I.* But since both Theodore of Mopsuestia and the 7th-c. Syrian influence on the Roman Mass antedate *Ordo I,* the 8th-c. date of the latter can hardly be said to exclude Syria as the ultimate source of the Roman commixture.

Could the opposite, then, be true, as some have proposed? Could the Roman fermentum rite, which probably goes back no further than the second half of the 3rd century—Hippolytus is silent on the subject—be the source of the eastern commixture first seen in Cilicia ca. 392 in the catechetical homilies of Theodore of Mopsuestia (†428) (see section VII.1 below)? In my view the normal direction of liturgical influence and borrowing among the various traditions makes a Roman influence on Syrian usage at this early date extremely unlikely.

At any rate the *Agnus Dei* sung at the fraction, already part of the Roman Mass in *Ordo I,* 104,[101] certainly came from the East, having been introduced by the Syrian Pope Sergius I (687–701), as the *Liber pontificalis* 86 claims,[102] if not earlier—Pope Theodore I (642–649) was a Palestinian. What is more, the *Agnus Dei* is intimately connected to the ideas concerning the fraction as symbolic of Christ's body "broken for us," in his passion,[103] ideas that were current in Syria and Palestine at the time, just as they were in the doctrine of the Quinisext Council "in Trullo" (691/2 AD) concerning the eucharist and representations of Jesus as Lamb of God.[104]

If the *Agnus Dei* came from the Syrian East, then so could the Roman commixture have. About this *possibility,* then, there can be no doubt whatever. Whether it in fact did originate there cannot be demonstrated, but I think it the most likely explanation, as does de Jong in his later writings on the topic.[105] As for the fermentum, it is probably a relic of the paschal eulogies. And the sancta is clearly derived from the fermentum.

But where did the late 4th-century eucharist described by Theodore of Mopsuestia get its purely symbolic commixture? The sources are silent, but it is possibly a derivative of the paschal eulogies suppressed in the East by the Council of Laodicea (ca. 360–390 AD) around the same time Theodore was preaching. The "Lamb of God" is, after all, a paschal theme, and the preservation under new symbolic cover of rites that once had another meaning and purpose is the very stuff of ritual history.

VII. Commixture/Consignation/Intinction

The fraction apart, the further elaboration of the "manual acts" in preparation of the sacred gifts just before communion is of decidedly Syrian provenance. The earliest witness is Ephrem (†373), who refers to a rite of consignation or "signing" of the eucharistic bread with the consecrated wine.[106] A similar rite is still practiced today in all eastern eucharists save the Byzantine and Armenian, either by the priest dipping his finger or a piece of the host into the chalice, then "painting" the sign of the cross on the Sacred Body with the Precious Blood.[107]

1. *Theodore of Mopsuestia (ca. 392 AD):*

Preached probably somewhere in Cilicia around 392 AD, *Homily 16,* 15–20 of Theodore, bishop of Mopsuestia from 392 until his death in 428,[108] is the earliest detailed description of such "manual acts" and their symbolism:

[15] **1.** The bishop...takes the bread in his hands and looks towards heaven. With his eyes fixed on high, he gives thanks for these great gifts, and breaks the bread. **2.** While breaking it he prays for the people that the grace of God may be upon them, saying: *"May the grace of our Lord Jesus Christ be upon all of you."* **3.** The people receive this [greeting] and answer with the usual words. **4.** And with the bread he marks the sign of the cross on the blood, and with the blood on the bread. **5.** And he joins them together, reuniting them in order to show everyone that, although two, they are one in power and are the memorial of the death and passion undergone by the body of our Lord when his blood was shed on the cross for all of us. This is what the bishop does in signing and joining and mingling them together. For every human body is one with its blood, and blood is throughout it. **6.** So from whatever slit or cut one makes in it, large or small, blood will necessarily flow according to the cut made...

[16] **7.** ...It is right, therefore, that according to this tradition we place both of them on the altar, to show what took place before, so we will know that both of them are one in power, as belonging to the one person who alone underwent the passion, that is to say the flesh of our Lord, from which also blood was shed. **8.** That is why the bishop, after completing the oblation, rightly breaks the bread and joins it with that [= the blood] while making the sign of the cross with it [= the bread], and then likewise brings the blood near the bread in order to show that both of them, which the passion affected, are one, and that we also are ordered to perform the memorial of the passion in this way.

[17] **9.** For this reason it is customary to drop the life-giving bread into the chalice little by little, in order to show that they are inseparable, that they are one in power and confer the same grace to those who receive them. **10.** The bishop does not break the bread to no purpose, but because Christ our Lord after his resurrection from the dead, appeared to all his followers...to show himself risen to them, and to reveal his resurrection and announce to them that they too will participate with him in those great benefits with which he greeted them...as to the women, to whom he appeared right after his resurrection, he said: "Peace be with you." **11.** For these reasons it is necessary that the bishop...break the bread in the way our Lord first appeared, now to this one, now to that one, and at another time showing himself to many, so that all could approach him...

[19] **12.** For this reason all the bread is finally broken, so that all of us who are present may be able to receive it...

[20] 13. ...When, therefore, the priest has finished all the service of the consecration, he rightly begins to break the bread, from which we must imagine that Christ our Lord, through each portion of the bread, draws near to the person who receives him, greeting him and speaking to him of his resurrection...[109]

This text is not exactly pellucid. First, the presiding celebrant takes the sacred bread in both hands, raises his eyes to heaven, and says, apparently, a prayer of thanksgiving for the gifts (**1**) Then he breaks the bread in two while greeting the people with the customary postanaphoral salutation, "The grace of our Lord Jesus Christ be upon you all" (**2**), to which the people respond with the usual, "And with your spirit" (**3**).

The next segment (**4–5**) I would take to be describing an intinction: "**4.** And with the bread he marks the sign of the cross on the blood, and with the blood on the bread. **5.** And he joins them together, reuniting them..." It seems that the bishop dips into the chalice one particle of the divided bread, making the sign of the cross with it while keeping it immersed in the Precious Blood. Then he removes from the chalice that same intincted portion of the bread and uses it to paint the sign of the cross with the Precious Blood on the rest of the broken loaf.

After this, he puts the bread into the chalice "one after another," or "little by little," "gradually," "by degrees" (**9**).[110] I cannot fathom what Theodore means here. Later (*Hom. 16*, 27–28) the faithful will receive the species separately, first the bread in the hand, then the chalice,[111] so the passage cannot mean that all the consecrated bread is put into the chalice piece by piece, as it is broken up.

After this commingling, Theodore mentions the comminution (**10–13**), saying that the rest of the bread is broken because our Lord, in his post-resurrection appearances, showed his desire to manifest himself to all, in order that they might have communion with him and enjoy the fruits of the resurrection.

Is the ritual Theodore describes in the passage cited above to be identified with the consignation still in use in the Syrian traditions? The text is not clear, though F.J. Dölger seemed to think so.[112] But this is not our problem. The consignation rite properly so called is unknown to the Byzantines, who contented themselves with a "dry consignation," making the sign of the cross over the chalice with the host before dropping it in.

2. *Narsai (†502):*

Somewhat later Narsai of Nisibis (†502), *Homily 21,* confirms the tradition of these "manual acts" in the Syrian liturgies:

> **1.** A corporal being [the priest] takes hold with his hands of the Spirit in the Bread; and he lifts up his gaze towards the height, **2.** and then he breaks it. **3.** He breaks the Bread and casts (it) into the Wine, **4.** and he signs and says: 'In the name of the Father and the Son and the Spirit, an equal nature.'

5. With the name of the Divinity, three hypostases, he completes his words; **6.** and as one dead he raises the Mystery, as a symbol of the verity. **7.** In verity did the Lord of the Mystery rise from the midst of the tomb; and without doubt the Mystery acquires the power of life. **8.** On a sudden the Bread and Wine acquire new life; and forgiveness of iniquity they give on a sudden to them that receive them. **9.** He (the priest) makes the Bread and Wine one by participation, forasmuch as the blood mingles with the body in all the senses (of man). Wine and water he casts into the cup before he consecrates, forasmuch as water also is mingled with the blood in things created.

10. With these (elements) the priest celebrates the perfect mysteries; then he makes (his) voice heard, full of love and mercy. Love and mercy are hidden in the voice of the word of his mouth; that the creature may call the Creator his Father. In the way of his voice run the voices of them that are become obedient, while they are made ready to call the hidden Divinity 'Our Father'...

11. With the voice of praise they seal the words of the completion of the Mysteries; and they render holiness to the Father and to the Son and to the Holy Spirit: 'Holy is the Father, and holy is His Begotten, and the Spirit who is from Him (*sc.* the Father); and to them is due holiness and praise from all mouths.'

12. After the utterance of sanctification and the rendering of praise they stretch the gaze of their minds towards the Gift. With their senses and mental faculties together they are eager to approach the Bread and Wine in the midst of which is hidden forgivenes of iniquity. By faith they acquire power to see things hidden; and, as it were the King, they bear in triumph the Sacrament in the midst of their palms. They hold it sure that the Body of the King dwells in the visible bread; and in it the resurrection of the dead is preached to him that eats of it.

13. 'The Body,' says the priest also when he gives it [in communion]; and 'the Blood' he calls the mingled Wine in the midst of the cup. He gives the Bread and says: 'The Body of King Messiah' (*or* 'of Christ the King'); and he gives to drink the Wine, and in like manner (he says): 'The Blood of Christ.'[113]

Frustratingly, the déroulement of the ritual is clear except for the one point that interests us. The priest takes the consecrated bread in his hands (**1**), breaks it (**2**), performs the "union" of the Body and Blood while invoking the name of the Holy Trinity (**3–5, 9**), then elevates the sacred species (**6**). These ritual gestures signify the vivifying quality of the Body and Blood of the Risen Christ (**7–8**). There follows the traditional Our Father before communion (**10**), the East-Syrian *Sanctum sanctis* and its response (**11**), and communion (**12–13**).

Just how the "union" of the Body and Blood, sign of the fulfillment in the resurrection, is performed is not clear. The priest seems to plunge a piece of the sacred bread into the consecrated chalice (**4**), making with it the sign of the cross "In the name of the Father and of the Son and of the Spirit, one equal nature" (**5**). Whether that means he makes the sign of the cross while holding the host submerged in the Precious Blood; or dips the host into the Precious Blood, then removes it and uses the moistened host to sign the rest of the Body with the Blood, as now in the Assyro-Chaldean tradition; is not altogether clear, though the latter seems more probable.

3. *John Chrysostom? (†407):*

Another early source, *In illud: Credidi propter quod locutus sum (Ps. 115:1–3)*, a homily of doubtful authenticity attributed to John Chrysostom, concludes with a comment on Ps. 115:4 ("I will take the chalice of salvation, and call upon the name of the Lord") which van de Paverd thinks could be a reference to the commingling.[114] The homilist says the chalice is "sealed in the name of the Lord (ἐν ὀνόματι κυρίου ἐσφραγισμένον); one who drinks from it, filled with the joy of the Holy Spirit, will be introduced into the holy choir of the martyrs, in Christ Jesus our Lord, to whom be glory and majesty unto the ages of ages. Amen!"[115]

VIII. Conclusion

The historical data reviewed above seem to yield the following results:

1. From the middle of the 2nd century we hear of the eucharist sent as eulogies to neighboring churches.
2. In Rome, certainly by the end of the 4th century, and probably from the time the *tituli* multiplied around 250 AD, this took the form of the fermentum, a particle of the eucharist from the papal Sunday mass sent around to the absent presbyters, who were away holding Word services in the urban *tituli*.
3. In the East, the sending of eulogies is outlawed at the Synod of Laodicea ca. 360–390, for reasons not difficult to imagine.
4. Around the same time (ca. 392), Theodore of Mopsuestia is the first to describe a symbolic commixture rite, possibly suggested by the recently defunct eulogies—though we have no evidence that the paschal eulogy was added to the chalice via a commixture rite.
5. This symbolic Syrian commixture may have been brought to Rome along with the *Agnus Dei* in the 7th century. It went everywhere else, and there is no reason to suppose Rome was an exception.
6. In Rome it was introduced as a *second* commixture, i.e., in addition to the already existing fermentum or its derived sancta rites, which had survived even after the old Sunday Word service of the *tituli* had been replaced by the complete mass.

42   ROBERT F. TAFT, S.J.

NOTES

1. The situation is somewhat better, though by no means ideal, in the Christian East. On the whole question see R.F. Taft, "Melismos and Comminution. The Fraction and its Symbolism in the Byzantine Tradition," in G. Farnedi, ed., *Traditio et progressio. Studi liturgici in onore del Prof. Adrien Nocent, O.S.B.* = Analecta liturgica 12 = Studia Anselmiana 95 (Rome 1988), 531–552.

2. In the Assyro-Chaldean tradition of the "Church of the East" there still exists an analogous rite at the preparation of the dough for baking the eucharistic bread, when a particle of consecrated eucharistic bread is added like "yeast" to the mix. Cf. J.-M. Hanssens, *Institutiones liturgicae de ritibus orientalibus* (Rome, 1930, 1932), 2:§§302–309; E.S. Drower, *Water into Wine. A Study of Ritual Idiom in the Middle East* (London, 1956), 57–9; F.E. Brightman, *Liturgies Eastern and Western* (Oxford, 1896), 247.12.

3. See, for instance, the 11th-c. diataxis of the Liturgy of the Presanctified in the Typikon of Casole from the letter of the patriarch of Constantinople to bishop Paul of Gallipoli in 1174, ed. by G. Cozza-Luzi, "Excerpta e Typico Casulano," in A. Mai, G. Cozza-Luzi, eds., *Nova Patrum Bibliotheca,* 10 vols. (Rome, 1852–1905) X.2: 169; Symeon of Thessalonika (†1429), *Resp. ad Gabrielem Pentapolitanum* 57–8, PG 155:909BC. On the whole question of "consecration by contact," the basic work is M. Andrieu, *Immixtio et consecratio. La consécration par contact dans les documents liturgiques du moyen âge* (Université de Strasbourg, Bibliothèque de l'Institut de droit canonique, Paris, 1924), esp. chapters 6, 8–9. See also M. Jugie, *Theologia dogmatica Christianorum orientalium ab Ecclesia Catholica dissidentium,* 5 vols. (Paris, 1926–1935), 3:218–27; J. de Jong, "L'arrière-plan dogmatique du rite de la commixtion dans la messe romaine," *Archiv für Liturgiewissenschaft* 3.1 (1953), esp. 85–93; id., "Le rite de la commixtion dans la messe romaine, dans ses rapports avec les liturgies syriennes," I: *Archiv für Liturgiewissenschaft* 4.2 (1956), 245ff.; Hanssens, *Institutiones* 2:§§169–73; N. Ouspensky, "Le schisme dans l'Église russe au XVIIe siècle comme suite de la collision de deux théologies," in A.M. Triacca, A. Pistoia, eds., *La liturgie expression de la foi.* Conférences Saint-Serge—XXVe Semaine d'études liturgiques, Paris, 27–30 juin 1978 = Bibliotheca *Ephemerides liturgicae,* Subsidia 16 (Rome, 1979), 241ff. and esp. the Russian sources and literature cited there.

4. See note 1.

5. G. Dix, *The Shape of the Liturgy* (London, 1945),16, italics in original.

6. *Ibid.*, 21.

7. SC 10:138–40; trans. adapated from FC 1:121.

8. SC 10:84–86; trans. adapted from FC 1:97–8. See also *Eph.* 5:1–3, 20:2, *Philad.* 4, 6:2, SC 10:60–63, 76–77, 122–25.

9. SC 248:192–93 = FC 1:182.

10. K. Bihlmeyer, *Die apostolischen Väter.* Neubearbeitung der Funkischen Ausgabe = Sammlung ausgewählter kirchen- und dogmengeschichtlicher Quellenschriften, 2. Reihe, 1. Heft, 1. Teil (Tübingen, 1924), 53 = FC 1:36.

11. Bihlmeyer, 14 = FC 1:196.

12. Repeated prohibitions against celebrating eucharist separately, or in private houses, etc., can be taken as a reflection of the same concern: canons 5–6 of the Synod of Gangres in Paphlagonia ca. 340 AD (P.-P. Joannou, *Discipline générale antique [IIe–IXe s.]* 2 vols.

plus Index = Fonti codificazione canonica orientale, fasc. 9 (Grottaferrata, 1962–1964, I.2:91); canon 5 of the Synod of Antioch in 341 AD (*ibid.* I.2:108–9); canon 58 of Laodicea ca. 360–390 AD (*ibid.* I.2:153); canon 31 "of the Apostles" ca. 400 AD (*ibid.* I.2:22); canon 31 of the "Quinisext" Council in Trullo in 691/2 AD (*ibid.* I.1:162); etc.

13. GCS 9.2 (= Eusebius 2.2) 882 = SC 55:101–2; cf. P. Nautin, "Le rite du «fermentum» dans les églises urbaines de Rome," *Ephemerides liturgicae* 96 (1982):517.

14. Joannou, *Discipline* I.2:22, 108–9.

15. CSEL 3.2:594 (capitalization modernized).

16. *Ibid.*, 776.

17. PL 35:2001; cf. Nautin, "Fermentum," 513–4.

18. CSEL 52:632 = PL 43:468.

19. PL 54:626C–627A: "Ut autem in omnibus observantia nostra concordet, illud quoque volumus custodiri, ut cum solemnior quaeque festivitas convenium populi numerosioris indixerit, et ea fidelium multitudo convenerit, quam recipere basilica simul una non possit, sacrificii oblatio indubitanter iteretur; ne his tantum admissis ad hanc devotionem, qui primi advenerint, videantur hi, qui postmodum confluxerint, non recepti, cum plenum pietatis atque rationis sit, ut quoties basilicam, in qua agitur, praesentia novae plebis impleverit, toties sacrificium subsequens offeratur. Necesse est autem ut quaedam pars populi sua devotione privetur, si unius tantum missae more servato, sacrificum offerre non possint, nisi qui prima diei parte convenerint." Cf. Nautin, "Fermentum," 517.

20. G.W.O. Addleshaw, *The Beginnings of the Parochial System*, St. Anthony's Hall Publications 3 (London, 1953), 4.

21. For a recent Orthodox study of this early unitary ecclesiology as expressed in the local eucharistic unity of one congregation, one bishop, one altar, one eucharist, see Jean de Pergame (Zizioulas), *L'Unité de l'Église dans la divine Eucharistie et dans l'évêque aux trois premiers siècles* (Paris, 1994).

22. *Ibid.* 6. Current western sacramental theology is pleased to call the bishop "the ordinary minister of confirmation." History shows that the bishop used to be the ordinary minister of *everything*. Confirmation is what he managed to retain in the West.

23. I put "concelebration" in quotation marks to avoid being anachronistic, since the term has acquired modern meanings not necessarily identifiable with the earlier practice I advert to here. On the issue of concelebration, see R.F. Taft, *Beyond East and West. Problems in Liturgical Understanding*, 2nd rev. and enlarged ed. (Rome, 1997), ch. 6.

24. For limitations on the right of presbyters to offer the eucharist, see, for example, canons 13–14 of the Synod of Neocaesarea ca. 314–319 AD, in Joannou, *Discipline* I.2:81–2. The development of presbyteral ministry is well-summarized in N. Mitchell, *Mission and Ministry. History and Theology in the Sacrament of Order*, Message of the Sacraments 6 (Wilmington, 1982), esp. 167–259.

25. Addleshaw, *Beginnings,* 6.

26. *Apostolic Tradition* 4–8, 21–22, 25–26, 31, 34, B. Botte, *La Tradition apostolique de S. Hippolyte. Essai de reconstitution*, Liturgiewissenschaftliche Quellen und Forschungen 39 (Münster, 1963), 10–81. Later documentation in Nautin, "Fermentum," 516–17.

27. Dix, *Shape,* 21.

28. Greek: G.W.H. Lampe, *A Patristic Greek Lexicon* (Oxford, 1961) 570D–F; Latin: *Thesaurus linguae Latinae* (Leipzig 1900–) 5:1048. On the whole question, in addition to the particular references below, see G. Galavaris, *Bread and the Liturgy. The Symbolism of*

Early Christian and Byzantine Bread Stamps (Madison/Milwaukee/London, 1970), 109–66; A. Stuiber, "Eulogia," RAC 6:914–28; A. Penna, "«Eucharistie» et messe," *Concilium* 40 (1968):66–8.

29. E.g., John Scholasticus, bishop of Scythopolis in Palestine (ca. 536–550 AD), *Scholia in Ecclesiasticam hierarchiam* (attributed to Maximus Confessor) III, 1, PG 4:137A; also III, 10, PG 4:148B.

30. Origen († ca. 254), *In Jerem. hom. 18 (19)*, 13, GCS 35 (Origenes 3) 169.32 = PG 13:489C; Cyril of Jerusalem (†387), *Cat. 13*, 6, PG 33:780A; Augustine (†430), *Ep. 36*, 8 (19), CSEL 34.2:48; Cyril of Alexandria (†444), *Comment. in Iohannis evangelium* 3, 6:35, PG 73:520D. The usage was typical of Cyril of Alexandria: several further references in A. Struckmann, *Die Eucharistielehre des heiligen Cyrill von Alexandrien* (Paderborn, 1910) 140ff, cf. index 166.

31. Struckmann, *Eucharistielehre,* 140.

32. §§26, 49, 133, *Acta apostolorum apocrypha*, ed. R.A. Lipsius, M. Bonnet, vols. 1–2 (Leipzig, 1898–1903) 2.2:141–42, 166, 240; A.F.J. Klijn, *The Acts of Thomas. Introduction—Text—Commentary*, Supplements to Novum Testamentum 5 (Leiden, 1962) 77, 90, 136. This seems to be its meaning still in the 10/11th c. *Constitutiones ecclesiasticae* 150, J.P. Pitra, ed., *Spicilegium Solesmense*, 4 vols. (Paris, 1852–1858, repr. Graz, 1963) 4:412, attributed to Patriarch St. Nicephorus I (806–815 AD) = V. Grumel, *Les Regestes du Patriarcat de Constantinople*, vol. 1: *Les actes des patriarches*, fasc. 1–3 = Le Patriarcat byzantin, série 1 (Kadiköy-Istanbul, 1932, 1936; Bucharest, 1947); V. Laurent, fasc. 4 (Paris, 1971); I, fasc. 1, 2nd ed. (Paris, 1972)—references are to the documents, which are numbered consecutively throughout—405–6.

33. *Apost. Trad.* 26, Botte, *Tradition apostolique*, 66–67; Socrates, *Historia ecclesiastica* VII, 12.9, GCS Neue Folge 1:357 = PG 67:759; *Constitutiones ecclesiae Aegyptiacae* xvii (xlvii), 5, and *Ex constitutionibus capitula* 10, F.X. Funk, ed., *Didascalia et Constitutiones apostolorum*, 2 vols. (Paderborn, 1905) II, 112, 138; Synod of Laodicea (ca. 360–390 AD), canon 32, Joannou, *Discipline* I.2:143 (and cf. below at note 67); canon 5 of the 10/11th c. canons attributed to Patriarch St. Nicephorus I (806–815 AD): PG 100:852B = Gumel, *Regestes*, 405–6; the 9th-c. *Vita* 26 of St. Mary of Egypt, see Alice-Mary Maffry Talbot, ed., *Holy Women of Byzantium. Ten Saints' Lives in English Translation,* Byzantine Saints' Lives in Translation 1 (Washington, D.C., 1996), 84. See also the references below in notes 34–38, 40–44; the Ethiopian code of laws and canons known as the *Fetha Nagast*, chap. VII ("On the deacons"), part III: *"Fetha Nagast" o "Legislazione dei re." Codice ecclesiastico e civile di Abissinia*, trans. and annotated by I. Guidi, Pubblicazioni scientifiche del R. Istituto Orientale di Napoli, Tomo III (Rome, 1899), 84; *The Fetha Nagast, The Law of the Kings*, trans. from the Ge'ez by P. Tzadua, ed. P.L. Strauss (Addis Ababa, 1968), 49.

34. *Apostolic Constitutions* VIII, 28:2, 31:2, SC 336:230–31 (and note 31), 234–35 (and note 31).

35. Augustine (†430), *Ep. 31*, 9, CSEL 34.2:9, and Paulinus of Nola (355–431), *Ep. 3*, 6 and *5*, 21, CSEL 29:18, 38–39 (the latter is cited below at note 55); the Greek *Vita Prima* 11, 13, 29–32, 43, of St. Matrona of Perge, a 5/6th c. Constantinopolitan nun (ca. 430–†510/15 AD): *AASS,* Nov. III (Brussels, 1910) 196, 805 (I am indebted to Jeffrey Featherstone for these references) = Talbot, *Holy Women* 30, 46–49, 57. Such

hagiographical references could doubtless be multiplied almost *ad infinitum*.

36. John Moschus (ca. 540/50–†619/34 AD), *Pratum spir.* 125, PG 87.3:2988AB; cited in Galavaris, *Bread*, 116.

37. *Ibid.*, 161–6.

38. Numerous examples in *ibid.*, 109–66.

39. SC 296:134–5, 170–3, 190–1, 222–3.

40. Ca. 1085–1095 AD, in *Protheoria* 9, PG 140:429A.

41. *Vita* 38, of St. Matrona of Perge (see note 36 above); Talbot, *Holy Women*, 53.

42. Hincmar of Rheims, *Capitula synodica* (852 AD), ch. vii, PL 125:774BC; cf. Penna, "Eucharistie," 58.

43. *Protheoria* 38, PG 140:465C; *Vita* 38 of St. Matrona of Perge (ca. 430–†510/15 AD), Talbot, *Holy Women*, 53; *Responses 8–10* of Patriarch Nicholas III Kyrdiniates Grammaticus (1084–1111 AD), J. Oudot, ed., *Patriarchatus Constantinopolitani acta selecta*, 2 vols. (Fonti codificazione canonica orientale, serie II, fasc. III–IV; Vatican, 1941/Grottaferrata, 1967) 1:16–8 (= Grumel, *Regestes*, 982.13).

44. See the medieval Typika mss: the Evergetis Typikon in 12th c. *Athens Ethn. Bibl 788* (which uses both terms, eulogia and antidoron, interchangeably); the Studite Hypotyposis in 13/14th c. *Athos Vatopedi 322 (956);* the Diatyposis of Athanasius the Athonite in 16th c. *Athos Ivirion 754 (228)* already employs the more common later term, "antidoron": A.A. Dmitrievskij, *Opisanie liturgicheskix rukopisej xranjashchixsja v bibliotekax pravoslavnago vostoka,* 3 vols. (Kiev, 1895, 1901; Petrograd, 1917), 1:233, 248, 603.

45. J. Mateos, "Un Horologion inédite de S. Sabas. Le Codex sinaïtique grec 863 (IXe siècle)," *Mélanges Eugène Tisserant* III: *Orient chrétien*, Studi e testi 233 (Vatican, 1964), 47–76.; J.E. Klentos, *Byzantine Liturgy in Twelfth-Century Constantinople: An Analysis of the Synaxarion of the Monastery of the Theotokos Evergetis* (codex *Athens Ethnike Bibliotheke 788*) (Ph.D. diss.: University of Notre Dame, 1995; Ann Arbor: University Microfilms International, 1997), 185–9; Hanssens, *Institutiones* 2:§§189–90.

46. *Vita* 7 of St. Theodora of Thessalonika (812–892 AD); Talbot, *Holy Women*, 224.

47. O. Nußbaum, *Die Aufbewahrung der Eucharistie*, Theophaneia 29, (Bonn, 1979), 27ff, 31ff. A practice still in force ca. 1185–1095 A.D., according to *Protheoria* 38, PG 140:465C.

48. E.g., 3rd. c. *Apostolic Tradition* 36–37 (ca. 215 AD), Botte, *Tradition apostolique*, 82–85; Tertullian († *post* 220 AD), *Ad uxorem* 2, 5:2ff, CCL 1:389ff; Cyprian (†ca. 258), *De lapsis* 26, CCL 3:235; 4th c. Jerome (ca. 347–419 AD), *Ep. 49*, 15 (= *Apologeticum ad Pammachium,* 393 AD), CSEL 54:377—for the dating of Jerome's life and works see F. Cavallera, *Saint Jérôme. Sa vie et son œuvre.* Première partie, Tomes 1–2 = Spicilegium Sacrum Lovaniense, Études et documents, fasc. 1–2 (Louvain, 1922), II, 153–65; 6th c. *Ep. 93*, attributed to St. Basil the Great (†379 AD), Y. Courtonne, ed., S. Basile, *Lettres*, 2 vols. (Paris, 1957, 1961), 1:203–4 = PG 32:484–5, but certainly not authentic according to S. Voicu, "Cesaria, Basilio (*Ep. 93/94*) e Severo," in M. Simonetti, P. Siniscalco, eds., *Studi sul cristianesimo antico e moderno in onore di Maria Grazia Mara,* I–II = *Augustinianum* (1995):697–703, who argues convincingly for Severus, monophysite patriarch of Antioch from 512–518 AD, as the likely author; further references in Nußbaum, *Die Aufbewahrung,* 266ff.; N. Mitchell, *Cult and Controversy: The Worship of the Eucharist outside Mass* (New

York, 1982), 10–19.

    49. Taft, *Beyond East and West,* 88–9.

    50. F.J. Dölger, "Die Eucharistie als Reiseschutz. Die Eucharistie in den Händen der Laien," AC 5 (1936):232–47; W.H. Freestone, *The Sacrament Reserved. A Survey of the Practice of Reserving the Eucharist, with Special Reference to the Communion of the Sick, during the first Twelve Centuries,* Alcuin Club Collections 21 (London/Milwaukee, 1917), 55–6; D. Callam, "The Frequency of Mass in the Latin Church ca. 400," *Theological Studies* 45 (1984):616–7, esp. n. 11.

    51. See for example Justin (ca. 150), *Apol.* I, 65:5, 67:5, PG:428–32; Pope Damasus I (305–384 AD), *Elogium S. Tarsicii,* no. 15 in A. Ferrua, ed., *Epigrammata Damasiana,* Sussidi allo studio delle antichità cristiane 2 (Vatican, 1942), 117; M. Ihm, ed., *Anthologiae Latinae supplementa,* 1: *Damasi epigrammata,* Bibliotheca scriptorum Graecorum et Romanorum Teubneriana (Leipzig, 1895), 21. Cf. F.J. Dölger, *ΙΧΘΥΣ. Das Fischsymbol in frühchristlicher Zeit,* 2 vols. (1, 2nd ed. Münster, 1928; 2, Münster 1922), 2:534–5; Taft, *Beyond East and West,* 88; Nußbaum, *Die Aufbewahrung,* 177–8; for further references, especially western, see Callam, "Frequency," 615ff.

    52. Though *1 Clement* 42:4 at the end of the first century already speaks of bishops being instituted for the faithful "in the countryside and towns—κατὰ χώρας οὖν καὶ πόλεις" (Bihlmeyer, *Die apostolischen Väter,* 58), it is generally accepted that through the 3rd century the Church was well ensconced only in the towns. The organization of a resident clergy in the countryside had to await the "Peace of Constantine" in 312/3 AD. This occurred more rapidly in some areas, more slowly in others. For instance, by the end of the 4th c. the bishop of Caesarea in Cappadocia was assisted by 50 "chorbishops" serving the surrounding countryside (P. Joannou, "Chorbishop," *New Catholic Encyclopedia* 3:625–6). On the whole question, see especially D. Baker, ed., *The Church in Town and Countryside,* Studies in Church History 16 (Oxford, 1979); also A. von Harnack, *The Mission and Expansion of Christianity in the First Three Centuries,* 2 vols., 2nd ed. (London/New York, 1908) 1:445–82, 2:89ff, 324–37; C. Rupe, "Parish," *New Catholic Encyclopedia* 10:1017; H. Dressler, "Asia Minor, Early Church in," *New Catholic Encyclopedia* 1:955–7; Addleshaw, *Beginnings,* 7ff. On the institution of chorbishops or "country bishops," see: F. Gillmann, *Das Institut der Chorbischöffe im Orient* (Munich, 1903); T. Gottlob, *Der abendländische Chorepiskopat,* Kanonistische Studien und Texte 1 (Bonn-Köln, 1928, repr. Amsterdam, 1963); H. Hess, *The Canons of the Council of Sardica, A.D. 343, A Landmark in the Early Development of Canon Law,* Oxford Theological Monographs (Oxford, 1958), esp. 100–3; E. Kirsten, "Chorbischof," RAC 2 (1954):1105–14; H. Leclercq, "Chorévêques," DACL 3.1:1423–52; id., "Périodeute," DACL 14.1:369–79; J. Parisot, "Les chorévêques," *Revue de l'Orient chrétien.* 6 (1901):157–71, 419–43.

    53. Severus of Antioch, *Ep. 93* (note 49 above), attributed to St. Basil, refers explicitly to the persecutions as a reason for this practice. See also Callam, "Frequency," 616; Freestone, *The Sacrament Reserved,* 44–5.

    54. CSEL 29:38–39.

    55. Ignatius of Antioch, *Magn.* 6–7, *Smyr.* 8; *Barnabus* 4:10; *1 Clement* 34:7, cited above at notes 8–9, 11–12.

    56. See Taft, *Beyond East and West,* 95–6, and further references there in notes 53–55.

57. Eusebius, *Church History* V, 25:15, GCS 9.1 (= Eusebius Werke 2.1) 496 = SC 41:70–1.

58. Cf. Lampe, *Patristic Greek Lexicon*, 1042; Addleshaw, *Beginnings*, 4; G. Dix, *A Detection of Aumbries* (Westminster, 1942), 16–7.

59. Eusebius, *Church History* V, 24:9, 14, GCS 9.1 (= Eusebius Werke 2.1) 494, 496 = SC 41:69–70.

60. Cf. Nußbaum, *Die Aufbewahrung*, 175–6; E. Peterson, "ΜΕΡΙΣ. Hostien-Partikel und Opfer Anteil," *Ephemerides liturgicae* 61 (1947):7ff.

61. P. Franchi de' Cavalieri, ed., "I dieci martiri di Creta," in *Miscellanea Giovanni Mercati*, vol. V: *Storia ecclesiastica—diritto*, Studi e testi 125 (Vatican, 1946), 39–40 (for the date, p. 28); further literature on these feasts in Peterson, "ΜΕΡΙΣ," 8, notes 20–21; Nußbaum, *Die Aufbewahrung*, 175–6.

62. Dix, *Aumbries*, 18.

63. Nußbaum, *Die Aufbewahrung*, 179–80, cites a variety of opinions.

64. CSEL 38:26.

65. F.J. Dölger, "Sacramentum infanticidii," AC 4 (1934):217, n. 53.

66. Joannou, *Discipline* I.2:136. Cf. Ch.J. Hefele, *A History of the Councils of the Church from the Original Documents* (Edinburgh, 1896), 2:308–9.

67. Cf. Nußbaum, *Die Aufbewahrung*, 180.

68. Contrary to contemporary mythology, which likes to view the West as the innovator that abandoned the ancient apostolic and patristic traditions still preserved by Eastern Orthodoxy, in Late Antiquity innovations almost without exception began in the East. Western innovations began somewhat later, when the demise of the empire and the rise of the barbarian kingdoms forced the Church to adjust to the birth of a new world order. In such matters the real issue, as history shows beyond cavil, is not who introduced innovations (all Churches did), but in what periods they chose to do it.

69. Addleshaw, *Beginnings*, 5.

70. L. Duchesne, ed., *Le Liber pontificalis.* Texte, introduction, commentaire, 3 vols. (Paris, 1886, 1892, 1957), 1:164.

71. See *ibid.*, 165, n. 4.

72. Here diocese means an ecclesiastical circumscription like the modern parish: *ibid.*, 165, n. 6.

73. Cf. Nautin, "Fermentum," 512–3.

74. Though many have commented on the question of the fermentum—M. Andrieu, *Les «Ordines Romani» du haut moyen âge*, 5 vols., Spicilegium Sacrum Lovaniense fasc. 11, 23, 24, 28, 29 (Louvain, 1956–1961), 2:59–64; F.C. Cabrol, "Fermentum," DACL 5:1371–1374; Dix, *Shape*, 134; J.A. Jungmann, "Fermentum. Ein Symbol kirchlicher Einheit und sein Nachleben im Mittelalter," in B. Fischer, V. Fiala, eds., *Colligere fragmenta. Festschrift A. Dold*, Texte und Arbeiten, I. Abt., 2. Beiheft (Beuron, 1952), 185–90; id., *The Mass of the Roman Rite. Missarum sollemnia*, 2 vols. (New York, 1951, 1955), 2:311–4; Mitchell, *Cult and Controversy*, 35–8, 57–61; Nautin, "Fermentum"; Nußbaum, *Die Aufbewahrung*, 179–85—the subject still awaits a definitive study.

75. Duchesne, *Le Liber pontificalis* 1:168, 216.

76. Nautin, "Fermentum," 518–20.

77. R. Cabié, ed., *La lettre du Pape Innocent Ier à Décentius de Gubbio (19 mars 416)*, Bibliothèque de la *Revue d'Histoire ecclésiastique*, fasc. 58 (Louvain, 1973), 27–8 = PL 20:556.

78. Literally "parishes," but meaning in this context the rural dioceses outside Rome: see Cabié, *ibid.*, 27, n. 2.

79. Cf. authors cited in Nautin, "Fermentum," 511–2.

80. *Ibid.*, 512, 518.

81. The problem of distance was one of security: in the second half of the 3rd c. St. Tarsicius, probably a deacon, was martyred while carrying the eucharist: "Christi sacramenta gerentem" (see note 52 above).

82. GCS 9.2 (= Eusebius 2.2) 618 = SC 41:156.

83. See note 3 above.

84. Andrieu, *Ordines* 2:115 (cf. 112), 3:474 (cf. 463). See also Amalarius of Metz (ca. 775–ca. 850), *Ep. ad Hilduinum* 91–96, J.-M. Hanssens, ed., *Amalarii episcopi Opera liturgica omnia*, 2 vols., Studi e Testi 138–139 (Vatican, 1948) 1:357–8. Cf. Nautin, "Fermentum," 511, 521–22; Jungmann, "Fermentum," 186ff; references to later sources in Nußbaum, *Die Aufbewahrung*, 181–4.

85. *Ordo I*, 48, 95, Andrieu, *Ordines* 2:82–3, 98. Cf. Andrieu's commentary, *ibid.*, 59–64; Jungmann, *Mass of the Roman Rite*, 2:311–4; Mitchell, *Cult and Controversy*, 57–61.

86. Andrieu, *Ordines*, 2:82–3.

87. *Ordo I* is from the beginning of the 8th c. See *ibid.*, 2:51–2.

88. E.g., the 10th-c. Romano-Germanic *Ordo Romanus V*, 82, Andrieu, *Ordines* 2:225 (cf. 195–6, 203–4); Amalarius of Metz, *Liber off.* III, 31:3, ed. Hanssens, *Amalarii episcopi opera*, Studi e Testi 138:361. On the relationship of these sources see Andrieu, *Ordines* 2:77–92.

89. Andrieu, *Ordines* 2:98–103; J. de Jong, "Le rite de la commixtion dans la messe romaine," *Revue bénédictine* 61 (1951):18–21.

90. Andrieu, *Ordines* 2:164–5, cf. 56–64.

91. *Ibid.*, 2:115, 132, 335.

92. de Jong, "Commixtion," 37.

93. Eusebius, *Church History* V, 24:16, GCS 9.1:497 = SC 41:71.

94. J.P. de Jong, "Fermentum," *New Catholic Encyclopedia* 5:889.

95. *Ibid.*, 28–9. T. Parayady, *A Communion Service in the East Syrian Church. Liturgical Study* (unpublished doctoral dissertion, Pontifical Oriental Institute, Rome, 1980), 326–33, proposes the same solution as a possible hypothesis for the East-Syrian eucharist, which was clearly influenced by the East-Syrian Liturgy of the Presanctified for days of "razanait" without a full mass. Indeed, in the Syrian traditions, Liturgy of the Presanctified is known as "the signing of the chalice."

96. de Jong, "Commixtion," 28–9.

97. In the East-Syrian Liturgy of the Presanctified, for instance, this was done only by adding wine from the consecrated chalice: Syriac text and English trans. in H.W. Codrington, "The Syrian Liturgies of the Presanctified. III. East Syrian, or Persian," *The Journal of Theological Studies* 5 (1904):545. Cf. also the Antiochene John of Tella (†538 AD): de Jong, "L'arrière-plan," 87–90.

98. Jungmann, *Mass of the Roman Rite*, 2:316ff (see also the later German ed., Vienna, 1952, 2:390–1, which incorporates de Jong's work not utilized in the 1949 German edition translated into English).

99. Jungmann, *Mass of the Roman Rite*, 2:316–8; L. Haberstroh, *Der Ritus der Brechung und Mischung nach dem Missale Romanum*, St. Gabriel Studien 5, (Mödling, 1937), 62–70.

100. de Jong, "Commixtion," 32–6; cf. Jungmann, *Mass of the Roman Rite*, 2:333–4; E. Bishop, *Liturgica Historica* (Oxford, 1918), 145–6.

101. Andrieu, *Ordines*, 2:100.

102. Duchesne, *Le Liber pontificalis*, 1:376.

103. Jungmann, *Mass of the Roman Rite*, 2:301–2, 334.

104. Cf. H.-J. Schulz, *The Byzantine Liturgy* (New York, 1986), 64ff, 89ff, 98–9, 184–90; K.Ch. Felmy, "Der Christusknabe auf dem Diskos. Die Proskomidie der orthodoxen Liturgie als Darstellung von 'Schlachtung des Lammes' und Geburt des Herrn," *Jahrbuch für Liturgie und Hymnologie* 23 (1979):99–101; G. Descoeudres, *Die Pastophorien im syro-byzantinischen Osten. Eine Untersuchung zu architektur- und liturgiegeschichtlichen Problemen*, Schriften zur Geistesgeschichte des östlichen Europa, Bd. 16 (Wiesbaden, 1983), 91–6, 116–21; M. Garidis, "Approche 'realiste' dans la représentation du mélismos," *Jahrbuch der österreichischen Byzantinistik* 32.5 (1982):495–502; Ch. Walter, *Art and Ritual of the Byzantine Church*, Birmingham Byzantine Series 1 (London, 1982), 200, 205–7, 238.

105. de Jong, "Rapports" (see note 3), I:252ff, 274–6.

106. *De fide 10*, 14–15, ed. E. Beck, Corpus scriptorum Christianorum orientalium 155, Script. Syri 74 (Louvain, 1955), 35; *Contra haereses 45*, 1, id. (Corpus scriptorum Christianorum orientalium 170, Script. Syri 77 (Louvain, 1957), 158; *De nativitate 16, 7*, id., Corpus scriptorum Christianorum orientalium 187, Script. Syri 83 (Louvain, 1959), 76. Cf. E. Beck, "Die Eucharistie bei Ephräm," *Oriens Christianus* 38 (1954):65; F.J. Dölger, "Die Signierung des eucharistischen Brotes mit dem eucharistischen Wein bei den syrischen Marcioniten und in der syrischen Liturgie des vierten Jahrhunderts nach einem Zeugnis Ephräm des Syrers," AC 5 (1936):275–81; id., "Eucharistischer Hostienstempel," AC 1 (1929):30; I.E. Rahmani, *Les liturgies orientales et occidentales* (Beirut, 1929), 234–5; F. Probst, *Liturgie des vierten Jahrhunderts und deren Reform* (Münster i. W., 1893), 317.

107. See note 1 above.

108. On the disputed date and place of his homilies see R.F. Taft, *A History of the Liturgy of St. John Chrysostom*, IV: *The Diptychs*, Orientalia Christiana Analecta 238 (Rome, 1991), 47.

109. R. Tonneau, R. Devreesse, *Les homélies catéchétiques de Théodore de Mopsueste*, Studi e Testi 145 (Vatican, 1949), 557–63.

110. *Hom. 16*, 17, Studi e Testi 145:558.

111. Studi e Testi 145:577–9.

112. Dölger, "Die Signierung," 279–80.

113. *The Liturgical Homilies of Narsai*, translated into English with an introduction by R.H. Connolly, with an appendix by Edmund Bishop, Texts and Studies VIII.1 (Cambridge, 1909), 59–60.

114. F. van de Paverd, *Zur Geschichte der Meßliturgie in Antiocheia und Konstantinopel gegen Ende des vierten Jahrhunderts. Analyse der Quellen bei Johannes Chrysostomos*, Orientalia Christiana Analecta 187 (Rome, 1970), 367.

115. S. Haidacher, "Drei unedierte Chrysostomus-Texte einer Baseler Handschrift," *Zeitschrift für katholische Theologie* 31 (1907):358.

Origen of Alexandria
Among the Renaissance Humanists
and their Twentieth Century Historians

Daniel J. Nodes
Hamline University

In 1481 Cristoforo Persona published in Rome his translation of Origen's apology *Contra Celsum*.[1] By that year several of Origen's writings were among the Christian classics that Western scholars were studying again with the textual critic's attention to detail, the philologist's love of eloquence, the theologian's scrutiny of argument, and the mystic's pursuit of divine wisdom. Although the West had never completely abandoned Origen, by the time *Contra Celsum* was printed in Latin translation, it was receiving more serious and multidisciplinary attention than it had for over a millennium. By 1503, when the Aldine press published its first edition of Origen's Homilies, Western scholars were deeply embroiled in a debate over their author and issues surrounding his doctrines and legacy.

This essay examines Origen's fifteenth–century revival with a focus on how its occurrence and nature are characterized in recent scholarship. The past forty years have seen several important histories of the revival, where reasons for the renewed interest in Origen follow perceived changes in the humanist movement in Italy.[2] In particular, the revival of Origen as a speculative thinker is seen to take place after the transformation from civic humanism to the more spiritual form of platonist humanism that would eventually be brought to fulfillment in the Florentine Academy. Emphasizing the turning point from a civic to a philosophical perspective as far as Origen is concerned, however, begs the question about his influence on the larger movement, that is, to what degree renewed interest in Origen contributed to rather than reflected a new *Zeitgeist*. The aim here is to show that the revival happened more cumulatively and less sequentially than emphasis on the transition from civic to philosophical humanism makes it appear. In the texts composed during the years when debate over Origen's orthodoxy raged, that is, between 1481, the year of the publication of the *Contra Celsum*, and 1510, the year of the dedication of Aldus' edition to Cardinal Egidio of Viterbo, interest in Origen was multidisciplinary and included elements of theology and philology. Further, this was the case even before Pico's encounter with a papal inquisitional committee and Bishop Pedro Garcia highlighted doctrinal issues.

Collectively, the fifteenth century scrutinized Origen's writings for various reasons, but the early decades of that century are difficult to assess when it comes to identifying the range of interest. Scholars' expressions of hope in acquiring copies of Origen's writings leave uncertainties about what they considered most appealing about them. As evidenced by the general praise for Origen's fame, as can be found in Coluccio Salutati, and general interest in collecting MSS of Origen's writings, as in the case of Niccolò Niccoli (1363–1437), early humanists refer to Origen as a brilliant writer and homilist, and that kind of praise lies at the foundation of the accepted reason for early humanist interest in Christian as well as non–Christian classics: philology and the appeal of "classic" and "patristic" eloquence and judgment.[3]

The early decades of the fifteenth century, however, also possessed the essential seeds for developing interest in Origen's thought. The Council of Florence of 1438–1439 that brought Orthodox Christian theologians to Italy not only furthered the already growing interest in Greek Patristic texts but stimulated efforts to incorporate Eastern mysticism and theology into the Latin humanist tradition. According to Max Schär, however, any importation of Origen's thought *per se* in this period was minor: only Cardinal Bessarion and Theodore Gazes were especially familiar with him, but they discussed Origen in Greek, and this limited their influence on Western scholars at this early period. Schär also suggests that even their interest was not in Origen the dogmatic or speculative thinker but Origen the confessor of the apology against Celsus.[4] Just as there was need in Origen's day to respond to the charges of an enlightened paganism, so was there in the fifteenth century the need to address the challenge from Islam.

Evidence for interest in Origen as a speculative thinker appears by the second half of the century. Italy was by then a healthy environment for synthesizing philological interests in ancient texts with Neoplatonism and other branches of ancient wisdom. That this environment was essentially Christian, as was Origen's, is no longer a serious point of contention. For some, the pall of heresy overshadowing Origen would lift as more accessible texts enabled his perspective to be reevaluated first–hand. Origen had eloquently proclaimed optimism regarding human potential within a Christian Middle–Platonic context more strongly than any of his contemporaries. His writings synthesize philosophy and the Bible, Platonic and Christian perspectives, reason and revelation, the *nova doctrina* and the *vetus doctrina*, to a degree and in a manner comparable to those of the Platonizing humanists, notwithstanding the absence of overt classical allusions in Origen. His theology offered a refreshing look at the doctrines of sin and grace. Origen's optimistic view of the potential of all rational creatures attracted thinkers despite his official condemnation. He was to become "the favorite theologian of the [Renaissance] Neoplatonists."[5] A more intense scrutiny of Origen's writings and thought occurred, however, even among those who rejected his theology. In the doctrinal arena the vote on Origen would be split, and the intensity of that split, characterized in Aldus' adoption of the commonplace assessment of Origen himself: *Ubi bene dixit, nemo melius; ubi male, nemo peius*, shows one aspect of the complex attraction and substantive caution connected with him.

Whatever Origen's role as cause or effect in the develop of philosophic humanism, Platonic mysticism became a prime characteristic of the late fifteenth–century perspective. Ethical philosophy was to place additional emphasis on the contemplative life with deeply religious overtones connected with a desire for mystical union with God. Speculative philosophy turned toward enlightened mysticism, the goal of which is well–expressed in the phrases *docta religio* and even more to the point, as it epitomizes the interdisciplinary nature of the movement, *theologia poetica*.[6] Paul Kristeller attests to the eventually mystical flavor of the *studia humanitatis*, wherein humanity is celebrated as the universal center, the cosmic bond between the spiritual and material worlds, drawing, to be sure, on Plato himself, as on the Phaedrus myth of the quest for union with the divine:

> This goal is pursued through a gradual ascent of the soul that turns away from all things external and through contemplation moves inwards and upwards. This ascent is accomplished by the two wings of the soul, will and intellect, through ever higher acts of loving and knowing that culminate in the direct enjoyment and vision of God. The ultimate union is attained during this earthly life only by a few persons and for a fleeting moment, but it must be postulated as an eternal possession in a future life for all those who have made an earnest effort in this present life.[7]

Patristic writers, however, were in the vanguard of the march toward philosophical and even mystical humanism that Ficino was to make centuries later, as Kristeller observes:

> The notion that man occupies a privileged place in the order of things, and that human problems should be our central concern, is frequently found in ancient and early Christian writers, and it had a great appeal to the Renaissance humanists who liked to call their fields of study the *studia humanitatis*.[8]

We see in this definition the broad application of "the humanities" extending far beyond philology.

What kind of role, then, did Origen play in enriching the Renaissance humanist perspective as evidenced, say, by an early text such as Matteo Palmieri's *Città di vita*? Schär recognizes this work for its "transitional" qualities, adopting the notion of the older literary humanism and the renewed Platonism of Ficino and his academy and suggesting that this poem falls not just chronologically but attitudinally between the two.[9] Composed between 1455 and 1464, when the Christian philosophical work of Ficino was just beginning, this poem relates the Christian–Platonic doctrine of the soul's struggle to be liberated from the body to Origen's teaching on the common nature of humans and angels. It was long asserted that Palmieri used Origen or a disciple of Origen as the point of departure for the idea.[10] Schär doubts the connection with Origen himself, pointing to several differences in detail between Origen's own teaching and the relationships in the *Città di vita*. Palmieri, for example, presents the human race as those angels who remained neutral in the primordial crisis over Lucifer and his followers, while in Origen man does not remain neutral but turns away from God, albeit to a lesser degree than do the angels.[11] We do know that Palmieri did not publish the poem during his lifetime, probably out of fear of public censure, and a commentary on the poem by Leonardo Dati, who went out of his way to promote the doctrine of the common nature of men and angels, was also kept within close circles. The controversy over Palmieri did not start until eight years after his death. When he died in 1475 there was praise for his book, but in 1483 there were instead charges that Palmieri had made heretical statements about angels. The matter of the precise nature of Origen's influence may never be resolved in this case.

The literature composed between the quarter century from Palmieri's poem to the emergence of Giovanni Pico as the champion of Origen in the mid 1480s has yielded more solid evidence of the increased attention to Origen as a thinker, and Ficino plays an undeniably key role in this period. Porphyry, as quoted in Eusebius, describes Origen as a Christian who tried to reconcile Plato and Moses by employing the figurative method of the Greek mysteries and applying it to Jewish writings. Edgar Wind points out that such a description "could have been invented for Marsilio Ficino."[12] Also like Origen, the founder of the Laurentian academy eventually became a priest, and he gave his Alexandrian predecessor a significant role in his Platonic revival, mentioning Origen often and quoting from his most expressive theological writings, *De principiis* and *Contra Celsum*. Ficino's *De Christiana religione* (*De authoritate doctrinae Christianae*), ch. 35, of 1477, even presents a list of Origen's virtues. As mentioned, Ficino was drawn to Platonism rather than Aristotelianism "precisely by the strain of religious mysticism that ran through the Platonic tradition, which he hoped might serve as a source of spiritual renewal for Christian piety."[13] He cherished the idea of man's ontological position in the center of the great chain of being, thus sharing in material and spiritual creation. Ficino knew that Origen was deeply committed to all these. He also knew of Palmieri's reputed use of Origen's theory on the angels. Even after following Origen to ordination Ficino kept his deep interest in religious syncretism, nor was he challenged for harboring heretical viewpoints as his pupil Pico was to be after the change of climate.

The works of astronomer/poet Lorenzo Bonincontri (1410–1491) show from the outset a disposition favorable to Origen's theological anthropology.[14] In his principal poems, composed between 1469 and 1475, Bonincontri includes numerous commonplaces of Christian Platonism. He insists, for example, on the free will of man, who must not blame the stars for human faults. The evil influences of the stars exist, he argues, but are punitive rather than malign, and each person is attended by a good and an evil angel who try to influence his conduct but who cannot touch the sovereign independence of the human will. Such speculations may reflect an awareness of certain central speculations of Origen, and although we cannot be certain that Bonincontri knew Origen's works directly at this early point, the similarity of such details in his early poetry to the doctrines of Origen, along with Bonincontri's residency at the humanistic center of Naples, makes it possible that he made an early acquaintance.

Bonincontri may even have harbored a tentative belief in metempsychosis, an idea that was also frequently if improperly read in Origen. Solid evidence exists in a later treatise for Bonincontri's familiarity with this aspect of Origen's speculations in *De principiis*. He moved to Florence and lived there as a member of the Medicean circle from 1475 to 1478, and after his encounter with the Florentine humanists he composed at Rome *De vi ac potestate mentis humane animeque motibus et eius substancia* between 1483 and 1491, in which he adapts a passage from Origen's *De principiis* and quotes from his *Commentary on Titus* in a reflection on the nature of the soul.[15]

Origenian influence on fifteenth–century Florentine painting and sculpture has also been a tempting issue over the past forty years. Ghiberti's "Gates of Paradise" (1429–1452), and a fresco of Uccello in Santa Maria Novella (ca. 1450), for example, two works depicting Noah's ark in the form of a pyramid, have been connected to Origen's Second Genesis Homily. The iconography of Botticelli's "Purification of the Leper" (1481–1483) in the Sistine Chapel, a work which incorporates three apparently disparate motifs, may depict a passage in one of Origen's homilies on the Gospel according to Luke. Also, the imagery in Botticelli's "Assumption of Moses" in the Sistine Chapel, dating from the same period, has been explained by reference to a lost work which Origen quoted often.[16]

As suggested at the start of this essay, the most well documented period of scrutiny of Origen begins with the published Latin translation of the *Contra Celsum* in 1481. Hard upon the ever–growing interest and use of his works, Origen came under renewed criticism, apparently as part of a growing religious intolerance in the years of the papacy of Innocent VIII. The decade even saw opposition arise within the Medici circle itself. Luigi Pulci's *Morgante Maggiore*, for example, whose first edition appeared in Florence in 1482, ridicules Origen's optimism regarding the ultimate salvation of all rational beings including, theoretically, the Devil himself. Pulci criticized this idea by opposing the impropriety of including Judas Iscariot among those who could eventually be saved.[17] Soon after this repudiation began the severe censure of Palmieri's *Città di vita*.

At this time of crisis, however, Origen's staunchest defender came forward. In 1486 Giovanni Pico published at Rome his *900 Conclusiones* featuring the well known proposition, *rationabilius est credere Origenem esse salvum quam credere ipsum esse damnatum*. A commission of Pope Innocent VIII, nominally headed by Jean Monissart, Bishop of Tournai, but guided mainly by the Spanish Bishop Pedro Garcia, included that proposition about Origen's salvation among thirteen it cited as heretical or dubious. Instead of revising the suspect opinions, Pico used the opportunity to develop them in an *Apology* (1487), which he dedicated to Lorenzo dei Medici. Although he had thirteen separate propositions to treat, Pico chose to spend over one fifth of the treatise defending his thesis about Origen's salvation, placing that discussion at the center of the treatise.[18] The theological optimism which was capable of producing such a statement also motivated Pico's celebration of human freedom as the potential for divinization through contemplation. Pico, incidentally, wrote in this spirit the *Oratio de hominis dignitate*, which, although published in full only posthumously, was intended to introduce the *900 Conclusiones*. Pico knew that doctrines derived from Origen had been condemned by two early church councils, but he argued that for one thing, the Synod of Alexandria (400), which included Origen's name on its list of anathemas, had the authority of a regional council but not that of the universal church. Further to the point, he noted that this synod was theologically suspect because of its involvement in regional politics.[19] As for the legacy of the Second Council of Constantinople (553), neither Pico nor Garcia, who in 1489 published the *Determinationes magistrales* condemning Origen, had access to the details of what had transpired there but knew only of an anathema (#11) and the famous Letter of the Emperor Justinian to Mennas, Patriarch of Constantinople, repudiating Origen's name. Pico seems to have sensed, however, that it was less Origen himself than certain teachings loosely attributed to him that had been the real target of condemnation.[20] Pico demonstrated that those doctrines for which Origen had been criticized had been either misunderstood or removed from their historical context, the formative years of Christian theology. As a result Pico was arrested and charged with heresy, and all his writings were condemned. It remained until 1493 for Rome, then under Alexander VI, to issue a pardon, when Pico, back in Florence, was living out the final year of his short life under Savonarola's influence, outwardly at least.

Pico's defense of Origen has justifiably been presented as a monument to the humanist spirit and Origen's revival. The case lasted ten years and occasioned written exchanges hardly rivaled by the disputes between Origenism's first defenders and detractors or by the debates between Luther and Erasmus over Origen which were still to come.[21] So great is Pico's fame that even the recent histories, including Schär's study published in 1979, have been content to make him stand virtually alone of all the Florentines as a student of Origen, friend or foe, during the last two decades of the Quattrocento, especially since there is hardly any mention of Origen in works by members of the Medici circle from those two decades, considered as an "austerity period" marked by Ficino's retirement and the reign of Savonarola. Do the lack of references mean that, Pico notwithstanding, the Florentines, because of despair and in deference to ecclesiastical pressure, generally abandoned whatever interest they had taken in Origen? If so, then perhaps Origen's influence on humanism of any description was never profound. Schär is reluctant, in fact, to attribute an intimate knowledge of Origen even to Pico despite Pico's many references to Origen's works.

But since the absence of direct references to Origen leaves open the question of his ongoing indirect influence (especially since Pico's ordeal made caution a virtue), it is natural to ask whether the continuity of Christian Platonism in Florence in some measure can reveal continued interest Origen. One expects that influential ideas would endure an austerity period even if the influence were not acknowledged. In order to learn whether this is true in the case of Origen, students of his thought must continue to examine the late Quattrocento Florentine writings.[22] Such work should proceed more readily as more of the Florentine literature of the 1480s and 1490s is edited. One may consider, as a case in point, the *Paradisus* of Ugolino Verino, which not only promotes Christian Neoplatonism in general but expresses particular themes that bespeak the influence of *De principiis*.[23] The poem is a dream–vision modeled after Dante in which Verino is borne upwards to the halls of the gods. There the poet learns, among other things, about the creation of men and angels, about the existence of good and evil angels and their dealings with humanity, but most important, about humanity's possession of sovereign freedom even after the Fall of Adam. Verino learns that while the loyal angels have remained in God's presence and celebrate his glory, the fallen angels tempt man. He also learns that each person has a good angel to assist him to salvation. The result is a familiar tug–of–war of the spirit:

> Hinc bonus, inde malus trahit in contraria pectus,
> ambiguus spectare bonus caelestia regna
> admonet et vanos vitae mortalis honores
> spernere virtutemque sequi per mille labores.
> Ille alter vitiis tentat corrumpere mete
> nunc magnos opes ostentat nunc ditia regna.[24]

But despite this conflicting angelic pressure, Verino holds, man remains absolutely free to direct his course where he wills:

> Ipse sed arbitrio liber deflectit habenas
> frenaque anhelantum spumantia volvit equorum
> nunc altos moles cursumque intendit ad astra
> et nunc illecebris captus percurrit apertum.[25]

That the emphasis on human freedom presented within the context of the contrary angelic influences is derived from Origen is suggested by two main factors. First, the idea that each person has both good and evil angelic influences to contend with is a central feature of Origen's theology. There are indeed numerous precursors to the general idea of angelic dealings with man in Hellenic, Jewish, Christian, and other ancient literatures which Origen knew and used. Plato's *Phaedrus*, for example, provided Origen with excellent support for the idea of guardian angels. But while the *Phaedrus* presents the function of spirits as guardians, it does not emphasize the conflicting functions of angels as both guardians and tempters. Origen, acknowledging the existence of angels as *definitum in ecclesiastica praedicatione*, that is, laid down in the Church's teaching, accepted the opportunity to speculate about the nature of their existence and their particular manner of dealing with mankind, issues which, as he says, are not defined in the teaching. Such speculations stress, as does Verino's poem, both the dual functions of the angels and the freedom of man to proceed in either direction:

> Est et illud definitum in ecclesiastica predicatione, omnem animam rationabilem esse liberi arbitrii et voluntatis; esse quoque ei certamen adversum diabolum et angelos eius contrariasque virtutes, ex eo quod illi peccatis eam onerare contendant, nos vero si recte consulteque vivamus, ab huiuscemodi labe exuere nos conemur. Unde consequens est intellegere, non nos necessitati esse subiectos, ut omni modo, etiamsi nolimus, vel mala vel bona agere cogamur. Si enim nostri arbitrii sumus, inpugnare nos fortasse possint aliquae virtutes ad peccatum et aliae iuvare ad salutem, non tamen necessitate cogimur vel recte agere vel male.[26]

Secondly, this passage, in which Origen encapsulates his speculation on men and angels, stands next to the passage that Bonincontri quotes verbatim in his above–mentioned treatise on the nature of the soul. Circumstances like these suggest the influence of *De principiis* by the late Florentine humanists.[27]

A more serious obstacle to Origen's continued influence than the centralized Roman opposition, however, has been seen in the dominance of Savonarola in Florence during the final decade of the Quattrocento.[28] By 1491 his influence over the general population was firmly established, but he had begun even earlier to criticize the Medici court and the intellectual Florentines for profligacy and unorthodoxy. It has been noted as well that among the members of the Laurentian academy "a new, stricter, more somber Christianity was developing, perhaps in reaction to the untimely death of Lorenzo, their great patron and protector in 1492."[29] Most to the point, Savonarola appears to have been one to consider Origen as a "heretic with no honorable philosophy but a Platonizing Christianity full of errors."[30]

Nevertheless, Savonarola's effect on the theological attitudes of the Florentine intellectuals is in many ways unclear, and this ambiguity extends to his effect on the interest in Origen among the members of the Laurentian circle. For one thing, Savonarola's own visionary and apocalyptic utterances reflect numerous Christian Neoplatonic doctrines which are often harmonious with Origen. And despite Savonarola's nominal rejection of Origen, he at least on one occasion (1484) included Origen's name among the "prophets" he cited.[31] In addition, the Mediceans were by no means unanimous in their support of the Dominican preacher. Pico and Benivieni, for example, may have been more prone to adopt a new, more austere mood while Ficino held to his old beliefs, although even he had been influenced by the Dominican preacher for a short while.[32] Ultimately, Savonarola's influence on other Miceceans was short–lived and of questionable effect. Ugolino Verino, for example, author of the above–mentioned *Paradisus*, became an admirer of Savonarola and in 1491 dedicated to him his *Carmen de Christiana religione ac vitae monasticae felicitate*. This work, however, a simple rhetorical appeal to reject the attractions of the world and to concentrate on matters of the spirit, still places an essentially Christian Neoplatonic emphasis on the fundamental spiritual nature of man, who must escape from the obstacles of the flesh:

> Mortale nihil durare videmus.
> Solus homo aeternus, coelestis patris imago...
> namque plagae aethereae civis non incola terrae est....
> Surgite, quis somnus, quae vos lethargica pestis
> opprimit, ignaros coeli vestraeque salutis?
> Brutorum tellus, nobis est mansio coelum.[33]

Soon after dedicating this poem, which is as amenable to Origen or Augustine as to the Friar, Verino rejected Savonarola outright and sent the Signoria a document sharply attacking him. The net effect on Verino's theological outlook thus appears to have been minor.

Similarly, Pico experienced his conversion to a more austere form of Christianity without abandoning his essentially eclectic theology. It was in 1486 that Pico had published his *900 Conclusiones*. Two years later he was seeking refuge after the disastrous episode of the planned disputation in Rome, and Ficino wrote to Lorenzo on behalf of Pico. Pico accepted an invitation to return to Florence and the two men resumed their friendship, although it has been suggested that since Pico was turning increasingly to a more austere form of religion, Ficino became somewhat more estranged from him. In the *Heptaplus*, completed in 1489, Pico quotes with impunity from Origen, if only from his less controversial homilies on Jeremiah and Genesis. Moreover, although it was probably Pico who persuaded Lorenzo to recall Savonarola to Florence, there is no reason to insist that Savonarola caused a profound theological conversion in Pico or turned Pico away from his admiration for Origen. It has been observed that when any of the young Laurentians came to Savonarola they "brought with them their Ficinian ideas as well as their individual talents and enthusiasms. Younger, less cautious, and perhaps less critical than Ficino, they readily saw in Savonarola the promise of the *renovatio* long heralded by their Platonic master."[34] Their philosophical outlook was essentially unchanged, therefore, only further subordinated to Christianity. The Neoplatonic synthesis with Christianity continued and posed no essential threat to the doctrines of Origen despite the stigma on his name.

Equally suspect writings were being produced by converts to Savonarola. Giovanni Nesi's *Oraculum*, for example, synthesizes Ficino's cosmology with aspects of the Savonarolan reform. It was as if Nesi was "no longer content with the mere rhetoric of philosophical piety, but unable to abandon its charms for the simpler, more literal Biblicism of his new spiritual master."[35] Nesi was trying to show that Savonarola heralded the fulfillment of all that Ficino and his followers had hoped for and worked for: namely an initiation into man's ultimate enlightenment, when spiritual renewal and moral perfection would at last permit humans to open all those mysteries to which they were heirs. This emphasis shows how the Savonarolan reform was interpreted by the younger Neoplatonists of the Medici circle. It shows the same spirit which occasioned Pico's defense of Origen against the criticisms of the Church, Savonarola's apparent rejection of Origen notwithstanding.

Thus it seems that Schär overstates the limitations of Origen's revival when he writes that with the condemnation of Pico's thesis, and in the heat of the Savonarolan austerity campaign, the newly opened Origen revival suddenly stops.[36] At very least, the syncretistic work of the Laurentian circle continued with a stronger flavor of a particular form of Christian Platonism and allegorical interpretation central to Origen's legacy. Scholars like Benivieni and Nesi responded to Savonarola by paying greater attention to Christian themes without abandoning the philosophical and eclectic character of their compositions. This resulted in an increased emphasis on the Christian faith by writers already thoroughly steeped in Neoplatonism. Consequently, their later works often reflect Christian– Platonist interpretations of biblical lore although it is difficult to isolate the specific influences. When Benivieni, for example, rejected his earlier compositions as "unfitting . . . for one who professed the laws of Christ," he replaced pagan motifs with Christian ones, by providing each of his *Eclogues* with a commentary demonstrating that the classical allusions were really spiritual allegories. This was common practice.[37] Moreover, the younger Florentines continued explicitly to refer to Origen. Mention is made of him by Jacopo Passavanti and Francesco Cattani da Diacceto (1466–1522). Passavanti published in 1495 in Florence *Lo speccio di vera penitenzia*, which included a translation of Pseudo–Origen's Homily on Mary Magdalen.[38]

The works produced in Italy at the end of the Quattrocento are as much in the tradition of Christian Platonism as are those composed during the mid–1480s, despite the renewed ecclesiastical censure and Savonarola's imposing presence. Historians, however, have been prone to connect this phase of the tradition with the names Plato, Plotinus, or Dionysius, for example, in places where Origenian theology was likely present as well. Although writers of the late Quattrocento were reluctant to name Origen, they continued to assume a theological stance harmonious with his teachings and speculations. At the beginning of the 16th century, Origen studies were taken up openly once again, in Venice and then in northern Europe. The line of the Alexandrian's admirers may best be described as unbroken, from Palmieri to Pico, Egidio of Viterbo to D'Étaples and Erasmus, the most celebrated students of Origen among the scholars influenced by humanism in Italy and in the North.

NOTES

1. *Origenis proaemium Contra Celsum et in fidei Christianae defensionem, Liber I* (Rome: Georgius Herolt de Bamburga, 1481) [Ludwig Hain, *Repertorium bibliographicum . . . usque ad annum MD*. 4 vols. Stuttgart/Paris 1826–1838; repr. Milan, 1966), 12078].

2. The present essay comments in particular on three studies: Edgar Wind, "The Revival of Origen" in *Studies in Art and Literature for Bella da Costa Green* (Princeton, 1954), 412–24; Henri Crouzel, *Une controverse sur Origène a la Renaissance: Jean Pic de la Mirandole et Pierre Garcia*, (Paris, 1977); Max Schär, *Das Nachleben des Origenes in Zeitalter des Humanismus* (Basel, 1979). See also Eugene Rice, "The Humanist Idea of Christian Antiquity: Lefevre d'Étaples and his Circle," *Studies in the Renaissance* 9 (1962): 126–60.

3. Eugene Rice has observed the predominantly literary interests of the early humanists. His argument can be summarized as follows: Humanism in its early phase mainly applies to a literary/stylistic movement. During the initial, "literary" phase of humanism in the cities of northern Italy, scholars experienced joy in discovering, among Christian authors no less than among classical ones, a desirable alternative to what they considered as the barbarism of medieval writing. The church fathers' works were sought out, edited, and published often with the same dedication and zeal accompanying work on the Greek and Roman classics. Like their medieval forerunners, the early humanists continued to look to Augustine as a principal authority from the early centuries, but Jerome and other Latin patristic authors received greater attention. But esthetics was connected to religion. The Fathers, who were almost all classically trained, had the same technical advantage over their medieval counterparts as did the ancient Greeks and Romans: patristic works reflected classical standards of eloquence. They were sometimes pure and concise, sometimes rich and elegant, but hardly ever were they unconsciously crude or rustic. Furthermore, the early humanists saw something of themselves in the Fathers, who were synthesizers of classical and Christian culture a millennium earlier: "An initial reason for admiring the fathers therefore was their eloquence: the Laconic brevity or Attic elegance of the Greeks; the Latins' clear sober concision, for which they were held to merit the praise traditionally given Sallust, that he offered as many ideas as he used words. Indeed the fathers themselves were considered classical men of letters." The interest in patristic theology that did exist was strongly influenced by a literary ethos. The humanists were attracted to the fact that to the fathers theology was not a *scientia* but a *sapientia* (thus they wrote no summas). They reasoned grammatically and explained allegorically the ceremonies of the law, adapting its teaching to the mysteries of faith and to the ethical problems of human life. Furthermore patristic exegetical method was admired: the fathers read Scripture in the original; they had developed critical techniques, they therefore provided a model for the humanist program. Rice, "The Humanist Idea of Christian Antiquity," 130–32.

See also Schär, *Das Nachleben des Origenes*, 90–100. Schär summarizes awareness of Origen in the fourteenth and early fifteenth centuries as indirect at best. Petrarch, for example, expressed himself about Origen as seriously erroneous, especially regarding his alleged doctrines of reincarnation and metempsychosis, but Petrarch, as well as Boccaccio, appears to know Origen only second–hand. Coluccio praises Origen for his use of allegory, along with Augustine and Gregory, but he knows Origen little in the original. Niccoli shows an interest in Origen and expressed hope that Poggio would bring back a MS. from England. In Rome, DaFiano includes Origen among the rhetorizing church fathers. Sacchi mentions Origen often and has second hand knowledge. Cardinal Arcimboldi used Origen first hand. Pius II makes only a rhetorical mention of Origen.

4. In general, according to Schär, the approach to Origen by the first three generations of Renaissance humanists may be summarized as follows: Indirect knowledge of him, an attitude characterized by rhetorical admiration, and restrained suspicion. For instance, Cardinal Bessarion paid attention to Origen's *Contra Celsum* in the fight against Turkish Islam, but he distanced himself from Origen as a speculative thinker. Theodore Gazes, however, had considerable interest in Origen's thought.

5. Nesca A. Robb, *Neoplatonism of the Italian Renaissance* (1935, repr. New York, 1968), 168.

6. Ibid., 63.

7. P. O. Kristeller, "The European Significance of Florentine Platonism," *Medieval and Renaissance Studies* (Chapel Hill, 1967), 219.

8. Ibid., 218–19.

9. Schär, *Das Nachleben*, 101–2.

10. See, e.g., the comments of P. D. Huetius, *Origeniana*, in PG 11: 1111 ff., as noted in G. Boffito, "L'Eresia di Matteo Palmieri 'Cittadin Fiorentino,'" *Giornale storico della letteratura italiana* 37 (1901): 25–43.

11. Schär, *Das Nachleben*, 102.

12. Wind, "The Revival of Origen," 419.

13. Wallace K. Ferguson, *Europe in Transition: 1300–1520* (New York, 1962), 514–16.

14. Bonincontri actually wrote his two most familiar works, the *Rerum naturalium* and *De rebus coelestibus*, while living in Naples between 1469–75. These works show that already at this time there were numerous philosophical influences on his general Christian orientation. The *Rerum naturalium* is the more religious of the poems, but *De rebus coelestibus* opens with an exposition of the mysteries of the faith, including the Trinity, Incarnation, the Atonement, and *creatio ex nihilo*, and several Platonic reflections on human nature. See Schär, *Das Nachleben*, 111.

15. The reference to *De principiis* is as follows: "Notice, I ask, what Origen, that man of extraordinary skill, perceived about the soul. He says that the soul, whether it is drawn from the transference of the seed in such a way that the principle or substance of the soul may be considered as from the seeds of the body itself, or whether, if it has another beginning, namely if it is begotten or not, or at any rate if it is imparted to the body from outside or not, none of this is clear enough in the [Church's] teaching. He says these things in his book on ecclesiastical doctrine"; quoted in Ruffo, "Lorenzo Bonincontri e alcuni suoi scritti ignorati." *Rinascimento* 5.2 (1965): 182. Latin text quoted in Schär, *Das Nachleben*, 111.

16. See Wind, "The Revival of Origen," 420–421.

17. Volt. 3, Canto 25 vv. 153ff. A second edition, with additional cantos, was published in the following year (ed. Volpi, Florence, 1863).

18. Schär, *Das Nachleben*, 131.

19. See Henri Crouzel, *Une Controverse sur Origène à la Renaissance: Jean Pic de la Mirandole e Pierre Garcia* (Paris, 1977), 63.

20. Ibid., 65.

21. Summing up the aftermath of the Origenian revival during the Renaissance, D.P. Walker equates it with the controversies over Origen, containing "the same mixture of veneration and ill–willed defiance, of passionate attacks and passionate defenses, which Origen's writings had excited in Antiquity" ("Origène en France au début du XVIe siècle," in *Courants religieux et humanisme a la fin du XVe siècle et au début du XVIe siècle* [Paris, 1959], 105).

22. See Schär, *Das Nachleben*, 138–39. Engelbert Monnerjahn, *Giovanni Pico della Mirandola: ein Beitrag zur philosophischen Theologie des italienischen Humanismus* (Wiesbaden, 1960) lists fourteen parallel theological emphases between Pico and Origen. His list provides a useful starting place for discovering points of affinity between Origen and other humanists: a) man's free will, b) man's being in God's image, c) the interpretation of man's fall and reconciliation, d) the ideas related to the degrees of recovery, e) the goal of mystical union through the obliteration of passion and through self–knowledge and ecstasy, f) the bride and lover motif, g) the idea that human affairs are related to the unity and harmony of the universe, h) the understanding of the logos as intermediary in the creation of the universe and the conduit of God's wisdom and power, i) allegorical interpretation, j) belief in the mystical power of words and numbers, k) distinction between simple and wise people, l) claiming of superiority of Jewish wisdom over Greek, m) a vacillating position regarding pagan philosophy, and n) the denial of eternal punishment for sin.

23. Ugolino Verino was born in Florence in 1438 and died there in 1516. He was a pupil of Landino and, like him, had an interest in harmonizing classics with strong Christian faith. This aim is especially apparent in his *Paradisus*. The date of composition remains uncertain but the earliest MSS. date from 1487.

24. *Paradisus*, MS. Florence. Laur. Plut. 39,40; 89v–90r.

25. Ibid., 90r.

26. "This is also laid down in the Church's teaching, that every rational soul is possessed of free will and choice; and also, that it is engaged in a struggle against the devil and his angels and the opposing powers; for these strive to weigh the soul down with sins, whereas we, if we lead a wise and upright life, endeavour to free ourselves from such a burden. There follows from this the conviction that we are not subject to necessity, so as to be compelled by every means, even against our will, to do either good or evil. For if we are possessed of free will, some spiritual powers may very likely be able to urge us to sin and others to assist us to salvation; we are not, however, compelled by necessity to act either rightly or wrongly." *De principiis*, Pref., 5, trans. G. W. Butterworth (New York, 1966), 4. See also *De principiis* 1.8 [on angels] and *De principiis* 3.2.4ff.

27. The Biblioteca Laurenziana contains manuscript copies of this and other works of Origen in the core of its collection. See, e.g., MS. Flor. Laur. Plut. 22.9 (A. M. Bandini *Catalogus codicum latinorum Bibliothecae Laurentianae*, 1774, vol. 1, col. 712).

28. Girolamo Savonarola (b. Ferrara, 1452), entered the monastery of St. Dominic in Bologna. He was sent to preach in Bologna in 1481 but was recalled and transferred to Florence that same year, where he entered the monastery of St. Mark. Lorenzo de' Medici died in 1492 and Savonarola's power increased with the accession of Lorenzo's son Piero.

In 1494 Charles VIII began to drive the Medici out (after a brief period of treaty). As a result Savonarola's power increased. In 1495 he was summoned to Rome but refused the summons. By 1496 many Florentines began to tire of his "virtue," and he was executed in 1498.

29. Donald Weinstein, *Savonarola and Florence: Prophecy and Patriotism in the Renaissance*, (Princeton, 1970), 191.

30. Schär, *Das Nachleben*, 143.

31. See Weinstein, *Savonarola and Florence*, 87.

32. As late as 1494 Ficino was praising Savonarola as a man of God. Ficino had been instrumental in joining Savonarola to the intellectual community of Florence. See Weinstein, *Savonarola and Florence*, 186.

33. Ugolino Verino, *Carmen de christiana religione*, in A. Gherardi ed., *Nuovi documenti e studi intorno a Girolamo Savonarola*, 2nd ed. (Florence, 1887, repr. 1972), 295.

34. Weinstein, *Savonarola and Florence*, 209.

35. Ibid., 194–95.

36. Schär, *Das Nachleben*, 142–43.

37. Weinstein, *Savonarola and Florence*, 216–17.

38. Schär (p. 143) acknowledges these references but thinks they were occasioned more out of sympathy with Pico than out of genuine interest in Origen.

Lady Wisdom's Final Call:
The Patristic Recovery
of Proverbs 8

Charles Kannengiesser
Concordia University

Lady Wisdom, a personified synthesis through which the simple or the erudite in Sumerian, Egyptian and Semitic cultures, expressed their sense of responsible human spirituality,[1] introduces herself in Proverbs 8 as a divine source of redeeming knowledge and eternal happiness. The whole book of Proverbs resounds with her voice, but chapter 8, striking for the very insistence of her self–defining statement, constitutes what may be termed her final call: "It is to you I call, to all humankind I appeal" (v.4). My purpose is to briefly analyze the patristic perception of Lady Wisdom's appeal to the Christian faith community in the aftermath of its experience of the gospel event.[2]

Already significant in Hebrew scripture as a powerful plea for honoring moral and religious values,[3] for Christian self–understanding the prosopopoeia of Wisdom in the Septuagint became a disclosure of the central mystery of the gospel. At first sight, a transvestite Lady Wisdom/Christ looks as foreign to the Old Testament as she/he might be to the New. At best, such a hybrid figure is an invitation to doctrinal fancies alien to any sound exegesis. However it is my claim that the Christological interpretation of the early church has more to teach us by its consistent logic than the letter of its polemics suggests. In a first stage let us face the antiquated polemics around Lady Wisdom, linked as they were with the intellectual culture of Late Antiquity. What actually remains relevant about them for us is the inner dynamic of faith at work as strongly in antiquated settings of Christian thought, as in today's believers. We shall come back to the spiritual event of that dynamic after having discussed some implications of the polemical reception of Proverbs 8 in ancient Christianity.

I. The Polemical Reception in the Fourth Century CE

Lady Wisdom immediately attracted the attention of New Testament writers.[4] She probably stands behind Paul's forceful proclamation of Christ "the power of God and the wisdom of God" in the first letter to the Corinthians.[5] In Rev. 3: 14, she identifies explicitly with the apocalyptic Christ: "These are the words of the

Amen, the faithful and true witness, the source of God's creation."[6] The quotation of Proverbs 8 runs through the writings of Justin of Rome,[7] Irenaeus of Lyons,[8] Clement of Alexandria[9] and Origen,[10] to mention only a few leading figures of second– and third–century thought. In the first book of his theoretical masterpiece, *On First Principles*, Origen elaborated a systematic notion of Christ partly based on the OT belief in divine Wisdom as a personified potentiality.[11] That initiative allowed him to oppose the Gnostic claim of a divine Plerôma, with the very first systematic outline of what would become long after him a Trinitarian doctrine.[12] But only in the Arian controversy of the fourth century would Lady Wisdom take on a new persona, definitely Christological. Along the interpretive trends from the New Testament to the fourth century, it becomes clear that the personified figure of Wisdom was read as an anticipated revelation of Christ. The high–sounding rhetorics of the Arian dispute rest on that presupposition.[13]

More precise information is needed on the fourth-century debate. The Alexandrian priest Arius had no difficulty in admitting the divine nature of Sophia and, as far as we can know, he kept true to her Christological significance carried on inside the Alexandrian tradition as Origen's legacy.[14] Arius' misfortune arose from his inability to reformulate that legacy beyond the mindset proper to theologians trained in the third century, before the so–called "great persecution" of Diocletian, which lasted in the Alexandrian church from 303 to 312, entailing a severe breakdown of her intellectual institutions. For Arius, Sophia in Proverbs 8 provided a self–identification of the heavenly Christ, which only confirmed his old–fashioned Monarchianism; in other words his Christianized biblical monotheism, according to which the μοναρχία, in Greek the "single principle" of deity was identical with the Father and included the Son and the Holy Spirit as two distinctive titles and entities thinkable only as one with the Father.[15] Thus Arius had no difficulty in admitting the "created" nature of Sophia, stated in Proverbs 8:22, as for him only the Father could be claimed to be radically uncreated.

Athanasius became bishop of Alexandria about ten years after Arius had been condemned by a local synod for his heretical preaching.[16] Athanasius was typical of the new generation issued from the time of the great persecution. Born with the century, probably in late 298 or early 299 (the seventeenth centennial of his birth should be celebrated at the Patristic conference in Oxford 1999!), he found himself willy–nilly involved in the theological and political turmoil of the Arian crisis during the agitated post–conciliar decades following the imperial synod held at Nicaea in the summer of 325.[17] Much younger than Arius, Athanasius shows nowhere in his writings any special interest in the personal theories of the condemned priest. At the repeated requests of his most militant parishioners, members of monastic communities in Egypt, he composed a polemical anti–Arian exposition of Christian faith, transmitted under the title *Orations against the Arians*.[18] The work was probably completed in 339, on the eve of Athanasius' second exile,[19] due to his flight to the West, when the Alexandrian see was taken over by a coalition of bishops favoring the Arian persuasion.

As I am dealing further on with the Arian crisis, my question will remain strictly limited to the hermeneutical procedures linked with Athanasius' reference to Proverbs 8: 22 in the *Orations against the Arians*.

In fact, we are contemplating here the most extended commentary on that biblical passage produced during the seven centuries of the patristic era. Still in his thirties, in office for less than a decade, and forced by monastic supporters into a public and formal statement about the heresy of Arius, Athanasius called on holy scripture as the only indisputable authority capable of showing him the critical questions to address, and the most appropriate answers to them. Thus he responded to Arianism on the sole basis of a scriptural argumentation. As a matter of fact the strategy of the young bishop was hardly a choice of his own. He followed the initiatives of Arius and his friends in focusing on the biblical quotations popularized by them for the past two decades.[20]

Athanasius' special aptitudes for interpreting scripture become clear as we follow the mature orchestration of his thought in the anti–Arian interpretations of disputed passages. His fresh approach to those passages results in a creative reading, giving them a new life, a consistency unheard of in previous thought, and above all an unexpected relevance in the contemporary crisis. The focus of Athanasius' polemics remains entirely hermeneutical, though the interpreter plunges into his polemical endeavor seemingly with scant scholarly preparation.[21] With an inner vision of his own, he builds up one argument after another, drawing on his ingrained familiarity with scripture.

There is a disconcerting clarity in the very process of his hermeneutics: even as a novice in exegesis Athanasius witnesses to the secret power of scripture which reshapes the whole meaning of Proverbs 8: 22 in the light of his faith in the gospel. Far from engaging in a scholastic exercise, he testifies to a spiritual event in which he finds himself literally overwhelmed by the truth of the text to be interpreted. The new content of his interpretation derives from the sacred source itself, not from any interpretive rules applied by him. Only one generation after Athanasius, in Roman Africa, the Donatist Tyconius would become the very first systematician of Christian hermeneutics to present the theological principles which underscore that same ancient form of biblical interpretation prevalent in the early church.[22] Tyconius wrote his *Liber regularis*, or *Book of Rules*, some time before 390, a set of logical precepts allowing Christian interpreters to perceive the "mystic rules," *regulae mysticae*, as he called them, applied by the Holy Spirit during the composition of the Old Testament.[23] The essential function of those *regulae mysticae*, as Tyconius understood them, was to keep the secrets of scripture out of reach of the unprepared or unworthy readers, hence the need for a propaedeutic introduction like the one he offered. Significantly enough, he entitled his essay *Liber regularis*, not meaning by it that he authored a "book" of his own "rules," but that he was writing on the Bible, itself a "regulated" book. For an appropriate reading of the Bible, Tyconius presented initiatory guidelines. On the other hand, Augustine, extensively quoting Tyconius in *De doctrina christiana*,[24] spontaneously changed the title into *Liber regularum*,[25] which announced a tractate with exegetical precepts, in line with the many such "rule books" on the market for traditional school rhetorics.

More immediately than Tyconius and Augustine, Athanasius experienced the mystical structuring of scripture without theorizing it. He spontaneously reacted to it as a young pastor educated in the Bible from childhood. Polarized by the ministerial duty to interpret scripture in the heat of a critical context, his attitude toward the sacred book was foremost one of admiration and celebration in faith. The believing identity of the interpreter, showing all the marks of a conversion–experience born of faith in the gospel–event, was completely involved in the exegetical task. The distinctive dynamic of gospel faith led Athanasius, first as believer, than as bishop constantly to perceive the present reality of the gospel–event in the church and the human condition at large.

So far I have tried to formulate the most basic inductive evidence at the core of Athanasius' familiarity with scripture. More needs to be clarified about the centrality of that evidence, which consistently actualized the gospel–event in Athanasius' self–awareness. For the moment I would attempt to explore briefly how far that same evidence highlights the procedures of his hermeneutics, which need to be explored in more detail in order to reach a constructive understanding of the reception of Proverbs 8 in the early church.

II. Procedures of Athanasian Hermeneutics

In the first *Oration against the Arians*, chapter 53 according to the numbering reproduced in Migne's Patrology, the citation of Proverbs 8: 22, "The Lord created me the beginning of his ways for his works," is introduced at the same time as Heb. 1: 4, "Being made so much better than the angels, as he has by inheritance obtained a more excellent name than they," Heb. 3: 1, "Wherefore, holy brethren, partakers of the heavenly calling, consider the apostle and high priest of our profession, Christ Jesus, who was faithful to him who made him," and Acts 2: 36, "Therefore all the house of Israel know assuredly, that God has made that same Jesus whom you have crucified both Lord and Christ." The choice of the four quotations is obviously dictated by Arian concerns.

Athanasius starts by changing the order of the references: he places Proverbs 8: 22 at the end of his comments to the whole series. Thus the discussion of Heb. 1: 4 and 3: 1, and of Acts 2: 36 prepares the reader for the consideration of the verse from Proverbs. For the interpretation of all four quotations a basic hermeneutical rule is first stated: "Now it is right and necessary, as in all divine scripture, so here, faithfully to expound *the time* (ὁ καιρός) of which the apostle wrote, and *the person* (ὁ πρόσωπον), and *the point* (τὸ πρᾶγμα); lest the reader, from ignorance missing either these or any similar particular, may be wide of the true sense."[26] The interpretive rule recommended here by Athanasius may not be unrelated to the fact that no other translation, and no critical edition at all, of his

Contra Arianos is currently available. For Athanasius' interpretive rule challenges the standard idea of an Alexandrian exegete. A one–sided focus on the political dimension of Athanasius' career during the past hundred years seems to have damped the enthusiasm even of historians of patristic exegesis from exploring the Athanasian scripture heritage as such. Indeed the Athanasian approach of scripture ill–fits the text–book categories of current research about the so–called "Alexandrian school" of interpretation. No allegorism, as inherited from Origen, can be found in his writings. No conventional typology serves with explicit support his theological thinking. He occupies a unique position among the intellectual leaders of the Alexandrian church, in that he wrote not a single commentary on a biblical book.

The hermeneutical rule of *Contra Arianos* 1, 54, quoted above, links instantly the verse of Proverbs 8: 22 with the *kairos* of salvation history. By identifying Lady Wisdom's "created" condition, proclaimed in Proverbs, with that of the divine Logos of John 1: 14, καὶ ὁ λόγος σάρξ ἐγένετο, the fourth–century Alexandrian interpreter turns her whole discourse toward the concrete world of his own spiritual experience, the Christian church. For there, and only there, does the personified Sophia repeat now her promise of earlier days: "Whoever finds me finds life and wins favor with the Lord" (Prov 8: 35). A truly Johannine promise in Athanasius' ear.[27]

After having refuted Arian interpretations of the other three quotations under scrutiny, Athanasius starts with a lengthy introduction of the commentary on Proverbs 8: 22. From chapter 18 to 44 of what is now known as the second *Oration against the Arians* (originally both treatises were a single one), he feels obliged to recapitulate the massive debate on the true divinity of the Son launched under his predecessor, Bishop Alexander, in opposition to Arius. Only in chapter 44, when, at long last, he starts to explain his own understanding of Proverbs 8: 22, his viewpoint sharpens again and, as in the hermeneutical rule of *C. Ar.* 1, 54 added to the very first mention of Proverbs 8: 22 , he demonstrates once again a strictly interpretive focus: "For it is written, 'The Lord created me a beginning of his ways for his works'; since, however, these are *proverbs* (παροιμίαι), we must not expound them nakedly in their first sense, but we must inquire into *the person* (τὸ πρόσωπον), and thus religiously put the sense on it. For what is said in *proverbs* (ἐν παροιμίαις), is not said plainly, but is put forth latently, as the Lord himself has taught us in the gospel according to John, saying: 'These things have I spoken unto you in proverbs (ἐν παροιμίαις), but the time comes when I shall no more speak to you in proverbs, but openly.'"[28]

Thus Athanasius concludes that the proper form of Lady Wisdom's discourse is found actualized in the gospel, the Johannine Jesus himself speaking "in proverbs." For that reason he would henceforth consider the proverbial form of Sophia's speech as a crucial key, provided by scripture itself, for the interpretation of Proverbs 8: 22; in particular, that key leads his hermeneutical inquiry "into the person," as he says, of Sophia. Thus the linking of the solemn self–disclosure of

Lady Wisdom with the *kairos* of God's incarnation is paralleled with the identification of *her* "proverbial" statements with those of *Jesus* in the fourth gospel. For Athanasius their identical diction signals their also identical, though hidden, *persona*. It seems obvious that such a hermeneutics was well fitted to secure a decisive blow against any Christology, like the one denounced by Athanasius in Arius, that would not essentially be incarnational.

In any event, Athanasius' response to the call of Lady Wisdom could only be in the context of the central *kairos* of salvation–history, as he knew it. The echoing of her voice in the liturgies of the church announced for him her actual rebirth in the person of Jesus, not by physical transmigration, but by her mystical transfiguration in the present reality of the gospel–event. To respond correctly to the actual message of Sophia as embodied in Christ, there was an imperative need for the submission of the interpreter to the proper form of her message, forming a scriptural link between past and present salvific revelation. In other words, it needed a "proverbial" interpretation of what is revealed in Proverbs.[29]

Throughout his comments from chapter 44 to 82, at the very end of the *Oration*, Athanasius holds firmly to that hermeneutical rule. He pours a rich doctrinal content into his reading of Proverbs 8: 22, but not without constantly legitimating his doctrinal exegesis by calling on the hermeneutical rule imposed by the proverbial form of the Wisdom message. Thus Athanasius' hermeneutical focus keeps him in line with a classical principle of literary "mimesis": being a creative interpreter means primarily reproducing the peculiar form of the literary source to be interpreted. Thereby the Christological reception of Proverbs 8: 22 turns into a profuse meditation on the "proverbial" (παροιμιωδῶς 240 C) or "latent" (κεκρυμμένως 241 A) nature of biblical statements as such, including, amazingly enough, the incarnational imperative of John 1:14: "For, as when John says, 'The Word was made flesh,' we do not conceive the whole Word himself to be flesh, but to have put on flesh and become man" (chap. 47: 248 A). More pointedly, to perceive the dogmatic truth of John 1:14, one has to keep a correct sense for the very nature of biblical statements.

All along his commentary on Prov 8: 22, the Alexandrian bishop confronts his opponents[30] with the texture and proper nature of the biblical passages under discussion: "And the very passage in question proves your irreligious spirit.... For the Word of God is not creature but Creator, and says in the manner of proverbs (παροιμιωδῶς) 'He created me' when he put on created flesh."[31] Even when debating in categories of the intellectual culture the notion of the Christian deity, the interpreter's attention never deviates from the biblical source. Each time when needed, Athanasius finds it normal and legitimate to receive from scripture itself the decisive criteria for his argumentation. For instance, Athanasius discusses the "point," or *pragma*, of Proverbs 8: 22, which means in fact the purpose of Sophia's self–disclosure: "And this is usual with divine scripture (ἔθος ἐστὶ τῇ θείᾳ γραφῇ); for when it signifies the fleshly origination of the Son, it adds also the cause (τὴν αἰτίαν) for which he became man; but when he speaks or his servants declare anything of his godhead, all is said in simple diction (ἀπλῇ τῇ λέξει) and with an absolute sense, and without reason (αἰτίας) being added."[32]

In short, the *hethos*, or "habit," of all scripture is to express the reality of divine and salvific revelation through the peculiarities of its own literary form. From syntactical structures to most ordinary grammatical or lexical devices the proper nature of scriptural discourse always conforms to the mysteries out of which the discourse originates. Marked by such a constant disposition, scripture's second nature, as Athanasius perceives it, consists in referring all its statements to the gospel–event as to the only focus capable of giving a coherent sense to any sacred writing belonging to salvation–history. Athanasian hermeneutics establishes such a close connection between the events and their written transmission inside the realm of salvation–history, that Athanasius' own style takes on a narrative shape. The Alexandrian bishop never tires of interpreting any biblical passage in light of the *kairos*, the *persona* and the *pragma*, that, to his mind, characterize the gospel–event.[33]

III. The Actualizing Dynamic of Christocentric Faith

"The personification of wisdom in the Old Testament has often received a christological interpretation. Especially in chapter 8, one must cast serious doubt upon the validity of this approach."[34] Indeed the question of "validity" remains crucial after any exercise, fragmentary and clumsy as it may be, in Athanasian exegesis; but "valid" for whom and in what sense? My purpose is not to justify Athanasius vs. Roland Murphy, nor is it to contemplate any dilemma between patristic hermeneutics and contemporary exegesis. Fifteen years ago, Sean McEvenue wrote a thoughtful essay, based on Bernard Lonergan's teaching, which he entitled with the question "The Old Testament: Scripture or Theology ?"[35] Among more complex and challenging ideas I found in it a crystal–clear definition of exegesis as currently understood: it is the "exact interpretation of a text in its original meaning" (236). In the light of such a definition, Athanasius' hermeneutical enterprise is not "exegetical" at all, the "meaning" of the sacred text being not seen by him as belonging to a past culture and bound to the circumstances which occasioned the original production of the text. In the Athanasian understanding "meaning" is best rendered by δύναμις, "power": the sacred text possesses a "power" that transcends its incidental provenance, a "dynamic" of its own which remains alive as long as the divine revelation carried on by the text makes sense. For a reader like Athanasius, as he insists precisely in the section of *Contra Arianos* which we are dealing with , "all these (biblical) texts have the same force and meaning," τὰ τοιαῦτα γὰρ πάντα ῥητὰ τὴν αὐτὴν ἔχει δύναμιν καὶ διάνοιαν.[36]

Therefore the text itself remains alive for such an interpreter. More explicitly, the actualizing reception of the text by people like Athanasius involves at once entire submission to form and content of the textual message, and personal identification with the text's *kairos*, *persona* and *pragma*: personified Wisdom becomes Christ for them, in the letter and the form of her discourse, not in substituting herself for the historical Jesus, but in being identified by their christocentric faith as signifying Christ. In their hermeneutics, the question of "validity" is irrelevant in terms of historical exactness, it can only be a question of spiritual value.

To refer casually to the "christocentric faith" of patristic hermeneutics without an additional comment would be superficial. In my following remarks I would like to point out only one aspect of that faith: it must be understood as producing the psychological conditions for the *actualizing* process: it operates the identification of the believing person with scriptural data in assimilating them to its self–definition as faith in Christ. Thus the sacred text remains alive for those believers because their christocentric faith breathes into it its own life. Hence their reading *actualizes* the text in the light of the gospel–event on which they actually participate in their faith.

Objectively Arius was correct in stressing "created me" in Proverbs 8: 22, but a narrow–minded literalism prevented him from a creative reading which would have orchestrated Lady Wisdom's speech by calling on the symphonic trends of all scriptures. In fact, his theological concerns were in need of a proof–text concerning what he considered the improper divine title of the Son, and "created me" could easily be isolated as a slogan; at least, such is the impression Athanasius gives about Arian exegesis. On the other hand, Athanasius' interpretation of the passage entails, first of all, a global vision of scripture. "Christological" as it is, that vision has nothing to do with punctual, or artificial, cases of typology, nor should it be reduced to pious forms of allegorism. It defines the basic reception of the Old Testament in the Christian faith community, a reception which by definition (being christocentric) transforms radically the meaning of all scripture. Just as the poetic personification of Lady Wisdom concentrates for us a whole tradition of learning and spiritual praxis throughout ancient cultures of the eastern Mediterranean, so does her christocentric identification in the early church fulfill the *actualizing* expectations of many Christian generations. Focusing on God's incarnate presence in his church and his contemporary world through an intense awareness of his christocentric faith, a still youthful leader like Athanasius could well dispense with the "original meaning" of any sacred verses; but he could not neglect to explore the relevance of all such verses in the light of the gospel–event in which he found himself included through the actualizing dynamic of his faith.

IV. The Amplification of Wisdom's Voice

A systematic analysis of the interpretive reception by which Athanasius and his contemporaries inculturated scripture in Late Antiquity is far beyond the limits of the present essay. I would limit my concluding remarks to the global effect of their exegesis, by which any passage in need of an explanation engaged them in quoting all existing books of the Bible according to their inner vision of the nature of biblical truth.

In the section of *Contra Arianos* directly dedicated to the discussion of Proverbs 8:22, namely chapters 18 to 72 of the second *Oration*, Athanasius quotes scripture 287 times, without counting the repeated mentions of Proverbs 8:22 itself. Lady Wisdom's call reaches here a supreme amplitude: her statement attracts other voices from near and far in the scriptural universe, and she orchestrates these voices, and plays with them distinctly on different levels of thought, in producing thereby an extraordinary display of doctrinal themes and lexical data.

In the introductory part of the commentary, chapters 18 to 43, fully 54 references of a total of 115 are to the Old Testament. Most frequently quoted are the Psalms (18 times). Some quotations from different chapters of Proverbs join additional mentions of Proverbs 8: 22. The book of Genesis is referred to 12 times, as the commentary espouses Sophia's claim to be the Creator's assistant, by celebrating the new creation inaugurated by God's incarnation. Exodus and Numbers appear occasionally. Among the prophets, Isaiah leads with 4 quotations, surrounded by Joel, Baruch, Zechariah, Daniel. Among the historical books figure Esdras and Judith, in addition to Judges. The book of Wisdom supplies only one reference. In the call on the New Testament, the gospel of John occupies a central position, with 23 references against only 11 to the other canonical gospels. Pauline literature is invoked 16 times, completed by only sporadic mentions of Acts and Revelation.

In the proper exegesis of Proverbs 8: 22 (*C. Ar.* 44–72), the Old Testament remains in the same proportion to the New Testament as in the introductory part, with 70 quotations of a total of 172. Psalms also remain prevalent with 24 quotations. Genesis is invoked only 9 times, but complemented with 6 references to Deuteronomy. Ten references are to other parts of Proverbs, in addition to Proverbs 8: 22. Isaiah returns 5 times, with isolated mentions of Jeremiah, Baruch, Daniel, Micah and Malachi, 2 Chronicles and Wisdom. Calling on the New Testament, the commentary includes this time 45 Pauline quotations against only 39 Johannine. The contrast between the latter and only 8 references to the other canonical gospels is striking. New are, in this part of Athanasius' development on Proverbs 8: 22, the quotations from Deuteronomy and others from Malachi, Micah, Baruch, 2 Chronicles and 1 Peter.

Athanasius' extended comments on Proverbs 8: 22 constitute only one among hundreds of similar cases, where intellectual leaders of ancient Christianity succeeded in harmoniously collecting a large number of biblical quotations in order to illuminate given scriptural books or passages of a book. This cannot be dismissed in a cavalier manner, as simple "proof–texts." The same creative interpretation of scripture by scripture itself, through the prism of individual selections of references, has been at work from Irenaeus of Lyons, before the end of the second century, to Maximus Confessor, in the second half of the seventh.

One may repeat what a critic recently observed about patristic allegorism: "I am intrigued by the quantity of allegorical commentary–enormous in terms of quantity but also in terms of authority. Like Mount Everest, it is there. What is to be made of it ?"[37] From what I have tried to emphasize, it seems clear that no real retrieving of ancient hermeneutics will ever be conceivable without a critical re–formulation of the faith–experience witnessed by patristic commentators. Their "Himalayan" contribution to the interpretation of Christian scripture overtowers at least fifteen centuries of Western culture. The current crisis in the Christian church and in post–Christian trends of our society includes the formidable task of recasting in our present mindset the dreams and the mystic fervor behind presently disqualified patristic hermeneutics.

NOTES

1. J.J.A. van Dijk, *La sagesse sumero–accadienne* (Leiden, 1953); E.I. Gordon, *Sumerian Proverbs: Glimpses of Every Day Life in Ancient Mesopotamia* (Philadelphia, 1959); W.G. Lambert, *Babylonian Wisdom Literature* (1960); S. Langdon, *Babylonian Wisdom* (London, 1923: texts translated); P. Humbert, *Recherches sur les sources égyptiennes de la littérature sapientiale d'Israël* (Neuchatel, 1929); H. Brunner, *Grundzüge der altägyptischen Religion* (Darmstadt, 1983); P. Heinisch, *Die persönliche Weisheit des Alten Testaments* (1926); H. Ringgren, *Word and Wisdom: Studies in the Hypostatization of Divine Qualities and Functions in the Ancient Near East* (Lund, 1947); M. Dahood, *Proverbs and Northwest Semitic Philology* (Rome, 1963); R.E. Murphy, *Wisdom Literature: Job, Proverbs, Ruth, Canticles, Ecclesiastes, and Esther* (Grand Rapids, 1981); W. Visher, "Der Hymnus der Weisheit in den Sprüchen Salomos 8, 22–31," *Evangelische Theologie* 22 (1962): 309–26; C. Bauer–Kayatz, *Studien zu Proverbien* (Neukirchen-Vluyn, 1986).

2. On the reception of Proverbs in the early church: J. Allenbach, ed., *Biblia Patristica*, Index des citations et allusions bibliques dans la littérature patristique, Centre d'Analyse et de Documentation (Paris, 1975–1991); J. Trublet, *La Sagesse biblique: De l'Ancien au Nouveau Testament*, Actes du XVème Congrès de l'Association Catholique Française pour l'Étude de la Bible, Lectio Divine, 160 (Paris, 1995); S. Leanza, "Sapienziali (libri)" in A. Di Berardino, ed., *Dizionario Patristico e di Antichità Cristiana* 2 (1984), 3085–87 = *Encyclopedia of the Early Church* 2 (1992), 878–81; M. Richard, "Les fragments d'Origène sur Prov. XXX, 15–31," in J. Fontaine and C. Kannengiesser, eds., *Epektasis*, Festschrift for Jean Daniélou (Paris, 1972), 385–94; L. Abramowski, "Dionys vom Rom (+258) und Dionys von Alexandrien (+264/5) in den arianischen Streitigkeiten des 4. Jahrhunderts," *Zeitschrift für Kirchengeschichte* 93 (1982): 240–72; A. Weber, *ARXH: Ein Beitrag zur Christologie des Eusebius von Caesarea* (München, 1965); A. Meredith,

"Proverbes 8, 22 chez Origène, Athanase, Basile et Grégoire de Nysse," pp. 349–57 in C. Kannengiesser, ed., *Politique et Théologie chez Athenase d'Alexandrie*, Actes du Colloque de Chantilly 23–25 septembre 1973 (Paris, 1973); M. Van Parys, "Exégèse et théologie trinitaire: Proverbes 8:22 chez les Pères Cappadociens," *Irénikon* 43 (1970): 362–79.

3. G. Von Rad, *Wisdom in Israel* (Nashville, 1972); R. Bultmann, Der dogmengeschichtliche Hintergrund des Prologs zum Johannes–Evangelium," in *Exegetica*, ed. E. Dinkler (Tübingen, 1967), 10–35.

4. P.–E. Bonnard, *La Sagesse en personne, annoncée et venue, Jésus Christ* (Paris, 1966); H. Conzelmann, "Wisdom in the New Testament," *The Interpreter's Dictionary of the Bible* (Nashville, 1976), Supp. Vol, 956–60; J. Ashton, "The Transformation of Wisdom: A Study of the Prologue of John's Gospel," *New Testament Studies* 32 (1982): 161–86.

5. Ἐριστὸν θεοῦ δύναμις καὶ θεοῦ σοφίαν (1:24).

6. Τάδε λέγει ὁ ἀμήν, ὁ μάρτυς ὁ πιστὸς καὶ ἀληθινός, ἡ ἀρχὴ τῆς κτίσεως τοῦ θεοῦ.

7. *Dialog with Trypho* 61,3; 126,1. For Prov. 8 in Justin and the other patristic authors here mentioned, see J. Wolinski, "La Sagesse chez les Pères de l'Église: De Clément de Rome à Augustin," pp. 423–65 in Trublet, *Sagesse biblique* (see n. 2).

8. *Against the Heresies* 2, 35.3; 4, 20.1–3; 5, 17.1, 24.1.

9. *Protreptikos* 80,1; *Paedagogos* 1, 90.1; 2, 79.4; 3, 35.3; *Stromatoi* 1, 58.3, 173.6; 2, 83.2; 5, 89.4; 6, 125.2, 138.4; 7, 7.4.

10. No precise reference available, but see J. Letellier, "Le Logos d'Origène," *Revue des sciences philosophiques et théologiques* 75 (1991): 587–612; Richard, "Les fragments d'Origène" (n. 2); Meredith, "Proverbes 8, 22" (n. 2).

11. *De Principiis* 1, 2.2; also 1, 4.405.

12. C. Kannengiesser, "Origen Systematician in *De Principiis*," pp. 395–405 in R.J. Daly, ed., *Origeniana Quinta* (Leuven, 1992); "Écriture et théologie trinitaire d'Origène," pp. 351–64 in G. Dorival et A. Le Boulluec, eds., *Origeniana Sexta* (Leuven, 1995).

13. Weber, *ARXH* (n. 2); M. Simonetti, *La crisi ariana nel IV secolo* (Rome, 1975).

14. "He called him Word, and Wisdom, and Son. . . . Wisdom through Wisdom existed by the wise God's will"; *Thalia* in *Contra Arianos* 1, 5 (PG 26: 21 B) and *De synodis* 15 (PG 26: 708 B).

15. On second-century Monarchianism, R.M. Hübner, "Εἰς θεὸς ᾽Ιησοῦς Ἐριστός. Zum christlichen Gottesglauben im 2. Jahrhundert—ein Versuch," *Münchener Theologische Zeitschrift* 47 (1996): 325–44. On Arius's notion of deity: A. Grillmeier, *Christ in Christian Tradition* I, 2nd ed. (Atlanta, 1975), Lit.; R. Williams, *Arius: Heresy and Tradition* (London, 1987) 95–116; C. Kannengiesser, *Le Verbe de Dieu selon Athanase d'Alexandrie*, Jésus et Jésus Christ, 45 (Paris, 1990), 96–101.

16. D. W–H. Arnold, *The Early Episcopal Career of Athanasius of Alexandria* (Notre Dame, Ind., 1991); A. Martin, *Athanase d'Alexandrie et l'Église d'Égypte au IVème siècle (328–373)* (Rome, 1996), 321–40.

17. In the vast literature, T.D. Barnes, *Constantine and Eusebius* (Cambridge, Mass., 1986); R.P.C. Hanson, *The Search for the Christian Doctrine of God: The Arian Controversy 318–381* (Edinburgh, 1988).

18. PG 26: 12–468; This essay uses Henry Newman's translation published in 1844, "the year before his secession," as noted by Archibald Robertson, who reproduced the same translation; NPNF, 2nd series, vol. 4 (1892, 1994), 303–432. Only in the Preface is Arius's

Thalia quoted; in the three books (the third possibly of a later date or by a different author) central issues remain hermeneutical: Athanasius teaches how to interpret scripture against Arianism; see my *Athanase d'Alexandrie évêque et écrivain: Une lecture des traités 'Contra les Ariens'* (Paris, 1983); or "The Bible in the Arian Crisis" in P.M. Blowers, ed., *The Bible in Greek Christian Antiquity* (Notre Dame, forthcoming).

19. Montfaucon's dating from Athanasius's third exile (356–362) was challenged by Loofs and others at the turn of the Twentieth Century; it still remains problematic because of the discrepancies between *C. Ar.* 1–2 and *C. Ar.* 3.

20. In particular, Phil. 2:9–10 and Ps. 44:7–8 (*C. Ar.* 1:35–52), Heb. 1:4, 3:2; Acts 2:36 (*C. Ar.* 1:53–2:18) and Prov. 8:22 (*C. Ar.* 2:18–61) received extended treatment in Athanasius's work.

21. It is striking to observe that after a "general introduction," written after completion of the whole work—which makes it the more surprising that the *Thalia* is never quoted in the bulk of the *Contra Arianos* as it is in that "introduction"—the author tried a first kind of exposition by refuting Arian slogans (1:11–22a), before introducing a new exegetical method in 1:22b with commentaries on Phil. 2:5–11 and Ps. 44:7–8. Again, in 1:53, he gives a new start to a more thorough study of other biblical references, culminating in a lengthy discussion of Prov. 8:22. Only in that last section, covering the rest of *C. Ar.*, the author seems to feel comfortable with his newly acquired methodology. Additional commentaries in *C. Ar.* 3 are organized in a systematic way alien to the pattern of two former books of *C. Ar.*; for more about this see my *Athanase d'Alexandrie*, or *Le Verbe de Dieu* (n. 18 and n. 15).

22. W.S. Babcock, trans., *Tyconius. The Book of Rules*, Society of Biblical Literature Texts and Translations 31, Early Christian Literature Series 7 (Atlanta, 1989); P. Bright, *The Book of Rules of Tyconius: Its Purpose and Inner Logic* (Notre Dame, 1988); C. Kannengiesser and P. Bright, *A Conflict of Christian Hermeneutics in Roman Africa: Tyconius and Augustine* (Berkeley, 1989); P. Bright, ed., *Augustine and the Bible* (Notre Dame, forthcoming).

23. [S]unt enim quaedam regulae mysticae quae universae legis recessus obtinent (Prologue) *per omnes scripturas* (8.6); they belong to the *mysteria caelestis sapientiae*, as due *magisterio spiritus sancti* (31.11–12), and identified as *regulas quibus spiritus legem signavit* (66.11).

24. Ed. R.P.H. Green (Oxford, 1995), 92 (30.42)–135 (37.56). The whole section of *De doctrina christiana* 3, added by Augustine with Book 4 after an interruption of three decades, consists of a summary of Tyconius, in which Augustine changes at his convenience most of the biblical quotations; cf. P. Bright, "Tyconius and His Interpreters: A Study of the Epitomes of the *Book of Rules*," pp. 23–39 in *A Conflict* (n. 22).

25. [F]ecit librum quem Regularum vocavit (Green edition, 92; 30.42).

26. PG 26: 124B.

27. T.E. Pollard, *Johannine Christology and the Early Church* (London, 1970).

28. John 16:25; 240 C–241 A; NPNF 4:372.

29. In conformity with the more general rule of patristic hermeneutics urging interpreters to impersonate prophets and other human agents of biblical revelation in appropriating scripture.

30. About whom he remains extremely vague, as if he never met any of them in the flesh.

31. Chap. 50: PG 26: 252 C–253 A; NPNF 4:375.

32. Chap. 53: PG 26: 260 B; NPNF 4:377.

33. That hermeneutical rule is replaced in *C. Ar.* 3:21 by the distinction of "a double account of the Saviour" (Robertson, 409) in accordance with Christ's two natures, whereas in all of Athanasius's later writings, from the 350s to 373, the rule of *C. Ar.* 1 and 2 obtains; see my essay on "Athanasius von Alexandrien als Exeget," pp. 336–43 in G. Schöllgen and C. Scholten, eds., *Stimuli: Exegese und Ihre Hermeneutik in Antike und Christentum*, Festschrift for E. Dassmann, Jahrbuch für Antike und Christentum, Ergänzungsband 23 (Münster, 1966).

34. R.E. Murphy, "The Kerygma of the Book of Proverbs," *Interpretation* 20 (1966): 5.

35. *Interpretation* 35 (1981): 229–42.

36. PG 26: 149 A; Robertson, 348.

37. Michael Cahill, "Reader–response Criticism and the Allegorizing Reader," *Theological Studies* 57 (1996): 91.

Seven Unidentified Sources
in Eusebius' *Historia Ecclesiastica*

Andrew J. Carriker
Columbia University

A distinguishing feature of the *Historia Ecclesiastica* (HE) is that its author, Eusebius of Caesarea, customarily names and quotes from his numerous sources. But, while citation of sources is the rule in the HE, in seven of its passages, namely, II.7; II.8.1; II.25.2; III.18.4; III.20.8; IV.2.5; and V.5.3, Eusebius refers to his sources generally and without identifying them.[1] Many editors and translators of the HE have noted the existence of other ancient discussions of the same material as Eusebius treats in these passages, but it is difficult to know what to make of these editors' references, since Eusebius leaves little clue about his sources here.[2] Perhaps the greatest frustration in locating Eusebius' sources is that so much ancient literature has disappeared and consequently cannot be compared with Eusebius' text. Indeed, one historian has, for a variety of reasons, pessimistically concluded that "hopeless uncertainties prevail in the field of source-criticism."[3] Nevertheless, the optimistic historian may hope that a fresh examination of these passages will be useful, even if only suggestions can be made about the sources of some of them, and that such an examination will serve as a modest tribute to the Reverend F. W. Schlatter, S. J., who introduced me to the study of sources in late ancient authors.

I

The first passage occurs at HE II.7. After reporting the tradition (κατέχει λόγος) that Pontius Pilate committed suicide, Eusebius states:

ἱστοροῦσιν Ἑλλήνων οἱ τὰς Ὀλυμπιάδας ἅμα τοῖς κατὰ χρόνους πεπραγμένοις ἀναγράψαντες.

Those of the Greeks who record the Olympiads together with the events of the times report this.

This hostile tradition about Pilate's fate is late (Eusebius provides the first evidence
of it), and it is very probably Christian, for who more than Christians would be
keen to establish Pontius Pilate's manner of death? Earlier, in his *Chronicon*,
Eusebius simply attributes the information to "historians of the Romans."[4] There
is, it seems, little hope of identifying Eusebius' source here, for the evidence bears
two different interpretations. It is possible that Eusebius' reference to the Olympiad
chroniclers, because it is more specific than the formula with which he introduces
the story (κατέχει λόγος), indicates that Eusebius possessed the evidence of a
written source.[5] On the other hand, it is also possible that Eusebius did not actually
have written evidence that Pilate took his own life. Now, it is unlikely that
Eusebius invented the story itself, since he probably believed that there was
evidence somewhere to support the tradition of Pilate's suicide. But, he may have
exaggerated when he named his source in order to make his information more
credible. The remaining vagueness in Eusebius' attribution to "those of the Greeks
who record the Olympiads" inclines one to the latter of the two possibilities.

II

At HE II.8.1 Eusebius records the inauguration of Claudius' reign and then
notes that under Claudius a famine beset the whole world:

> καθ' ὃν λιμοῦ τὴν οἰκουμένην πιέσαντος (τοῦτο δὲ καὶ οἱ πόρρω τοῦ καθ'
> ἡμᾶς λόγου συγγραφεῖς ταῖς αὐτῶν ἱστορίαις παρέδοσαν).[6]

> . . . under whose reign [Claudius'] a famine oppressed the world (and this event
> even those historians who are far from our teaching relate in their histories).

Eusebius goes on to say that this famine is also mentioned in Acts (11:28), from
which he then borrows the phrase ἐφ' ὅλην τὴν οἰκουμένην, a token of his direct
reliance here on the text of Acts. But who are these non-Christian historians who
refer to the Claudian famine? Tacitus (*Ann.* 12.43) and Suetonius (*Claud.* 18) both
record a severe famine that affected Rome, but it is highly unlikely that Eusebius
used these authors, since Eusebius was largely unfamiliar with works by Latin
writers.[7] Cassius Dio (60.11.1) also records the famine and similarly speaks of its
effect on Rome. Eusebius may possibly be thinking of Dio as one of the non-
Christian συγγραφεῖς, but, if, as seems more likely, Eusebius only loosely uses
the plural here, the single source he refers to is Josephus.[8] In his *Antiquitates
Iudaicae* (20.101) Josephus reports that a great famine struck Judaea, a report that
Eusebius quotes four chapters later (HE II.12) and connects directly to the account
in Acts.[9]

III

At HE II.25.1–2 Eusebius confronts Nero's depravity and, worst of all, his hostility to piety toward God. Eusebius refuses, however, to continue a discussion of this topic, since "many, indeed, have handed down the events under his reign in very accurate narratives": πολλῶν γε μὴν τὰ κατ᾽ αὐτὸν ἀκριβεστάταις παραδεδωκότων διηγήσεσιν. Eusebius then briefly observes that Nero killed many Romans, including his mother, brothers, and wife.[10]

Although Eusebius next quotes a Greek translation of Tertullian's *Apologeticum* (HE II.25.4 of *Apol.* 5.3) in order to expose Nero as the first imperial persecutor of Christians, Eusebius cannot be thinking of Tertullian as one of the many accurate historians of Nero's reign, since, apart from this passage, Tertullian only once more refers to Nero's reign.[11] Similarly, unless Eusebius exaggerates when he speaks of "narratives," it seems unlikely that he is referring to any of the chronicles that must have supplied him with information for his *Chronicon*.[12] The Latin authors Tacitus and Suetonius are again also unlikely to have been used by Eusebius. Nor does it seem that Eusebius is drawing upon Josephus, who at *Ant.* 20.154–156 refuses, like Eusebius, further discussion of Nero's various murders.[13] For, unlike Eusebius, Josephus does not characterize the many historians of Nero's reign as accurate, but he rather complains that they are untruthful, some as a result of their prosperity under Nero and others as a result of their hatred of Nero. Cassius Dio may seem a more attractive candidate for Eusebius' reference. According to the epitome that survives, Dio's account of Nero's reign began in Book 61 and was completed only in Book 63, with full descriptions of Nero's murders. Nero's depravity, however, is a commonplace, and it will consequently be difficult to consider Dio his immediate source without more decisive evidence. Perhaps Eusebius' whole statement is best considered to be nothing more than an exaggeration, rather like Josephus' statement in form, if not in content.

IV

At HE III.18.4 Eusebius explains that the teaching of Christianity shone so brightly that even non-Christian historians reported the persecution and martyrdoms under Domitian, including the exile of Flavia Domitilla:

... ὡς καὶ τοὺς ἄποθεν τοῦ καθ᾽ ἡμᾶς λόγου συγγραφεῖς μὴ ἀποκνῆσαι ταῖς αὐτῶν ἱστορίαις τόν τε διωγμὸν καὶ τὰ ἐν αὐτῷ μαρτύρια παραδοῦναι ....

... so that even those writers far from our teaching do not hesitate to relate in their histories both the persecution and the martyrdoms in it ....

Cassius Dio (67.14) also tells of the exile of Flavia Domitilla, but he is manifestly not Eusebius' source. Not only are Eusebius' details substantially different from Dio's—Domitilla is the niece of Flavius Clemens in Eusebius but she is his wife in Dio; Domitilla is exiled to Pontia in Eusebius but to Pandateria in Dio; Domitilla suffers for her Christianity in Eusebius but for atheism and "Jewish ways" in Dio—but also Eusebius himself in the *Chronicon* attributes his information on this matter to a certain Bruttius.[14] Even though in the HE Eusebius omits the name of his source, Bruttius, the ultimate source must undoubtedly be the same.[15] But is Eusebius likely to have taken his information directly from this Bruttius, who is nowhere else mentioned in Eusebius' works? A strong argument can be made that Eusebius actually drew the information on Domitilla's exile, which itself derived from Bruttius, from the *Hypomnemata* of the second-century Christian writer Hegesippus.[16]

Long ago, H. J. Lawlor collected the extant fragments of Hegesippus' *Hypomnemata*, primarily those from Eusebius and Epiphanius, but also those from independent manuscripts in England and France.[17] In reconstructing the text of the *Hypomnemata*, Lawlor was able to identify numerous passages in the HE that derived from Hegesippus, even though Eusebius often did not attribute them to Hegesippus, including much of HE III.11–20. A summary of Lawlor's conclusions (p. 54) about the content and sources of these chapters will be helpful here:

HE III.11: Symeon is elected bishop of Jerusalem. Hegesippus is the source, hidden behind the phrase λόγος κατέχει.

HE III.12: Vespasian seeks to destroy the descendants of David. Hegesippus is again the source behind the phrase λόγος κατέχει.

HE III.13–15: Eusebius relates the successions of the emperors Titus and Domitian, as well as of the Roman and Alexandrian bishops.

HE III.16: When referring to Clement of Rome's epistle, Eusebius again names Hegesippus.

HE III.17: Domitian begins the persecution of Christians. Hegesippus is the likely source, although no source is named.

HE III.18.1: St. John the Evangelist is banished to Patmos. Hegesippus is the source behind the phrase λόγος κατέχει.

HE III.18.2–3: Irenaeus is quoted on the date of the Apocalypse.

HE III.18.4: Flavia Domitilla is banished. Bruttius is the source, according to the entry in the *Chronicon*.

HE III.19: Domitian seeks to destroy the descendants of David. Hegesippus is the source behind the phrase παλαιὸς λόγος κατέχει.

HE III.20.1: Hegesippus is quoted directly and indirectly on the topic introduced above.

HE III.20.7: Tertullian is quoted for information on Domitian's reign.

HE III.20.8: Nerva reverses Domitian's policies. Eusebius refers to unidentified sources.

HE III.20.9: St. John returns from exile. Hegesippus is the source behind this λόγος.

Lawlor's conclusions are in general worth accepting, but one can go further, at least in the case of HE III.18.4. Lawlor attributed this passage to Bruttius because the two manuscripts, *Parisinus gr.* 1555A and *Barocc.* 142, with which he was comparing Eusebius' text in order to identify common passages (and therefore passages drawn from Hegesippus) did not contain HE III.18.4. Lawlor essentially believed that the Paris and Oxford manuscripts used Hegesippus directly, as did Eusebius, and that HE III.18.4 could not have come from Hegesippus because it was not common to both Eusebius and the two manuscripts. Lawlor, however, acknowledges that the Paris and Oxford manuscripts abbreviate the Hegesippean material that Eusebius reproduces in direct and indirect quotation, and Lawlor even concedes that the two manuscripts may have followed a different version of Hegesippus from that followed by Eusebius (pp. 43–45). There is therefore no security in the belief that HE III.18.4 did not come from Hegesippus.

Rather, Lawlor's own reconstruction of Hegesippus' text from HE III.11–20 provides a very plausible position for HE III.18.4 within the *Hypomnemata* itself. Lawlor convincingly argues that Eusebius used Hegesippus' text without holding to his text's arrangement. Thus, according to Lawlor, Hegesippus' text likely followed the order: HE III.12; III.17; III.19; III.18.1; III.20.9; III.20.1. Whether or not the whole of Lawlor's reconstruction is accurate is not important here.[18] What is important is that HE III.18.4 suits the context of the first passages derived from Hegesippus, namely, HE III.12, 17, and 19. Hegesippus, then, having reported Vespasian's hostile proceedings against the descendants of David (HE III.12), passed on to Domitian's persecution of Christians (HE III.17). He next recorded an instance of this persecution at Rome, the exile of Flavia Domitilla (HE III.18.4), an episode for which he also referred to Bruttius.[19] Thereafter, Hegesippus reported Domitian's attempt to destroy the descendants of David and the banishment of St. John (HE III.19 and 20.1 with III.18.1 and 20.9, in an uncertain order).

Hegesippus thus referred to Bruttius in his *Hypomnemata* for the story of Flavia Domitilla's exile. Eusebius, as he followed the text of Hegesippus, incorporated Bruttius' material into his HE, although it was only in the *Chronicon* that Eusebius named Bruttius as the original source of the story.[20]

V

In the fifth passage, at HE III.20.8, Eusebius introduces the reign of Nerva and adds that at this time Domitian's honors were cancelled and the Senate recalled exiles and restored property to them.[21] Eusebius refers again to unnamed historians for this information:

ἱστοροῦσιν οἱ γραφῇ τὰ κατὰ τοὺς χρόνους παραδόντες.

Those who hand down in writing the events of the times record it.

Eusebius next relates the popular story of St. John the Evangelist's settling at Ephesus after his banishment (HE III.20.9).

This last piece of information on St. John probably derives from Hegesippus' *Hypomnemata*, as was noted above, but it seems unlikely that the events of Nerva's accession come from that same source. Hegesippus seems to have concerned himself, at least in these passages, primarily with the affairs of Christians in Palestine, taking notice of the Roman emperors insofar as their activities affected Christians but without describing political affairs themselves.[22] The Latin writers, again, will hardly have served as Eusebius' sources (Suetonius, *Dom.* 23; Pliny the Younger, *Pan.* 52). Several close parallels, however, can be found in the extant epitome of Cassius Dio. After a brief notice of Nerva's elevation, Dio immediately reports that images of Domitian and arches in his honor were destroyed and that Nerva released those on trial for treason, recalled exiles (68.1), and even restored property to those who had lost it under Domitian (68.2). Dio's account is, of course, lengthier than Eusebius', but there is only one essential difference between them: Eusebius attributes the recall of exiles and restoration of property to the Senate, while Dio attributes these measures to Nerva himself. The evidence is by no means conclusive, yet there must remain a possibility that Eusebius knew this text of Dio.[23]

VI

The sixth passage appears at the end of Eusebius' account of the Jewish War of 115–117 (HE IV.2.5):

ταῦτα καὶ Ἑλλήνων οἱ τὰ κατὰ τοὺς αὐτοὺς χρόνους γραφῇ παραδόντες αὐτοῖς ἱστόρησαν ῥήμασιν.

Those of the Greeks who hand down in writing the events of the same time also recorded these things in their own words.

Dio (68.32) recounts this same rebellion, but in a significant detail Dio and Eusebius differ, Dio naming the Jewish leader as Andreas, Eusebius naming him as Lucuas (HE IV.2.3–4). Other possible sources are lost, including books Appian wrote on the Roman conquests.[24] But, a simple explanation of Eusebius' use of sources is that Eusebius used the same source from which he later drew some information for his account of the subsequent Jewish War of 132–135. At HE IV.6.3 Eusebius relates how, after the rebellion had been quelled, Hadrian closed Jerusalem to the Jews. This information Eusebius attributes to Ariston of Pella.[25] Eusebius does not name the title of Ariston's work, and, although Ariston of Pella is ordinarily credited with only one work, the *Altercatio Iasonis et Papisci*, a debate between a Jewish Christian and an Alexandrian Jew, it is yet possible that Ariston composed a historical work. Ariston's history would thus have treated the Jewish War under Trajan as well as that under Hadrian.[26]

VII

The final passage concerns the famous "rain miracle" that occurred in the year 172, which Eusebius records at HE V.5.[27] As Eusebius reports the story (λόγος ἔχει, V.5.1–2), when Marcus Aurelius was arranging his troops for battle against the Sarmatians and Germans and because the Roman soldiers suffered severely from thirst, the troops of the legion Melitene knelt and prayed to God. The story continues (λόγος ἔχει) that a rain storm saved the Romans from their thirst and put the enemy to flight. Eusebius next reports that this story exists both among non-Christian historians of the affairs of Marcus Aurelius and Lucius Verus and among Christian writers:

ἡ δ᾽ ἱστορία φέρεται μὲν καὶ παρὰ τοῖς πόρρω τοῦ καθ᾽ ἡμᾶς λόγου συγγραφεῦσιν οἷς μέλον γέγονεν τῆς κατὰ τοὺς δηλουμένους γραφῆς, δεδήλωται δὲ καὶ πρὸς τῶν ἡμετέρων (V.5.3).

The story survives even among those historians far from our teaching, whose care it is to write of the events of those [emperors] mentioned, but it is also known among our people.

Furthermore, although non-Christians record the miracle, they do not, notes Eusebius, attribute it to the prayers of Christians. Meanwhile, Christians record the miracle in a "plain and innocent" manner.[28] Of these Christian writers, Eusebius adduces a certain Apolinarius, who explains that, as a result of the efficacy of its prayers, the emperor granted to the legion Melitene the title κεραυνοβόλος, "Thundering" (HE V.5.4).[29] Eusebius turns then to introduce a quotation from his Greek translation of Tertullian's *Apologeticum*, V.5.7, about the unwillingness of various emperors to prosecute Christians, by summarizing Tertullian's statement (*Apol.* V.5.6) that a letter of Marcus Aurelius confirms the Christian interpretation of the "rain miracle" (HE V.5.5–6).

What is the source of Eusebius' statement that non-Christians record a version of the "rain miracle"? Tertullian cannot be the source because, apart from Marcus Aurelius' letter, he does not report the existence of an account in non-Christian histories. Presumably, the letter of Marcus Aurelius to which Tertullian refers was not in Eusebius' possession, else Eusebius would not have appealed to Tertullian for the evidence of its existence.[30] Some extant non-Christian sources do, however, record this miracle, of which one should not be overlooked.[31] Dio (71.8–10), as epitomized by Xiphilinus, reports that in one of Marcus' wars against the Quadi the

Romans were saved from thirst and the enemy by a sudden rain storm. The story continues (λόγος ἔχει), according to Dio, that the prayers of the Egyptian magician Arnouphis effected this miracle. Eusebius may have known Dio's version of this story, but two details tell against this possibility. First, Eusebius names the enemy as Germans and Sarmatians, while Dio calls them Quadi. In his *Chronicon* Eusebius admittedly says that the Romans were in the region of the Quadi, but he again names Germans and Sarmatians as the enemy.[32] Second, in the *Chronicon* Eusebius also names the commander, Pertinax, the future emperor. Dio, at least in the form in which his work survives, does not name any commander.[33]

The most economical solution is that Eusebius drew his information from the Apolinarius whose inaccurate explanation of the name of the legion Melitene Eusebius reports. This Apolinarius is no doubt Apolinarius of Hierapolis, who in approximately 176 composed an *Apologia* on behalf of Christianity addressed to Marcus Aurelius.[34] Some scholars, it should be noted, have suggested that, because Pertinax appears in the entry on the "rain miracle" in the *Chronicon* but not in the account in the HE, Eusebius relied on Julius Africanus in the *Chronicon* but utilized Apolinarius for the HE.[35] But, Africanus may have been only a minor source for events in the Roman Empire (see note 12), and Eusebius could well have omitted the detail of Pertinax's name when he recounted the miracle in the HE.[36] Eusebius most likely relied on Apolinarius' *Apologia* for his whole account of the "rain miracle" in both the *Chronicon* and the HE.[37]

* * * * *

When he composed his HE, Eusebius naturally relied on sources that were ready at hand, those he was already using to compose books or even sections of books or particular topics. Josephus is used extensively throughout the first three books of the HE and was thus in Eusebius' mind when he turned to the famine under Claudius at HE II.8.1; Ariston of Pella was a convenient source in HE IV for the Jewish Wars under Trajan and Hadrian; and Apolinarius of Hierapolis, used at HE V.5, was a source contemporary with Marcus Aurelius' reign and one whose writings were surveyed in just the previous book of the HE (IV.27). Hegesippus, whose *Hypomnemata* furnished Eusebius with much material in HE III, especially in the sequence of HE III.11–20, was likewise a ready source from which Eusebius could draw Bruttius' information on the exile of Flavia Domitilla.

Cassius Dio is a problematic source, since there is no evidence of Eusebius' use of his history elsewhere in the HE. He is clearly not the unnamed source in three passages (HE II.8.1; III.18.4; IV.2.5) and is probably not in two (HE II.25.1–2; V.5.3), yet he is a plausible source for Nerva's policies after his accession (HE III.20.8). Allowance must be made for the possibility that Eusebius knew and used Dio for this passage and, therefore, for other passages in other works.[38] Perhaps Cassius Dio was featured in the *Chronicon's* list of sources for

Roman imperial history, and Eusebius' general reference to his source at HE III.20.8 derives from his earlier entry in the *Chronicon*.

Eusebius, it seems, had no single reason for cloaking the identity of his sources in these seven passages. The general reference might be used for rhetorical effect, as is the case with HE II.8.1, when Josephus, whom Eusebius elsewhere in the HE cites by name, becomes one of the generic non-Christian historians who provide corroborating evidence of the events in Eusebius' history. Similarly, Eusebius elsewhere exaggerated the number of his sources to enhance the plausibility of his information, as when he referred to the many sources for Nero's depravity at HE II.25.2, when he lumped Ariston of Pella among Greek historians at HE IV.2.5, and perhaps when he referred to the Olympiad chroniclers at HE II.7. To some extent, such exaggeration is simply imprecision. If the vague reference at HE II.7 is not the product of carelessness, two more passages surely are: Eusebius probably omitted Cassius Dio's name (or the name of whoever his source was) from HE III.20.8 because he was following the information that he had already compiled for his *Chronicon*; and he omitted Bruttius' name at HE III.18.4 even though he had included it in the *Chronicon*. In the account of the "rain miracle," Eusebius followed Apolinarius of Hierapolis, who must have made reference to a pagan version of the miracle in the course of his *Apologia*. Eusebius' repeated use of the phrase λόγος ἔχει to introduce the story may indicate Eusebius' own hesitation about the credibility of the miracle,[39] perhaps because Eusebius was aware, if only through oral tradition, of the existence of such a pagan version.

NOTES

1. The problem of determining the sources behind Eusebius' repeated usage of the phrase λόγος (κατ)έχει will not be considered here, although the present inquiry will touch on some uses of this expression. The work against Artemon quoted by Eusebius at HE V.28 (ἔν τινος σπουδάσματι κατὰ τῆς Ἀρτέμωνος αἱρέσεως) may be considered unidentified, but its author is one of those interpreters of Scripture whose names Eusebius does not know (HE V.27), and the work itself may be the *Little Labyrinth* (ὁ σμικρὸς Λαβύρινθος) named by Theodoret at *Haereticarum fabularum compendium* II.5 (PG 83:392). The text of the HE used in this paper is that of E. Schwartz, ed., *Eusebius Werke 2: Die Kirchengeschichte*, GCS 9, 3 vols. (Leipzig; 1903, 1908, 1909). All translations are my own. I thank Professors W. V. Harris and D. Kries and Dr. C. Tkacz for reading versions of this paper and suggesting improvements to it.

2. See, for example, the references ad loc. in A. C. McGiffert's translation in NPNF, second series, vol. 1 (New York, 1890); K. Lake, *Eusebius, the Ecclesiastical History*, vol. 1 (London and New York, 1926); H. J. Lawlor and J. E. L. Oulton, *Eusebius, Bishop of Caesarea, the Ecclesiastical History and the Martyrs of Palestine*, 2 vols. (London, 1927–28); G. Bardy, *Eusèbe de Césarée, Histoire Ecclésiastique*, SC 31 (Paris, 1952) and 41 (Paris, 1955). To be sure, these editors ordinarily list references in other ancient sources as helpful *comparanda*, but in some cases the editors go as far as to identify Eusebius' sources. For example, McGiffert believes that Eusebius followed Cassius Dio at HE IV.2.5, and Lawlor and Oulton imply the same in their note. The standard edition of E. Schwartz, *Die Kirchengeschichte*, provides no comparative references.

3. F. Millar, *A Study of Cassius Dio* (Oxford, 1964), 34.

4. Eusebius, *Chronicon*, p. 178c Helm: *Pontius Pilatus in multas incidens calamitates propria se manu interficit. Scribunt Romanorum historici.* Eusebius already mentions the *Chronicon* at HE I.1.6, and the work seems to have served as a chronological frame for the HE. The exact dates of the composition of the *Chronicon* and HE, however, have not been conclusively established. The HE has traditionally been dated after 311; cf. A. Louth, "The Date of Eusebius' *Historia Ecclesiastica*," *JTS* 41 (1990): 111–23. The *Chronicon* appeared before this date; cf. A. A. Mosshammer, *The Chronicle of Eusebius and Greek Chronographic Tradition* (Lewisburg, PA, 1979), chapter one. T. D. Barnes, *Constantine and Eusebius* (Cambridge, MA, 1981), pp. 111, 113, and 128, alternatively dates first editions of both works to before 300. The standard edition of St. Jerome's translation of Eusebius' *Chronicon* (really, his *Chronological Canons*), is that of R. Helm, *Eusebius Werke 7.1: Die Chronik des Hieronymus*, GCS 24 (Leipzig, 1913), also in a second edition, GCS 47 (Leipzig, 1956).

5. Cf. H. J. Lawlor, *Eusebiana: Essays on the Ecclesiastical History of Eusebius Bishop of Caesarea* (Oxford, 1912), p. 22 and note 1. Lawlor interprets the words κατέχει λόγος, which Eusebius uses to introduce the story, as referring to an actual document, no doubt the unidentified Olympiad chronicler. Contrast P. L. Maier, "The Fate of Pontius Pilate," *Hermes* 99 (1971): 369, who seems to attribute Eusebius' report to a current tradition. Cf. also J. Lémonon, *Pilate et la gouvernement de la Judée: textes et monuments* (Paris, 1981), 267–68.

6. Cf. Eusebius, *Chronicon*, p. 179f Helm: *Profetia Agabi, qua in Actis Apostolorum famem in toto orbe futuram dixerat, sub Claudio expletur.*

7. See G. Bardy, *La question des langues dans l'église ancienne* (Paris, 1948), 129–30; Barnes, *Constantine and Eusebius*, 142–43.

8. B. Gustafsson, "Eusebius' Principles in Handling His Sources, as Found in His Church History, Books I–VII," *Studia Patristica* 4 (1961) (Texte und Untersuchungen 79), 437, is in this case wrong to suggest Dio or Phlegon of Tralles.

9. Josephus, *Ant.* 20.101: ἐπὶ τούτοις δὲ καὶ τὸν μέγαν λιμὸν κατὰ τὴν Ἰουδαίαν συνέβη γενέσθαι . . . . Cf. Lawlor and Oulton, *Eusebius*, 2: 15, for this identification.

10. Cf. Eusebius, *Chronicon*, p. 182f Helm: *Nero Agrippinam matrem suam et sororem patris interficit.* Also, p. 184c Helm: *Multi nobilium Romae a Nerone interfecti*; and p. 184h Helm: *Nero cum ceteris viris insignibus et Octaviam uxorem suam interficit Cornutumque philosophum praeceptorem Persii in exilium fugat.*

11. *Apol.* 21.25. This passage, too, simply names Nero as a persecutor of Christians.

12. Unfortunately, Eusebius' list of the main sources he used for the chronology of the Roman imperial period is missing from the *Chronographia*, the first book of Eusebius' *Chronicon* (the second being the *Chronici canones,* or *Chronological Canons*), which provides summaries of the histories of the major peoples of the world. In the *Chronographia*, Eusebius lists his main sources, but the extant text breaks off before he names his sources for the Roman imperial period. The text, extant in Armenian, is available in J. Karst, ed., *Eusebius Werke 5: Die Chronik aus dem Armenischen übersetzt,* GCS 20 (Leipzig, 1911). Eusebius may, however, have utilized for the Roman period some of the chronicles that are named as sources for Greek history, such as Porphyry's *Chronica,* which, if it actually existed as a separate work (cf. B. Croke, "Porphyry's Anti-Christian Chronology," *Journal of Theological Studies* 34 [1983], 168–85), extended from the fall of Troy to the emperor Claudius (Gothicus?); Phlegon of Tralles' Olympiad chronicle to Olympiad 229 (AD 137–140); or Cassius Longinus' Olympiad chronicle to Olympiad 249 (AD 217), all of which are listed at p. 125 Karst. (On Longinus' Olympiad chronicle, see Mosshammer, *Chronicle,* 141–45.) Julius Africanus also composed a *Chronographiae,* which covered the period from Creation to the year 221. Eusebius used this work as a source for Hebrew history in the *Chronicon* (cf. pp. 34, 47–48, and 61 Karst), but it is unclear to what extent Eusebius could have drawn information on the Roman Empire from Africanus. At p. 193 Karst and p. 113a Helm, Eusebius cites Africanus as a source for the Roman period, but here he may be referring to events concerning the Hebrews. Photius, *cod.* 34, moreover, explains that Africanus did not give detailed information about events in the Empire.

13. Josephus, *Ant.* 20.154: ἀλλὰ περὶ μὲν τούτων ἐῶ πλείω γράφειν. πολλοὶ γὰρ τὴν περὶ Νέρωνα συντετάχασιν ἱστορίαν, ὧν. . . .

14. Eusebius, *Chronicon,* p. 192e Helm: *Scribit Bruttius plurimos Christianorum sub Domitiano fecisse martyrium, inter quos et Flaviam Domitillam, Flavii Clementis consulis ex sorore neptem, in insulam Pontiam relegatam quia se Christianam esse testata sit.* J. B. Lightfoot, *The Apostolic Fathers,* 2 vols. (London, 1890; reprinted Hildesheim, 1973), vol. I, part 1, pp. 46–49, traces back to Scaliger the identification of this Bruttius with a correspondent of Pliny the Younger (*Ep.* VII.3). Barnes, *Constantine and Eusebius,* p. 348, note 31, accepting this attribution, refers to R. Syme, "Pliny's Less Successful Friends," *Roman Papers,* E. Badian, ed. (Oxford, 1979), 2: 477–95 [=*Historia* 9 (1960): 362–79], for what is known of his career, although he admits that this particular Bruttius is unlikely to have considered the cause of Domitilla's exile her Christianity. Lightfoot himself thinks Eusebius' Bruttius was an early Christian chronographer, and he cautions that Bruttius could simply have been a freedman or some other of the Bruttian clan's many clients.

15. Lawlor and Oulton, *Eusebius,* 2: 88, think that Eusebius simply forgot the name of his source.

16. Lightfoot, *Apostolic Fathers,* vol. I, part 1, p. 48, proposes that Eusebius drew Bruttius' information from the Christian chronographer Julius Africanus, but he offers no evidence for this view.

17. Lawlor, *Eusebiana,* 1–107. Lawlor's essay is an expansion of his article in *Hermathena* 11 (1901).

18. For example, III.19 and III.20.1 may have been sequential in Hegesippus' text, just as they are in Eusebius. The precise order of Hegesippus' lost text is, however, a matter of speculation.

19. Whether Bruttius is to be identified with the Bruttius Praesens whose career extended from around the year 89 to around 140 or with some client of the Bruttian clan (see note 14 above), whatever work he composed would presumably have been available for Hegesippus' consultation when Hegesippus visited Rome around 155. On the other hand, so little is known of Hegesippus' methods and sources that one must consider the possibility that no Bruttius ever really existed, despite Hegesippus' citation of him, or that the name of Hegesippus' source, "Bruttius," was inaccurately transmitted to Eusebius.

20. Eusebius therefore knew and used Hegesippus for both his *Chronicon* and his HE. R. M. Grant's view in *Eusebius as Church Historian* (Oxford: Clarendon, 1980), 67–68, that Eusebius became acquainted with Hegesippus only after he wrote the *Chronicon* must be rejected. T. D. Barnes, "Some Inconsistencies in Eusebius," *Journal of Theological Studies* 35 (1984): 471 and note 5, points out that Grant earlier stated that Eusebius had used Hegesippus in his *Chronicon* ("Eusebius and Gnostic Origins," *Paganisme, Judaisme, Christianisme: Mélanges offerts à Marcel Simon* [Paris, 1978], 201).

21. Cf. Eusebius, *Chronicon*, p. 193b Helm: *Senatus decrevit, ut omnia, quae Domitianus statuerat, in irritum deducerentur. itaque multi, quos iniuste eiecerat, de exilio reversi, nonnulli bona propria receperunt.*

22. On Eusebius' use of Hegesippus in HE III.17–20, again, see Lawlor, *Eusebiana*, 40–62.

23. Alternatively, Eusebius may have drawn this information on Nerva from one of the lost sources he used for Roman imperial history in the *Chronicon*, including, perhaps, Porphyry's *Chronica* or the Olympiad chronicles of Phlegon of Tralles and Cassius Longinus.

24. Lawlor and Oulton, *Eusebius*, 2: 119, suggest Appian. Of his history, books 18–21 treated Egypt, where the rebellion began, and books 23 and 24 treated Dacia and Parthia, respectively, up to Trajan's conquests.

25. Eusebius simply writes: Ἀρίστων ὁ Πελλαῖος ἱστορεῖ (HE IV.6.3).

26. For the traditional view of Ariston of Pella, see E. Schürer, *The History of the Jewish People in the Age of Jesus Christ (175 B.C.–A.D. 135)*, new English version revised and edited by G. Vermes and F. Millar (Edinburgh, 1973) 1: 37–39. But, F. Jacoby, *Die Fragmente der griechischen Historiker* 201, Commentary II D, 627–28, acknowledges that Ariston may have composed a history, and Grant, *Eusebius as Church Historian*, p. 48, accepts Ariston as a source for the Jewish War under Trajan.

27. On the date of the miracle, see J. Guey, "La date de la 'pluie miraculeuse' (172 après J–C) et la Colonne Aureelienne," *Mélanges d'archéologie et d'histoire de l'École Francaise de Rome, Antiquité* 60 (1948): 105–127; 61 (1949): 93–118. Cf. also G. Barta, "Legende und Wirklichkeit—das Regenwunder des Marcus Aurelius," *Marc Aurel*, R. Klein, ed. (Darmstadt, 1979), 347–58. M. M. Sage, "Eusebius and the Rain Miracle: Some Observations," *Historia* 36 (1987): 106 and note 60, dates the miracle to 173.

28. HE V.5.3: ἀλλὰ τοῖς μὲν ἔξωθεν ἱστορικοῖς, ἅτε τῆς πίστεως ἀνοικείοις, τέθειται μὲν τὸ παράδοξον, οὐ μὴν καὶ ταῖς τῶν ἡμετέρων εὐχαῖς τοῦθ᾽ ὡμολογήθη γεγονέναι. τοῖς δέ γε ἡμετέροις, ἅτε ἀληθείας φίλοις, ἁπλῷ καὶ ἀκακοήθει τρόπῳ

τὸ πραχθὲν παραδέδοται.

29. Apolinarius' explanation is, in fact, incorrect. According to Cassius Dio, 55.23.5, the legion had been called *fulminata* since the time of Augustus.

30. A version of this letter appears in the MS of Justin Martyr, *Parisinus gr.* 450; see Appendix II in M. Marcovich, ed., *Iustini Martyris Apologiae pro Christianis*, Patristische Texte und Studien, 38 (Berlin, 1994). Eusebius' reference to the letter in the Latin text of the *Chronicon* seems to have been excerpted from Tertullian. Cf. Eusebius' *Extant litterae Marci Aurelii gravissimi imperatoris, quibus illam Germanicam sitim Christianorum forte militum precationibus impetrato imbri discussam contestatur* (pp. 206i–207 Helm) with Tertullian's *At nos e contrario edimus protectorem, si litterae Marci Aurelii, gravissimi imperatoris, requirantur, quibus illam Germanicam sitim Christianorum forte militum precationibus impetrato imbri discussam contestatur.* St. Jerome is probably the source of this approximate quotation, because Eusebius did not know the original Latin of Tertullian's *Apologeticum*. This conclusion is supported by the fact that other versions of the *Chronicon* omit the word *sitim*: cf. the Armenian version (p. 222 Karst) and the Greek of the *Chronicon Paschale*, 260d.

31. For a complete list of the sources that record this miracle, see Barta in *Marc Aurel*, p. 356, note 1. The other ancient testimonies to this miracle are much later than Eusebius and are for this reason better left aside, although the evidence of the *Historia Augusta, M. Ant.*, 24, may be important, since its sources are so little known. The author of this *vita* could have used Cassius Dio, but if he did not, his source was probably Latin ("Ignotus" or Marius Maximus), and Eusebius is unlikely to have known these Latin sources. Cf. T. D. Barnes, *The Sources of the Historia Augusta*, Coll. Latomus, 155 (Brussels, 1978), 78–89 and 108–9 on the little use of Dio; and 124–25 for conclusions.

32. Eusebius, *Chronicon*, pp. 206i–207 Helm: *Imperator Antoninus multis adversum se nascentibus bellis saepe ipse intererat, saepe duces nobilissimos destinabat, in quis semel Pertinaci et exercitui, qui cum eo in Quadorum regione pugnabat, siti oppressis pluvia divinitus missa est, cum e contrario Germanos et Sarmatas fulmina persequerentur et plurimos eorum interficerent. Extant litterae Marci Aurelii gravissimi imperatoris, quibus illam Germanicam sitim Christianorum forte militum precationibus impetrato imbri discussam contestatur.*

33. A. Birley, *Marcus Aurelius: a Biography*, revised edition (London: B. T. Batsford, 1987), p. 173, tends to accept the genuineness of Eusebius' evidence here. Although Marcus is named in Dio, he need not have been the commander at the time and place of the miracle's occurrence.

34. The date of his *Apologia* is given by R. M. Grant, *Greek Apologists of the Second Century* (Philadelphia, 1988), p. 83, and, in essentially the same words, "Five Apologists and Marcus Aurelius," *Vigiliae Christianae* 42 (1988): 4–5. Sage, "Eusebius and the Rain Miracle," 110–11, conjectures that Eusebius used not Apolinarius' *Apologia* but his five books Πρὸς "Ελληνας. This suggestion rests in part on dating Apolinarius' *Apologia* to 170/1. For what little is known of the writings of Apolinarius of Hierapolis, HE IV.27.

35. See Sage, "Eusebius and the Rain Miracle," 107–8, expanding on A. von Domaszewski, "Das Regenwunder der Marc-Aurelsäule," *Rheinisches Museum* 49 (1894): 616, note 2.

36. Sage himself argues that Eusebius omitted Pertinax's name in order to emphasize Marcus Aurelius' role in the miracle and that he "purposely adopted the nomenclature of Marcus Aurelius Caesar for the emperor of the Rain Miracle to distinguish him from Antoninus whose reign he considered to be one of persecution" ("Eusebius and the Rain Miracle," 108).

37. Bardy, SC 41 (Paris, 1955), p. 30, note 4, recognizes the possibility that Eusebius drew all of his information on the "rain miracle" from Apolinarius. Note that Sage, "Eusebius and the Rain Miracle," 111, concludes that Eusebius introduced into his account the commander "Marcus Aurelius Caesar" and the idea that the legion Melitene remained Christian. Apolinarius' own source for the non-Christian version of the story is not known.

38. This suggestion would, of course, be considerably strengthened if a copy of Dio's history were to be connected directly with the library of Caesarea. C.M. Mazzucchi's attempt to do this by connecting the codex *Vat. gr.* 1288 to the Caesarean library of the late fifth and early sixth centuries, however, is unpersuasive, since the evidence is so tenuous: the MS apparently comes from Syria-Palestine, but it is not certain that it comes from Caesarea. Mazzucchi's argument appears in "Alcune vicende della tradizione di Cassio Dione in epoca bizantina," *Aevum* 53 (1979): 94–114.

39. On the implications of Eusebius' use of the expression λόγος ἔχει, cf. Sage, "Eusebius and the Rain Miracle," 101–4 and 111–12.

Quid Facit Cum Psalterio Horatius?
Seeking Classical Allusions
in the Vulgate

Catherine Brown Tkacz
Spokane, Washington

When Jerome rhetorically asked his spiritual daughter Eustochium, "Quid facit cum Psalterio Horatius? cum evangeliis Maro? cum apostolo Cicero?" he also posed intriguing questions for modern scholars interested in the role of classical allusions in Jerome's translations of the books of the Bible.[1] In the early centuries of Christianity, Jewish and Christian biblical scholars, such as Philo of Alexandria and St. Jerome, deliberately considered and praised the literary aspects of the Bible.[2] Medieval biblical scholars, including the Venerable Bede, Theodulf, and Alcuin, also treat the theme of respect for the Bible as literature.[3] Yet early and medieval appreciation of the Bible as literature is only now being recovered by modern scholars, with the result that the study of the Vulgate as literature is a new field, and a broad one. It is comprised of 1) literary aspects of the *creation* of the Vulgate in the fourth and fifth centuries; 2) the *reception and uses* of the Vulgate as literature, involving the next thousand years of commentary, education, liturgy, and literature; and 3) the *influences* of the Vulgate on vernacular languages and literatures. Because this field is so new and still unfamiliar to people, it is useful to sketch what has been done to date.

A 1983 dissertation inaugurated study of the Vulgate as literature by treating the biblical topos of the Tormentor Tormented and its influence in medieval hagiography and Old English literature.[4] In 1990 a study of formulaic expressions in the Vulgate treated two formula systems—"secundum opera manuum eorum" and "super caput"—affecting twenty-four books of the Bible, and demonstrated that the primary Christian text as experienced by the Western Europeans is in part formulaic.[5] This is culturally important and has implications for vernacular poetry. No wonder that, as shown in 1993, the Anglo-Saxons, with formulaic composition in both their Germanic and their Christian traditions created fresh, explicitly Christian formulas in Old English to express biblical ideas.[6] Groundwork for research on the literary aspects of the creation of the Vulgate exists in the form of an article in *Vigiliae Christianae* (1996) which covers who translated which books of the Bible, when, using what source texts and comparanda in which languages.[7]

It includes the chronology of Jerome's work on the Vulgate (summarized in Table One below) and a guide to editions of both the Vulgate and the Vetus Latina.[8]

The most provocative contribution in this new field of literary Vulgate studies is a paper presented at the Twelfth International Conference on Patristic Studies at Oxford in 1995, since published in *Studia Patristica*: "Ovid, Jerome, and the Vulgate" shows that, when translating the Bible, Jerome evidently drew on Ovid's diction in similar narrative contexts. Specifically, Jerome uses the wording of *Metamorphoses* 2:44, Phoebus's rash promise to Phaeton, in both the Gospel of Mark (6:22), Herod's rash promise to Salome, and the Book of Esther (5:3, 5:6, and 7:2), Ahasuerus's rash promises to Esther.[9] The idea that Jerome used diction to construct classical allusions in the Vulgate is utterly novel, but the biblical and classical scholars who hear the research find it convincing. And indeed, it is just what one would expect from St. Jerome. As Fredric W. Schlatter has recently shown, Jerome's commentary on Ezekiel (written 410–14) contains "an astonishing statement expressing Jerome's willingness to see the wisdom of Hellenism absorbed into the teaching of the Church."[10] Jerome's classical quotations in biblical commentaries and his prologues and prefaces to his biblical translations are well documented; now that it has been shown that he evidently constructed classical allusions through diction in the biblical translations themselves, more work is needed to clarify this technique of his. A tantalizing topic is what in fact Horace has to do with Jerome's two extant translations of the Psalter, a topic all the more provocative because Jerome quotes Horace in his preface to his Vulgate Psalter.[11] In order that other scholars may begin to research such specific possibilities, the present study briefly recapitulates the parameters of Jerome's non-intrusive allusions in the Vulgate and then outlines how the researcher may proceed in exploring which texts by which classical authors it may be likely that Jerome drew on, and for which biblical books.

Parameters. Obviously Jerome would not interpolate into his translation an actual quotation from Ovid or Horace or any other author. Nor would he grossly intrude with flagging references such as *poeta, comicus*, or *nobilis historicus*, as he refers to Virgil, Terrence, and Sallust respectively in his commentary on Ecclesiastes.[12] Classical allusions in the Vulgate, if any exist, would appear to be limited to diction; this is also consonant with his "reminiscences in phraseology" to classical authors in his original works.[13] Other forms of allusion short of quotation would include imitating syntactical patterns, although without dictional borrowings as well such patterns would be hard to recognize and even harder to demonstrate convincingly. Such means are less likely than dictional allusion, however: Jerome's pastoral attentiveness made him retain word orders already familiar from earlier translations when this did not prevent improving the accuracy of the translation.[14] But for Jerome to consider a dictional borrowing, the classical and biblical contexts must be consonant. He scorned the *Vergiliocentones* precisely because of their stupid and sacrilegious disregard for context, as when Proba (v. 403) uses Venus's words to Cupid in the *Aeneid* to supply God the Father's pronouncement about Christ at the Transfiguration.[15] To sum up, Jerome might have recognized in a given biblical passage similarities to a particular classical text, or topos, and fittingly borrowed diction from that text or commonplace to use in his translation. Note well that such dictional allusions are by their nature unprovable. Nonetheless, if they exist, neither the Vulgate nor the patristic era can be well understood until these allusions are recognized.

Method. Ideally in reading the Vulgate one may simply be struck by what seems to be a dictional allusion to a specific classical passage. Or one may deliberately set out to answer Jerome's rhetorical questions and investigate just what Horace has to do with the Psalter, or Virgil with the Gospels, or Cicero with the Apostle Paul. After all, these three classical authors are in fact the ones Jerome quotes most often in his original compositions.[16] But if instead one simply wants to explore more generally, without the starting point of a specific biblical text and a specific classical one, how does one begin?

A practical concern deserves mention. In such research, one will compare the Latin of Jerome's Vulgate and of the classical passage to all other pertinent biblical versions, i.e., Hebrew, the Greek, the Old Latin.[17] Therefore, one's work will be vastly easier if the Old Latin of the biblical book under scrutiny has already been edited by the Beuron Institute. Otherwise one must use the partial and long outdated edition by Pierre Sabatier and, for the New Testament, Adolf Jülicher's edition.[18] The books already published in the new Vetus Latina edition are Genesis, the Song of Songs (part), Wisdom, Sirach, Isaiah and, from the New Testament, the Letters to the Romans (part), First Corinthians (part), Ephesians, Philippians, Colossians, Thessalonians, Timothy, Titus, Philomen, Hebrews, and the Catholic Epistles.[19] For the Gospels, the late Bonifatius Fischer had published four studies toward the full edition, treating numerous verses, before poor health intervened; the full editions are not even scheduled at present.[20] Thus, Vetus Latina editions of biblical books to be compared with Vulgate books known to be Jerome's work (see Table One, note) are Genesis, the Song of Songs, and Isaiah. So anyone with a bright idea about the *Georgics* and Genesis is in luck.

An obvious pointer both to which authors Jerome might favor in biblical translation and also to his manner of allusion is the role of classical quotation in his original compositions. Harald Hagendahl extensively studied Jerome's use of the classics, and his books and articles are an invaluable guide to which passages by classical authors Jerome used, and when and how.[21] Famous for his erudition, Jerome is known to have drawn on at least forty-six classical authors in his original compositions (see Table Two).[22] His three favorite writers account for nearly four hundred quotations in his original compositions, so probably he draws on them in his biblical translations as well. Jerome quotes Virgil, especially the *Aeneid*, at least 174 times; Horace he quotes at least sixty-five times; and Cicero is the prose-writer Jerome cites most, over 136 times.[23] In contrast, Ovid he cites only six times. Yet he cites the very book and the very passage now identified as the source for his allusion in Mark and Esther.[24] If Jerome alludes even to a classical poet he rarely quotes, how much more likely that he alludes dictionally to the authors he admires and quotes frequently.

Jerome's manner of quotation also suggests how he might have proceeded in constructing a dictional allusion to a classical text. Hagendahl, with scholarly rigor, accepts as definite only a quotation of at least a half verse, and he catalogues several quotations that are each two full lines. When looking for dictional borrowings, one should bear in mind that Jerome would probably derive a given set of terms from within two lines of verse or from a single sentence of prose. Also, the greater the similarity between the classical and biblical passages in context and syntax as well as diction, the more likely it is that an allusion exists. Because the evidence can never go beyond plausibility, research on possible dictional allusions in the Vulgate must be done with rigor. Scholars have alleged classical allusions in Jerome's original compositions on the shallowest of grounds, as when J. J. Thierry asserts that Jerome's account of his dream is modeled on *Aeneid* 6 on the basis of little more than that each account has a judge and the one word *superos* (*Aeneid* 6.568), and Robert Godel and Franciscus Glorié have suggested additional allusions to Ovid on equally unconvincing grounds.[25] Any argument for a dictional allusion in the Vulgate should adduce more credible grounds than these. In the allusion to Ovid, three words are involved, drawn from a single sentence of direct discourse in Ovid and deployed in a single sentence of direct discourse in the Vulgate, and the narrative contexts are strikingly similar.[26]

There may be a more specific correlation between Jerome's use of dictional allusions in his Vulgate books and some directly related categories of his original compositions, namely his biblical prefaces and commentaries. The prefaces are related quite closely to the translations in time of composition, but are quite brief and so contain few classical quotations. Nevertheless, those few may be valuable signals. In his earlier prefaces to his translations from the Septuagint, classical allusions are few, though perhaps they have not been fully identified: Cicero, Pliny, and Virgil in the preface to Paralipomenon and Sallust in the preface to Job.[27] In the later sixteen prefaces to his fresh translations from the Hebrew, however, classical allusion is more frequent. Indeed, if one sets aside the distinctive Prologue to Kings, Jerome's classical allusions outnumber his biblical ones. The editors of the Stuttgart Vulgate have identified the classical and biblical allusions in the margins of the prefaces. The list of classical authors cited by Jerome in these prefaces is headed by his favorite trio of classical authors: Virgil Jerome quotes three times; Cicero and Horace twice, and once each Sallust, Valerius Maximus, and an unknown author (see Table Two). Could the classical texts referred to in a given preface correlate with the texts and authors Jerome had alluded to in the book he had just finished translating? As a corollary, could the unusual Prologue to Kings indicate an unusual aspect of the translation of those books? This one prologue is different from the other prefaces in that it is a defense, a response to criticism of Jerome's whole enterprise and manner of retranslation; here uniquely Jerome uses only biblical allusions with no whiff of classicism. This is rhetorically shrewd, as he is stressing his competence as a biblical scholar and his authenticity as a Christian. But the question arises: are his translations of the Books of Kings also devoid of classical allusion, or did he assume (rightly, one suspects) that his detractors would lack the sophistication to recognize classical allusion through diction? Or did the detraction come to his attention after he had translated Kings but before he had written the prologue?

Could the classical allusions Jerome makes when writing a commentary on a given biblical book indicate what may have been in his mind when he was translating that particular book? Here one must pay careful attention to the dates of composition (see Table One), for Jerome commented on Genesis years before he translated the biblical book, he commented on Matthew years after translating it, and his commentaries on the individual prophet books in some cases were contemporary with his translation, but in other cases years before or years after the labor of translation. In his twenty-two biblical commentaries he certainly names and quotes a wide range of classical authors.[28] He wrote commentaries on four Pauline epistles (Philemon, Galatians, Ephesians, Titus, ca. 386–87), on Ecclesiastes (ca. 388–89), then *Quaestiones hebraicae in genesim*, on five of the minor prophets (Nahum, Micah, Zephaniah, Haggai, Habakkuk, by 392), a bit later on Jonah and Obadiah (ca. 396), a single Gospel commentary upon request and swiftly, just before Easter in 398 (*In Matthaeum*), and then commentaries on the rest of the prophets: Zachariah, Malachi, Hosea, Joel, Amos in 406; Isaiah in 408–10; Ezechiel next, but interrupted by the sack of Rome and so finished only in 414, and an unfinished commentary on Jeremiah.[29] In these commentaries, in addition to his naming classical authors, nearly two hundred times he actually quotes or paraphrases substantial passages from at least twenty authors. As usual, Virgil heads the list, at seventy-six quotations, followed by Cicero (forty-one), Horace (twenty), and Terence (seventeen). It is perhaps instructive that whom he quotes and how frequently he uses classical allusion and quotation varies markedly from one commentary to another, even between commentaries written sequentially. For instance, *In Isaiam* has an average of 1.3 quotations from classical poetry for every one hundred columns in Migne and a total of eight lines of Virgil, while *In Ezechielem* has an average of 5 quotations per hundred columns and fully thirty lines of Virgil (232). Sometimes the constraint of a deadline kept Jerome's overall use of quotation in a work to a minimum, yet even then a passage within the work might break out in rich allusion, as in the preface to Book 2 of his commentary *In Zachariam*, written in 406 (216). Similarly, his *Quaestiones hebraicae in genesim* rarely uses classical material, yet its preface is a virtual *cento* of nine classical passages from seven authors (130–32). In two passages in his commentary *In Michaeam* "borrowings from secular literature are so numerous that they fit into one another like the *tesserae* of a mosaic" (135–38). While poets provide most of his classical quotations, in *In Habacuc* most of the citations are from prose, and the solitary classical allusion in *In Matthaeum* is also from prose (134, 212). Sometimes a specific passage is in his mind, as when he draws three of his four quotations from Horace in *In Ecclesiasten* from Horace's Epistles 1 and 2 (128). Notably, Virgil is ubiquitous, with Jerome in his final biblical commentary, on Jeremiah, quoting with greater frequency than in any other commentary and using passages from Virgil he had never quoted before (244–46).

As noted, comparing classical allusions in the commentaries to the possible allusions in the biblical translations involves comparing works that have been composed as much as twenty years apart, as in the case of the book of Jeremiah. To reconstruct the chronological context for Jerome's biblical translation more fully, one could look at all of his texts, regardless of genre, from a specific period, seeking patterns of allusion which might bear on his possible selection of classical allusions for biblical translation. The obvious caveat here is that far more important than the readiness with which a quotation might come to his mind would have been the aptness of the allusion to the biblical passage at hand. One could digest Hagendahl's research and construct a chronology of classical texts and authors Jerome used. The results could then be compared to the chronology of his work on the Vulgate (see Table One).

Another consideration with regard to the Old Testament is Jerome's growing facility with Hebrew. Benjamin Kedar-Kopfstein's study of Jerome's translation of the Hebrew Bible bears on research into possible classical allusions. He finds Jerome rigorous in handling the Hebrew, Greek and Old Latin materials, rejecting a series of terms used repeatedly in the Old Latin. He concludes, "Indirectly . . . Jerome stamped also those words and clauses which he took over from others: by approving them he made them his own."[30] Moreover, Kedar-Kopfstein discerns a development in Jerome's facility with Hebrew and therefore in his technique of translating. The Latin of the Psalter and Prophet books he considers "rigid, imitative"; of Samuel, Kings, and Job, "imitative, detached"; of Ezra, Nehemiah, Chronicles, "detached"; of Proverbs, Ecclesiastes, Canticles, Pentateuch, "detached, transformative"; and finally, of Joshua, Judges, Ruth, and Esther, "transformative" (271–74). He concludes:

> In the case of the Vulgate, the reader generally has been offered a smoother translation in the historic books, but he faces a cruder Latin text, imitative of Hebrew, in the Psalter and Prophets. Here, the reader is compelled to wrestle with each single verse of the text itself and search for its meaning. It would be unwarranted to assume that this was Jerome's intention; the relatively free rendering of theologically important sections of the Pentateuch (e.g. Ex 20; Dt 5) refute[s] any such assumption. According to the evidence we have adduced above, it seems that changes in the translation technique follow a chronological pattern rather than an ideological motivation. However, the result is a most fortunate blending of a strict adherence to the Hebrew structure in texts where the single words and verses are loaded with profound meaning and a fine literary version of the biblical narrative (284–85).

This would imply that in the later translations his increased facility with Hebrew may have allowed him more latitude for incorporating classical allusions through diction. The Book of Esther is among the last translations from the Hebrew, and it seems to have an allusion to Ovid. On the other hand, if even his early translations from the Hebrew, such as Jerome's Hebrew Psalter, already hold dictional allusions to classical texts, that itself will be a valuable finding.

Hitherto only Jerome's name has been mentioned. But not all the Vulgate books are his work. In the Old Testament, he certainly translated into Latin all of the Hebrew Bible, and he also undertook to translate Tobit and Judith, assisted by a colleague who translated these books from the Aramaic into Hebrew, which Jerome then translated into Latin. And he reworked from the Septuagint and Theodotion the last two chapters of Daniel. But he did not retranslate from the Greek those books he considered non-canonical, namely Wisdom, Sirach or Ecclesiasticus, Baruch and the four Books of Maccabees. These "are pure Old-Latin and untouched" by Jerome or any other reviser.[31] Did the Old Latin of these texts incorporate dictional allusions to classical texts? If so, one need not assume that Jerome's favorite authors were also the favorite authors of the unknown translators of the Old Latin.

The authorship of the Vulgate translation of the New Testament other than the Gospels is debated. Certainly it is a revision of Old Latin versions by consultation with the Septuagint, that is, Jerome's technique is followed throughout the New Testament. The name most often put forward as the translator of the post-Gospel New Testament is Rufinus the Syrian, a student of Jerome in Bethlehem ca. 398, who arrived in Rome in 399.[32] Perhaps when several studies on classical allusions through diction in the Vulgate have been completed they will reveal patterns that indicate Jerome or Rufinus or a third party as the probable translator of Acts, the Epistles, Revelation.

Research into Jerome's classical allusions through diction in the Vulgate is just beginning. Presumably it will take scholars well into the next century to begin to understand the role of this technique in the Vulgate as a whole. In the process, we are bound to learn more about the Christianized imagination in the early centuries of the Church, and eventually we may be able to answer Jerome's own question, "What *has* Horace got to do with the Psalter?"

TABLE ONE
Chronology of Jerome's Work on the Vulgate*

Date	Biblical book	Commentary
382–85	revision of Gospels[†]	
ca. 386–87		Philemon, Galat., Ephesians, Titus
ca. 388–89		Ecclesiastes
ca. 390–94	1–2 Samuel, from the Hebrew	Genesis,
	1–2 Kings "	Nahum, Micah, Zephaniah, Haggai,
	Psalter "	Habakkuk (by 392)
	the Prophets "	
	Job "	
394/95	Ezra and Nehemiah "	
395	1–2 Chronicles "	
ca. 396		Jonah, Obadiah
398	books of Solomon "	Matthew
	(Proverbs, Song of Songs, Ecclesiastes)	
398–404/5	Octateuch "	
	(Genesis, Exodus, Leviticus, Numbers, Deuteronomy, Joshua, Judges & Ruth, and Esther)	
406		Zach., Malachi, Hosea, Joel, Amos
before 407	Tobit and Judith (from Aramaic)	
408–410		Isaiah
410–414		Ezechiel
414–16		Jeremiah (unfinished)

* The information on the Vulgate is derived from Tkacz, "*Labor tam utilis,*" 50–53. The following Old Testament books were not the work of Jerome, but were taken from the Old Latin into the Vulgate: Wisdom, Sirach or Ecclesiasticus, Baruch, 1–4 Maccabees. The information on Jerome's commentaries is drawn from Hagendahl, *Latin Fathers and the Classics.*

† Against the Old Latin. If Jerome was the reviser of the rest of the Latin New Testament, he did it at this time, too.

TABLE TWO
Classical Authors Used by Saint Jerome

The list of authors at the left derives from Jerome's entire corpus. The biblical prefaces are to the Vulgate unless parenthetically identified with (LXX) as pertaining to his translations from the Septuagint. With nearly two hundred classical citations in the biblical commentaries, and some authors cited in a dozen or more commentaries, this table simply indicates the rough number of times an author is cited in the commentaries, not which commentaries cite him. Details on the individual classical authors and on the specific biblical commentaries can be retrieved through the index of Hagendahl, *Latin Fathers and the Classics*.

Author	biblical prefaces*, books	biblical commentaries
Aristophanes, *Nubes*		2 in 2 commentaries
Arnobius		
Cato		
Cicero[†]	prol. Paralipomenon (Vulg./LXX)	41 in 13 " " " "
Cornelius Nepos		1 in 1 " " " "
Ennius		
Florus		
Hesiod		1 in 1 " " " "
Horace	prol. Job, 2nd pref. Psalms	20 in 10 " " " "
Juvenal		
Livy		1 in 1 " " " "
locus incertus (Gr.)		1 in 1 " " " "
loci incerti (Lat.)	both prefaces to the Psalms	6 in 4 " " " "
Lucan		3 in 2 " " " "
Lucilius		
Lucretius[‡]		2 in 2 " " " "
Martial		
Ovid	Mark, Esther[§]	4 in 4 " " " "
Perses[**]		
Persius		1 in 1 " " " "

* Jerome's classical allusions in the biblical prefaces and prologues are noted in the margins of the Stuttgart Vulgate.

† Neil Adkin, "Hieronymus Ciceronianus: The Catilinarians in Jerome," *Latomus* 51.2 (1992) 408ff.

‡ Ilona Opelt, "Lukrez bei Hieronymus," *Hermes* 100 (1972) 76–81.

§ Tkacz, "Ovid, Jerome and the Vulgate."

** G. Burzacchini, "Nota sulla presenza di Persio in Girolamo," *Giornale italiano di filologia* 27 (1975):50–72.

TABLE TWO (continued)

Plato		1 in 1 commentary
Plautus		
Pliny the Elder		1 in 1 " " " "
Pliny the Younger[*]	prol. to Paralipomenon (LXX)	
Plutarch		
Porphyry		
Publius Syrus		
Quintillian		4 in 4 " " " "
Pseudo-Quintillian		1 in 1 " " " "
Rhetorica ad Herennium		
Sallust	prol. Ezra; pref. Job (LXX)	12 in 8 " " " "
Seneca the philosopher[†]		
Seneca the rhetorician		
Suetonius		1 in 1 " " " "
Tacitus		1 in 1 " " " "
Terrence		17 in 9 " " " "
Valerius Maximus	prol. Paralipomenon	
Varro		
Virgil[‡]	prols. to Joshua, Ezra, Daniel;	76 in 17 " " " "
	prol. to Paralipomenon (LXX)	
Xenophon		1 in 1 " " " "

[*] F. Trisoglio, "San Girolamo e Plinio il Giovane," *Rivista di studi classici* 21 (1973):343–83.

[†] K. A. Neuhausen, "Hieronymus, Seneca und Theophrasts Schrift «Über die Freundschaft,»" in *Vivarium: Festschrift Theodor Klauser zum 90. Geburtstag* (Münster, 1984), 257–86.

[‡] Mary Alberi, "Jerome, Alcuin and Vergil's 'Old Entellus,'" *Journal of Medieval History* 17 (1991):103–13; Douglas Kries, "Virgil, Daniel, and Augustine's Dialogic Pedagogy in *De Magistro*," in the present collection.

NOTES

1. Ep. 22.29.7 (CSEL 54:188–89).

2. Adam Kamesar, "Philo and the Literary Quality of the Bible: A Theoretical Aspect of the Problem," *Journal of Jewish Studies* 46.1–2 (1995) 55–68; Kamesar, "The Literary Genres of the Pentateuch as Seen from the Greek Perspective: The Testimony of Philo of Alexandria," *Festschrift for David Winston = The Studia Philonica Annual* 9 (1997):143–89; and Tkacz, "*Labor tam utilis*: The Creation of the Vulgate," *Vigiliae Christianae* 50.1 (1996):43–44.

3. Bede, *De schematibus et tropis* (CCL 123a); Theodulph, *Praefatio bibliotheca exametris ac pentametris versibus composita*, edition in *Biblia Sacra iuxta latinam vulgatam versionem ad codicum fidem* [hereafter Vatican Vulgate], vol. 1 (Vatican, 1926) 52–60); Alcuin, *Prologus*, in Vatican Vulgate 1:44–51. These texts are discussed by the author in "The Medieval Reception of the Vulgate as Literature," paper presented at the Thirtieth International Congress on Medieval Studies, Kalamazoo, 1995, in a session sponsored by the Medieval Latin Association of North America.

4. C. B. Tkacz, "The Tormentor Tormented: Study of a Topos in Selected Works of Old English Hagiography" (University of Notre Dame: Ph.D. diss., 1983).

5. C. B. Tkacz, "Literary Studies of the Vulgate: Formula Systems," *Proceedings of the Patristic, Medieval, and Renaissance Conference* 15 (1990):205–19.

6. C. B. Tkacz, "Christian Formulas in Old English Literature: *Næs hyre wlite gewemmed* and Its Implications," *Traditio* 48 (1993):31–61.

7. C. B. Tkacz, "*Labor tam utilis*" 42–72.

8. For a related guide, see C. B. Tkacz, "The Bible in Medieval Literature: A Bibliographic Essay on Basic and New Sources," *Religion & Literature* 19 (1987):63–76.

9. C. B. Tkacz, "Ovid, Jerome, and the Vulgate," *Studia Patristica* 33 (1996):378–82.

10. F. W. Schlatter, S. J., "The Two Women in the Mosaic of Santa Pudenziana," *Journal of Early Christian Studies* 3.1 (1995):20.

11. Horace, *Satirae* 1.10,34, quoted in second preface to the Psalter, in *Biblia sacra iuxta vulgatam versionem*, ed. Robert Weber et al., 4th rev. ed. (Stuttgart, 1994) [hereafter Stuttgart Vulgate], 769.

12. Harald Hagendahl, *Latin Fathers and the Classics: A Study on the Apologists, Jerome and Other Christian Writers* (Göteborg, 1958), 127.

13. Hagendahl discusses such reminiscences of Terence and Virgil in *In Sophoniam; Latin Fathers and the Classics,* 133.

14. See ll. 30–32 of Jerome's letter to Pope Damasus which prefaces his revision of the Gospels, Stuttgart Vulgate 1515. See also Rebecca R. Harrison, "Jerome's Revision of the Gospels" (Ph.D. diss.: University of Pennsylvania, 1986), 195–99, and Benjamin Kedar-Kopfstein, "The Vulgate as a Translation: Some Semantic and Syntactical Aspects of Jerome's Version of the Hebrew Bible" (Ph.D. diss.: University of Jerusalem, 1968), passim.

15. Hagendahl, *Latin Fathers*, 188–89.

16. Tkacz, "Ovid, Jerome and the Vulgate," 382.

17. For details, see Tkacz, "*Labor tam utilis*," passim.

18. Pierre Sabatier, ed., *Bibliorum sacrorum latinae versiones antiquae seu vetis italica et ceterae quaecunque in codicibus manuscriptis et antiquorum libris reperiri potuerunt* (Reims, 1739–49; repr. in 3 vols., Turnhout, 1976); Adolf Jülicher, ed., *Itala: Das Neue Testament in Altlateinische Überleiferung*, 4 vols. (Berlin, 1938, 1940, 1954, 1963).

19. *Vetus Latina: Die Reste der Altlateinische Bibel* (Freiburg, 1949–).

20. Bonifatius Fischer, O.S.B., *Die lateinischen Evangelien bis zum 10. Jahrhundert*, 4 vols., Aus der Geschichte der lateinischen Bibel 13, 15, 17, 18 (Freiburg, 1988–1991).

21. Hagendahl, *Latin Fathers and the Classics*. Other comprehensive studies include Hagendahl, "Jerome and the Latin Classics," *Vigiliae Christianae* 28 (1974) 216–27; and Hagendahl, *Von Tertullian zu Cassiodor: Die profane literarische Tradition in dem lateinischen christlichen Schrifttum* (Göteborg, 1983).

22. A. S. Pease, "The Attitude of Jerome towards Pagan Literature," *Transactions of the American Philological Association* 50 (1919): 150–67; William C. McDermott, "St Jerome and Pagan Greek Literature," *Vigiliae Christianae* 36 (1982): 372–82; and, less successfully, Robert Godel, "Réminiscences de poètes profanes dans les lettres de St Jérôme," *Museum Helveticum* 21 (1964): 65–70. For studies on Jerome's use of individual authors, see Table Two.

23. Hagendahl, *Latin Fathers and the Classics*, 101–2, 281–83 (Horace), 276–79 (Virgil) and 284–92 (Cicero); and Hagendahl, *Von Tertullian zu Cassiodor* 75–76. For Virgil also see Hagendahl, "Jerome and the Latin Classics" 216–17.

24. Tkacz, "Ovid, Jerome and the Vulgate" 380.

25. J. J. Thierry, "The Date of the Dream of Jerome," *Vigiliae Christianae* (1963): 28–40, esp. 32–34; Godel, "Réminiscences de poètes profanes"; and Franciscus Glorié, "Nouvelles sources de saint Jérôme," *Sacris erudiri* 18 (1967–68): 472–77.

26. Tkacz, "Ovid, Jerome and the Vulgate."

27. Hagendahl, *Latin Fathers and the Classics*, 132.

28. This paragraph draws heavily on Hagendahl, *Latin Fathers and the Classics*, 119–38, 209–13, 215–46. The citations covered are by no means exhaustive: Reiter lists an additional sixty passages in the index of his edition (CSEL 59) of Jerome's *In Jeremiam*; Hagendahl, 245.

29. Hagendahl, *Latin Fathers and the Classics*, 119, 126, 130, 133, 209, 211, 215, 227, 236, 244.

30. "The Vulgate as a Translation" 58–60. See also Albert Condamin, S.J., "Un procédé littéraire de St. Jérôme dans sa traduction de la Bible," in *Miscellanea Geronimiana: scritti varii publicati nel XV centenario dalla morte di San Girolamo* (Rome, 1928), 89–95.

31. Stuttgart Vulgate xx.

32. Herman Josef Frede first advanced this view in 1966; see Tkacz, "*Labor tam utilis*," 53.

The Vulgarity of the Vulgate

Edward A. Synan
Pontifical Institute of Mediaeval Studies

To deal in a thorough way with the "Vulgate" text of the Christian Bible, the "generally accepted" Latin version of the Sacred Scriptures, would impose a twofold duty upon us, each worthy of a volume or, indeed, of several volumes. First, to say nothing of our own time, there are well-established interventions by personalities from at least three significant periods in the long history of that text: the Patristic, the Medieval, and the Renaissance eras. This last, of course, was the period when our text was designated "the ancient and commonly used edition," *vetus et vulgata editio*, at Session IV of the Council of Trent on 8 April, 1546.

In addition to adducing historical facts, a second desideratum would be to uncover psychological and sociological motivations pertinent to the history of the Vulgate: intentions harbored, objections met, values defended. Since comparable controversies on language in the Church are with us still—only the formulations of those positive or negative attitudes are new—it will not be useless to advert to those painful continuities. May their persistence justify the present modest discussion!

Despite our human uncertainty as to what developments will mark the future, we may be sure that the translation of sacred texts will never cease to pose difficulties for the Church. Apart from high level scholarship which must always be an arena for the *tournaments des clercs* (was there really a "Q" or is it no more than a construct of the scholarly imagination?), the determination of authentic biblical texts will not fail to engage "the many," "the *polloi*," the *vulgus*, as well as learned believers. The translation of those texts into our various vernaculars and especially their use in our liturgies, now as in times past, constitute pastoral minefields. As will be seen, Saint Augustine was chary about just such textual changes, not only on what we should call today a "theological" ground, but especially on a "pastoral" concern: What disturbing effect might the reading of an unaccustomed text have on his congregation? There is today a significant section of both lay and clerical opinion that regrets the relegation, in the wake of Vatican II, of the "Tridentine" Latin mass along with its Vulgate biblical texts and echoes to exceptional times and places with *ad hoc* clearance by Church authorities. The nostalgia of those disconsolate believers has made them quick to note infelicities in the new liturgical formulae and in the new vernacular translations of Scripture.[1] It will be appreciated that many an intriguing by-path must wait for another day.

I. Origins

Here the primary intention is to deal briefly with the turmoil that surrounded the establishment of the Vulgate.[2] To that end, it will be necessary that we advert to the roles of Pope Saint Damasus I (ca. 304–384) and to that of Saint Eusebius Hieronymus (ca. 342–420), whose hellenic name, pious to the point of pleonasm,[3] has come down to us as "Jerome." Pertinent in a mode other than that of Jerome's relationship with Damasus is the correspondence between Saint Jerome and Saint Augustine (354–430) on the text of the Latin Bible. The Bishop of Hippo, it can be maintained, was the greatest of the Latin Fathers; he was surely a most notable correspondent on our theme with Jerome, at times by letters that are dismayingly acerbic.[4] Augustine's final position would be in opposition to what was then a "new" version of the Latin Scriptures. That version was to be so successful that it could be termed by the Fathers of the Council of Trent "the Vulgate edition" of Holy Writ, that is to say, the Latin translation in widespread use, an edition which for good reasons has been closely associated with Jerome.

As for the medieval use of the Latin Vulgate, we ought to mention the crucial place then held by that version of the Scriptures in university theological education. Candidates for university degrees in theology were "bachelors of the Bible," normally for not fewer than two years before becoming, for two more years, "bachelors of the *Sentences*." In that four-volume work Peter Lombard had collected (ca. 1150) the "views," the *sententiae*, of authoritative writers; from the early thirteenth century on, this work functioned as the basis for theological speculation. This sequence, first Scripture, then speculation, and the importance it assigned to biblical study for theologians, is not always given full value when scholastic theology is evaluated. Nor ought it to be forgotten that Latin, "vulgar" rather than "Golden Age" Latin, was in more than one medieval circle a *lingua franca*. This was the case, not only in the medieval universities, outside as well as within their faculties of theology, but for solemn transactions and records in general. The "Christian Latin" of the Middle Ages with its vulgate echoes has become the object of sophisticated scholarship in our time.

Finally, within living memory, my own as well as that of others, seminary theology under Roman Catholic auspices was everywhere conveyed through Latin source books and, at least where the seminarians came from diverse language groups, lectures and examinations were often conducted in Latin. For us too, although formal courses in the Holy Scriptures necessarily included reference to Hebrew and Greek texts, the Scriptural basis for theology was still the Vulgate, so resoundingly approved by the Council of Trent. A most respected modern authority, the late and regretted J.N.D. Kelly, has gone so far as to say "... his

[Jerome's] Old Testament raised the vulgar Latinity of Christians to the heights of great literature."[5] Emerging vernacular literatures too were marked by biblical themes and turns of speech. That biblical presence to those literatures was not confined to miracle and morality plays; in the English-speaking world we have only to think of Chaucer. It can be argued that the vernacular languages of the medieval west themselves reflect the Latin of the Vulgate. Brief reflections on the Vulgate and on our own liturgical and Scriptural difficulties, will exhaust both the space available and my limitations.

II. An Extra-Biblical Parable

The two major Covenants proclaimed in Sacred Scripture both teach us in "parables," that is, by fictional, exemplary tales. An extra-Biblical parable that may go some distance toward illuminating our theme was in circulation during the second and third consulates of Franklin and Eleanor when my generation of seminarians was first engaged in Scriptural studies. A number of Renaissance Cardinals, so the tale went, feared that the daily recitation of their Office in Latin—the overwhelming bulk of it texts from the Vulgate version of the Bible—would be inimical to their newly-acquired Ciceronian Latinity. The Cardinals appealed to the Roman Curia, therefore, requesting permission to recite that daily Office in Greek. The Curia replied "affirmatively," *affirmative*, but with a curial qualification: The erudite Cardinals were granted permission to recite the Office in Greek, but only after having recited it in Latin, that is, with Psalms and biblical readings according to the Vulgate's Latin, "warts and all."

Since even the Apostles were accustomed to request, and to receive, explanations of the Lord's parables, no one should take umbrage at an explanation of this "parable"; it makes three points:

First, ecclesiastical eminence (here that of fictitious Cardinals), does not exclude the possibility of a certain awkward elitism and language is often the area in which such elitism especially flourishes.

Second, Papal Rome, above all when acting through the Curia, knows how to get its own way even when apparently giving way to petitioners. Furthermore, from the day of Pope Damasus I and his dealings with Jerome, the Holy See has understandably intervened in serious Scriptural issues, not only on their interpretation and on the solution of crucial problems, but on the very text to be interpreted.

Third, because our Church esteems sacred texts, the language of biblical texts is of enormous importance; that language must honor a delicate balance of concerns. The inspired words must be intelligible to the generality of the faithful and Vatican II recognized this concern by authorizing use of our vernaculars. Still, it can hardly be denied that those translations ought to be as little unworthy of divine revelation as our scholars can make them. In our present ecumenical climate no offense will be taken by members of other Churches if we note the role that has been played in the English-speaking Christianity of the Anglican Church by the literary excellence of the King James Version of the Scriptures. If Professor Kelly was right to speak of the "vulgar Latinity of Christians" at the "heights of great literature" owing to the influence of Saint Jerome's work, we may make a parallel observation, namely, that the King James Version has been responsible in no insignificant degree for certain of the achievements of English literature.

III. A Biblical Parable

Having ventured to introduce a non-biblical parable, one well may search the Scriptures for a parable with more impressive claims. Of all the many human missteps recorded in the Bible, only the unfortunate episode in the Garden of Eden has had more far-ranging ill effects that did that doomed project, the effort to reach the sky by building a brick tower at Babel (Gen. 11:1–9). The very name "Babel"—the Hebrews, our spiritual ancestors, were not sorry to think of the obnoxious site as the "Babylon" of their exile—that name "Babel" expresses what went wrong. For ever since that day, we have been no longer a unitary human race; each of our various language groupings has seemed to all others to be "babbling"; we confuse and annoy each other with our varied ways of speaking. Indeed, to the degree that we human beings can be defined, that is, to the degree that our very essence can be captured in a pithy formula, we are "the speaking human," *homo loquax*, as well as the somewhat more flattering "the knowing human," *homo sapiens*, or the obviously practical "human maker," *homo faber*, the artisan who produces tools and clothes and space-craft.

Consider the consequences of that audacious and frustrated project at Babel: Most of us would be bewildered by Swahili; many of us are uncomfortable with the French way of pronouncing the letter "u" and, in their turn, native French speakers have small sympathy with our mispronunciation of that subtle vowel. Even within a single language community, Babel has tormented us since the day the builders despaired of finishing their arrogantly conceived tower. There were Hebrew speakers who had trouble with pronouncing "Shibboleth"; "Sibboleth" said the Ephramites and, thus identified by their vulgar mispronunciation, they died at the hands of the better-spoken Gileadites (Judg. 12:6). In Bernard Shaw's London (as Henry Higgins's slight exaggeration has it) a sharp ear could distinguish, not only the neighborhood, but even within two streets, where a humble speaker had been reared—all hands speaking "English," but in permutations so extreme as to justify Higgin's efforts to teach "correct" English.[6]

There really was no tower at Babel? No matter; at the very least the account is a parable and a pointed one. We humans are insufferably proud of the particular ways we talk, a pride that destroys our unity and peace as one human family; the Holy One cannot be expected to bless that pride. If the Church provides redemption from our more substantive ills, she herself suffers all the ill effects of Babel and this is nowhere more evident than in the history of our traditional Latin text of the Sacred Scriptures, "The Vulgate."

IV. "Vulgar" and "*Vulgus*"

To avoid misunderstandings it will be useful to recognize that the term "vulgar" and its derivatives can convey two meanings, one evaluative in an offensive direction, the other neutral as to value and merely factual. As all scholars know, the Latin word *vulgus* (or, as will be seen, also spelled *volgus*) is a term that signifies primarily the human masses, the "common people"; in the pagan world of antiquity it evoked the lower orders who were generally despised by their "betters." It must be insisted that when our text was designated by the Fathers of the Council of Trent as the *vetus et vulgata editio*,[7] the "edition, ancient and *in general use*," the Latin translation since called, in accord with their formula, the "Vulgate Text," no pejorative air was conveyed (such as is inseparable from our normal use of the term "vulgar"). True enough, in the humanist period of the Council of Trent, the pejorative use of the term also was known. A conspicuous instance of this negative usage (the passage is to be found as an illustration of the word *ministrare* in at least one standard Latin dictionary) occurs in a passage from Virgil:

> ac veluti magno in populo cum saepe coorta est
> seditio, saevitque animis ignobile volgus,
> iamque faces et saxa volant furor arma ministrat
> *Aeneid* 1.148–50.

Since Latin has long since disappeared from general academic experience (at least in North America) may no one think my effort to translate these lines condescending:

> and, as often happens in a great crowd,
> sedition arose, and in their minds the ignoble vulgar rages;
> now too do firebrands and rocks take flight: fury provides those weapons...

The Council Fathers at Trent knew their Latin as well as the next man, but had no thought of demeaning the humble crowd of believers who did not share their own expert Latinity. What was intended was no more than to indicate the approval of the "text in general use" by the Council, despite the strictures, not only of Reformers, but of Catholic humanists as well. As for those latter critics, from within the Church, one thinks of Desiderius Erasmus with his more than legitimate concern for better Scriptural texts so often conveyed with an acidulous pen. The use of the ambivalent term by the Council Fathers was a world removed from that of Virgil; *vulgata* at Trent signified nothing more than the widespread use of that version of the Latin Bible. A logician would tell us that their term was "descriptive" merely, not "prescriptive," not evaluative. That Latin Bible text had been in use since Patristic times; for the Bishops and Cardinals at Trent in the sixteenth century, that use had begun more than a thousand years in the past, from the late fourth, and early fifth, century.

V. Jerome and Augustine

As for that Patristic period, the Latin Vulgate for which the Council of Trent was to have a good word more than a millennium later was partly at least the product—in their diverse ways—of two Saints: Jerome (he had been a pupil of no less a literary light than Donatus), and Pope Damasus I, whom Jerome served for a time as secretary, as *os Damasi* in Jerome's own phrase, "the mouth of Damasus." On 1 October 366, Damasus had been elected Bishop of Rome; epigraphs he had himself composed, set out in scarlet capitals that have been cut into white marble slabs, are still to be seen in the catacombs of Rome where they mark the graves of martyrs. Both Pope and scholar recognized that the Latin texts of Scripture, circulating in what had become a Latin-speaking population, suffered grievous limitations, not the least of which was the confusing diversity of the various versions. As will be seen, on this at least, Augustine agreed with Jerome. Given that he was not to agree with Jerome on the relative merits of the "Septuagint," henceforth the "LXX," and the "Hebrew verity," it must be conceded that the two Fathers of the Church did agree that the profusion of Latin versions of Scripture circulating in their time was intolerable. In Augustine's words to Jerome: "Here too you would be extremely useful if you would render in accurate Latin, *Latinae veritati*, that Greek Scripture which the Seventy wrought since what is found in diverse codices varies so much as to be hardly tolerable. . . ."[8]

As is so often the case, a passage from a work by that younger contemporary of Damasus and Jerome not only posed their common problem sharply, but even indicated shrewdly how it might be solved. We must remark, however, that in the event Augustine did not welcome the application of the solution he himself had suggested. In the course of his treatise *On Christian Doctrine*, a work on his table for more than a decade, Augustine juxtaposed two current Latin translations of the Prophet Isaiah's ominous warning to King Achaz who, threatened by invasion, was tempted to put his trust in alliances with surrounding kinglets rather than to trust in the Lord of history. One current version of the Latin Isaiah 7:9 was a translation of the Greek LXX, and thus a translation-of-a-translation that long would justify Christian reflection of the sort that, from the day of Peter Abelard forward has been termed "theological." That translation of the verse is: "Unless you shall have believed, you will not understand," *Nisi credidistis, non intellegetis*. We cannot forget Saint Anselm's fruitful reflections on this formula;[9] no doubt the translation is at fault, but we may be excused for counting that fault a happy one, *felix culpa*. In another circulating Latin version, this time a literal translation of the Hebrew

Isaiah, incidentally the translation which was to be adopted by the Vulgate, the same line must be understood as referring to the threatened siege of Jerusalem: "Have firm faith, or you will not stand firm," *Nisi credidistis, non permanebitis.*[10] Only the Holy One is worthy of unreserved trust, surely not the fool's gold of alliances with petty local princes.

As he so often did, the Bishop of Hippo in his next two lines proposed a most intelligent procedure in the presence of these variant interpretations: "Which of these sayings might be the one to follow is uncertain unless texts in the preceding language (*exemplaria linguae praecedentis*) be read." By the term "preceding language" Augustine would seem to have intended that the languages preceding the two dissident Latin versions ought to be read (the source of the first is the Greek of the LXX, of the second, the Hebrew Isaiah) if we are to judge between them.[11] Augustine, however, (may we say this without irreverence!) immediately fell victim to his own ingenuity in solving insoluble puzzles: He ignored his own excellent suggestion and proceeded to say:

Still, for those who read them knowledgeably (*scienter*), something important is conveyed by both translations. Difficult it would be for translators [of the same line] to be so diverse that they would not converge in the same neighborhood! Hence, since "understanding" belongs to eternal vision, whereas "faith" belongs with the swaddling-clothes of temporal things, with the milk, as it were, that nourishes infants [1 Pet. 2:2]: "we now walk through faith, not through vision" [2 Cor. 5:7]. Unless we do walk through faith, we cannot attain to the vision which does not pass away, but will remain with us as we cling to the Truth through a purged understanding. Hence one says: "Unless you shall have believed, you will not understand," and one says: "Have firm faith, or you will not stand firm."[12]

In short, Saint Augustine has given a clever analysis of how, for one who reads the two sentences "knowledgeably," the apparently diverse translations might be thought to end "in the same neighborhood." For him, both formulae can be taken to contrast the transitory life through which we walk in the obscurity of faith with the eternal security of the vision to which we aspire. Our contemporary exegetes may regret, or at least, can hardly be expected to adopt, Augustine's ingenious interpretation with its appeal to firm vision as analogous to the understanding of the blessed in heaven, an eternal grasp of Truth Itself, contrasted with the obscure and passing faith this side of the tomb (1 Cor. 13:13), analogue of our imperfect grasp of Truth while on the road to eternal understanding, toward the vision in which the blessed are eternally at rest.

Since Augustine's exegesis, with its appeals to transitory faith and to permanent understanding, can hardly survive application to the Hebrew text of Isaiah, it is all the more to be regretted that (as will be seen) he did not stay with his own recommendation that texts in the "preceding language" be consulted. In this case, of course, the Hebrew which speaks of the coming siege of the Holy City ought to have been consulted, for the translation that missed the siege is that of the

LXX and, through that text, of the *Vetus latina*, that Latin version itself a translation of what is here an inept Greek translation and in no sense the *ultimate* "preceding language." Augustine, of course, was convinced that the LXX translators had been "inspired." Did his pastoral concern, visible below, push him to this view of the inspiration of the LXX translators or did that conviction, for which he gave reasons—the Apostles themselves had used LXX readings—compel him to accept this reading?

In the end Pope Damasus and Jerome would both be committed in theory to precisely the solution Augustine had proffered, but had not followed: the consultation of the appropriate "preceding language" of each text, Hebrew and Aramaic for the Ancient Covenant, *Koinê* Greek for the New Covenant. They reached this solution gradually in their effort to heal the confused condition of the *Latin* translations of those Scriptures as they then circulated in the Church.

The first step that Jerome took, however, was to go, not to the ultimate "preceding language," but to the Greek texts to be found in Origen's *Hexapla*, from an aristocratic standpoint as "vulgar" as was the popular Latin into which all translations had then to be made if they were to be intelligible to the bulk of believers. This was the *Koinê*, the "common" Greek, in which the Christian Scriptures had been written from the beginning and into which the Hebrew Scriptures had been translated for the sake of Diaspora believers, of Jews "sown" like seed outside The Land. That translation had generated the myth of "seventy" (or as some versions had it, seventy-two) learned translators, shut in separate cells, who produced identical translation of the Pentateuch. This alleged origin of the Greek Pentateuch (along with the rest of the Ancient Covenant in *Koinê*) is the "Septuagint" usually, as here, referred to as the "LXX." This legend Augustine accepted.[13] In that acceptance he was moved by his conviction that the primitive Church, Apostles and immediate disciples of the Lord included, had done so before him. *Koinê* Greek has been characterized by the author of a modern manual of Attic Greek as far from aristocratic:

> By the end of the fourth century [BCE], a new, "common" dialect had emerged: the Koine.... From the mid-fourth century on, spoken Greek begins a long and gradual process of change affecting pronunciation, accentuation, vocabulary and syntax, with Koine eventually suppressing the old dialects... These changes in the language are also evident in nonliterary works written in Greek of the time,... writings without high cultural aspirations, including the Greek New Testament...[14]

To the New Testament, written originally in *Koinê*, our manual author might have added the LXX Testament translated into the same *Koinê* Greek, but from its "preceding language," Hebrew. As the Bishop of Hippo knew, his formula referred both to *Koinê* Greek and to Hebrew.

All this throws light on otherwise obscure pericopes in the Scriptures of the New Covenant that refer to the "Greek" and "Hebrew" languages. It illumines, for instance, the passage recorded in Acts between the "Tribune" (the "Chiliarch"—his title in Greek announces that he commanded a thousand soldiers, if his troop were up to strength) and The Apostle, Paul of Tarsus. When Paul addressed that officer in *Koinê*, the Tribune asked him in surprise: "You know Greek?" for he had thought Paul an Egyptian trouble-maker, presumably from so far up The River that he likely would not have known *Koinê*. Paul permitted himself a mild boast: "I am a Jew from Tarsus in Cilicia, citizen of a not unknown city" (Acts 21:37–40). What is important to us is that Paul could write and speak *Koinê* Greek; he used it in writing his Epistles and he used it now to address the Tribune. When Paul then proceeded to address the Jewish crowd, he used the dialect that then passed as "Hebrew." For the "Hebrew" in which Acts tells us Paul addressed his fellow Jews was not strictly speaking Hebrew, but Aramaic, a dialect current in The Land. There are other indications in the Christian Scriptures that the Jewish public (as distinguished from the educated classes: Pharisees, Scribes, the priesthood) could no longer be counted on to understand the Hebrew of their own ancient Scriptures. That venerable language was so little known, even in Jerusalem, that the public notice of his "crime" on the cross of Jesus—He had made Himself "King of the Jews"—had to be written in the Latin of the Roman overlords, in Greek for the sake of strangers, as well as "in Hebrew letters" for the sake of the native population (Luke 23:38; John 19:20). The crucifixion account has supplied another striking evidence that biblical Hebrew was not universally known in the Holy City, not even by the native population. When Jesus cried out on the cross in the biblical Hebrew of Psalm 21(22):2: *Eli, Eli, lamma sabactani*, there were some in the crowd, certainly Jews (for what pagan could have been expected to recognize the name "Elijah" in that cry to the Holy One?) who thought he was calling on Elijah (Matt. 27:46; Mark 15:34, 35).

This highlights a curious and significant parallel between an overarching detail of Jewish religious experience and our own contemporary Christian population. The scattering of the Jews throughout the pagan world, we have noted, was such that it received the Greek name *Diaspora*, the "sowing through" the gentile world of the People Chosen by the Holy One. Living among foreigners for whom other tongues were native, the Jews thus "sown" forgot the language of their Scriptures; Jews needed and received their Bible translated into a language they could understand. Knowledge of biblical Hebrew became the exclusive province of the learned and of the exceptionally pious; *Koinê*, language of the "gentile" Mediterranean world, became the language of the humbler Jewish masses outside The Land. The Jewish *polloi*, if we may so speak of the Chosen People in their exile, no longer could speak and read the Sacred Language.

Yet another modification was in the "canon," the list of biblical Books accepted as inspired. That list was widened in the Diaspora, well beyond the "Palestinian" canon. A major repercussion in Christian circles has been that the Church accepted the extended, Diaspora canon, but sixteenth-century Reformers returned to the more restricted Palestinian canon. In our more courteous times those additional Books (and parts of Books) are now called the "deutero-canonical," rather than the "apocryphal," Books, that is to say, they are often termed "Books of the second canon" rather than "spurious Books." It is a curiosity that Jerome held for the Palestinian canon, but despite the stubbornness of which he gave so many signs, under pressure would translate into Latin certain Old Testament Books of the "second canon," Tobit and Judith.

Our contemporary parallel to the Jewish experience is twofold, negative and positive. First, Latin, so regretted by numbers of contemporary Catholics (who do not necessarily understand it) was introduced to replace the *Koinê* Greek precisely because even that popular dialect was no longer intelligible in the western Church; it gave way to "vulgar" Latin that could be understood by the mass of believers. The Latin, esteemed for its air of "mystery," for its "solemnity," was adopted because even *Koinê* Greek had become intolerably mysterious for the teaching, worshipping, western Church.

Second, because most Christian believers in our day no longer understand the Latin in which, not only the Bible, but (as has been noted) education and much solemn business was conducted, the Church has authorized the various vernaculars for liturgical use. No single language has replaced the ancient *Koinê* and the less ancient "Christian Latin." One may hear that English (or Spanish) is understood "everywhere"; travelers will be wise not to count on this. Hence, after strong medieval reluctance on the part of Church authorities to authorize translations of the Bible into contemporary vernaculars, we now have everywhere a vernacular Bible and a vernacular liturgy. English-speaking believers with strong emotional and traditional ties to hearing the Vulgate in the liturgy (with, to be sure, a Rheims-Challoner translation of the Epistle and the Gospel readings at mass) have been as reluctant to accept a vernacular liturgy as were many believers (Augustine among them!) to accept Jerome's revision of the Latin Scriptures.

VI. The Issues for Damasus and Jerome

Saint Jerome, as everyone knows, is one of the four major Fathers of the Church in the Latin tradition. In his case the phrase "as everyone knows" is deceptive: everyone is apt to "know" much about him that is not true. For instance, we "know" from many a renaissance painting that the fourth- and fifth-century Jerome was a cardinal, a rank not to be established until the eleventh century. There are few works of scholarship to rival *The New Jerome Biblical Commentary* of 1990 and every contributor to that monumental work most certainly knows that the El Greco painting of Jerome in the robes of a Cardinal on the dust jacket is an instance of artistic license. It is hard to see what harm this venerable myth can do; in the same category must be the tale (also widely represented in Christian art, Leonardo for one has left his version unfinished) that Jerome had an unlikely pet, a lion, with him in his cave at Bethlehem. According to this legend, Jerome had been good to the lion when the poor beast had a thorn in a paw. What is less open to pious interpretation and by no means unusual, is the flat statement, pronounced in my hearing not a thousand days ago by a university professor: "He [Jerome] translated the New Testament into Latin." In fact Jerome "translated" the four Gospel accounts by revising and correcting prior Latin translations, but no one seems to know who made comparable revisions and corrections of earlier Latin versions to produce the Vulgate text of the rest of the New Testament: Acts, Epistles, Revelation.[15]

While Jerome was given the excessive credit of having put the whole New Testament into Latin, his labors on the Old Testament tend to be diminished, even passed over. Here his complicated interventions ought to be untangled. A complicating factor is that Jerome held out for the Old Testament "canon" of the Land, not for the list of inspired Books accepted by the Diaspora and thus present in the LXX version, all of the latter accepted by the Council of Trent and, in our day, known as "deutero-canonical" writings. Nor is this the sole source of confusion on his Old Testament interventions.

VII. The Psalters

The Book of the Psalms, the Psalter, has attracted persistent scholarly attention from the day of Jerome to that of Pope Pius XII. First, the most influential of Jerome's efforts to produce an improved Latin Psalter must be noted. This is his "Gallican Psalter," completed by 389, and called "Gallican" thanks to its early popularity in Gaul. This version is mentioned first because, despite its many limitations, that Psalter dominated Catholic liturgy from the time of Jerome to the day of Pius XII who in 1945 ordered that it be replaced in the Roman Breviary by a corrected Latin version designed to eliminate the defects of the Gallican Psalter of Jerome. Jerome's source for that Psalter was the *Hexapla* of Origen, a volume to which Jerome had access at Caesarea, which is to say that a number of *Koinê* translations, including the LXX text, lie beneath Jerome's Latin.

A Latin Psalter, earlier than the Gallican and also a translation of the LXX Greek text, has long been ascribed to Jerome. Because that text has been used in Italy, and especially in Saint Peter's Basilica, this version has been dubbed the "Roman" Psalter. Today the ascription of this Psalter to Jerome is seriously challenged; it may be the Latin version that Jerome corrected in 384, but seems not to be the corrected version.[16]

After Jerome learned Hebrew in the Holy Land, however, he produced yet another translation of the Psalter; this time his translation honored the suggestion of Augustine that "texts of the preceding language" be followed. It remained on the shelves of libraries while the "Roman" and the "Gallican" Psalters dominated the liturgical prayer of the Church. This situation persisted from the day of Jerome until the new version under the patronage of Pope Pius XII. Today a "Liturgy of the (canonical) Hours," *Liturgia horarum*, revised once more after Vatican II, is widely used in vernacular translations of the approved Latin edition. The Ciceronian cardinals of the parable could have welcomed this development. The

Psalter translated is still the one produced under Pius XII, along with appropriate "canticles" from other books of Scripture here included along with Psalms. Antiphons have been chosen from other sources as before, but in general they are still from the alternative Psalter. Perhaps it not necessary to mention that apart from psalmody the Breviary of Pius XII has been revised radically since the Second Vatican Council, but the Psalms and their antiphons still represent generally that great Pope's revisions.

VIII. The Jerome-Augustine Correspondence

As is well known, the exchange of letters between the older Jerome and Augustine, begun when the latter was not yet in bishop's orders, are revelatory of two strong personalities, not always in harmony on every problem. The fact that a letter then could be sent in good faith by Augustine to Jerome in The Holy Land, yet not be delivered for five years because a messenger changed his mind about his destination, became an occasion of major distrust on Jerome's part: How could a letter, addressed to him, have been read all over Italy, yet not by the only one addressed—and the whole thing take five years to come to the surface? Even worse was the "leaking" (and exaggeration) of controverted points before the letter reached Jerome.[17] Like many an intellectual, Jerome was sensitive; Augustine was younger and in education (it might be argued) inferior to Jerome, at least in linguistic breadth. Jerome was to learn, as Augustine did not, the Hebrew language, indispensable for the study of the Ancient Covenant. Here limited space suggests that their dissent on the interpretation of other controversies touched on in their letters be omitted: the controversy at Antioch between Peter and Paul (Gal. 2:11–14),[18] the origin of the human soul, original sin, and a last on the text of James 2:10. Dissent between the two Latin Fathers of the Church on those controversies proceeded from dissent on what we post-Abelardians would term their "theological" issues, rather than on their exegetical or scriptural views; they hardly touch our precise issue of the Vulgate text. There remains, however, the prolonged and serious dissent between these two major Latin Fathers of the Church on that most fundamental of scriptural issues, the text to be used in the day-by-day life of the Church.

Damasus and Jerome had begun with the project of bringing into harmony the mass of variant Latin texts circulating in the west. This inevitably entailed comparison, not only with the LXX, but with the other texts preserved in Origen's *Hexapla*, to which Jerome had access at Caesarea. Moved by his academic interests in language, Jerome learned Hebrew after his remove to Bethlehem and there understandably began to translate a number of Old Testament Scriptures from the Hebrew text now accessible to him, from what he called "the Hebrew verity," *ex veritate Hebraica*. This he did with varying degrees of attention and always under pressure to finish quickly. His translation of the Pentateuch is enormously esteemed, even today, but that of other Books less so.

What is of primary interest here is that, in the end, Augustine objected, not precisely to Jerome's program of producing an acceptable Latin translation of the Hebrew rather than of the LXX Greek, but to the reading in the churches of such a text. Although he recognized the value of better translations, whether from Hebrew or from the Septuagint, Augustine noted what he foresaw would be the ill effects on his congregation of that innovation:

> For this, therefore, I desire your translation from the Septuagint... may they understand that I do not want your translation from the Hebrew to be read in the churches for this reason: lest we, by bringing forth something novel, against the authority of the Septuagint, disturb with an immense stone of stumbling *(magno scandalo)* the People of Christ whose ears and hearts are accustomed to hear that translation, one which was approved even by the Apostles![19]

There is wry satisfaction in recording that before Jerome's death the two towering figures ended in a degree of harmony. Jerome had come to see that the younger man had not intended that a delay of five years in the delivery of a letter should be an opportunity for circulating objections to Jerome's work before he himself had seen those objections. Furthermore, Augustine's command of rhetoric allowed him to write a conciliatory letter that Jerome willingly accepted. On the other hand, the humanity of both is visible in the fact that what finally brought them together was a common enemy. The doctrine of Pelagius on the basic issue of grace, and also explanations of the origin of our souls and of original sin they agreed were heretical. Strongly opposed to heresy as they were, the two Fathers no longer opposed each other.

Jerome's dream of a complete Latin Old Testament, grounded on "the Hebrew verity" and universally accepted in the Church, remained a dream. In our time serious efforts have been made to fulfill this ambition for a vernacular version, grounded on Hebrew and Greek, and acceptable to experts in the vernacular used. One thinks of the Hebraists, classicists, and "Immortals" from the French Academy (Etienne Gilson, for instance, participated owing to his command, neither of theology nor of philosophy, but of the French language), and others who collaborated in producing the *Bible de Jérusalem*. From Jerome's day until our own, the Vulgate text with its extended canon has held sway in Catholic circles. Except for scholarly use, the Vulgate has been replaced because it is no longer "vulgar" enough; it is hardly accessible to our mass of believers, our *vulgus*. As the masses once forgot their *Koinê* Greek and began to need Latin, so now ours has long forgotten Latin and so needs innumerable vernaculars—the linguistic chaos to which we all have been condemned by our arrogance at Babel.

NOTES

1. See William D. Dinges, "Roman Catholic Traditionalism in the United States," *Fundamentalisms Observed*, ed. M.E. Marty and R.S. Appleby (Chicago, 1991), 1:66–101.

2. See also Catherine Brown Tkacz, "*Labor tam utilis:* The Creation of the Vulgate," *Vigiliae Christianae* 50.1 (1996): 42–72 and her essay in the present volume.

3. The Greek adjective *eusebes* means "pious," "religious"; *ieros* means "pertaining to the gods," "holy," "sacred" as against profane; "Eusebius Hieronymus," strictly taken, and as doubtless it sounded to his contemporaries who knew Greek, means literally "A Pious man, Religiously named."

4. Their exchanges have been collected in a convenient publication, *SS. Eusebii Hieronymi et Aurelii Augustani epistolae mutuae*, ed. Josephus Schmid (Bonn, 1930)= Florilegium patristicum tam veteres quam medii aevi auctores complectens, ed., B. Geyer and J. Zellinger, fasc. 22; this collection is cited here as *Epistolae mutuae*.

5. J.N.D. Kelly, *Jerome: His Life, Writings, and Controversies* (New York and San Francisco, 1975), 163; news of the passing of this great scholar arrived as this paper was being prepared.

6. "You can spot an Irishman or a Yorkshireman by his brogue. *I* can place any man within six miles. I can place him within two miles in London. Sometimes within two streets." G.B. Shaw, *Pygmalion*, Act 1.

7. "Insuper eadem sacrosancta Synodus considerans, non parum utilitatis accedere posse Ecclesiae Dei, si ex omnibus Latinis editionibus, quae circumferuntur sacrorum librorum, quaenam pro authentica habenda sit, innotescat: statuit et declarat, ut haec ipsa vetus et vulgata editio, quae longo tot saeculorum usu in ipsa Ecclesia probata est, in publicis lectionibus, disputationibus, praedicationibus et expositionibus pro authentica habeatur, et quod nemo illam reicere quovis praetextu audeat vel praesumat." Council of Trent, Session IV, 8 April 1546; H. Denzinger, *Enchiridion Symbolorum. Definitionum et declarationum de rebus fidei et morum*, ed. C. Bannwart, I.B. Umberg, S.J., editio 21–23 (Freiburg im B., 1937), no. 785, p. 280.

8. "Ac per hoc plurimum profueris, si eam Scripturam Graecam, quam Septuaginta operati sunt, Latinae veritati reddideris, quae in diversis codicibus ita varia est, ut tolerari vix possit...", *Epistolae mutuae*, no. 71, p. 43, ll. 19–21.

9. See Anselm, *Proslogion* 1, in his *Opera omnia*, ed. F.S. Schmitt (Stuttgart, 1968) 1:100.17–19; and *Epistola de incarnatione Verbi* (prior recensio),[4], in ibid. 1:284.1–2 and 26–27; and his *Cur Deus homo* in ibid. 2:40.8.

10. "... illud eiusdem Esaiae: *Nisi credideritis, non intellegetis*, aliud interpretatus est: *Nisi credideritis, non permanebitis*." Augustine, *De doctrina christiana* 2.12 (CCL 32:43). The English translation given is that of *The New English Bible with the Apocrypha* (Oxford and Cambridge, 1970).

11. "Quis horum uerba secutus sit, nisi exemplaria linguae praecedentis legantur, incertum est." *De doctrina christiana* 2.12 (CCL 32:21–22).

12. "Sed tamen ex utroque magnum aliquid insinuatur scienter legentibus. Difficile est enim ita diuersos a se interpretes fieri, ut non se aliqua uicinitate contingant. Ergo, quoniam intellectus in specie sempiterna est, fides uero in rerum temporalium quibusdam cunabulis quasi lacte alit paruulos; nunc autem per fidem ambulamus, non per speciem; nisi autem per

fidem ambulauerimus, ad speciem peruenire non possumus, quae non transit, sed permanet per intellectum purgatum nobis coherentibus ueritati. Propterea ille ait: *Nisi credideritis, non permanebitis*, ille autem: *Nisi credideritis, non intellegetis.*" *De doctrina christiana* 2.12 (CCL 32:22–32).

 13. See the *City of God*; 8.11, 15.11, 14, and 23, 18.42–43.

 14. D.J. Mastronarde, *Introduction to Attic Greek* (Berkeley/Los Angeles, 1993), 5.

 15. For the state of the question, see Tkacz, "*Labor tam utilis*" 52.

 16. See Kelly, *Jerome*, 89.

 17. Augustine's letter provoked Jerome's understandably bitter response; *Epistulae mutuae*, nos. 40 and 102.

 18. On this controversy, see Anne P. Carriker, "Augustine's Frankness in his Dispute with Jerome over the Interpretation of Galatians 2:11-14," in this volume.

 19. "Ideo autem desidero interpretationem tuam de Septuaginta... intellegant propterea me nolle tuam ex Hebraeo interpretationem in ecclesiis legi, ne contra Septuaginta auctoritatem tamquam novum aliquid proferentes magno scandalo perturbemus plebes Christi, quarum aures et corda illam interpretationem audire consuerunt, quae etiam ab apostolis adprobata est." *Epistulae mutuae*, no. 82. 5.35 on p. 93, ll. 11–14.

Augustine's Frankness in his Dispute with Jerome over the Interpretation of Galatians 2:11–14[1]

Anne P. Carriker
Columbia University

Augustine and Jerome never met, but they corresponded intermittently between 394/5 and Jerome's death in 419/20. Seventeen letters of this correspondence are extant, and at least three have been lost.[2] The first eleven letters were exchanged between 394/95 and 405, and, after a decade's hiatus, in 415, the correspondence resumed and the remaining letters were exchanged. In the latter stage of the correspondence Augustine sought Jerome's assistance with certain questions that emerged in the Pelagian controversy, though Jerome's response was brief and of little help to Augustine.[3] The earlier stage of the correspondence, however, witnessed a more vigorous relationship between the two scholars. Two important issues were discussed in these first eleven letters: whether the Septuagint or the Hebrew Old Testament is the more authoritative, and how to interpret Galatians 2:11–14.

The question of the authority of the Hebrew Bible arose when Augustine learned of Jerome's decision to translate the Old Testament from the original Hebrew rather than from the Septuagint. Augustine was convinced of the divine inspiration of the Septuagint and hence its authority, a conviction that arose from faith and, particularly, pastoral experience. A single word in Jerome's revised version of the Book of Jonah, Augustine relates, had so troubled the nearby congregation at Oea that it had forced its bishop to revert to the more familiar reading.[4] Jerome, on the other hand, appealed to the authority of the older version after noting disagreements not only between the Hebrew version and the Septuagint but also between different versions of the Septuagint itself (*Ep.* 112.5.19). Although Augustine refused to consider the Hebrew Bible as a legitimate source for a translation meant for common use, he did concede its usefulness for scholarly purposes in *Ep.* 82 (at 5.34, ca. 405), the final letter of the first stage of the correspondence.

The second issue discussed by Augustine and Jerome, the proper interpretation of Gal. 2:11–14, is the topic that I have selected to honor the Reverend F. W. Schlatter, S. J., with whom I first read Galatians as an undergraduate. I intend to set the dispute between Augustine and Jerome over the interpretation of Gal.

2:11–14 in the context of Augustine's ideas about frankness in human relations by first reviewing the exegetical problem of Gal. 2:11–14, then surveying the modern scholarship on this subject, and finally concluding with an evaluation of Augustine's ideas about frankness and how they influenced his relationship with Jerome and his interpretation of Gal. 2:11–14.

I. The Incident at Antioch

Jerome's interpretation of Gal. 2:11–14 prompted Augustine's first letters to him and became the chief topic of controversy between them. The history of this issue begins with the passage in Galatians itself, which represents the first major challenge to the authority of the Christian Church. Shortly after Christ's death, some converts from Judaism thought it necessary that the first Gentile converts observe Mosaic Law.[5] St. Paul argued to the contrary and obtained approval for his view at the Council of Jerusalem, at which St. Peter was also present.[6] It is furthermore recorded that Peter had received a vision that lent divine support to Paul's position.[7]

Nevertheless, in the Incident at Antioch recorded at Gal. 2:11–14, Peter acted contrary to the agreement made at the Council of Jerusalem as well as to his personal revelation by withdrawing from the Gentile table in order to avoid the disapproval of Judaizing Christians. Paul then openly rebuked Peter for his inconsistency and recorded the incident to illustrate to the Galatians the superiority of the position that Gentile Christians need not observe Mosaic Law.

The passage of Gal. 2:11–14 provided ancient heretics with some of their favorite ammunition against Christianity.[8] Marcion, for example, used the Incident to support his Gnostic position that Christianity was fundamentally incompatible with Judaism.[9] The third-fourth century Ebionite author of the Pseudo-Clementine *Homilies*, on the other hand, attacked Paul's confrontation of Peter in order to support his own allegiance to Jewish Law.[10] Most troublesome to Christians, the argument in the first of Porphyry's fifteen volumes against Christianity seems to have been based on the Incident at Antioch, which, according to Porphyry, undermined the authority of the principal leaders of the infant Church and, by extension, Christianity itself.[11]

II. Jerome's Interpretation

Jerome's own *Commentarii in epistolam ad Galatas*[12] appears to have been written precisely in order to respond to the concern of his friends Paula and Eustochium over Porphyry's interpretation of the Incident at Antioch. In his preface he summarizes Porphyry's position:

> Bataneotes et sceleratus ille Porphyrius . . . Petrum a Paulo obiecit esse reprehensum, quod non recto pede incederet ad evangelizandum: volens et illi

maculam erroris inurere, et huic procacitatis, et in commune ficti dogmatis accusare mendacium, dum inter se Ecclesiarum principes discrepent [al. discreparent].[13]

That accursed Batanean[14] Porphyry . . . objected to Paul's rebuking Peter for not evangelizing properly: he intended to brand Peter with the stain of error and Paul with that of impudence, and to accuse both of deceitful, fictitious teachings, on the grounds that the very first leaders of the Church disagreed among themselves.

Jerome further writes that he himself follows the Greek tradition of exegesis, the greatness of which, he insists, he cannot hope or presume to surpass. He cites Didymus of Alexandria, Apollinaris of Laodicea, Alexander the heretic, Eusebius of Emesa, and Theodore of Heraclea as among the many commentators who have gone before him, and, though failing to state specifically which exegete he follows, he explains the confrontation between Peter and Paul as a staged event. According to this explanation, Peter merely pretended to observe the Jewish Law as essential to salvation, while Paul, aware that Peter was dissimulating, pretended to rebuke him. The staged scene thus achieved the intended result of demonstrating that observance of the Law was not essential to salvation, while it did so without directly confronting the Judaizing Christians who were present.

This interpretation also solves another problem Jerome brings up in his *Commentary*.[15] He cites three instances in which Paul recounts his own observation of the Law: Acts 16:3, in which Paul circumcises Timothy; Acts 18:18, in which he cuts his hair according to Judaic practice in keeping with a vow he had made; and Acts 21:17, in which he purifies himself in keeping with the law of Moses. These actions, in addition to Paul's statement, "to the Jews I became as a Jew so that I might gain the Jews,"[16] Jerome insists, would condemn Paul of hypocrisy if he had in reality rebuked Peter for supporting Judaizing Christians. Yet if Paul had merely pretended to observe the Law and to "become as a Jew," Jerome contends, he would then not be guilty of hypocrisy.

III. Augustine's Response
and the Confusion That Followed

In *Ep.* 28, the first letter of his correspondence with Jerome, Augustine writes that he is troubled by the interpretation Jerome advocates and hopes it can be disproved. If Christians admit in one instance that Scripture can contain a falsehood, how can individuals be prevented from accepting as literally true only what they like, while discarding the rest as figurative?[17] The deliverer of *Ep.* 28, however, never reached Bethlehem, so Augustine then sent Jerome *Ep.* 40, in which he begs him to engage in debate by mail (*adgredere, quaeso, istam nobiscum litterariam conlocutionem*, 40.1.1) and elaborates his own position. Augustine also

entreats Jerome to recant his interpretation, jokingly emphasizing his point with the
only direct classical allusion he uses in the entire correspondence:

> Quare arripe, obsecro te, ingenuam et vere Christianam cum caritate severitatem
> ad illud opus corrigendum atque emendandum et παλινῳδίαν, ut dicitur, cane.
> Incomparabiliter enim pulchrior est veritas Christianorum quam Helena
> Graecorum. . . . Neque hoc ego dico, ut oculos cordis recipias, quos absit ut
> amiseris, sed ut advertas, quos cum habeas sanos et vigiles, necscio qua
> dissimulatione avertisti, ut non intenderes, quae consequantur adversa, si semel
> creditum fuerit posse honeste ac pie scriptorem divinorum librorum in aliqua sui
> operis parte mentiri (*Ep.* 40.4.7).

> Consequently, take up, I implore you, a frank and truly Christian severity
> combined with love in order to correct and amend your work, and, as they say,
> sing a palinode. For Christian truth is incomparably more beautiful than Helen of
> the Greeks. . . . And I do not say this so that you recover the eyes of your heart–far
> be it from me to consider that you had lost them–but that you give attention to
> your eyes, which you have averted by some dissembling unknown to me, since
> they are healthy and alert, so that you were not attentive to the troubles that would
> follow, if it should once be believed that a writer of divine Scripture honestly and
> piously could lie in some part of his work.

Unfortunately, this letter never reached Bethlehem. Having somehow been
misplaced, it was then published and circulated in Rome, where Jerome had many
enemies.

As a result, Jerome received a copy of *Ep.* 40 only after many of his critics had
already seen it. For a time he refused to answer it and instead demanded that
Augustine either acknowledge or deny his authorship of the letter that criticized
him.[18] Meanwhile, he alluded to classical passages depicting rash youths who
challenge slower but more powerful elders and attached his *Apologia contra
Rufinum* to one of his letters to Augustine.[19] Since Augustine did not consider *Ep.*
40 to be an attack against Jerome, there was some confusion until he realized that
Jerome was referring to *Ep.* 40, which he then acknowledged to be his own.[20] He
further explained that its misplacement had occurred in spite of the greatest care he
had taken to ensure its reaching its destination, expressed his inability to carry on
a candid correspondence with someone who seemed prepared to injure him, and
passionately lamented the implications of the fracture, made clear in the *Apologia
contra Rufinum*, of Jerome's previously famed friendship with Rufinus[21]:

> In cuius sensus tota se proiciat secura dilectio? Quis denique amicus non
> formidetur quasi futurus inimicus, si potuit inter Hieronymum et Rufinum hoc,
> quod plangimus, exoriri? . . . O infida in voluntatibus amicorum scientia
> praesentium, ubi nulla est praescientia futurorum! (*Ep.* 73.3.6)

> Into whose thoughts can love completely and safely enter? What friend is not to
> be feared as a future enemy, if that which we bewail could happen between Jerome

and Rufinus? O treacherous knowledge of the affections of present friends, when there is no foreknowledge of future friends!

In his lengthy *Ep.* 112 Jerome at last responded to some of Augustine's criticisms, but he first summoned the weapons of God, portraying himself as a heavenly warrior battling Satan.[22] He next appealed to the preface of his *Commentary*, in which he had set forth his method of drawing upon previous exegetes, and stated that he had followed Origen's interpretation of the Incident at Antioch.[23] He further named the commentaries of Greek exegetes who had preceded him, just as he had in the preface of his Commentary.[24] Although Jerome does not state explicitly that they follow Origen, Augustine took him to mean that they did (*Ep.* 82.3.23–3.24). Jerome also referred to a long work by John Chrysostom devoted to the same interpretation of Gal. 2:11–14 that Jerome had endorsed.[25] Finally, he accused Augustine of the Ebionite heresy, which permitted the observance of Jewish Law.

Augustine responded with *Ep.* 82, a detailed argument in favor of the literal interpretation of Gal. 2:11–14. Here he maintains that Peter had provided a Christian example of humble acceptance of rebuke, all the more worthy of emulation since it came from so distinguished an apostle. Further, Augustine argues in this letter that in apostolic times the Law was not deadly but inconsequential for those who practiced it. It was then allowed a slow burial appropriate to its superiority to pagan customs, which were always forbidden to Christians. In this way, Augustine answers Jerome's accusations of heresy and, more fully than had been done before, the objections of the Ebionites and Gnostics. There is no evidence that Jerome ever responded to Augustine's *Ep.* 82, but, in 402, before writing his *Ep.* 112 to Augustine, he gives in his *Contra Pelagianos* support for the view that Peter had sinned at Antioch: at 1.22 he uses "Peter's sin" at Antioch in defense of his position that bishops cannot be infallible, and at 3.19 he mentions Agustine with praise. This change of opinion was noticed by Augustine, whose interpretation of the Incident at Antioch eventually came to predominate in both West and East.[26]

IV. Survey of Modern Scholarship

Since the correspondence between Augustine and Jerome provides much material for assessing their characters, one strategy modern scholars have adopted is to analyze Augustine's and Jerome's differences in personality as depicted in their correspondence. In 1839 Möhler published a brief history of the theological issues treated by Augustine and Jerome that ends in an evaluation of their characters.[27] Möhler agrees with Augustine's interpretation, but he is sympathetic to Jerome's suspicion of Augustine's criticisms, which he judges to be the cause of Jerome's avoiding dispute.[28] Jerome's recent confrontation with Rufinus, Möhler maintains, may have led him to avoid confrontation with others, and

Augustine's apparent unfamiliarity with problems of translation probably caused Jerome to be suspicious of his motives for criticizing him. On the other hand, Möhler concedes that Augustine should not be accused of arrogance for challenging Jerome in a friendly letter that was never intended for publication.

Möhler judges that the argument ended because, as stated above, in his *Dialogus contra Pelagianos* Jerome adopts the interpretation of the Incident at Antioch for which Augustine had originally argued.[29] Möhler then draws a parallel between this passage in Jerome and Augustine's judgment that Peter had accepted Paul's rebuke "humbly." Jerome's humility and Augustine's noble conduct, he writes, put an end to the argument: "Auch große Männer können Streit anfangen; aber nur große werden ihn also endigen; das erste theilen sie mit Jedermann, das zweite nur mit sich selbst."[30] This passage is frequently cited by later scholars. It is quoted favorably by Asslaber in 1908, who also contends that after Augustine's *Ep.* 73, Jerome's letters become more tender, while Augustine's effusion of feeling diminishes as he focuses on the issues themselves.[31] It is quoted favorably again by Buchwald (1920) and Malfatti (1921), the latter of whom also holds that Jerome is the wiser of the two since he confessed that he had erred,[32] even though there is only evidence for his having changed his view and not for his having acknowledged to Augustine that he had changed his opinion. Tourscher (1917–18) does not refer to Möhler but shares the same view that Jerome had no means by which to judge Augustine's sincerity and intentions in criticizing him.[33]

In 1877 Overbeck responded to Möhler's judgment that Augustine's interpretation of Gal. 2:11–14 was correct.[34] In his view, although Augustine apparently had the last word in the argument, he never answered the chief point of Jerome's objections. Jerome was arguing, he claims, that the *character* of Peter's action (in observing the Judaic Law) was simulated, while Augustine asked whether or not his *motive* was truthful. This defense gives more nuance to Jerome's argument than does Jerome himself, who in any case later endorsed in his *Contra Pelagianos* the interpretation for which Augustine had argued. It also presupposes that Scripture can contain falsehoods, but Overbeck does not give any guidelines on how to determine what in Scripture is false and what true. Overbeck's support for Jerome's theological interpretation is followed by Grützmacher (1908), who nevertheless gives the credit to Augustine for keeping the argument as civil as it was.[35] In response to Möhler's "Auch große Männer können Streit anfangen," he writes: "Gewiß ist das richtig; aber das Verdienst, daß der Streit nicht in häßliches Gezänk ausartete, gebührt in erster Linie der herzlichen Liebenswürdigkeit, vornehmen Ritterlichkeit und aufrichtigen Bescheidenheit Augustins."[36] The theological positions of Overbeck and Grützmacher were never followed by later scholars,[37] and, similarly, Grützmacher's view that Augustine's chivalry and modesty were chiefly responsible for keeping the dispute from degenerating into a bitter squabble found disfavor among Möhler's followers[38] and was overlooked by later scholars.

An important study undertaken by Dorsch (1911) documents the developments of Augustine's and Jerome's philosophies of biblical exegesis and shows that in his interpretation of Gal. 2:11–14 Jerome had gone against the philosophy he had presented to Pope Damasus, that Scripture cannot contain something that is not true.[39]

Among the more recent specialized studies of the correspondence between Jerome and Augustine is Cole-Turner's (1980), in which he traces the chronological development of Augustine's argument against Jerome's interpretation of Gal. 2:11–14 and shows that it parallels his anti-heretical writings against the Manichees, Donatists, and Pelagians. Jamieson (1987) argues that Augustine's request for a Stesichoran palinode predisposed Jerome against Augustine, since Rufinus had requested the same of Jerome after accusing him of heresy. She points out how Augustine, who would have understood the ire his allusion had caused only after reading the *Apologia contra Rufinum* that Jerome had sent, employed rhetorical techniques to win back Jerome's respect and trust. In 1990 White published the first complete English translation of the correspondence with a limited but helpful commentary, while in 1994 Hennings published an analysis of the first stage of the correspondence, thoroughly documenting patristic precedents on the issues raised.[40]

Among general treatments of the controversy after 1940 is Semple's (1950). His investigation of "the clash between their temperaments and attitudes" unabashedly reveals Jerome's vindictiveness and readiness to take offense.[41] He shows that while Augustine is ready to admit his own faults and to apologize to Jerome for unintended mistakes, Jerome emphasizes Augustine's faults while minimizing his own. Semple's observations are central to the differences between the two saints over criticism within friendship, but he himself does not make this clear.[42]

Bonner (1963) refers briefly to the correspondence between Jerome and Augustine in his book on Augustine's life and controversies.[43] He gives as chief reason for the "misunderstandings" between Jerome and Augustine the difficulties in relying on private carriers to convey letters in the conditions of late antiquity, but he also writes that Augustine's language was "tactless." Citing *Contra Pelagianos* 1.22, in which Jerome follows Augustine's interpretation of Gal. 2:11–14, Bonner oddly maintains that it is unclear whether Jerome ever came to agree with Augustine.

Brown (1967),when discussing the correspondence between Jerome and Augustine in his biography of Augustine, characterizes both men as exhibiting "elaborate gestures of humility," "showing their claws" in their use of classical allusions, and refusing to "give an inch" to each other's point of view.[44] Brown furthermore claims that "there is no doubt that Augustine provoked Jerome" without discussing Augustine's motivation and intentions, and Brown asserts that Augustine was "anxious to be innocent of his own aggressive behaviour" in "declar[ing] himself always ready to accept criticism." Such a cynical assessment of Augustine's honesty in his dealings with Jerome would seem to require proof, but Brown offers none.[45]

Kelly (1975) treats the controversy in his study of Jerome's life and writings. He describes Augustine as "pompous" at one point but gives a balanced narration of the correspondence between Augustine and Jerome, admitting the "hostile insinuations, distrust, cantankerousness" of Jerome's *Epp.* 102 and 105, and concludes, "What he yearned for in their relationship, [Augustine] insisted emphatically, was not simply mutual love, but that freedom of speech without which true friendship is impossible."[46]

O'Connell (1979) attempts a diplomatic balance between the views of Brown and Kelly. While Brown, he contends, is "gentler to Jerome than to Augustine," Kelly "shows more kindness to Augustine than to Jerome. It may just be that there are dangers, for a man of contemporary sensibility, in getting too 'close' to either of these volcanic individuals." Nevertheless, O'Connell follows what, as he acknowledges, Brown implies, and he thus speaks of the "bully" in Augustine.[47]

V. Augustine's Regard for Frankness in Human Relations

The most accurate assessment of the interpersonal relations between Jerome and Augustine is surely Grützmacher's, for he writes that we owe it to Augustine's chivalry and modesty that the dispute did not degenerate into a bitter squabble.[48] It is Augustine who pleads that Jerome and he be able to conduct a friendship that does not suffer injury or envy when one corrects the other (*Ep.* 73.3.9) but who at the same time admits that Jerome may justly feel injury for something Augustine unwittingly said:

> Nec omnino arbitror te suscensere potuisse, nisi aut hoc dicerem, quod non debui, aut non sic dicerem, ut debui, quia nec miror minus nos scire invicem, quam scimur a coniunctissimis et familiarissimis nostris.[49]

> I certainly do not think that you could have got angry unless I said something which I ought not to have or did not say it in the way I ought to have, for it is not surprising that we know each other less well than we are known to our closest and most intimate friends.

Furthermore, Augustine became more cautious with Jerome after the misplacement of *Ep.* 40. In about 410, Jerome wrote to Marcellinus and Anapsychia that it would be easier for them to learn his own views on the creation of souls if they simply consulted Augustine, who was closer at hand (*Ep.* 165). When Augustine learned of this, he responded (*Ep.* 190) that, being unsure himself in this matter, Jerome should express his views in a letter to Augustine. When Jerome had still not responded eight years later, Augustine refused to betray any of the contents of his

Ep. 190, in which he had outlined several alternatives for explaining the creation of souls. "This book," he writes, " . . . can be read at my house, but it ought not to be sent anywhere or given to anyone outside, unless when, the Lord helping, I have received an answer about what he thinks."[50] Jerome, on the other hand, refused to the end to engage in candid discussion, proffering one excuse after another. He suggests that the appearance of disagreement would lend their mutual enemies ammunition against them; he complains that he has no time to respond to Augustine or that he lacks stenographers; he writes that rather than state his own opinion he prefers to praise Augustine. Although Jerome eventually took up Augustine's interpretation of the Incident at Antioch, it was by indirect means that Augustine learned of it, for Jerome did not admit openly to this change of opinion.[51] The deeper problem in the dispute between Jerome and Augustine, which Kelly correctly identifies, namely, that freedom of speech is a necessary element of friendship, was never resolved.

It is one of the central aspects of Augustine's thought that disagreement can exist within friendship. In his *Confessions* Augustine cites in a catalogue of the many pleasures of friendship the ability of friends to accept and give criticism:

> simul legere libros dulciloquos, simul nugari et simul honestari, dissentire interdum sine odio tamquam ipse homo secum atque ipsa rarissima dissensione condire consensiones plurimas, docere aliquid invicem aut discere ab invicem. (*Conf.* 4.8.13–14)

> to read sweet books together; to joke together and to be serious together; to disagree at times without offense as a man might disagree with himself, and from that most infrequent disagreement to produce very many agreements; to teach something to each other and to learn from each other.

Friends will naturally, if infrequently, disagree, but their disagreements are without spite, and the disagreements themselves yield many more agreements. It is in this way that friends instruct each other, for disagreement, it seems, is closely related to mutual instruction. Yet in order to progress from disagreement to agreement, one friend must correct the other–he must be frank with his friend. True Christian friendship, indeed, requires frankness. Augustine, we may recall, when he disputed Jerome's interpretation of Gal. 2:11–14 and asked Jerome to sing a palinode, urged his friend to correct his view by taking up a severity that was mixed with love (*caritas*), one that was Christian and *ingenua*, frank (*Ep.* 40.4.7).[52]

One ought, then, according to Augustine, to teach one's friend when appropriate, and this necessarily includes candidly pointing out a friend's error. Interestingly, we note that Augustine elsewhere extends the duty of frankness beyond friendship to human relations in general. Augustine, in writing of one's duty to reprove the sinner in *De civitate dei*, explains that, while no one is free from sin, good men must not evade their responsibility to correct the sinner.[53] Correcting others and subjecting oneself to correction, or teaching and learning, are not to be confined to friendship alone but ought to be practiced among all so that others may aim at life eternal.

The aim of friendship and, indeed, of all human relations, after all, is the attainment of God. In his *De doctrina christiana* (1.22.20–1.23.22), Augustine writes that it is not right to enjoy another person. People cannot truly be enjoyed because they are subject to change and error. God alone can be enjoyed, and the people He created can help lead others to Him. Thus, properly speaking, we use, rather than enjoy, other people, for the sake of loving and enjoying God. In his opening letter to Jerome, Augustine writes that, by sharing with each other their common pursuit of Scriptural studies, it is Christ (not the one or the other of them) who will "supply us generously with many benefits and provisions . . . for the journey which he has revealed to us."[54]

Augustine's conception of Christian friendship and the importance in all human relationships, but particularly within friendship, of frank, mutual correction are not simply abstract ideas, for Augustine conducts himself according to his principles. People who had never met or previously corresponded with Augustine sent questions to which he provided lengthy and detailed replies, even as his duties increased as he became a priest in 391 and a bishop in 395.[55] Many of Augustine's works, in fact, are responses to questions posed by his various correspondents. The composition of *De haeresibus* was prompted by Quodvultdeus' insistence for a list of all heresies in existence (*Epp.* 221, 223), and it is well known that the composition of his *De civitate dei* was prompted by his correspondence with Marcellinus and Volusianus (*Epp.* 135–138), who objected to Christianity on the grounds that it had caused the fall of the Roman Empire.

Augustine's zeal for truth, however, is not tainted by that personal investment in the outcome of an argument that lesser men often have. Rather than return personal attack in his disputes with pagans, for example, he argues point by point to specific objections. Of particular interest is the example of *Ep.* 17 to Maximus, a grammarian in Madaura, whose defense of paganism includes expressions of disdain for Christian martyrs and the Christian cult. Although he doubts Maximus' desire to engage in serious discussion,[56] Augustine provides a full response to the points Maximus raises. He is equally ready to assist others in their discussions with pagans, as, for example, in *Ep.* 102, in which he responds at length to questions that were posed to Deogratias by a pagan friend, and in *Ep.* 138, in which he responds to questions posed to Marcellinus by unbelievers on such subjects as the Incarnation.

Similarly, in his correspondence with Donatist leaders, it appears that Augustine wished their conversion to come about as a result of sober reflection and the conviction of the superiority of the arguments in favor of orthodoxy.[57] To this end, it is particularly noteworthy that he wishes to avoid crowds in this debate, especially in light of his renowned effectiveness as a public speaker.[58] Instead, he insists that frank, open discourse requires the absence of distracting spectators. For instance, in *Epp.* 43 and 44, Augustine suggests a quiet countryside as the venue for open discussion rather than a public square. In *Ep.* 49 to the Donatist bishop Honoratus, Augustine approves of a plan to carry on an epistolary debate to settle theological differences, "where no disturbance of the crowds can disrupt our debate, which ought to be undertaken and conducted with all peace and gentleness of mind."[59] He furthermore insists on Scripture, rather than the opinions of himself or his Donatist opponents, as the basis for the truths they should hold.

Finally, Augustine seeks candid criticism of his own views. He asks the little-known Caelestinus (*Ep.* 18) to give his frank impression of his books against the Manichees and to tell Augustine what "armor" he thinks is needed to overcome Manichaeism.[60] But Augustine does not seek criticism solely in order to oppose unorthodox views more effectively; he also does so in order to advance his own understanding of theology. He takes the opportunity to ask Simplicianus, his former instructor at Milan, for correction once he learns that Simplicianus is reading his writings. When Simplicianus requests that Augustine assist him in turn, Augustine agrees on condition that he pray for Augustine's weakness and that he read carefully and undertake to correct his writings, both those written specifically for Simplicianus and any others that Simplicianus might read.[61]

VI. Conclusions

Augustine's view of human relations and his regard for truth provided him with the insight to argue for the literal interpretation of Gal. 2:11–14. The duty of frankness allows disagreement to exist in the context of Christian friendship, and, in a wider sense, among Christians and all good men. Disagreement should not be misinterpreted as a sign of broken or weak relations. Instead, it signals an opportunity for faults to be laid open, confronted, and set right–for the person correcting to be a means of advancement in holiness for the person who is corrected.

When Paul rebuked Peter at Antioch, Peter *vere correctus est et Paulus vera narravit* (*Ep.* 40.4.5). Because Paul spoke the truth and rightly corrected Peter's hypocrisy, Paul cannot be faulted. Clearly, Augustine understood the broad implications of Jerome's interpretation of the Incident at Antioch: if Peter and Paul dissimulated, then Scripture justifies lying, and how then can Scripture be believed? But Augustine's acceptance of the literal meaning of Paul's words also necessarily supports the rightness of Paul's open rebuke of Peter. I consider the Incident at Antioch, then, to be an instance of Paul's own frankness toward his Christian brother.[62] It is this frankness, this open rebuke, that is problematic for Jerome, who worries about defending the Church's earliest leaders against the criticism of Porphyry. For Augustine, such frankness would be a natural part of the relationship between the two apostles, two friends in Christ.

Augustine's and Jerome's attitudes toward frankness, manifested already in their differing interpretations of Paul's rebuke of Peter, inevitably affected their own relationship. Augustine's devotion to truth and insistence on frankness as an obligation of Christian friendship made Augustine a demanding correspondent, as evidenced by his persistent attempts to obtain responses from Jerome, even until Jerome's death, on problems he found difficult to solve. This persistence must be interpreted in the context of Augustine's understanding of Christian friendship. Möhler and his followers see too much humility in Jerome. Augustine may have required this humility of a true friend, but he certainly did not receive it from Jerome. It is, rather, Augustine who evidences humility in his own willingness to receive, as well as to give, candid criticism. Perhaps Möhler's parallel between Jerome's late acceptance of Augustine's interpretation of Gal. 2:11–14 and Peter's humble acceptance of Paul's rebuke ought instead to be revised into a parallel between Augustine's and Paul's similar frankness in pursuit of the truth. Grützmacher, correct in observing that Augustine's chivalry and modesty kept his relations with Jerome civil, fails to notice that, although the maintenance of civility was one of Augustine's priorities (cf., for example, *Ep.* 82.5.36), his higher purpose was to determine answers to specific theological problems, because solving these problems brings men closer to God. Jamieson is too narrow in her assessment of Augustine: while rhetorical strategy figures prominently in all of Augustine's writings, it is not his primary concern when he faces such a fundamental question as the veracity of Scripture. Bonner gives too little credit to Augustine's concern for truth when he characterizes Augustine's language as "tactless." Nevertheless, in the preface to the second edition of his book Bonner rightly emphasizes the need to understand Augustine in all the facets of his personality and thought, and he consequently reveals the weakness in Brown's influential general treatment of Augustine:

> It is . . . important to remember Brown's self-imposed limitation: ". . . I am acutely aware that I have been led along the side of a mountain-face: I found myself, for instance, above the plains of Augustine's routine duties as a bishop, and far below the heights of his speculation on the Trinity" [Brown, p. 9]. The problem here, I have come increasingly to feel . . . is that it is precisely the plains and heights which between them give the true measure of the man. It is the combination of parochial concern and theological speculation, of action and contemplation, which make the saint; for whatever Augustine was, he was never average.[63]

In my view, Bonner points to the the precise difficulty of evaluating the participants in this controversy. It is the combination of humble frankness, theological acumen, and dedication to truth that characterizes Augustine's side of the correspondence. Brown, as was observed earlier, describes Augustine and Jerome as exhibiting "elaborate gestures of humility," "showing their claws" in their use of classical allusions, and refusing to "give an inch" to each other's point of view. While this may be true of the irascible Jerome (on this point Semple's earlier contribution is to be commended), it is not at all true of Augustine, whose humility is deeper than gestures, who uses only one classical allusion (and with many qualifications), and who reaches some agreement with Jerome on translating from the Hebrew. Likewise, Brown is unjustifiably suspicious of Augustine's willingness to benefit from criticism.[64] Because he valued truth, and because the frank correction of error enables one to pursue truth more effectively and therefore to progress in holiness, Augustine not only expected to correct others but also hoped that he would himself be corrected.

Studies such as Cole-Turner's do the greatest justice to Augustine's concern for the frank discussion of theological problems, since he shows that important questions that Augustine discusses in his correspondence with Jerome are present at the same time in Augustine's other works. And while Kelly recognizes that Augustine considered frankness to be an essential part of friendship and White is aware of the intimate connection between friendship and the theological disputes in the correspondence,[65] one can still go further. Augustine's insistence on frankness in his relations with Jerome can also be seen active in his interpretation of Gal. 2:11–14. How else than with candor and honesty could St. Paul have acted at Antioch and written his inspired letter to the Galatians?

Moreover, because Augustine's dispute with Jerome over the interpretation of the Incident at Antioch integrates theological speculation and Augustine's own understanding of human relations, the dispute may be seen as a microcosm of Augustinian thought. Augustine approached Scripture just as he engaged in personal relationships, with the intention of obtaining truth and advancing in holiness. His thought is unsystematic, but its consistency reveals itself when Augustine's private beliefs and behavior are examined together with his theological writings, as in the case of Augustine's relationship with Jerome and his interpretation of Gal. 2:11–14.[66]

NOTES

1. I thank Professor E. TeSelle, Professor W. Race, and Mrs. J. Barr for reading portions of this paper at an early stage of its composition, as well as Professor D. Kries and Dr. C. Tkacz for their guidance at a later stage. Unless otherwise indicated, the translations in this paper are mine.

2. The lost letters are: a greeting from Augustine sent prior to Jerome's *Ep.* 103; Jerome's response to it; and another letter to which Jerome responds in *Ep.* 105. See C. White, *The Correspondence (394–419) between Jerome and Augustine of Hippo* (New York, 1990), pp. 23 and 82 for a list of the letters and their dates. The edition of the correspondence used in this paper is that of J. Schmid, ed., *SS. Eusebii Hieronymi et Aurelii Augustini epistulae mutuae*, Florilegium Patristicum tam veteris quam medii aevi auctores complectens, fasc. 22 (Bonn, 1930).

3. Augustine's *Ep.* 166 was devoted to the origin of the human soul. In *Ep.* 167 Augustine asked Jerome to critique his interpretation of James 2:10. Jerome responded with *Ep.* 134.

4. Augustine, *Ep.* 71.3.5; cf. Jerome, *Ep.* 112.6.21. The word that caused the uproar was "ivy" in place of "gourd" in Jonah 4:6–10. The congregation was probably familiar with the *Vetus Latina*: see White, *Correspondence*, 94.

5. The extent to which these converts observed Jewish Law is uncertain, but according to Paul they were unable to observe it in its entirety (see, e.g., Gal. 6:13).

6. Paul was responding in particular to the unauthorized preaching of Judaizing Christians to his communities. See Acts 15:24; Gal. 1:6; 3:1–3; 5:7; 6:12. For the Council of Jerusalem, see Acts 15:1–29 and Gal. 2:1–10.

7. Acts 10:9–16; cf. Acts 11:4–10.

8. See J. B. Lightfoot, *Commentary on Galatians,* 10th ed. (London, 1890), 61; Schmid, *Epistulae*, 14–16. Both give treatments of the history of the exegesis of the Incident at Antioch up to the time of Augustine and Jerome.

9. Tertullian, *Adv. Marc.* 1.20 and 5.3; *De praescr.* 100. 23; cf. Irenaeus, *Adv. haer.* 3.12.15 (cited in Lightfoot, *Commentary*, 129, n. 2).

10. *Hom. Clem.* 17, 19. See Lightfoot, *Commentary*, 329.

11. A. B. Hulen, *Porphyry's Work Against the Christians: an Interpretation* (Scotdale, PA, 1933), reconstructs the evidence for this treatise, the Κατὰ Χριστιανῶν. For the fragments, see A. von Harnack, *Porphyrius, "Gegen die Christen," 15 Bücher: Zeugnisse, Fragmente und Referate*, Abhandlungen der königlichen preussischen Akademie der Wissenschaften, Phil.-hist. Klasse 1 (Berlin, 1916).

12. Jerome probably composed this work in 387–88: J. N. D. Kelly, *Jerome: His Life, Writings, and Controversies* (London, 1975), 145.

13. *Comm. in ep. ad Gal.* 371–372 (PL 26.310C–311A). Incidentally, Jerome is our only source for this argument by Porphyry. His other references to it are at *Comm. in ep. ad Gal.* 409 (PL 26.341); *Ep.* 112.6.11; and *In Isaiam* 15.54. See Hulen, *Porphyry's Work*, p. 45.

14. "Bataneotes" is probably a term of abuse (cf. R. Beutler, "Porphyrios [21]," RE 22.1 [1953], col. 276), referring to Porphyry's place of origin, Batanea, east of the Jordan River (cf. I. Benzinger, "Batanaia [1]," RE 3.1 [1897], cols. 115–17), though Porphyry was in fact from the cultured city of Tyre (Porphyry, "Vita Plotini" 7 and 20).

15. *Comm. in ep. ad Gal.* 407 (PL 26.339).

16. 1 Cor. 9.20, cited by Jerome in *Comm. in ep. ad Gal.* 407 (PL 26.399).

17. Augustine's experience with Manichaeism may have sensitized him to the dangers of this view.

18. *Ep.* 102.1; *Ep.* 105.1 and 2.4.

19. In *Ep.* 102.2 he alludes to the story of Dares and Entellus (Virgil, *Aen.* 5.368–464). In *Ep.* 105.2.3 he remarks that Q. Fabius Cunctator's patience outdid Hannibal's "youthful self-confidence," and, quoting from Virgil's *Ecl.* 9.51–54, he suggests that Augustine is a wolf driving him from his peaceful farm. Later, he cites the story of David and Goliath (*Ep.* 112.1.2). Although Jerome was probably about seventy when he wrote his letter in 402 (but see Kelly, *Jerome*, 337ff, for the difficulties in ascertaining Jerome's date of birth) Augustine was almost fifty.

20. Augustine, *Ep.* 73.1.1. In *Ep.* 67.2 Augustine protests against a rumor he has heard that someone told Jerome he had published a book against Jerome in Rome. Jerome, *Epp.* 102.1 and 105.1, comments that he has only received a copy of *Ep.* 40, and in *Ep.* 105.2.4 he writes that a letter that Augustine says he did not write is circulating throughout Italy.

21. This childhood friendship ended when it was shown that ideas contained in Origen's writings, which both Jerome and Rufinus had read avidly, were heretical. Jerome immediately renounced Origen, but Rufinus did not, and in 399, when the climate at Rome was rife with anti-Origenism, a bitter conflict between the two ensued. See Kelly, *Jerome,* 195–209 and 245ff.

22. Jerome refers to Eph. 6:13 and 14–17; 2 Chron. 26:19–20; 2 Cor. 12:14; 1 Chron. 12:17–18; Ps. 56:8–9 (57:7–8); 107:2–3 (108:1–2); 80:11 (81:10); and 67:12 (68:11) in *Ep.* 112.1.2.

23. Jerome's statement is the sole evidence that Origen first expounded this interpretation.

24. *Ep.* 112.3.4. Lightfoot, *Commentary,* 130, n. 3, points out that it is questionable whether Didymus, one of Jerome's teachers for a short time (cf. Kelly, *Jerome,* p. 75, n. 31; pp. 85 and 142–43) held this theory, "for in two passages in his extant works he speaks of St Peter's conduct as an instance of human infirmity, *De Trin.* 2. 13; 3. 19." In the same passage, Lightfoot also notes that another of Jerome's instructors, Gregory of Nazianzus, "had . . . attribut[ed] St Peter's error . . . not to cowardice but to mistaken policy, *Carm.* 2."

25. Jerome's *Ep.* 112.3.6, referring either to Chrysostom's commentary on Galatians (PG 61) or to his homily *In faciem ei restiti* (PG 51).

26. Augustine refers to Jerome's change of opinion in a letter to Oceanus (*Ep.* 130) without acknowledging his own authorship of the interpretation, attributing it instead to Cyprian. While Augustine's interpretation was accepted in the West almost immediately, it took approximately one hundred years for Greek exegetes to abandon Chrysostom's interpretation (Lightfoot, *Commentary,* 132 and n. 3).

27. J. A. Möhler, "Hieronymus und Augustinus im Streit über Gal. 2, 14," *Gesammelte Schriften und Aufsätze,* J. Döllinger, ed., vol. 1 (Regensburg, 1839), 1–18.

28. Möhler, *Gesammelte Schriften,* 5.

29. Lightfoot, *Commentary,* 132 and n. 1, shows sympathy toward this view.

30. Möhler, *Gesammelte Schriften,* 16.

31. P. Asslaber, *Die persönlichen Beziehungen der drei grossen Kirchenlehrer Ambrosius, Hieronymus und Augustinus,* Studien und Mitteilungen aus der kirchengeschichtlichen Seminar der Theol. Fak. der Universität in Wien, 3 (Vienna, 1908), 117.

32. R. Buchwald, "Augustinus und Hieronymus im Streit über Galater 2, 11ff," *Schlesisches Pastoralblatt* 41 (1920): 19–23. E. Malfatti, "Una controversia tra S. Agostino e S. Girolamo," *La Scuola Cattolica* 49, s. 5, v. 20 (1921): 321–338 and 402–426; see especially p. 426.

33. F. E. Tourscher, "The Correspondence of Saint Augustine and Saint Jerome: a Study," *American Ecclesiastic Review* 57 (1917): 476–492 and 58 (1918): 45–56. Tourscher also has equal regard for the theological positions of both, maintaining that though Jerome "piles up difficulties which seem at first to obscure the main issue . . . [he] proves . . . his power to take in at a glance the wider problems which the minor question about the text of

136 ANNE P. CARRIKER

St. Paul must surely comprehend" (pp. 490–491). Here Tourscher fails to understand that it is Augustine, not Jerome, who has the power to grasp the more important problems involved in the interpretation of Gal. 2:11–14.

34. F. Overbeck, *Über die Auffassung des Streits des Paulus mit Petrus in Antiochien (Gal. 2, 11ff.) bei den Kirchenvätern* (Basel, 1877).

35. G. Grützmacher, *Hieronymus*, 3 vols. (Leipzig, 1901–8). See especially 3: 134–35 and 134, n. 3.

36. Grützmacher, *Hieronymus*, 3: 136–37.

37. P. Auvray, "Saint Jérôme et Saint Augustin: la controverse de l'incident d'Antioch," *Recherches de science religeuse* 29 (1939): 594–610, however, may be excepted, since he argues that observation of the Law for the sake of appearance is legitimate because it is not a real observation and that Augustine's weakness was his inability to overcome a presupposition that a third element of dissimulation had to be involved, namely that of Paul in recording the episode in Galatians. But, like Overbeck and Grützmacher, Auvray fails to explain Jerome's eventual adherence to Augustine's interpretation.

38. A. Dufey, "Controverse entre S. Jérôme et S. Augustin d'après leurs lettres," *Revue du clergé francais* 25 (1901): 141–49, although he does not cite Grützmacher, portrays Augustine's attitude as consistently peace-seeking, while Jerome's attitude gradually became so.

39. A. Dorsch, "St. Augustinus und Hieronymus über die Wahrheit der biblischen Geschichte," *Zeitschrift für katholische Theologie* 35 (1911): 421–48; 601–64. Grützmacher, *Hieronymus*, 1: 211–12, also refers to this philosophy, but he does not point out its inconsistency with Jerome's interpretation of Gal. 2:11 ff, which he supports.

40. R. S. Cole-Turner, "Anti-heretical Issues and the Debate over Galatians 2.11–14 in the Letters of St. Augustine to St. Jerome," *Augustinian Studies* 11 (1980): 155–66; K. Jamieson, "Jerome, Augustine and the Stesichoran Palinode," *Rhetorica* 5 (1987): 353–67; R. Hennings, *Der Briefwechsel zwischen Augustinus und Hieronymus und ihr Streit um den Kanon des alten Testaments und die Auslegung von Gal. 2, 11–14*, Supplements to Vigiliae Christianae, 21 (Leiden, 1994). For White, see above note 2.

41. W. A. Semple, "Some Letters of St. Augustine," *Bulletin of the John Rylands Library* 33 (1950): 111–30; for the quotation, see p. 123.

42. Semple also vouches for a theological consistency in Augustine's interpretation of the Incident at Antioch and his reverence for the Septuagint because he grants "an absolute authority to the Canonical Scriptures" (p. 130). But, persuaded by Jerome, Augustine changed his attitude towards the Septuagint and not his interpretation. The consistency in Augustine in this correspondence lies in his objective reception of criticism and his application of it, if necessary, to his theological positions.

43. G. Bonner, *St. Augustine of Hippo: Life and Controversies* (Norwich, 1963; revised edition 1986); see especially 147–48.

44. P. Brown, *Augustine of Hippo* (Berkeley, 1967); see especially 274–75.

45. White, *Correspondence*, p. 3, observes, "[Augustine's] criticisms and questions are expressed in a polite and respectful, if firm manner, without the provocative or aggressive tone which Peter Brown appears to find in them."

46. Kelly, *Jerome*, 271 (in answer to Jerome's request that they not "sport in the field of Scripture"); p. 267; conclusion at p. 271.

47. R. J. O'Connell, "When Saintly Fathers Feuded: the Correspondence between Augustine and Jerome," *Thought* 54 (1979): 344–64; see especially 358, n. 7.

48. Grützmacher, *Hieronymus*, 3: 136–37.

49. *Ep.* 73.3.10. The translation is that of White, *Correspondence*, 108.

50. *Ep.* 190.21: *Qui liber meus . . . apud me legi potest; mitti vero uspiam non debet vel cuiquam foras dari, nisi cum rescripta domino adiuvante percepero id, quod ille sentit.*

51. Bonner, *St. Augustine*, 147, is wrong to state that we cannot know for certain that Jerome eventually endorsed Augustine's interpretation. By using Gal. 2:11–14 as an example of imperfection in a bishop, Jerome necessarily imputes fault to Peter, a contradiction of his earlier position. It is almost certain that Jerome never stated his change of opinion to Augustine, even though Augustine noticed Jerome's new position. In his *Ep.* 134 to Augustine, Jerome refers to the high praise with which he commended Augustine in the *Contra Pelagianos*. Since his re-evaluation of Peter's action is contained in the same *Contra Pelagianos*, he could, if he had wished, surely have mentioned this change of view with his reference to his praise of Augustine.

52. On the need for frankness in Augustine's conception of friendship, see Sister M. A. McNamara, *Friendship in Saint Augustine* (Fribourg, 1958), 207–10 (and cf. her *Friends and Friendship for Saint Augustine* [New York, 1964], 224–26), with additional evidence of this point in Augustine's writings. It is interesting that in the Christian idea of friendship *caritas* (ἀγάπη) often replaces the classical *amicitia* (φιλία): cf. D. Konstan, "Problems in the History of Friendship," *Journal of Early Christian Studies* 4 (1996): 97–106, on which is based his *Friendship in the Classical World* (Cambridge, 1997), 156–62. Like Augustine's view of Christian friendship, the ancient conception of friendship, at least since the Hellenistic period, demanded frankness: see Konstan, *Friendship*, 103–14.

53. *De civ. dei* 1.9. Augustine insists that Christians must even correct the godless.

54. Ep. 28.2.1: *. . . qui nobis multas utilitates et viatica quaedam demonstrati a se itineris . . . ministrare dignatur.* The translation is that of White, *Correspondence*, 66. Augustine also acknowledges here that Jerome is an instrument of Christ.

55. In 398, for example, Augustine answered some rather technical questions presented by a certain Publicola, such as whether a starving Christian may eat food set out for idols (*Ep.* 47). In around 400 he provided a lengthy answer to the stenographer Januarius' query about why Christmas is on the same day each year, while the date of Easter changes (*Ep.* 55).

56. *Ep.* 17.5: *Disserentur ista latius ipso vero et uno deo adiuvante, cum te graviter agere velle cognovero.*

57. Cf. Bonner, *St. Augustine*, 259. It is true that Augustine eventually enlisted the use of force by secular authorities in order to convert Donatists, but it should be borne in mind that other issues governed this decision, such as the violent tactics of the Donatists themselves that endangered his own congregation. Also, it appears that force was used primarily against the rank and file, whom Augustine regarded as deceived by their leaders.

58. See, for example, Possidius, *Vita Aug.* 7 and 9.

59. *Ep.* 49.1: *. . . ubi nullus turbarum tumultus perturbare possit dispositionem nostram, quae cum tota pace et lenitate animi suscipienda et agenda est.*

60. *Ep.* 18.1: *Peto itaque, ne differatis eos remittere cum rescriptis, quibus nosse cupio, quid de illis geritis vel adhuc ad illum expugnandum quid armaturae vobis opus esse arbitremini.*

61. *Ep.* 37.3: *Tantum illud quaeso, ut pro infirmitate mea depreceris deum et sive in his, quibus me exercere benigne paterneque voluisti, sive in aliis, quaecumque nostra in tuas sanctas manus forte pervenerint, quia sicut dei data sic etiam mea errata cogito, non solum curam legentis inpendas, sed etiam censuram corrigentis adsumas.*

62. Note D. E. Fredrickson, "Παρρησία in the Pauline Epistles," *Friendship, Flattery, and Frankness of Speech: Studies on Friendship in the New Testament World,* J. T. Fitzgerald, ed., Supplements to Novum Testamentum, 82 (Leiden, 1996), 163–83, for the evidence of Paul's frankness at Phlm. 8–9; 1 Thess. 2:1–12; Phil. 1:12–20; and 2 Cor. 1–7.

63. Bonner, *St. Augustine of Hippo,* 2.

64. See, for example, Brown, *Augustine,* 274–75, citing *Ep.* 73.1.1: "Like many people anxious to be innocent of his [sic] own aggressive behaviour, Augustine declared himself always ready to accept criticism: 'Here I am, and in whatever I have spoken amiss, tread firmly on me'." Curiously, Brown earlier links this, to him, anxiety to be innocent of aggression to Augustine's imperfect parents: "Augustine was the son of a violent father, and of a relentless mother. He could uphold what he considered objective truth with notable innocence of his own aggressiveness: he will, for instance, badger the elderly and eminent Jerome in a singularly humourless and tactless manner" (p. 208).

65. For example, White (*Correspondence,* 3) explains that the dispute over the interpretation of the Incident at Antioch "caused Jerome to display much fury and sarcasm and Augustine great tact and determination in his desire to establish friendly relations with this man and to enlist his help in grappling with a number of Scriptural problems."

66. See, similarly, Bonner, *St. Augustine,* 8: "The interrelation between Augustine's life and thought seems to me to be one of the crucial elements in contemporary Augustinian studies."

Virgil, Daniel, and Augustine's Dialogic Pedagogy in *De Magistro*

Douglas Kries
Gonzaga University

In our time, philosophers usually write treatises. Sometimes the treatises are lengthy and constitute an entire monograph; usually they are shorter and constitute an article or an essay. In any case, the work is characterized by its transparency. The author does not hint at the teaching but comes right out and says it. The contemporary philosophical treatise has all the tact and subtlety of a three-year old child who innocently asks the most embarrassing questions and blurts out the most impertinent remarks. In antiquity, philosophers frequently wrote in the more opaque genre of the dialogue—a genre much more reserved in the expression of the author's views than the treatise. Plato's dialogues are of course the finest and most famous fruits of that genre, yet Aristotle also wrote dialogues, and Cicero transported this form of philosophical expression into the Latin world. Although we would like to have more information on the matter, it was apparently from Cicero that the young Augustine learned about the genre of the dialogue.

Through the dialogue, the careful author can ask the deepest questions and teach the most sublime truths; however, a dialogue is anything but transparent. The dialogue respects the differences between readers. It often appears opaque to less able or less diligent readers, but it delivers hints, allusions, gentle suggestions, and individual pieces of a puzzle that lead the curious and inquiring toward the most profound considerations. Rather than stating its most lofty teachings forthrightly before a soul that does not yet appreciate the true, the dialogue first seeks to turn the potential knower toward the true. While revealing its teachings to the best readers, it also masks or veils them from the unworthy or unprepared.

Because of its concern with language analysis and semiotics, Augustine's *De magistro* has received at least its fair share of attention among twentieth-century philosophers.[1] Nevertheless, most contemporary approaches to the dialogue read it as though it were a treatise, focussing simply on the content of the arguments, taking statements out of their conversational context, and more or less ignoring the dynamics of the dialogic structure.[2] Yet Ernest Fortin suggests that a very different approach is necessary for understanding the teaching of Augustine's dialogues, claiming that "Until the zetetic quality of these dialogues is fully appreciated and explored, it is doubtful whether the mystery that they pose can be resolved in a completely satisfactory manner."[3] The adjective "zetetic" is derived from ζήτησις—a discussion, an investigation, an inquiry, or a seeking. Despite all the attention given to Augustine's dialogues over the past century, their zetetic quality has not been sufficiently appreciated. Only if *De magistro* is read precisely as a dialogue will it be properly understood, for the work has a coherence and poignancy that is otherwise overlooked. The magisterial way in which Augustine constructs and comments upon the dialogic structure of the *De magistro* points to the meaning of the work as a whole, and the key quotations from Virgil and Daniel point to that same meaning—if one pays attention to the contexts that the quotations invoke. Indeed, the teaching of the dialogue extends far beyond a crabbed theory of signs and points to the whole role of poetics in Christianity. In order to explain these aspects of the dialogue, it is best to begin with a consideration of the position occupied by *De magistro* in the corpus of Augustine's works.

I. The Position of *De magistro* among Augustine's Dialogues

Roughly speaking, Augustine seems to have been most captivated by the genre of the dialogue from about the time of his conversion until around the time of his ordination to the priesthood. Certainly, he used other forms of literary expression during this period, but the dialogue seems to have been his favorite. *Perhaps* one could argue that the *Confessions* preserves a vestige of the dialogue genre in the form of Augustine's conversations with God, especially since the *Confessions* has a certain kinship to the *Soliloquia*, but it seems more accurate to say that the *Confessions* is a genre unto itself, and that a short time prior to his becoming bishop and beginning to write the *Confessions* Augustine discarded the dialogue and never returned to it. Augustine the bishop devoted himself to other genres: polemical writings, catechetical writings, sermons, and theological treatises. Somehow the dialogue was no longer an appropriate voice for him.

Unfortunately, Augustine does not tell us—at least not directly—what prompted him to pursue this genre originally, nor does he tell us—again, at least not directly—what prompted him to abandon it. It is clear that his use of the dialogue corresponded more or less to the period of his life in which he was fascinated with the liberal arts as an instrument for turning the soul away from the corporeal and toward the incorporeal—*a corporalibus ad incorporalis,* or *per corporalia . . . ad incorporalia,* as he puts it in the *Retractationes.*[4] B. Darrell Jackson notes,

> In Augustine's own intellectual development one of the major stumbling blocks to his acceptance of Christian doctrines had been that he could not conceive of anything incorporeal. Right after his conversion he seems to have thought that the

liberal arts could be useful in training the mind to conceive of the incorporeal and hence of God.[5]

The tradition of the liberal arts has its origin in a dialogue, particularly Book VII of the *Republic*, and it continued to be associated frequently with that genre. Though Augustine had been engaged in studying the liberal arts, or at least some of them, since his early reading of the *Hortensius*, he explains in the *Retractationes* that, around the time of his conversion and baptism, he had conceived of a grand project to write on each of them. The only one of these *disciplinarum libri* that was actually completed was *De musica*—written in the form of a dialogue.[6] The *De magistro*, concerned as it is with the early education of Adeodatus, is replete with discussions of grammar and contains echoes of dialectic as well. Hence, it is not hard to see some sort of connection between it and Augustine's general concern with the liberal arts.[7]

Although this concern with the arts is not unique to *De magistro*, in several other ways, *De magistro* is unique among Augustine's dialogues. For starters, the title of the work is different from the titles of the other dialogues. Most of Augustine's titles name the subject matter of the dialogue: *De beata vita, De ordine, De quantitate animae, De libero arbitrio, De musica,* and so forth. The *De magistro*, on the other hand, has a title that names an occupation, a person who does something. One is reminded of the titles of two of Plato's dialogues, the *Statesman* and the *Sophist*, but of course there is no reason to think that Augustine knew those dialogues. The title of the *De magistro* also reminds one immediately of the title of Clement of Alexandria's *Pedagogue*, but even though both works speak about Christ as the true teacher, there is no reason to assert that Augustine was familiar with Clement's work, which is not, after all, even a dialogue. The reader eventually learns that Augustine's title is intentionally mysterious. Although the reader wonders from the outset who the teacher is or what the teacher does, the question is not directly addressed until the final section of the work.

The *De magistro* is also unique in that it seems to have been the final dialogue that Augustine began. From the initial chapters of Book I of the *Retractationes*, it seems that the geographical locations in which the dialogues were composed are basically threefold. First, there are the four dialogues associated with the time spent at Cassiciacum in 386–87, just prior to Augustine's baptism: *De beata vita, De ordine, Contra academicos,* and *Soliloquia*. A second group is associated with conversations involving Evodius that occurred in Rome in 387–88, following the death of Monica: *De quantitate animae* and *De libero arbitrio*. Augustine explains in the *Retractationes* that only the first book of *De libero arbitrio* was actually completed in Rome. Thirdly, there were the dialogues composed in Africa, following Augustine's return there in 388. The titles associated with this time period are *De libero arbitrio, De musica,* and *De magistro*. However, *De libero arbitrio* was, as has just been noted, begun in Rome, and the *De musica* was originally conceived as part of Augustine's treatment of the whole of the liberal arts. This project was begun prior to his baptism, even though the books on music were not actually written until after the return to Africa. Thus, even though both the *De musica* and the final two books of the *De libero arbitrio* were finished after *De magistro*, which is thought to have been composed in 389, *De magistro* seems to have been the only dialogue with roots in conversations that occurred in Africa, and it therefore seems to have been the last one begun. This accords with Augustine's view of the matter as it is preserved in the *Retractationes*, which treats both *De libero arbitrio* and *De musica* prior to treating the *De magistro*. The ordering of the dialogues in the *Retractationes* is particularly significant because Augustine goes out of his way to explain at the end of the prologue of that work that he will list his books in their appropriate order so that readers can survey the progress of his thought.

The dialogic form and the interlocutors of *De magistro* also separate it from the other dialogues. First, the *De magistro* is not a narrated dialogue like the Cassiciacum dialogues; it does not tell us when or where the conversation took place, nor does the dialogue recount any of the circumstances surrounding it. Rather, the dialogue is performed, which seems to have been Augustine's preference after the Cassiciacum works. The initial words of *De magistro* are Augustine's query to Adeodatus, and the conversation simply begins.

Secondly, the interlocutors of *De magistro* are unique. It is generally the case with ancient dialogues that the chief interlocutor (Socrates, Scipio, Augustine, etc.) converses with a less-sophisticated interlocutor. According to the *Confessions*, the *De magistro* is based on the sorts of conversations Augustine had with Adeodatus when the latter was a youth of only sixteen.[8] Thus, we cannot expect that Augustine will discuss thoroughly and profoundly the most sublime truths he knows with Adeodatus. Even though the *Confessions* testifies that Adeodatus was a most talented youth, the conversation of the *De magistro* is not between equals. Neither are the conversations of the other dialogues, but the junior partner in *De magistro* is unique, for this is the only dialogue in which Augustine speaks exclusively and extensively with Adeodatus. Adeodatus appears briefly in the Cassiciacum conversations, but here he is the sole discussant with Augustine. The commentator thus needs to keep in mind that it is possible that what Augustine needs to say to Adeodatus may differ from what he needs to say to Evodius or the other interlocutors.

Finally, Augustine's treatment of the *De magistro* in the *Retractationes* is unique in that he does not make any corrections or qualifications concerning the teaching of the dialogue. Apparently referring to the Cassiciacum dialogues, he says in the prologue of the *Retractationes* that his first works were written when, although a catechumen, he was still puffed up with pride in secular learning. He states that those works can be read with profit and he commends them to his readers, but only with qualifications. He also makes corrections to the dialogues associated with Evodius and Rome, but he seems satisfied with the *De magistro* just as it is.

II. The Dialogic Structure of *De magistro*

Scrutiny of the surface structure of the dialogue's conversation—as opposed to its doctrinal content—demonstrates rather clearly that the dialogue can be divided into three parts that are separated from each other by two transitional passages.[9] A summary of the preceding part is found in both of the transitional passages. The first part of the dialogue (1.1–6.18) raises the problem of moving from signs to the things signified by the signs and then explores the category of signs that signify other signs. In the first transitional passage (7.19–8.22), Adeodatus is asked to summarize the teaching of the first part, which he does in great detail, although he almost forgets to mention the class of reciprocal signs. Augustine approves of Adeodatus's memory and reassures him that, although they are proceeding along a roundabout way (*ambages*) that might make it seem as though they are pursuing childish little questions (*pueriles quaestiunculae*), in fact he has a most important and sublime destination in mind, namely, the truth. The discussion, he says, has not been aiming at *vilia ludicra* and he asks Adeodatus to pardon him for his initial playing around (*praeludere*), but he plays (*ludere*) in order to exercise the powers and sharpness of the mind (*exercendi vires et mentis aciem*). Such playful exercise is necessary to prepare them for the blessed life, but it is best to move by stages because of their weak step (*infirmus gressus nostrus*). In this transitional section, then, Augustine the author is explaining to the reader—even while Augustine the interlocutor is explaining to Adeodatus—that the conversation, while appearing playful and rambling, is being carefully constructed with a definite and lofty purpose in mind. This transitional passage alone should warn the interpreter not to read the dialogue as a treatise.

The second part of the dialogue (8.22–10.30) returns directly to the issue of the realities signified by the signs. The problem of the "gap" between signs and the things they signify is paramount, and the interlocutors compound the problem by stating that even though knowledge of the realities signified by the signs is more valuable than the knowledge of the signs, it seems impossible to teach such knowledge without the signs. In the transitional section following the second part (10.31), Augustine again asks for a summary of the preceding part but provides a brief sketch of it himself, referring to its circuitous route (*circuitus*) along which the interlocutors have been throwing about words (*inter nos verba iaculamur*). Adeodatus admits that they have been travelling along circumlocutions and bends (*ambages atque anfractus*), but Augustine applauds him for his cautious attitude of mind in not accepting arguments too quickly, for if the arguments one has accepted are always dissolving and changing, the result will eventually be a kind of hatred and fear of reason (*in tantum odium vel timorem rationis*). Thus, whereas in the first transition Augustine says that his purpose has been to exercise the mind of Adeodatus with the circuitous questioning, now he is concerned that such questioning might eventually make Adeodatus hate argumentation.

Given what he has just said, the reader is not surprised that Augustine begins the third part of the dialogue (10.32–14.46) by saying that he will now expedite matters. He straightaway goes back on the position reached earlier that it was virtually impossible to teach anything without the use of signs. In fact, he now argues that human beings learn all sorts of things without the help of any signs whatsoever. Signs themselves do not teach us anything at all, but only by consulting the interior teacher, Christ, can human beings actually be said to learn. The fundamental paradox of the dialogue—that we can learn nothing without signs, but that we learn everything that we learn without signs—is resolved when one grasps that the ground of all knowing is not simply the sign, but that the sign is known only after the reality is known through consulting the inner light of truth. The form of this final part of the dialogue is most unusual in that the dialogic form is almost abandoned in favor of a monologue by Augustine, whose *oratio continua* fills up virtually all of this section. At the very end of the work Augustine asks Adeodatus if he approves of Augustine's monopolizing the conversation, and the student responds in the affirmative. In this way, Augustine the author calls attention to the fact that the conversational style of the dialogue has been abandoned—a procedure apparently required because of the concern, mentioned at the end of the second part, about excessive playing with arguments leading to hatred of reason.

Thus, it seems that the first two parts of the dialogue are devoted to the construction of a central paradox or even contradiction, a contradiction that is resolved only in the third part. R.A. Markus has stated the basic problem posed by the dialogue rather nicely:

> The conclusion [of the second part of the work] that we cannot get to know the meaning of signs without knowing the realities they stand for appears to contradict the conclusion of the first part of the work, namely that we require signs in order that we may get to know things. But Augustine means both these positions to be taken quite seriously, and indeed reiterates the conclusions of the first part in the course of this argument. His thesis is precisely that no knowledge can either be acquired or communicated on the basis of the account so far given.[10]

Brian Stock articulates the dialogue's central contradiction more succinctly: "We cannot learn anything from anyone without the use of signs, [Augustine] points out, nor can we learn anything from anyone for certain by the use of signs alone."[11] The paradox created by the first two parts of the dialogue is only resolved by the doctrine of the inner teacher, which is introduced in the third section. We begin, then, to see the accuracy of Augustine's brief statement on *De magistro* in the *Retractationes* (I, 11), namely, that in this dialogue it is debated (*disputare*), sought (*quaerere*), and discovered (*invenire*), that God is the only teacher who teaches man knowledge. It would seem that the first parts of the dialogue are collectively devoted to the debating and the seeking, the third part to what is found or discovered.

III. Quoting Virgil

A skilled author of dialogues sometimes uses a quotation not only to illustrate the immediate point being made by the interlocutors in the course of their discussion, but a secondary and unstated point as well. The quotation is thus ambiguous, in that it has two meanings. Augustine's *De magistro* gives us an example of a masterful and brilliant use of this technique, but discerning the secondary point requires the interpreter to do more than merely name the source of the quotation.

The dialogue opens with Augustine asking Adeodatus about the purpose of using words, and it quickly reaches the position that words are signs that signify things. At this point (2.3), Augustine gives Adeodatus a line of eight words from Virgil (*Si nihil ex tanta superis placet urbe relinqui*; If nothing from such a city pleases the gods to remain) and asks Adeodatus to show him the realities for which these words are signs. It quickly becomes clear that Adeodatus is able only to give other signs that can be substituted for the ones used by Virgil. Adeodatus seems to be able to show that the first word, *si*, signifies doubt, but he has a difficult time showing how *nihil* could signify anything. Augustine permits him to continue anyway, but the boy then flounders completely on the third word, *ex*, since he is unable to show what it could possibly mean except by substituting other prepositions for this one, other signs for this one. This problem, that it seems to be impossible to teach or even refer to things without using signs, is the problem that drives the dialogue forward for several chapters and forms the first horn of the dialogue's central paradox.

The line from Virgil that Augustine quotes is taken from Book II of the *Aeneid,* from the famous scene of Aeneas's escape from Troy, which is being sacked by the Greeks. Realizing that the battle is hopelessly lost, Aeneas desperately makes his way through the burning city to his own house, only to find that his father, Anchises, refuses to flee into exile, preferring to die with his city. Unwilling to leave his father behind, the despondent Aeneas dons his armor again, knowing that all is lost. He delivers a mournful speech, toward the beginning of which he utters the line that Augustine quotes (1. 659). At the conclusion of the speech, his wife Creusa clasps his feet at the threshold, holds up their son Iulus to him, and in a pitiful scene pleads with Aeneas not to go. Suddenly, a wonderous portent (*mirabile monstrum*; 1. 680) occurs. A sacred fire bursts forth around the cap (*apex*) on Iulus's head. Water is used to put it out, but Anchises interprets the fire as holy and prays to Jupiter for an augery (*augurium*) to confirm the omen (*omen*; 1. 691). No sooner has he finished than Jupiter sends a shooting star with a fiery tail to confirm the omen. Anchises interprets the augery as declaring that they should all flee into exile and he now goes willingly.

It is often the case in dialogues that the entire passage from which the quotation is taken needs to be considered by the careful reader. Here, Augustine the interlocutor does not tell us in so many words that we need to consider the entire passage, but by giving us the protasis without the apodosis he surely invites us to consult the subsequent lines of Virgil's poem. Moreover, it soon becomes clear in *De magistro* that Adeodatus himself recognizes the entire passage from which the example is taken (2.4; *ut in hoc versu non manente urbe poterant aliqui ex illa esse Troiani*). Augustine the author of the dialogue could expect at least the better-educated of his readers to know the context of the quotation. As is well-known, Virgil was commonly used in Roman pedagogy; indeed he became the poet of the empire, the one who explained to the Romans what it meant to be Roman. In the *Confessions* (I, 13.22), Augustine recalls how delighted he was with Virgil as a young boy, and he explicitly mentions events from Book II of the *Aeneid*, including the burning of Troy and the shade of Creusa. The testimony of the *Contra academicos* is that the philosophical discussions at Cassiciacum were often interrupted, not only because the participants took time off to help with the farming chores but also because they were busy studying Virgil. According to the *De ordine* (I, 8.26), half a book of the *Aeneid* was read in common before dinner.

Now, if one considers the entire passage from which the quotation is taken, one sees immediately that it serves to illustrate the teaching of the dialogue as a whole. There was an apparent sign from Jupiter—the flaming cap of the boy. However, the sign is not intelligible all by itself. The sign by itself teaches nothing; indeed it is not really a sign until one knows what it signifies. But in order to connect the sign with what is signified divine confirmation is needed. Anchises cannot "read" the sign until the god makes it clear. And is this not precisely what is taught in the dialogue? Signs make no sense unless the god confirms them, for signs cannot teach all by themselves. The god has to enable one to understand the reality to which the sign refers. The goal of the dialogue—its final teaching—is already implied and anticipated here in the allusion to Virgil; but of course Adeodatus is not yet in a position to be able to grasp the meaning of the allusion. Augustine the interlocutor introduces this quotation as though it were simply a line of poetry that just happened to come to mind; any other quotation would have served as well. But Augustine the author clearly selected this example very carefully.

This quotation from the *Aeneid* must be paired with another quotation that is prominent in the dialogue. Augustine's lengthy *oratio continua* begins with a quotation, one word in which has a meaning that he admits is unclear: *et sarabarae eorum non sunt commutatae;* and their sarabarae were unchanged. The unclear word is of course *sarabara*. Augustine the interlocutor uses the quotation to explain to Adeodatus that the sign *sarabara* cannot of itself teach him what a *sarabara* is. The sign does not teach anything by itself. In order to know the sign, he first has to know what the significate of the sign is, the reality to which the sign refers. Once he knows what *sarabarae* actually are, then he will know the meaning of the sign *sarabarae*. Until such time, the sign necessarily remains a mystery to him.

Once again, Augustine uses this example as though it were simply one of an innumerable set that could have been used; however, once again, it is necessary to consider the broader context in which this quotation occurs. This time the quotation under consideration comes from Sacred Scripture, from the book of Daniel (3:27; 3:94 in the Vulgate). The line occurs in the famous story of the three young Hebrews who were put in the furnace by Nebuchadnezzer for refusing to commit idolatry. Nebuchadnezzer sees that the three young men were not burned in the fire, nor were their *sarabarae* consumed in the flame. He interprets the rescue from the fire as a mark of divine favor and publishes a decree that no one should blaspheme the God of the three Hebrews. In fact, he calls the rescue from the fire *signa*.[12]

In delivering the quotation from the *Aeneid*, Augustine does not tell the reader what its larger context is. Likewise, in introducing this quotation, he does not tell us its source or remind us of its context. Nevertheless, if the reader considers the larger passages from which these quotations are drawn, the parallelism between them becomes apparent. Most obviously, each involves a divine sign. The sign in each case has to do with fire, and specifically with the heads of boys or young men being on fire without being burned up. It was Iulus's *apex* or cap that was on fire without his hair being burned. Augustine says that he does not know what *sarabarae* are for sure, but says that they may be some sort of head coverings (*quaedam capitum tegmina*).

G. N. Knauer has shown that Augustine's view that *sarabarae* are head coverings of some sort separates him from all other exegetes in his time and puts him over against a line of interpretation that thought that *sarabarae* were much larger pieces of clothing such as pants. That was the view of Tertullian and Jerome, among others. Knauer thinks that Augustine's understanding of the word is actually the correct one, but he wonders how Augustine could possibly have come up with it on his own. He suggests that perhaps Augustine remembered a translation of a Manichean hymn in which *sarabara*, or a related form of the word, was rendered in Latin as having something to do with head coverings.[13] Whatever the truth about this hypothesis, it seems appropriate to point out that by departing from the traditional view and surmising that the word has something to do with headgear, Augustine is better able to extend the parallelism between the passage from Virgil and the passage from Daniel.

In comparing the two passages, the other important parallel involves Anchises and Nebuchadnezzar. Each accepts the divine origin of the sign; Anchises's response is to go with his family into exile; Nebuchadnezzar's is to publish a decree proclaiming that the God of the Hebrews is not to be blasphemed. One important difference in the two accounts is that Anchises asks for the confirmation of the sign, and actually prays aloud to Jupiter for it, whereas Nebuchadnezzar believes the sign without recourse to a second, confirming sign. Given Augustine's doctrine of the necessity of the inner teacher, which is the basic point of the dialogue as a whole, it would seem to follow that Anchises is fundamentally mistaken to ask for a second, external sign to confirm the first one. Since external signs do not by themselves teach anything, a second one could not possibly illuminate a first one, anyway. How could Anchises know that the comet meant that the flaming cap meant that fleeing was the will of the god rather than not fleeing? There is no second or confirming sign in the Daniel story. Apparently we are to conclude that Christ, the true inner teacher, enabled Nebuchadnezzar to understand the significance of the external sign with which he was presented.[14]

Not only do these two quotations embody the basic point of the dialogue regarding the necessity of a divine teacher for grasping the meaning of signs, but one wonders if, perhaps, the quotation from Virgil is not somehow self-referential, i.e. if somehow it does not describe Augustine the author's own situation. Robert J. O'Connell suggests that Augustine's portrait of Monica in *Confessions* V (8.15) is inspired by Virgil's depiction of Dido in the *Aeneid*. O'Connell says that Monica appears there as a "Christian Dido" who remains "weeping on the Carthaginian shore as her new Aeneas, having tricked and deserted her, sails off in quest of the city of his heart's high dream."[15] Is it possible that just as Augustine has the audacity to cast himself as a new Aeneas in the *Confessiones*, he might already be doing something similar in *De magistro*? In the passage in question in the *Aeneid*, there is a father (Aeneas), a son (Iulus), an ancestor (Anchises), and a spouse (Creusa) whom death keeps behind as the others depart for Africa. In the dialogue *De magistro*, there is a father (Augustine) and a son (Adeodatus) who have recently come to Africa. Monica has been left behind, death making it impossible for her to travel to Africa. Is she meant to be Creusa here, as she was, according to O'Connell, meant to be Dido in the *Confessions*?[16]

The suggestion that Augustine uses the sample quotation from Virgil as self-referential may be supported by citing another self-referential passage in *De magistro*. In the first part of the dialogue, while discussing the thesis that nothing can be taught without using signs, the interlocutors consider whether performing an action that someone asks about immediately after the person asks about it constitutes teaching without using signs. That is, when someone asks what walking is and the teacher immediately gets up and begins to walk, is teaching going on without the use of signs? As is typical in dialogues, the interlocutors frequently change their minds on this issue. At the beginning of the third section of the dialogue (10.32), however, Augustine the interlocutor clearly goes back on what he had asserted earlier and argues that there are many self-exhibiting activities. The example he uses in order to convince Adeodatus of this is that of a birdcatcher (*auceps*). He asks Adeodatus to imagine someone who does not know anything about tricking birds who comes across a birdcatcher carrying his tools (*arma*). This person marvels at the birdcatcher and reflects upon him and his equipment (*ornatus*) and follows him. The birdcatcher notices this man following him and so he performs his art and catches some little bird (*aliqua avicula*) while the *spectator* looks on. Adeodatus is not convinced that simply by observing one could learn the whole of birdcatching, so Augustine is forced to add that the observer is so intellegent that he is able to learn the art as a whole from what he sees (*ut ex hoc quod vidit totum illud genus artis agnosceret*).

A careful reader of dialogues should immediately begin to be suspicious when Augustine introduces this example. Even though he says it is just one of many different examples he might have used, it is not, after all, the first example that springs to mind—walking or some other common activity would seem to serve the purpose better. A little reflection, though, suggests that the example of the birdcatcher is not only useful to Augustine the interlocutor to explain his point to Adeodatus, but that it also explains the dialogue as a whole—it is a self-referential allegory. In the example, there is the birdcatcher with his tools or equipment, some little bird, and an observer who looks on from afar. In the *De magistro* as a whole we have a master (Augustine the interlocutor) who uses his tools (in this case grammar and dialectic) to catch some little bird, Adeodatus, i.e. to catch his mind and turn it toward the most sublime truth. The observer is the reader of the dialogue—the person with great intelligence who, by watching the master teacher work, should be able to learn the whole of his art, to see how to pose a paradox to a young student and thereby prod him toward the highest things.[17] Yet, if Augustine is using the birdcatcher example as self-referential, is it not possible that the Virgil quotation is meant to be self-referential as well?

IV. Conclusion

Harald Hagendahl is surely correct to argue that Augustine's most profound and extended consideration of Virgil is contained in the *De civitate Dei*, in which the great poet of imperial Rome is found wanting in that he is ultimately attached to the earthly rather than the heavenly city. Hagendahl is also aware of the presence of Virgil in the Cassiciacum dialogues, but he seems to miss entirely the importance of Virgil in certain of the dialogues after Cassiciacum, and especially the significance of Augustine's encounter with Virgil in the *De magistro*.[18] The reason Hagendahl underestimates Virgil's presence in the *De magistro* is that, because of his adopted method, he is devoted to counting explicit references in Augustine's works. The techniques of accountants, while having a certain utility and a dominant role in modern research methods, are hardly sufficient for the delicate task of grappling with dialogues, for such techniques do not understand the subtle allusions that form part of the zetetic character of the dialogue. Even more disappointing is O'Connell's remark that the *De magistro* is simply "a grammarian's sterile analysis of a great line of Vergil."[19]

But what is Augustine attempting to do with these subtle, even hidden allusions to Virgil in the *De magistro*? They emerge only if one reads the work as a dialogue rather than as a treatise, and they make us appreciate the sophisticated composition of the dialogue and inspire us to consider the other dialogues anew, looking for subtleties we might have missed earlier. But what do they teach? In approaching this question, it is first necessary to appreciate the decisive power poets have over entire peoples. Homer told the Greeks how they should live, and through his charm made them love that life. Virgil was able to do something similar for imperial Rome. A careful reading of the *Republic* reveals that Plato's goal in that work was to replace the poet Homer as the teacher of the Greeks with the philosopher Socrates. It would seem that Augustine is attempting something similar in *De magistro* (and possibly elsewhere); namely, to replace the poet Virgil as the teacher of the Romans with another *magister*, Christ. The parallel quotations from the *Aeneid* and Daniel suggest that the *Aeneid* must give way to new signs, a higher poetry, as it were. The self-referential nature of the quotation suggests that Augustine understands himself as playing a decisive role in the transformation. He must be a new Aeneas, embarking upon the task of providing a new foundation for the new Romans. The new poetry that will be needed is, of course, principally the Scriptures, but one wonders if Augustine did not also understand the *Confessions* as providing, among other things, a substitute for Virgil's poetry. Fr. Fortin states the matter with lucidity:

> Poets . . . are not mere entertainers. Their power is such that they are able to mold the character of an entire nation. Reading the *Aeneid* was thus more than a matter of shedding a few idle tears over the plight of the abandoned Dido; through it one learned what it meant to be a citizen of the Roman empire. The challenge that it posed to Christian faith was not one to be readily ignored. At stake was the ultimate worth of the ideal of humanity embodied in the way of life of the pagan hero, conceived as a total way of life. Little wonder that, in spite of his deep admiration for the sheer loveliness of the *Aeneid*, Augustine should have continued to view it with suspicion. The point was not to attack art or to defend it but to determine how it could be placed in the service of an ideal that was even loftier than that to which in its unadulterated form the subtle charm of Virgil's poetry was likely to lead; a new Aeneas and a new Dido were called for. Both were provided by the *Confessions*. . . . [20]

Surely the *De magistro* does not provide that new poetry found in the *Confessions*; nor, for that matter, does it attack Virgil as profoundly as the *De civitate Dei*. Yet, even while treating the apparently mundane matters pertaining to grammar in the *De magistro*, Augustine is already at work replacing the old teacher of the Romans with a new one. In this, his mission has been nobly imitated by Fr. Fredric Schlatter, S.J., *magister meus*, who, even while pursuing his grammatical tasks, has always attempted to point his grateful students toward Christ, the true teacher.

NOTES

1. Those pursuing Augustine's theory of language analysis might reflect on the fact that in stating the goal and purpose of *De magistro* in the *Retractationes*, Augustine does not even mention the theory of signs. This leads us to wonder whether or not the articulation of such a theory was really a significant part of his goal in constructing the dialogue. See R.A. Markus, "St. Augustine on Signs," *Phronesis* 2 (1957): 69–70. An earlier version of the present essay was read at the 1997 Patristics, Medieval, and Renaissance Conference at Villanova University. I thank Catherine Brown Tkacz, Roland J. Teske, Laurie Douglass, and Uchechukwu B. Obisike for their help with this essay.

2. A recent and rather egregious example is G. Christopher Stead, "Augustine's 'De Magistro': A Philosopher's View," in *Signum Pietatis: Festgabe für Cornelius Petrus Mayer, OSA zum 60. Geburtstag,* Adolar Zumkeller, OSA, ed. (Würzburg, 1989).

3. Review of *St. Augustine's Early Theory of Man, A.D. 386–391,* by Robert J. O'Connell, in *The Birth of Philosophic Christianity: Studies in Early Christian and Medieval Thought,* vol. 1 of *Ernest Fortin: Collected Essays,* ed. J. Brian Benestad (Lanham, Maryland, 1996), 311. For an approach to the *De quantitate animae* (written not long before *De magistro*) that takes seriously its dialogic or zetetic character, see Fortin's essay, "Augustine's *De quantitate animae* or the Spiritual Dimensions of Human Existence," in the same volume.

4. *Retractationes* I, 3 and 5. On the whole issue of Augustine and the liberal arts, see Henri-Iréné Marrou, *Saint Augustin et la fin de la culture antique* (Paris, 1958), esp. 187–327.

5. Introduction to *Augustine: De dialectica* (Dordrecht, Holland, and Boston, 1975), 3. Cf. *Confessiones* VII, 1, 5, 10, and 20.

6. An unfinished version of Augustine's treatment of another of the liberal arts, *De dialectica,* may also have come down to us. See Jackson, Introduction to *De dialectica.*

7. Of all the commentators, Peter Harte Baker has seen this most clearly. See "Liberal Arts as Philosophical Liberation: St. Augustine's *De magistro*," in *Arts libéraux et philosophie au moyen âge: Actes du quatrième congrès international de philosophie médiévale* (Montreal, 1969).

8. *Confessions* IX, 6.14. I set aside here the question of the historical accuracy of the dialogue, except to point out that *De magistro* is a carefully crafted piece of writing. In no way is it a haphazard conversation such as actual, historical conversations normally are.

9. The division of the dialogue adopted here is quite close to that advocated by Frederick J. Crosson ("The Structure of the *De magistro*," *Revue des Études Augustiniennes* 35 [1989]: 120–27). However, whereas Crosson views Chaps. 1–3 of the dialogue as an introduction, with the first part of the dialogue beginning at Chap. 4, it seems to me that Chaps. 1–6 should be viewed as a unit. Textual support for Crosson's division is found in Chap. 4, par. 7; support for my division is provided by Chap. 7, wherein Adeodatus includes the contents of all of chaps. 1–6 in his summary. See also the discussion of the outline of the dialogue by Goulven Madec, "Analyse du *De magistro*," *Revue des Études Augustiniennes* 21 (1975): 63–71.

10. "St. Augustine on Signs," 68–69.

11. Brian Stock, *Augustine the Reader: Meditation, Self-Knowledge, and the Ethics of Interpretation* (Cambridge, Mass., 1996), 148.

12. Since there appears to be no surviving Old Latin text for this part of the Book of Daniel, it is harder to establish the exact wording of the context from which the quotation about the *sarabarae* is taken. However, in *Letter 105*, Augustine quotes, apparently from the Old Latin, a part of Daniel 3:99, in which Nebuchadnezzar calls the deliverance from the fire *signa et ostenta*. Cf. the Vulgate's *signa et mirabilia*.

13. G.N.Knauer, "Sarabara: (Dan. 3, 97 [27] bei Aug. Mag. 10, 33–11, 27," in *Glotta: Zeitschrift für griechische und lateinische Sprache* 23 (Göttingen, 1954): 100–18.

14. On the conversion of Nebuchadnezzar, see the intriguing remarks of Catherine Brown Tkacz, "The Seven Maccabees, the Three Hebrews and a Newly Discovered Sermon of St. Augustine (Mayence 50)," *Revue des Études Augustiniennes* 41 (1995): 72–75.

15. *Art and the Christian Intelligence in St. Augustine* (Cambridge, Mass., 1978), 128.

16. Or perhaps the parallelism between Augustine and Aeneas should proceed somewhat differently. Perhaps the analogue to Creusa is not Monica but Augustine's departed concubine, and then Monica is meant to parallel Anchises, the symbol of ancient piety. The advantage of this interpretation is that the concubine, unlike Monica, was in fact Adeodatus's mother and Augustine's lover, just as Creusa was Aeneas's wife and mother of Iulus. Still, if Augustine is willing to portray his mother as Dido, the lover of Aeneas, in the *Confessiones*, it does not seem unlikely for him to portray her as Creusa, Aeneas's wife, in *De magistro*.

17. This suggestion is supported by the fact that the term *auceps* had a double meaning, which Augustine may be playing upon in this passage of *De magistro*. Although the primary sense of the term is birdcatcher, at least by the time of Cicero the word came to have the secondary meanings of one who spies or eavesdrops on another or one who tries to catch or trick anyone or anything else. Thus, in the *Contra academicos* (III, 7.16), Augustine quotes a lengthy passage from Cicero (otherwise lost to us) in which Cicero refers to Epicurus as an *auceps voluptatum*, a catcher of pleasures. The word also comes to refer to those who use language to trick or catch others. Cicero speaks of an *auceps syllabarum* (*De oratione* I, 236); Ambrose of *aucupes verbis* (*Hex.*5, 12, 37). More relevant to this passage in *De magistro*, perhaps, is Augustine's reference to *aucupes verborum* in *Ennarationes in Psalmis* (55, 10); the birdcatcher, then, may also be a trickster with words. See especially the entry in the *Thesaurus Linguae Latinae*. Among his early writings, Augustine also uses the word in *Soliloquia* I, 14.24; *De quantitate animae* 21.36; *De utilitate credendi* I, 2. The Vulgate uses the term three times: Prov. 6:5; Jer. 5:26; Amos 3:5.

18. *Augustine and the Latin Classics* (Göteborg, 1967), 447–59, esp. 447, n. 2.

19. *Augustine's Early Theory of Man, 386–391* (Cambridge, Mass., 1968), 280.

20. Ernest Fortin, Review of *Art and the Christian Intelligence in St. Augustine*, by Robert J. O'Connell, in *The Birth of Philosophic Christianity*, 318–19.

The Definition of Sacrifice
in the *De Civitate Dei*

Roland J. Teske, S.J.
Marquette University

In his *Contra aduersarium legis et prophetarum*, written in 419 or 420 in reply to the work of an unidentified heretic, most probably someone in the Marcionite tradition, Augustine of Hippo was forced to deal with the topic of sacrifice because the anonymous heretic strongly objected to the animal sacrifices of the Jewish religion and cited Saint Paul as maintaining that all who offer sacrifice offer sacrifice to demons.[1] In a communication for the Oxford Patristics Conference in 1995 I summed up what Augustine said about sacrifice in that seldom read work and pointed out that Augustine presented in it a short, but brilliant treatise on sacrifice in which he showed the relationship between the sacrifices of the Old Law, the sacrifice of Christ on Calvary, and the sacrifice of the Church.[2] I was particularly struck by his apparently universal claim that visible sacrifices—whether of the Old Law or of Christ or of the Church—are signs of divine realities and in fact all signify the same great divine reality: "the grace of God through Jesus Christ our Lord."[3] Augustine says, for example, that David's sacrifice in 1 Kings 2:4 by which he asked that God would spare the people was a sign that "God shows mercy regarding the salvation of the people through the one sacrifice of which David's was the symbol."[4] Hence, in this volume in honor of Fredric W. Schlatter, S.J., it seems appropriate as an offering from one Jesuit priest to another to return to the topic of sacrifice in Saint Augustine and examine some of the aspects of its treatment in book ten of *De ciuitate Dei*, a passage which Gerald Bonner has described as "a wonderful *tour de force* . . . one of the most profound discussions of the nature of sacrifice in Christian literature."[5] Of particular interest is the definition of sacrifice which Augustine, it seems, presents in book ten, a definition which has been the subject of considerable controversy. In fact, one distinguished theologian has forcefully argued that Augustine did not offer—and did not intend to offer—a definiton of sacrifice in the passage,[6] though almost all other scholars who have written on chapters five and six of book ten have, nonetheless, taken Augustine as having presented there a definition of sacrifice.[7] Moreover, the definition that he apparently offers, along with his further claim that every act of mercy done for the sake of God is a sacrifice, seems to present a view of true sacrifice as something without any obvious relation to the two actions which the Church has consistently spoken of as sacrifices, namely, the death of Christ on Calvary and the Mass.[8] Augustine's definition of true sacrifice in fact sounds as though it fits any act of mercy that anyone might do for one's fellow human beings for the sake of God.[9]

I. A First Look at the Definition of Sacrifice

In chapter five, while discussing the sacrifices of the Jewish people recorded in scripture, Augustine points out that we are to understand that the animal sacrifices offered by the patriarchs of old signified "the things which are done among us in order that we might cling to God and assist our neighbor toward the same end. The visible sacrifice, then, is the sacrament, that is, the sacred sign of the invisible sacrifice."[10] In support of this claim he cites Psalm 51 to show that God is not pleased with holocausts, but that "sacrifice to God is a contrite spirit," for God will not reject "a heart that is contrite and humbled."[11] He points out that God speaking through the Psalmist does not reject sacrifice, but substitutes one sort of sacrifice for another. "He does not, then, want the sacrifice of a slaughtered animal, and he does want the sacrifice of a contrite heart."[12] Similarly, Augustine uses Psalm 50 to show that God did not demand animal sacrifices for their own sake, but to show that they were signs of the sacrifices that God does require.[13] He quotes the Prophet Micah to show what God does require of us, namely, "to practice justice and to love mercy and to be ready to walk with the Lord your God."[14] So too, he cites Hebrews 13:16, "Forget not to do good and to be generous, for God is pleased by such sacrifices."[15] Hence, he interprets the statement in Hosea 6:6, "I desire mercy rather than sacrifice," not to mean that God rejected sacrifice, but to mean that he preferred one sort of sacrifice to another.[16] "For what everyone calls a sacrifice," Augustine explains, "is a sign of the true sacrifice. Mercy is, in fact, the true sacrifice."[17] He adds that "all the sacrifices which we read that God commanded to be offered in many ways in the ministry of the tabernacle or the temple are directed to the love of God and of the neighbor."[18] Hence, at the beginning of chapter six, he says, "Thus true sacrifice is every work by which it is brought about that we cling to God in a holy society, every work, that is, which is directed to that final good by which we can be truly happy."[19] Augustine adds, "Hence, even an act of mercy itself by which a human being is helped is not a sacrifice if it is not done for the sake of God."[20] Augustine explains, "For even if a human being performs or offers it, sacrifice is, nonetheless, a divine reality (*res diuina*), so that the ancient Latin people even referred to it by that name."[21] Still later in this chapter Augustine repeats that "true sacrifices are works of mercy either toward ourselves or toward our neighbors which are referred to God."[22]

Augustine's discussion of sacrifice raises several questions: One, did he mean to offer a new definition of "true sacrifice" as an interior act of mercy or love such that visible acts of sacrifice are not genuinely sacrifices? Two, does his definition of sacrifice apply to every work of mercy done on account of God, even if the one who performs the act of mercy is not a Christian? And three, how are many true sacrifices related to the one and only true sacrifice of Christ? For elsewhere Augustine is quite clear that the sacrifice of Christ is the one true sacrifice. For example, in *De trinitate* IV, 13, 17, he speaks of Christ's death as "the one most true sacrifice"[23] and in *De spiritu et littera* 11, 18, he clearly refers to the Eucharist as "the singular and most true sacrifice."[24]

II. A New Definition of Sacrifice?

In his study of the meaning of "true sacrifice" in this book of *De ciuitate Dei*, Guy de Broglie has strongly argued that Augustine did not intend to offer a new and better definition of sacrifice, since such a move would imply that the visible sacrifice—"what everyone calls a sacrifice"—is not a true sacrifice. As de Broglie sees it, such a move would, after all, imply that the visible death of Christ on Calvary and the visible offering of the Mass are not "true sacrifices."[25] De Broglie distinguishes three senses in which Augustine uses the term "true" of various things. First, in its basic or elementary meaning the term "true" means that a thing embodies the given idea in the proper sense as opposed to something which embodies it only in an improper or merely apparent sense. With this meaning Augustine spoke, for example, of a "true Catholic" as opposed to a "false Catholic."[26] Second, in its pregnant meaning the term "true" presents as "true" something that not merely realizes the idea in its proper sense, but also possesses such a degree of perfection that the thing is thought to embody the proper sense of the term in a richer or doubled sense. With this meaning the Gospel speaks of Nathaniel as a "true Israelite," and in this sense Augustine says that the only true life is the happy life.[27] Third, in its typological meaning the term "true" transfers to the reality symbolized the name of the symbol. In this sense Christ is not merely called the Lamb of God, but is said to be the true Lamb of God, or the true light, the true manna, and the true vine.[28] Here de Broglie comments, "But nothing is also more in harmony with the Platonic tendencies of the great African Doctor, for whom the interest of the sensible world is reduced—or almost—to that of the spiritual realities which it symbolizes."[29] In this sense, Augustine not only speaks of Christ as the "true light" or of the Church as the "true temple," but claims that "true health" is not what the doctors tell us about and that "true freedom" is what sets us free from slavery to sin.[30] De Broglie claims that the originality of the typological sense of "true" lies in the fact that it in no sense calls into question the appropriateness of the ordinary meaning of the term, though many things which fit that ordinary meaning are said to be less true than some other reality quite different from them and of which they are merely the signs or symbols.[31]

When Augustine says that a true sacrifice is what is signified by the visible sacrifice, he is, then, not denying that the visible sacrifice is a sacrifice in the proper sense, but stressing that it is the interior act which in the pregnant sense realizes the proper meaning in a fuller or richer way and that in the typological sense the term "sacrifice" which properly applies to the visible sign is transferred to the reality symbolized. Though Augustine does not, as de Broglie has shown, deny that the visible sacrifice—"what everyone calls sacrifice"—is properly a sacrifice, he clearly does place the emphasis upon the interior act of the one who offers sacrifice rather than upon the external and visible sign. An examination of the larger context of the discussion of sacrifice can provide a plausible explanation of this fact.

III. The Context of the Discussion of Sacrifice

Augustine's discussion of sacrifice in *De ciuitate Dei* is found in book ten, the final book of the first part of the work which he himself described as "*magnum opus et arduum*."[32] The context of the definition of sacrifice in this work, which is every bit as large and difficult for the contemporary reader as it was for its author, offers a key to understanding what Augustine was about. Its author left explicit instructions in a letter to Firmus, who served as a sort of literary agent for him in Carthage, about how the twenty-two books of the work were to be divided for future publication, if they could not be published as a whole.[33] The bishop explained that the work falls into two parts: the first ten books which refute the vanities of the unbelievers and the last twelve which defend the Christian religion.[34] The first five books of the first part argue argue "against those who maintain that the worship not of the gods, but of demons contributes to the happiness of this life," while the next five argue against "those who think that either such gods or many gods of any sort ought to be worshipped by ceremonies and sacrifices on account of the life which is to come after death."[35] Central to the first ten books, then, is the question of the proper object of worship. The final twelve books, on the other hand, describe, in three clusters of four books each, the origin of the two cities, their development, and their ends.[36]

The discussion of sacrifice is found in the final, climatic book of the first part. In it Augustine continues to confront the Platonists who had in so many ways hit upon the truth about God and about human existence, though they ultimately rejected the incarnation of the Word. In praise of the Platonists, Augustine says, for example,

> We have chosen the Platonists who are rightly the most noble of all the philosophers, precisely because they were able to know that the human soul, though immortal and rational or intellectual, could be happy only by participation in the light of that God who created it and the world, and they claim that none will attain that which all human beings desire, that is, the happy life, unless by the purity of chaste love they cling to that one perfect Good which is the immutable God.[37]

Augustine's praise for the achievements of the Platonists whose philosophy had earlier made possible the intellectual dimension of his conversion to Catholic Christianity could hardly be more fulsome.[38] In book eight he explained that he prefers the Platonists to all other philosophers because

> they agree with us about the one God who is the author of this universe, who is not only above all bodies insofar as he is incorporeal, but is also above all souls insofar as he is incorruptible, who is our principle, our light, our good.[39]

Later in book ten Augustine even credits Porphyry with having come to a knowledge of "God the Father and God the Son, whom he called in Greek the paternal Intellect or paternal Mind"[40] and with having admitted the need for grace for those few who come to God by the power of their intelligence.[41] In fact, according to Augustine, Porphyry acknowledged that a universal way for the liberation of the soul existed, though he had not found it—the way which Augustine maintained is found in the Christian religion and which is ultimately the Way, Christ himself.[42] On the other hand, Augustine clearly reproaches Poryphry for refusing to accept the incarnation of the Son of God, the one mediator between God and human beings, the one Way by whom alone we are to be saved.[43]

In the beginning of book ten, Augustine is engaged in confrontation with the Platonists on the subject of sacrifice. Though they agreed with the Christians that human happiness is only to be found in clinging to the one God, which is the goal of sacrifice in Augustine's definition, they, nonetheless, held that in some cases immortal spirits inferior to God deserved the worship which Greek Christians called λατρεία, the worship which is owed only to the one true God.[44] Against this view Augustine argues that any immortal spirit that worships God and loves us will not want to be worshipped in place of God and that any such spirit that does not worship God is wretched and undeserving of our worship. Moroever, whatever may be the case with other acts of worship, Augustine argues that "no one would dare to claim that sacrifice ought to be offered to anyone but God."[45] He also argues that God has no need of the sacrifices we offer him, whether these be the animal sacrifices of the Old Law or the sacrifice of our own righteousness, for everything we do as part of the correct worship of God benefits us, not God. Augustine then explains, as we have seen above, that the animal sacrifices offered by the patriarchs signified the same actions that we carry out in order that we might cling to God and bring our neighbor to that same end. And there follows his definition of true sacrifice as "every work by which it is brought about that we cling to God in a holy society, every work, that is, which is referred to that ultimate good by which we can be truly happy."[46] Given that definition, Augustine goes on to list things which are sacrifices and, in fact, true sacrifices.

IV. Examples of True Sacrifices

Augustine first offers three examples of true sacrifices. First, he states that "a human being consecrated by God's name and dedicated to God insofar as one dies to the world in order to live for God is a sacrifice. For this belongs to the mercy one shows to oneself."[47] Second, our body is a sacrifice, when we chastise it with temperance "if we do this as we ought on account of God so that we do not offer our members to sin as weapons of wickedness, but to God as weapons of righteousness."[48] So too, and for even better reasons, our soul is a sacrifice "when it offers itself to God so that, enkindled with the fire of his love, it loses the form of worldly love and is reformed for him, now subject to the immutable Form and pleasing to him because it has received some of its beauty."[49] Each of these sacrifices, whether of the whole human being, or of the body, or of the soul, might at first glance seem to involve nothing specifically Christian, even though the mention of each of these sacrifices is followed by a text of scripture that justifies our calling it a sacrifice. Yet this absence of anything specifically Christian is more apparent than real, for the words "consecrated by God's name" connote baptism, as a search of the Augustinian corpus readily shows.[50] Moreover, Augustine wrote De ciuitate Dei during the height of the Pelagian controversy so that, when he mentioned the virtue of temperance, he certainly had in mind the Christian virtue which was rooted in faith and in the love of God poured out in the heart by the Holy Spirit.[51] Yet, there is nothing in the description of these sacrifices that a non-Christian would necessarily find unacceptable. Augustine, that is, emphasized the interior and spiritual character of true sacrifice as part of his strategy to convert contemporary Platonists to Christianity and specifically to the worship of the Christian God in the Church. A Platonist exploring the possibility of becoming a Christian would not necessarily find anything off-putting or incompatible with Platonic spiritualism at its best.

Later in book ten Augustine mentions certain people who wanted to offer visible sacrifices to the lesser gods, but wanted to offer to the one God who is invisible, who is the greatest and the best, only the invisible sacrifices of a pure mind and a good will. There the bishop of Hippo insists that visible sacrifices are the symbols of invisible offerings and that "visible sacrifice must be offered only to him to whom we ourselves ought to be an invisible sacrifice in our hearts."[52] Gerald Bonner suggests that Porphyry is the "most obvious subject of these remarks" and points to a saying ascribed to Apollonius of Tyana which Porphyry cites to the effect that "the highest god has no need of sacrifices at all, and that the only fitting offering is man's reason."[53] Bonner rightly concludes that, though Augustine was influenced by Neoplatonic thought, "it is not necessary, and may indeed be positively misleading, to emphasize that influence at the expense of the more obviously immediate influence of the Bible, on which his mature theology is fundamentally based."[54]

What explains Augustine's emphasis upon the interior and invisible forms of sacrifice in *De ciuitate Dei* is not so much his being under the influence of Neoplatonist thinking as his concern to present the Christian understanding of sacrifice in a way that would be most acceptable to some contemporaries who were deeply attracted to the spiritualism of Platonism. In his recent study of *De ciuitate Dei* Johannes Van Oort has argued that the work was basically a work of Christian apologetics meant to prepare converts—educated ones, we must suppose—for the reception of baptism.[55] In this light, one can maintain that, while in no sense being unfaithful to the understanding of sacrifice he learned in the teachings of scripture and in the writing of such patristic authors as Tertullian and Cyprian,[56] Augustine may have emphasized the spiritual and interior character of the Christian understanding of sacrifice in a way that would allow contemporary Platonists to see that Christianity was capable of incorporating the highest ideals of Platonic spiritualism.

V. The Universal Sacrifice

After the three examples of true sacrifice, Augustine repeats his claim that "true sacrifices are works of mercy, whether toward ourselves or toward our neighbors, which are offered to God," and points out that "works of mercy have no other purpose than than that we may be set free from misery and, in this way, be happy."[57] He adds that we can be happy only by clinging to God. Hence, he concludes that

> the whole redeemed city, that is, the assembly and society of the saints, is offered to God as the universal sacrifice through the great priest who also offered himself for us in his Passion in the form of the servant so that we might be the body of so great a head.[58]

The truly great work of mercy, then, is the work of our salvation, the universal sacrifice by which we are set free from the misery of sin and reconciled to God through the great priest.[59] In all his writings Augustine used the expression "universal sacrifice" only in this passage, and the most frequent use of "*universalis*" in all his works is as an adjective with "*via*" in the same book of *De ciuitate Dei*.[60] Such a pattern of usage suggests that Augustine linked in his mind the universal sacrifice with the universal way, the existence of which Porphyry acknowledged, but did not discover, and which Augustine knew was the incarnate Christ. Again we have evidence that in his discussion of sacrifice Augustine has the great Platonist in mind—not, of course, to convert Porphyry, but to nudge contemporary Platonists, those who were in agreement with the Christians on so many important points, to take the step and enter the City of God and become part of the universal sacrifice that is the people of God. Such, after all, was Augustine's message to Firmus in *Letter* 2*.[61]

Yves de Montcheuil commented on the meaning of "*opus*" in Augustine's definition of sacrifice with these insightful words,

> If we take things from the point of view of human history in its entirety, as God sees them, we must say that there is but one sole sacrifice in the complete sense: the act by which predestined humanity . . . passes from the sin in which it is found to the full reality of salvation. "Opus"—"the great work" of human history, that by which humanity attains its goal: "that we cling to God in a holy society," so that we may be truly happy.[62]

This universal sacrifice, then, is not merely a work of mercy, but the one all-inclusive work of mercy, because it is the sacrifice which Jesus Christ offered on Calvary in the form of the servant as the head of his body, the Church, and which is re-presented in each Eucharistic sacrifice. Christ as head offered that sacrifice in the form of the servant so that the whole city of God might as his body be the universal sacrifice offered to God.[63] In accord with his theme of the unity of sacrament and sacrifice, de Montcheuil adds,

> "A work" which is broken down into a series of "works," because humanity itself is made up of distinct and successive human beings, because each human beings is also subject to time and it is not by one single "action" that one realizes perfect society with God. . . . [64]

In his discussion of sacrifice in book ten Augustine mentions the sacrifice of Calvary only here, and he does not explicitly say that it is an act of mercy, though it is surely implied.[65] The sacrifice of Calvary is THE work of mercy, the work of our redemption by which we are reconciled to God, for as Augustine puts it in book ten: "Human beings are, after all, separated from God only by sins, which in this life are washed away not by our strength, but by God's compassion, by his pardon, not by our power. . . ."[66] And he explains, "the forgiveness of sins is brought about in him as priest and sacrifice, that is, through the mediator of God and human beings, the man Jesus Christ, through whom we are reconciled to God by the washing away of sins."[67] Because Augustine stressed the reality of the unity between Christ the head and his members, he saw every act of mercy performed by a member of the whole Christ as part of that universal sacrifice, the great act of mercy offered by Christ to reconcile us to the Father.[68]

NOTES

1. The heretic's text of 2 Cor 10:20 read: *Sed qui sacrificant, daemonibus sacrificant* instead of the text which Augustine had: *Sed quia quae immolant daemonibus, et non Deo immolant.* See *Contra aduersarium legis et prophetarum* I, 19, 38: CCL 49, 68.

2. See my translation of the work in *Augustine: Arianism and Other Heresies* (Hyde Park, NY, 1995).

3. See my "Sacrifice in Augustine's *Contra aduersarium legis et prophetarum,*" forthcoming in *Studia Patristica* XXXIII.

4. *Contra aduersarium legis et prophetarum* I, 18, 37: CCL 49, 67: "Unde illud quod Dauid obtulit, ut populo parceretur, umbra erat futuri, qua significatum est, quod per unum sacrificium, cuius illa figura erat, saluti populi spiritaliter parcitur." All translations in the present essay are by the author.

5. Gerald Bonner, "The Doctrine of Sacrifice: Augustine and the Latin Patristic Tradition," in *Sacrifice and Redemption. Durham Essays in Theology.* Edited by S. W. Sykes (Cambridge, 1991), 101–17, here 105.

6. Guy de Broglie, "La notion augustinienne du sacrifice 'invisible' et 'vrai,'" *Recherches de science religieuse* 48 (1960): 135–65.

7. Studies on sacrifice in the *De ciuitate Dei* are many. Besides Bonner's and de Broglie's, among the best are: Joseph Lécuyer, "Le sacrifice selon saint Augustin," in *Augustinus Magister* (Paris, 1946) II, 905–14; Yves de Montcheuil, "L'unité du sacrifice et du sacrement dans l'Eucharistie, in *Mélanges théologiques* (Paris, 1946), 49–70; Bernard Quinot, "L'influence de l'Épitre aux Hébreux dans la notion augustinienne du vrai sacrifice," *Revue des études augustiniennes* 8 (1962): 129–168; Ghislain Lafont, "Le sacrifice de la Cité de Dieu. Commentaire au *De Civitate Dei* Livre X, ch. I– VII," *Recherches de science religieuse* 53 (1965): 177–219; John F. O'Grady, "Priesthood and Sacrifice in 'City of God,'" *Augustiniana* 21 (1971): 27–44; Basil Studer, "Das Opfer Christi nach Augustins 'De civitate Dei' X, 5–6, in *Lex Orandi, Lex Credendi. Miscellanea in onore di P. Cipriano Vagaggini,* ed. G. Békés and G. Franedi (Rome, 1980), 93–107; and Marcel Neusch, "Une conception chrétienne du sacrifice: Le modèle de saint Augustin," in *Le sacrifice dans les religions.* Sciences théologiques et religieuses 3, ed. by Marcel Neusch (Paris, 1994), 117–38.

8. Such is the heart, I take it, of de Broglie's objection to taking what Augustine says here as a definition of sacrifice. He says, "Il suffit, comme on voit, d'interpréter le dogme catholique en partant de la définition dite 'augustinienne', pour voir s'envoler presque tous les problèmes, parfois délicats, que la théologie catholique du 'sacrifice' peut conduire à poser; et peut-être cette considération n'est-elle étrangère au succès que cette définition a quelquefois rencontré.—Mais il reste permis de se demander si une si merveilleuse simplification de la théologie ne menaçerait pas le contenu du dogme lui-même. Car, si toute action inspirée par l'amour de Dieu et qui fait avancer l'humanité dans la voie du salut, méritait *proprement, pleinement, et indistinctement,* le nom de 'sacrifice', on comprend mal que l'Église puisse attacher quelque importance à nous entendre qualifier de ce vocable *deux* actions particulières, *et deux seulement*: celle qui s'accomplit jadis sur la Croix et celle qui se renouvelle quotidiennnement sur nos autels" (de Broglie, "La notion augustinienne,"

140).

    9. Such a view was articulated by John F. O'Grady in "Priesthood and Sacrifice in 'City of God,'" when he spoke of "[t]he notion of Augustine on sacrifice as any work which unites us with God, or any work directed to our final end" (p. 43). He says, "The christian accepts the same demands of the Jew and of any other religious person. God wishes the offering of self, the interior sacrifice animated by charity, essentially involved in works of mercy in favor of others. . . . True sacrifice unites man to God in a holy society; the invisible sacrifice forms the heart of sacrifice and signifies the offering of man himself. Further it was seen that these notions are not limited to christianity nor even to Judaism, but Augustine sees them involved in man's nature as a person called to union with his God" (pp. 40–41).

    10. *De ciuitate Dei* X, 5: CCL 47, 276–7: "Nec quod ab antiquis patribus alia sacrificia facta sunt in uictimis pecorum, . . . aliud intellegendum est, nisi rebus illis eas res fuisse significatas, quae aguntur in nobis, ad hoc ut inhaereamus deo et ad eundem finem proximo consulamus. Sacrificium ergo uisibile inuisibilis sacrificii sacramentum, id est sacrum signum est."

    11. *De ciuitate Dei* X, 5: CCL 47, 277: "*Sacrificium Deo spiritus contritus; cor contritum et humiliatum Deus not spernet*" (Ps 51:19).

    12. *De ciuitate dei* X, 5: CCL 47, 277: "Non uult ergo sacrificium trucidati pecoris, et uult sacrificium contriti cordis."

    13. *De ciuitate Dei* X, 5: CCL 47, 277–8: "Et in huius prophetae uerbis utrumque distinctum est satisque declaratum illa sacrificia per se ipsa non requirere Deum, quibus significantur haec sacrificia, quae requirit Deus."

    14. Micah 6:8 in *De ciuitate Dei* X, 5: CCL 47, 277: "*Aut quid Dominus exquirat a te nisi facere iudicium et diligere misericordiam et paratum esse ire cum Domino Deo tuo.*"

    15. *De ciuitate Dei* X, 5: CCL 47, 278: "*Bene facere . . . et communicatores esse nolite obliuisci; talibus enim sacrificiis placetur Deo.*"

    16. *De ciuitate Dei* X, 5: CCL 47, 278: "Ac per hoc ubi scriptum est: *Misericordiam uolo quam sacrificium* nihil aliud quam sacrificium sacrificio praelatum oportet intellegi."

    17. *De ciuitate Dei* X, 5: CCL 47, 278: "illud, quod ab omnibus appellatur sacrificium, signum est ueri sacrificii. Porro autem misericordia uerum sacrificium est. . . ."

    18. *De ciuitate Dei* X, 5: CCL 47, 278: "Quaecumque igitur in ministerio tabernaculi siue templi multis modis de sacrificiis leguntur diuinitus esse praecepta, ad dilectionem Dei et proximi significando referuntur."

    19. *De ciuitate Dei* X, 6: CCL 47, 278: "Proinde uerum sacrificium est omne opus, quo agitur, ut sancta societate inhaereamus Deo, relatum scilicet ad illum finem boni, quo ueraciter beati esse possimus."

    20. *De ciuitate Dei* X, 6: CCL 47, 278: "Unde et ipsa misericordia, qua homini subuenitur, si non propter Deum fit, non est sacrificium."

    21. *De ciuitate Dei* X, 6: CCL 47, 278: "Etsi enim ab homine fit uel offertur, tamen sacrificium res diuina est, ita ut hoc quoque uocabulo id Latini ueteres appellauerint."

    22. *De ciuitate Dei* X, 6: CCL 47, 279: "Cum igitur uera sacrificia opera sint misericordiae siue in nos ipsos siue in proximos, quae referuntur ad Deum. . . ."

23. *De trinitate* IV, 13, 17: CCL 50, 164: "Morte sua quippe uno uerissimo sacrificio pro nobis oblato quidquid culparum erat unde nos principatus et potestates ad luenda supplicia iure detinebant purgauit, aboleuit, exstinxit, et sua resurrectione in nouam uitam nos praedestinatos uocauit, uocatos iustificauit, iustificatos glorificauit."

24. *De spiritu et littera* XI, 18, CSEL 60, 170: "Unde et in ipso uerissimo et singulari sacrificio, Domino Deo nostro, agere gratias admonemur."

25. De Broglie's article, "La notion augustinienne," was written in opposition to the claims of Yves de Montcheuil in *Mélanges théologiques* (Paris, 1946), 49–70, in which de Montcheuil presented, as de Broglie saw it, "le don spirituel que l'homme fait de soi à Dieu par la charité comme le seul 'sacrifice', *au sens plein et complet du terme*" (de Broglie, "La notion augustinienne," p. 138, note 10). De Broglie saw it as dangerous to suppose "qu'en parlant de 'vrai' sacrifice le grand Docteur entendait nous fournir du 'sacrifice' en tant que tel *une définition plus propre, plus profonde et plus satisfaisante* que toutes celles auxquelles le vulgaire était préparé à souscrire" (p. 141). For such an interpretation of Augustine would imply that the sacrifice of Calvary and the sacrifice of the Mass were something less than *true* sacrifices.

26. De Broglie, "La notion augustinienne," 144; Augustine, *De natura et origine animae* III, 2: Bibliothèque Augustinienne 22, 522.

27. See John 1:47 and Augustine, *Enchiridion de fide, spe, et caritate* XXIII, 92: CCL 46, 98.

28. See John 1:9, 6:32, 15:1. So too, Hebrews 8:2 speaks of the true tabernacle.

29. De Broglie, "La notion augustininne," 147: "Mais rien aussi n'était plus conforme aux tendances platoniciennes du grand Docteur africain, pour qui l'intérêt du monde sensible se réduit, ou peu s'en faut, à celui des réalités spirituelles qu'il figure."

30. *Ibid.* See Augustine, *De ciuitate Dei* XI, 9: CCL 48, 330; *Enarrationes in Psalmos*: In Psalmum 130, 2: CCL 40, 1899; *Sermo* 385, 6–7: PL 39, 1693–94.

31. De Broglie, "La notion augustininne," 148.

32. *De ciuitate Dei* I, Praefatio: CCL 47, 1.

33. The Letter to Firmus was published for the first time by Dom C. Lambot in "Lettre inédité de saint Augustin relative au 'De Civitate Dei,'" *Revue Bénédictine* 51 (1939): 109–121; it is now numbered as *Epistula* 1A in CSEL 88. *Epistula* 2A, one of the letters discovered and first published by Johannes Divjak in 1981 in CSEL 88 and newly edited in Bibliothèque Augustinienne 46[B] as *Epistula* 2*, reveals that the Firmus in question was not, as had been supposed, a Carthaginian priest and disciple of Augustine, but a pagan who was hesitating about receiving baptism.

34. *Epistula* 1A, 1: CSEL 88, 7: "decem quippe illis uanitates refutatae sunt impiorum, reliquis autem demonstrata atque defensa est nostra religio. . . ."

35. *Epistula* 1A, 1; CSEL 88, 7: "Si autem corpora malueris esse plura quam duo, iam quinque oportet codices facias, quorum primus contineat quinque libros priores quibus aduersus eos est disputatum qui felicitati uitae huius non plane deorum sed daemoniorum cultum prodesse contendunt, secundus sequentes alios quinque <aduersus eos> qui uel tales uel qualescumque plurimos deos propter uitam quae post mortem futura est per sacra et sacrificia colendos putant."

36. *Epistula* 1A, 1; CSEL 88, 7: "Iam tres alii codices qui sequuntur quaternos libros habere debebunt; sic enim a nobis pars eadem distributa est, ut quattuor ostenderent exortum illius ciuitatis totidemque procursum, siue dicere malumus, excursum, quattuor uero ultimi debitos fines."

37. *De ciuitate Dei* X, 1: CCL 47, 271–2: "Elegimus enim Platonicos omnium philosophorum merito nobilissimos, propterea quia sapere potuerunt licet immortalem ac rationalem uel intellectualem hominis animam nisi participato lumine illius Dei, a quo et ipsa et mundus factus est, beatam esse non posse; ita illud, quod omnes homines appetunt, id est uitam beatam, quemquam isti assecuturum negant, qui non illi uni optimo, quod est incommutabilis Deus, puritate casti amoris adhaeserit."

38. For a recent and excellent discussion of the role of the Neoplatonists in Augustine's conversion and intellectual formation, see Robert J. O'Connell, *Images of Conversion in St. Augustine's Confessions* (New York, 1996), especially pp. 93–203 in which O'Connell describes Augustine's gradual absorption of the philosophical insights of the Platonists.

39. *De ciuitate Dei* VIII, 10: CCL 47, 277: "In quo autem nobis consentiunt de uno Deo huius uniuersitatis auctore, qui non solum super omnia corpora est incorporeus, uerum etiam super omnes animas incorruptibilis, principium nostrum, lumen nostrum, bonum nostrum, in hoc eos ceteris anteponimus." See also my "Ultimate Reality according to Augustine of Hippo," *Journal of Ultimate Reality and Meaning* 18 (1995): 20–33.

40. *De ciuitate Dei* X, 22: CCL 47, 296: "Dicet enim Deum Patrem et Deum Filium, quem Graece appellat paternum intellectum uel paternam mentem. . . ."

41. *De ciuitate Dei* X, 29: CCL 47, 304: "Confiteris tamen gratiam, quando quidem ad Deum per uirtutem intelligentiae peruenire paucis dicis esse concessum."

42. *De ciuitate Dei* X, 32: CCL 47, 309–11: "Haec est religio, quae uniuersalem continet uiam animae liberandae, quoniam nulla nisi hac liberari potest. . . . Unde tanto post ex Abrahae semine carne suscepta de se ipso ait ipse Saluator: *Ego sum uia, ueritas et uita.*"

43. *De ciuitate Dei* X, 29: CCL 47, 304: "sed incarnationem incommutablis Filii Dei qua salvamur . . . non uultis agnoscere."

44. Augustine discusses at length the lack of a single Latin term suitable to translate λατρεία and points out the shortcomings of *cultus, servitius, religio,* and *pietas.* See *De ciuitate Dei* X, 1: CCL 47, 271–74.

45. *De ciuitate Dei* X, 4: CCL 47, 276: "Nam, ut alia nunc taceam, quae pertinent ad religionis obsequium, quo colitur Deus, sacrificium certe nullus hominum est qui audeat dicere deberi nisi Deo."

46. *De ciuitate Dei* X, 6: CCL 47, 278: "Proinde uerum sacrificium est omne opus, quo agitur, ut sancta societate inhaereamus Deo, relatum scilicet ad illum finem boni, quo ueraciter beati esse possimus."

47. *De ciuitate Dei* X, 6: CCL 47, 278: "Unde ipse homo Dei nomine consecratus et Deo uotus, in quantum mundo moritur ut Deo uiuat, sacrificium est. Nam et hoc ad misericordiam pertinet, quam quisque in se ipsum facit."

48. *De ciuitate Dei* X, 6: CCL 47, 278: "Corpus etiam nostrum cum temperantia castigamus, si hoc, quem ad modum debemus, propter Deum facimus, ut non exhibeamus membra nostra arma iniquitatis peccato, sed arma iustitiae Deo, sacrificium est."

49. *De ciuitate Dei* X, 6: CCL 47, 278: "quanto magis anima ipsa cum se refert ad Deum, ut igne amoris eius accensa formam concupiscentiae saecularis amittat eique tamquam incommutabili formae subdita reformetur, hinc ei placens, quod ex eius pulchritudine acceperit, fit sacrificium!"

50. See, for example, *Epistula* 23, 4: CSEL 34/1, 67: "Cur non dicis: ego unum baptismum noui Patris et Filii et Spiritus Sancti nomine consecratum atque signatum; hanc formam ubi inuenio, necesse est ut adprobem; non destruo, quod dominicum agnosco, non exsufflo uexillum regis mei?" or *Sermo* 352: PL 39, 1551: 40: "Sed quia baptismus, id est, salutis aqua non est salutis, nisi Christi nomine consecrata, qui pro nobis sanguinem fudit, cruce ipsius aqua signatur."

51. See *De nuptiis et concupiscentia* I, 4, 5: CSEL 42: 216, for Augustine's use of Rom 14:23 and Heb 11:6 to argue that there is no true virtue without faith. The fact that the specifically Christian elements are understated rather than explicit may explain how O'Grady missed them; see above note 9.

52. *De ciuitate Dei* X, 19: CCL 47, 293: "ita sacrificantes non alteri uisibile sacrificium offerendum esse nouerimus quam illi, cuius in cordibus nostris inuisibile sacrificium nos ipsi debemus."

53. Bonner, "The Doctrine of Sacrifice," 102, where he refers to Prophyry's *De abstinentia* II, 34. See *Porphyre. De l'abstinence* II. Livres II et III, ed. and tr. J. Bouffartique and M. Patillon (Paris, 1979), 100–101: θύσομεν τοίνυν καὶ ἡμεῖς· ἀλλὰ θύσομεν, ὡς προσήκει, . . . διὰ δὲ σιγῆς καθαρᾶς καὶ τῶν περὶ αὐτοῦ καθαρῶν ἐννοιῶν θρησκεύομεν αὐτόν.

54. Bonner, "The Doctrine of Sacrifice," 104.

55. Johannes Van Oort, *Jerusalem and Babylon: A Study into Augustine's City of God and the Sources of the Doctrine of the Two Cities* (Leiden, 1991), especially Chapter Three: "The 'City of God' as an Apology and a Catechetical Work." See pages 173–175 where Van Oort points to Letter 2* in which Augustine urges Firmus to enter the city of God by baptism if he wants to enjoy the fruits of the work: "neque enim ille fructus est eorum, quod delectant legentem, nec ille, quod multa faciunt scire nescientem, sed ille, quod ciuitatem dei persuadent vel incunctanter intrandam uel perserueranter habitandam" (*Epistola* 2*, 3: Bibliothèque Augustinienne 46^B, 64).

56. For the influence of Tertullian and Cyprian upon Augustine's thought on sacrifice, see once again Bonner, "The Doctrine of Sacrifice," 107–11.

57. *De ciuitate Dei* X, 6: CCL 47, 279: "Cum igitur uera sacrificia opera sint misericordiae siue in nos ipsos siue in proximos, quae referuntur ad Deum; opera uero misericordiae non ob aliud fiant, nisi ut a miseria liberemur ac per hoc ut beati simus. . . ."

58. *De ciuitate Dei* X, 6: CCL 47, 279: "profecto efficitur, ut tota ipsa redempta ciuitas, hoc est congregatio societasque sanctorum, uniuersale sacrificium offeratur Deo per sacerdotem magnum, qui etiam se ipsum obtulit in passione pro nobis, ut tanti capitis corpus essemus, secundum formam serui."

59. In "Das Opfer Christi," Basil Studer points out the puzzling fact that Augustine does not explicitly apply his definition of sacrifice to the sacrifice of Christ on the Cross. He says, for example, "Es ist schwer auszumachen, warum Augustin selbst nicht auf die naheliegende Möglichkeit aufmerksam geworden ist, seinen ohne Zweifel persönich tiefempfundenen Opferbegriff auf das Verständnis des Sterbens Christi auszudehnen" (p.

104). He does not explicitly apply his definition to Christ's death, I suggest, because he sees that death as the chief part of the universal sacrifice by which the whole Christ, head and body, is offered to the Father.

60. The adjective "*universalis*" appears in Augustine's works 75 times. It occurs most frequently with "*via*"—19 times— and 18 of these in book ten of *De ciuitate Dei* where the context is Porphyry's search for a universal way of salvation. Sixteen times the adjective accompanies "*concilium*," and another 6 times "*ecclesia*."

61. *Epistula* 2*, 3: Bibliothèque Augustinienne 46ᴮ, 62–64: "Nam quod in alia tua epistola te ab accipiendo sacramento regenerationis excusas, totum tot librorum quos amas fructum recusas; neque enim ille fructus est eorum, quod delectant legentem, nec ille, quod multa faciunt scire nescientem, sed ille, quod ciuitatem dei persuadent uel incunctanter intrandam uel perseueranter habitandam; quorum duorum primum regeneratione, secundum iustitiae dilectione confertur."

62. Yves de Montcheuil, "L'unité du sacrifice et du sacrement dans l'Eucharistie, in *Mélanges théologiques* (Paris, 1946), p. 51: "Si nous prenons les choses du point de vue de l'histoire humaine dans son ensemble, comme Dieu les voit, nous devons dire qu'il n'y a qu'un seul sacrifice au sens total: l'acte par lequel l'humanité prédestinée . . . passe du péché où elle se trouve à la consommation du salut. 'Opus', 'grand oeuvre' de l'historie humaine, celui par lequel l'humanité parvient à sa fin: 'ut sancta societate inhaereamus Deo,' en sorte qu'elle soit vraiment heureuse."

63. The Latin "societas" in Augustine definition of sacrifice, which has often been translated into English as "fellowship" loses the power of the Latin term which here clearly refers to the whole Christ, the City of God, for there is no other "sancta societas qua inhaereamus Deo." See Donald J. Keefe, *Covenantal Theology: The Eucharistic Order of History*. 2 vols. (Lanham, MD, 1991), II, 369.

64. Ibid.: "'Opus' qui se décompose en une série d''opera', parce que l'humanité se compose elle-même d'hommes distincts et successifs, parce qu'aussi chaque homme est soumis au temps, et que ce n'est pas par une seule 'action' qu'il réalise sa société parfaite avec Dieu. . . ." Yves de Montcheuil, S.J., a member of the faculty of the Institut Catholique de Paris, was executed on the night of August 10–11, 1944 at Vecors, France, after his capture during a Nazi attack upon a group of young resistance fighters. He was visiting the group during his summer vacation in order to provide them with some spiritual care. During the attack he remained behind with the wounded and was subsequently executed—an end which surely fits the Augustinian characterisation of sacrifice as a work of mercy toward other human beings for the sake of God. See the Préface to *Mélanges théologiques*, 7–12, by H[enri] de L[ubac].

65. See Basil Studer, "Das Opfer Christi," 95.

66. *De ciuitate Dei* X, 22: CCL 47, 296: "Non enim nisi peccatis homines separantur a Deo, quorum in hac uita non fit nostra uirtute, sed diuina miseratione purgatio, per indulgentiam illius, non per nostram potentiam. . . ."

67. *De ciuitate Dei* X, 22: CCL 47, 296: "in ipso sacerdote ac sacrificio fieret remissio peccatorum, id est per mediatorem Dei et hominum, hominem Christum Iesum, per quem facta peccatorum purgatione reconciliamur deo."

68. The theme of the whole Christ (*totus Christus*) underlies the unity of the many acts of sacrifice with the one sacrifice of Christ. See, for example, *Enarrationes in Psalmos*: In Psalmum 26, enar. 2, 2: CCL 38, 155: "Sacrificium obtulit Deo non aliud quam seipsum. Non enim inueniret praeter se mundissimam rationalem uictimam, tamquam agnus immaculatus fuso sanguine suo redimens nos, concorporans nos sibi, faciens nos membra sua, ut in illo et nos Christus essemus. . . . Inde autem apparet Christi corpus nos esse, quia omnes ungimur; et omnes in illo et christi et Christus sumus, quia quodammodo totus Christus caput et corpus est."

Equal Before God:
Augustine on the Nature and Role
of Women

Katherin A. Rogers
University of Delaware

When at Gonzaga University in November, 1996, to deliver the lecture on which
this essay is based, it was my pleasure to meet Fredric W. Schlatter, S.J., and to
enjoy some delightful time in conversation with him.[1] As he enthusiastically
supported the series in which I spoke, "Women in the Early Church," it is fitting
that this essay should appear in the collection that honors him.

The essay gives me the opportunity to clarify some common misconceptions
regarding St. Augustine and medieval philosophy generally, misconceptions of
which I was recently reminded by a student of mine who, repeating one of the
standard criticisms from that long list of charges one hears leveled against things
medieval, asked me how I could be a scholar of medieval philosophers when they
held such terrible views about women. "Which views are these?" I asked. He did
not have an answer, but since my academic focus is metaphysics and epistemology,
I wondered if I had somehow missed the misogyny which allegedly rages through
medieval thought. Most of the major medieval philosophers simply do not have
much to say about women. Could that in itself be a sign of misogyny? Upon further
consideration I decided that there are basically two innocent reasons why the
medieval philosophers do not make an issue of women.

One is that they are mostly concerned with finding out what is the case about
God and creation, and, unlike many contemporary philosophers, the medievals
believed in an objective truth to things that any rational person can aim to discover.
Nowadays one hears about the "woman's view" and "listening to women's voices"
because in contemporary academia it is popular to believe that how one sees things
depends entirely on who and where one is, what gender and color one is, and so
forth. This idea is at least as old as the pre-Socratic sophists, though in its recent
guise it is greatly indebted to the influence of Marx. We all see things differently
so "truth" is relative to the perceiver. Thus women's "truth" may be different from
men's "truth." The medievals would have thought such a view foolish. The truth
is there, like a mountain of diamond, and the fact that different people may
approach it from different angles does not change the mountain itself, so the idea
of "women's philosophy" would strike them as bizarre. Human beings, male and

female, are rational animals, naturally equipped to think about a world which is not the construct of their own place in society. A second reason why the medievals did not generally have a great deal to say about women in particular is that the consensus was that, fundamentally, women are in the same situation as men. As Augustine himself insists, women are as capable of salvation as men, and in the final analysis, that is not only the most important fact, but the only truly important one.

Why, then, all these accusations? That the Middle Ages have been getting a bad press for centuries is surely not news. My tenth grade daughter reports that high school students are still being told that in the Middle Ages people thought the earth was flat.[2] Professional academicians still sometimes make the claim that in the Middle Ages no one was interested in science because they thought everything worked by magic. Is such ignorance of medieval thought simply due to the fact that some people who ought to know better are woefully misinformed? The case could be made that it is especially people who are dissatisfied with religion who make a point of criticizing the Middle Ages, since that was the golden age of an intellectually powerful religious philosophy. If one can paint the medievals as superstitious and ignorant one does not have to engage in the arduous task of arguing with them point by point. If one can add "misogynistic" to the list, then the thinkers of the Middle Ages were not just stupid, but evil, and one can claim that anything they might have said is already discredited.

Furthermore, if one is dissatisfied with the entire European tradition, then the thinker to attack is Augustine. Augustine lived just as the western Roman empire was crumbling; he is the author who took the philosophy of the Greeks and synthesized it with biblical revelation to lay the foundation for the western tradition. As a bishop, he devoted himself to combating various heresies, so his thought came to be constitutive of orthodox Christianity. Virtually every educated person in the Latin West throughout the Middle Ages was conversant with Augustine, and when one studies the Reformation one finds Augustine's thought pervasive. Martin Luther, for example, claimed that one of the principal problems with the church was that she had gotten too far from Augustine. In sum, it is simply impossible to overestimate Augustine's influence on Western civilization, and hence, if one can show that Augustine was thoroughly misogynistic, one has indeed laid the axe to the roots of our culture.

It is my goal to defend Augustine against the charge that he hated women. Nevertheless, I do think it should be stated at the outset that the medievals in general and Augustine in particular do not believe that women are as strong physically and intellectually as men. "Strong" and "smart" are, of course, notoriously difficult to define, and I take it that the question of whether or not men and women really are equally strong and smart is an empirical one. If we disallow the evidence of history, since it is claimed that all previous ages have distorted the issue because they were all inherently misogynist, then the most that can be said is that the question is still an open one. Hence it is surely unfair to characterize this position as "terrible." And if, as I suspect, most men from the dawn of history up until about twenty-five years ago would have felt perfectly comfortable expressing the view that women were physically and intellectually weaker than men, it seems unreasonable to characterize the view as specifically "medieval" either, and even less that it is specifically "augustinian." That being said, is it true, as some have charged, that Augustine hates women?

I. The Charge

It has been suggested that Augustine hated women because he hated sex. Basically, two sorts of support for this claim have been proffered. The first is a psychological argument which claims that Augustine hated women because he had an Oedipus complex or some sort of sexual problem.[3] Clearly, such psychological discussions must start from the assumption that it is *possible* for us to psychoanalyze this genius, who belongs to a culture quite different from our own, and to do so on the basis of his writings, and at the temporal distance of sixteen hundred years. This is a most implausible assumption, and consequently the psychological approach is not likely to be very helpful.

A variant on the psychological approach is rooted in the contemporary feminist position that what sex is really about is power. Hence, the claim is made that Augustine's views constitute a veiled attempt to perpetuate patriarchy. The underlying assumptions of this claim seem to be, first, that the essential fact which characterizes the human condition is that all human beings are engaged in an unending struggle for power, and, second, that there is no natural inequality between men and women to account for the fact that in almost all times and cultures men have dominated. Apparently it is not that men have a greater aptitude for power than women, but somehow men have managed to become dominant, and then, subsequently, other men such as Augustine have used their talents to defend the injustice of male domination. These are sweeping assumptions, and certainly they are difficult to prove from the texts. Of course, according to this claim, Augustine cannot be expected actually to *say* that his views on women are intended as instruments of oppression. Rather, one must uncover and tease out the hidden message, thereby revealing the deeper (conscious or unconscious) motives at work.[4]

There are a number of fundamental difficulties with this approach. To begin with, one has to accept the metascientific feminist assumptions about the human condition. Then there is the assumption that the work of influential men has consistently aimed at the subjugation of women. Accepting such assumptions entails that one will uncover in the text just what one set out to dig for. Since one already knows that it is there one just keeps digging until it is 'found'.[5] This scholarly question-begging surely casts doubt upon the interpretive value of the method at work. Further, it seems rather arrogant to claim of anyone, much less of one of the West's greatest philosophers, that what he said is not what he meant. It seems even worse to claim that what he said is suspect since what he really meant was motivated by a desire for power. Ultimately, this approach seems to be simply a very impolite version of the genetic fallacy, and surely it is prudent to be skeptical that anyone is up to the task of uncovering such hidden motives in Augustine.

The other sort of argument that seeks to establish Augustine's misogyny is philosophical. According to this view, Augustine hated women because he hated sex, and he hated sex because he hated the human body, and such hatred of the body is due to his being a Platonist (or a Manichean). This is a simplified statement of an argument that is variously expressed, with myriad qualifications, by Kari Elisabeth Børresen, Rosemary Radford Ruether, and others.[6] Unlike the first sort of argument, this one can be discussed from the text. It will be useful, then, to examine what Augustine does say about women in theory, as well as his practical advice on how men and woman should deal with each other and how he himself treated the women in his own life.

II. Women in Theory

Does Augustine hate the body because he is a Platonist? The standard interpretation of the Platonic or Neoplatonic view, which is generally attributed to Plato himself, as well as to Plotinus, whose work had enormous influence on Augustine, is that according to Platonism the real person is the soul.[7] The soul is spiritual and eternal, whereas the body is a sort of unhappy accident. Matter, even if not always understood as evil *per se*, is still what lies farthest from Plato's Good or Plotinus' One. Base and corruptible, the body is a prison which traps the soul and keeps it from flying off to eternal wisdom. So death, as Socrates explains in the *Phaedo*, is not necessarily a bad thing (at least for the philosopher) because it frees the soul from the body. Manicheanism is even more negative towards the body than Platonism, in that it holds that matter is the very principle of evil, a palpable wickedness which is produced by that dark divinity which in the Manichean cosmos wages eternal war on its equal and opposite, the Good, which is light and spirit.

If the only extant writings of Augustine were his earliest works, one could perhaps make the argument that Augustine accepts this view. In my estimation, this interpretation of Augustine's early work would be wrong, but not wildly wrong. However, considering Augustine's work as a whole, and especially his most mature writings such as the *City of God*, this case is not even plausible. In *The City of God* Augustine asserts that the body is good. This is expressed not merely in an isolated sentence or two, nor does it require a carefully nuanced reading of the text to detect a positive attitude towards the body. To the contrary, Augustine goes on for chapter after chapter describing how the Platonists were wrong (e.g. XIII, 16–18). Augustine asserts that the whole human being is soul *and* body. Death is awful because it is the tearing apart of this unified thing (XIII, 6). At the resurrection, human beings will receive their bodies back, and the everlasting life of enjoying

God in paradise will be an embodied existence. In Augustine's time, the concept of the resurrection was hotly debated, and some of his contemporaries wanted to say that the resurrected "body" is only body in some metaphorical sense, especially since Paul himself calls it a "spiritual" body. Augustine, though, is adamant in asserting that the resurrected body is a physical body, with all that that entails. What Paul says, according to Augustine, is that even though the resurrected body will be perfectly governed by the spirit, it will still be flesh and blood (XIII, 19–23). The common contemporary idea that people "die and their souls (only their souls) go to heaven" does not find its origin in Augustine.

All of this is not to say that Augustine holds there are no problems connected with the body. The source of the problems is original sin, though. At the pre-dawn of history the first people disobeyed God and in doing so ensured that all of humanity would be infected by the horrible disease of sin. Though human beings are rational and social, and in some ways very capable creatures, it is also the case that something seems to have gone terribly wrong with the race from the very beginning. It is sometimes argued that this is a pessimistic view of human nature, but it is the person who can look at human history and conclude that humanity is doing about as well as can be expected who is the real pessimist. Augustine thinks that human beings were made much better originally and so our current condition requires a radical explanation.

For Augustine, the body in itself is made by God, is an essential aspect of the human being, and is therefore intrinsically good. The body has become a problem for fallen man, as Augustine explains in the *City of God*, because the consequence of sin is that the soul, in disobeying God, threw itself and the whole world into disorder, with the result that it can no longer control itself or the body it is supposed to govern. The fault for this tragedy belongs not to the body, but to the soul. Only something capable of reasoning and choosing can be held morally blameworthy, and of course reason and will are not in the body but the soul (XIV, 3–5).[8] Because the fallen soul cannot govern the body's appetites properly, the body can indeed become the catalyst for all kinds of sins of the flesh. It ought to be noted, though, that Augustine always argues that sins of the flesh are intrinsically less serious than sins which are more properly or purely the soul's. Pride is the worst sin, and it belongs to the soul alone. Satan is the worst sinner, but he is an entirely disembodied creature (*City of God* XIV, 3).

Augustine, then, does not hate the body. But does he hate sex? For Augustine, the problem, again, is not sex *per se* but fallen sex. A number of Augustine's contemporaries held that sexual procreation—or even the division of the human race into two genders—was a consequence of the fall, but Augustine rejects such a theory, arguing instead that Adam and Eve would have procreated sexually in the garden of Eden. Prior to sin, they would have had total control over their bodies, which would not have moved "on their own" so to speak. Rather, the first humans would have moved their bodily parts the way fallen human beings can move their arms or legs.[9]

The problem, then, is *fallen* sex, about which Augustine certainly does say that there is something intrinsically shameful. In this fallen world all intercourse inevitably involves a lack of control of the soul over the body (*City of God* XIV, 16–18). Augustine explains in *On the Good of Marriage* (Chapter 6) that even within licit marriage sex is a problem. If the married couple engages in sex for the purpose of having children, the good purpose overcomes the element of shame and the act is not sinful, but if the couple engages in sex just for pleasure then the act is sinful—not especially sinful, but sinful nonetheless. Many of Augustine's critics have pointed out that he does not seem to allow that sex might sometimes properly be used only to express love or to solidify the marriage relationship.[10] Such an omission seems mistaken to most people today, myself included, though an age in which sex has replaced the beatific vision as the supreme mystical experience for human beings perhaps ought to be cautious about accusing others of adopting an unrealistic approach to such a tricky business.

Augustine does indeed have a negative view of fallen sex.. Does he then hate women because of this? We know from Augustine's *Confessions* that he himself had a real problem with lust. He records that he struggled for years to find a true belief to live by, and that finally, after enormous effort, he had returned to Christianity, the faith which his mother had taught him when he was a child. That is, he became convinced *intellectually* that Christianity was the truth. However, he also felt that for him a total commitment to the Christian way of life meant embracing celibacy, and since he had a concubine and did not want to give up sex, he hesitated to be baptized. He says that he used to pray the marvelous prayer, so indicative of the human condition, "O Lord, Give me chastity and continence . . . but not yet!" (VIII, 7). Eventually, of course, he found the strength to live the life he chose.

Did Augustine blame women because he had such a struggle over lust? Obviously, it would be foolish to blame the chocolate cake because one abandoned one's diet, but the fact that such a move is illogical does not prevent some people from making it. Certainly there have been men who viewed women as wicked based on the evil desires they aroused.[11] There is, however, none of that anywhere in Augustine's works; indeed, he explicitly makes the point that a woman cannot be blamed because her natural, God-given beauty should tempt someone. "When a miser prefers his gold to justice," he says, "it is not the fault of the gold, but of the man" (*City of God* XV, 22).[12] Again, writing explicitly to console victims of rape, Augustine asserts unequivocally that, regardless of what may have been forced bodily against the woman's will, she remains utterly innocent and all fault falls upon the rapist (*City of God*, I, 16).

To sum up, then, the argument that Augustine hated women because he hated sex because he hated the body is indefensible. What, in fact, does he say about women? Augustine does think that in general women are weaker physically and intellectually than men, though, of course, for Augustine, whether one is strong or smart is not the most important thing about onself. What is really important is that one can be saved and live an eternal (embodied) life with God, and in this women are equal to men. Augustine makes this point very explicitly when he is discussing the first account in Genesis of the creation of human beings. Genesis says that God "made man to His image . . . male and female He made him." Some of his contemporaries, and Augustine himself in some earlier works, had been inclined to give this passage a figurative interpretation. Nevertheless, in his mature discussion in *On the literal meaning of Genesis* (III, 22, 34), he insists that the passage means that original human nature in its perfection was made male and female, and that "inasmuch as woman was a human being, she certainly had a mind, and a rational mind, and therefore she also was made to the image of God." It follows, of course, that women can be restored to the image of God just as men can and that hence, where it really counts, men and women are equal. Presumably this would largely explain why one does not find Augustine or later medieval philosophers particularly worried about "listening to women's voices." Insofar as women are rational beings made in the image of God, they will see the same truth that men see.

The second of the two Genesis stories of the creation of human beings has Eve created from Adam as his helper. Augustine explains that God did not make another man because he wanted people to procreate sexually so that the whole human race would come from the same parents and have a sort of family feeling toward each other. Augustine sees this generation of Eve from Adam as affirming the view that in marriage the wife should obey her husband, though it should also be noted that such a view, so at odds with the temper of our own time, does not originate with Augustine. The original culprit may be St. Paul, or, depending on the nature and status one accords to Scripture, perhaps a higher authority.[13]

Some of Augustine's detractors have seen his interpretation of these biblical passages as a justification of the oppression of women, even coming close to suggesting that Augustine condoned wife-beating.[14] This is, of course, a deep misunderstanding of Augustine's view; a misunderstanding which may stem from a failure to take the notion of sin as seriously as does Augustine. Augustine holds that the human condition as it is actually given in the world is thoroughly flawed. The relationships between people in this fallen world are inevitably colored by the pride and lust which are ubiquitous for the human race. There is nothing "normal" or "acceptable" about the fallen condition, and there is no "justification" for the oppression to which it gives rise. Augustine sees all human power relationships as intrinsically disordered if power means the ability to make people do what they do not want to do. In an unfallen world people would be responsive to the one proper authority which is God and one human being would not have power over another—whether it be the master over the slave, the husband over the wife, or the government over the citizen. The fall *explains* why there is oppression of all sorts, but it does not justify it.

Augustine does say that the husband and wife relationship, unlike the master/slave or the government/citizen relationship, would have existed in an unfallen world. But it would not have been a relationship of power in the contemporary sense of the term. On Augustine's assumption, Adam is smarter than Eve and hence she does owe him obedience. Given that assumption, Augustine's view is rather like saying that one ought to "obey" one's doctor. It must also be pointed out that not all the obligations within marriage fall on the shoulders of the wife, for the husband has to love his wife and promote her interests. The interpreter who holds all human relationships to be about power will take Augustine's assumption about the relative intelligence of men and women and the mutual obligations entailed to be a mask for his desire to maintain male domination, but Augustine holds that it is the desire for power which is the problem, whether it is manifested by a man or a woman. Of course, in the eyes of some, women will be happier and more fulfilled if only they are accorded more earthly power, but Augustine would view this as more of the same old wicked game: we do not like people making us do things, so we want to make them do things. On the Augustinian analysis, power is not the solution, but a large portion of the problem.

In summing up Augustine's "philosophy" of woman, it is safe to conclude that he is not, at least in theory, a misogynist. The argument that he somehow blames women for leading men into carnal temptations which bind them to the evil material side of the universe is indefensible. Matter in general and bodies and women in particular are all made by God and are good. There are physical and mental inequalities between men and women, but this does not justify the oppression of women by men, because nothing justifies an intrinsically disordered relationship. It does mean that (at least among those who are attempting to lead what Augustine sees as the Christian life) wives owe their husbands obedience. The next question is to consider how Augustine thinks this theory works out in practice.

III. Practical Advice

For Augustine, gender differences are for procreation, and so it is within marriage that being male and female is especially relevant to the task at hand. When one actually comes to look at Augustine's teaching on marriage and the marriage relationship, he seems surprisingly egalitarian, and when one considers him in light of his own era he is *quite* surprisingly egalitarian. This is not to say, of course, that his views reflect the standards for equality of our own day. An example is a letter (262) in which he chastises a woman, Ecdicia, for disposing of some property without her husband's permission.[15] Surely no modern wife of good character would sell the family car, even if it were in her name, without discussing it with her husband, but from Augustine's talk about the obedience Ecdicia owes to her husband as her "head" (quoting Paul), one suspects that had her husband sold the property without consulting Ecdicia, Augustine would have had no criticism to make. On the other hand, if we were to discuss the matter with Augustine today, perhaps he would agree with the view that a husband's love should include a policy of open fiscal communication with his wife.

In any case, Augustine's treatment of marriage is hardly "negative." At least on the key issue of sex, he is quite even-handed. Some of his contemporaries had taught that marriage was not intrinsically good, but only relatively good in comparison to fornication. Augustine discusses this attitude in *On the Good of Marriage* (Chapter 8), and finds it ridiculous. One might as well say that adultery is good because incest is worse, he points out. Rather, Augustine thinks that, for those who can manage it, celibacy is better, but marriage is a positive good, ordained by God from the beginning. It is good, moreover, not simply for the children, but also for the sake of the friendship between the couple and for the sake of the sacramental nature of marriage as a symbol of the union of Christ and the church. Regarding the issue of sexual rights, the issue which affects the couple as a married couple, the wife has as much authority as her husband. For example, apparently it was very common in Augustine's day, as it has been since, to treat infidelity on the part of the husband as a minor peccadillo, whereas no punishment seemed too much for an adulteress wife. Augustine condemns such a view in no uncertain terms, holding that the husband owes fidelity to his wife just as much as the wife to her husband.[16]

Augustine also argues that neither husband nor wife should refuse their partner's requests for sex. He believes that people will be able to pursue the God-centered life more single-mindedly if they refrain from sex, so he applauds married couples who decide to live a celibate life. However, he says to both wife and husband that if one partner should decide, out of this desire to dedicate himself to God, to eschew sex, unless the other partner consent he must fulfill his marital obligations, because otherwise his spouse may be led into temptation. Even though seeking the honor of the celibate life, one would fail in the more important duty of charity to spouse. This obligation is binding even if one's spouse makes very frequent demands which clearly go far beyond the desire for children, so this mutual obligation of wife and husband to keep each other out of danger of temptation is a very powerful duty indeed (*On the Good of Marriage*, Ch. 6).[17]

Can any of this be translated into a systematic analysis of how Augustine would view "women in the workplace"? He is certainly not a champion of women in positions of authority within the church, though again, this is not a position he originated. What about other roles? He says explicitly in the *City of God* (XIX, 17) that the particular mores of different societies are not especially important. Since there is no such thing as an "ideal" state, if one lives in a society in which one can meet one's material needs and worship God, one pretty much has the goods that society can offer. Constitutions and books of etiquette come and go; Augustine's concern is with the most basic and perennial issues of the human condition. Would he have any objections to women working at non-domestic tasks? It is hard to know, but perhaps not. In an early dialogue, *On Order*, which apparently records an actual philosophical discussion he and his friends had, one of the participants is his mother.[18] He suggests that Monica join in, but she hesitates at first, stating that she does not remember hearing that women usually engage in philosophical debate. Augustine's response is, basically, that just as there are stupid men, there are smart women, and since she is one of the latter, she should join in. In fact she does and she makes a significant contribution to the conversation. So apparently, at least if the issue is doing philosophy (surely one of the highest human enterprises), women can do the job, and since they can, they should.

Would Augustine be deeply concerned that women have not been able to break through that glass ceiling? Would he worry that there are very few female CEO's? Augustine is opposed to injustice, but he thinks it is inescapable in a fallen world. What one must do, practically speaking, is to improve what one can and live with what one must. There is, however, a deeper problem at work here. Augustine sees the pursuit of wealth and power as intrinsically foolish for anyone. If one's primary concern is to "succeed" in the eyes of the world, one has already failed as a citizen of the City of God. Those who aspire to worldly success have a horribly debased notion of their own value; such ambition represents a true lack of self-esteem, not to mention ignorance of God. The *real* goal is eternal beatitude with the loving Creator of all, and with respect to this goal Augustine is adamant that men and women are equal. There is no glass ceiling to keep anybody out of heaven.

IV. Women in Practice

How did Augustine treat the women he knew? It is generally inappropriate to judge a philosopher's thought on the basis of whether or not he actually practiced what he preached, for it is entirely possible to have a clear view of what should be done and yet not do it. On the other hand, Augustine is very concerned to expound a philosophy that will be a way of life, and if he did practice what he preached this will be evidence that he knew what he was talking about, and that what he preaches can indeed be practiced. Augustine preaches that where it counts, women are equal to men. Did he practice what he preached?

According to Augustine's biographer Possidius, after Augustine became a bishop he chose not to have any women living in his house. Apparently there was no rule against having his sister or his nieces, all of whom had chosen to live celibate lives, in the same house, but Augustine's house seems to have been rather more like a monastery, with other men living there. He felt that, even though probably there would not be any problem with his sister or his nieces, they would have friends coming to visit, and it would just be difficult for everybody to avoid temptation. If nothing else, women living in the same house with the men would give rise to gossip in the community.

The manner in which contemporary scholars treat this information is very revealing. Those who want to see Augustine as a misogynist cite this passage in Possidius as evidence of Augustine's extreme hatred of women—a hatred so powerful that he could not stand to be around them. At least one of Augustine's defenders is worried enough about the passage to suggest that maybe Possidius was engaged in an exercise of hagiography and was not actually reporting Augustine's lifestyle but was echoing a Life of St. Martin of Tours.[19] However, Augustine's reasoning on this matter strikes me as irreproachable. Surely, if one is concerned about chastity and the reputation for chastity, one does not turn one's house into a co-ed dorm.

Why, then, can contemporary scholars not take Augustine at his word? Perhaps they believe that decent, well-intentioned men and women can live together celibately quite comfortably without giving rise to temptation and gossip. If that is the assumption then one simply has to note that, unlike Augustine, these academics are rather naive. Another possibility could be that these scholars are so entirely out of sympathy with the idea that celibacy is a valuable way of life that they cannot imagine that Augustine would be motivated by a concern for safeguarding the chastity of his friends and relatives. A third possibility is that some scholars are willing to abuse the text in their zeal to discredit Augustine, and this may be an instance.[20] I do not see any reason not to take Augustine at his word when he explains why he did not have his sister and his nieces live in his house.

Moreover, we have a number of Augustine's letters to women, and these are very instructive. His writing style is the same when writing to women as when writing to men. He answers their theological questions and quotes Scripture, so he clearly believes that he is writing to intelligent, educated people.[21] He assumes his female correspondents have a high degree of literacy and have intellectual authority and competence, including the ability and responsibility to maintain their own orthodoxy; without remark, he relies on the advice of the *domina* Faviola in the matter of Antoninus.[22] In a charming letter to Florentina (267), Augustine praises the young student for her erudition and encourages her to continue her studies. Clearly he treats these female correspondents with respect.

Even more important, we know from the *Confessions* that there were two women who significantly influenced Augustine's life. One was his concubine, or maybe it would be better to call her his common-law wife, with whom he lived together faithfully in his pre-conversion years. The union, which lasted about ten years, produced a child by accident: Adeodatus, little gift of God. But Augustine had ambitions for worldly success and his concubine was low-born, so he sent her away in order to marry a rich, upper-class woman. At this time the bride-to-be was a little girl, so he had to wait two years before he could marry her. Apparently he was deeply wounded at having to send the concubine away, for he seems genuinely to have loved her even though the original attraction was purely physical. Then, while he was waiting to marry one woman and grieving for the loss of the first, he took yet another to be his mistress. This whole episode is quite sordid and one might be tempted to say that it shows that Augustine was simply a selfish libertine. But of course, Augustine hardly attempts to excuse himself for this behavior; instead, he thoroughly condemns and excoriates himself, confessing the whole affair in a tone of shame and sorrow.

Apparently this practice whereby a man would take a concubine until he could find a suitable wife was accepted in Augustine's day, but when he came to evaluate the practice later in his own life he says that a man who plans to leave a concubine and marry another woman has, in his soul, committed adultery with the concubine. However, if the concubine should remain faithful to him (as Augustine's had sworn to do), then he cannot call her an adulteress (*On the Good of Marriage*, Ch. 5). The conclusion is that concubinage is a bad idea all around; one should either plan to be celibate or get married and be faithful. Augustine never attempts to justify his treatment of this woman, and he clearly sees the pain caused to everybody, and especially to the woman, in this sort of relationship. It seems safe to say that the sad history of the concubine may be part of what motivated Augustine's uncompromising defense of marriage and fidelity.[23]

The other important woman in Augustine's life was his mother, Monica, and certainly the testimony of the *Confessions* is that the relationship was very close. Monica told her son stories about her own childhood, and not always flattering ones, since he hints that as a girl she may have had a bit of a drinking problem. Monica can err in a typical motherly fashion, as when she sends her brilliant son off to school in the iniquitous Carthage, caring more that he should cut a fine figure in the world than that he should stick to the path of self-restraint and virtue, but Augustine credits her unceasing prayers for bringing him back to the faith. In the earliest dialogues he wrote after his conversion, his mother participates and he praises her wisdom.

Augustine devotes the concluding pages of the first part of the *Confessions* to praising his mother, especially for her ability to get along even with difficult people (IX, 9). Her husband, Augustine's father, Patricius, was not a Christian, not faithful to his wife, and very hot tempered. Nevertheless, Monica paid him the patient obedience that she felt was due from a Christian wife, avoided his anger when it was extreme, and learned how to communicate her views to him in his better moments. This is yet another passage, though, where a look at the scholarly interpretations is illuminating, for at least one feminist scholar has treated Augustine's account of the relationship between his parents as a proof text for suggesting that Augustine justifies male oppression of women.[24] Such an interpretation is unjust, though, both to Augustine and to Monica. First, it ignores the fact, reported by Augustine, that Monica went to great lengths to win the favor of her mother-in-law, whom Patricius was very concerned to please. Since she seems to have been at least part of the cause for the hard feelings between Monica and Patricius, Augustine is obviously not describing a simple case of "men oppressing women." More important, though, is that Augustine does not in the least approve of Patricius' behavior toward Monica. Rather, what he records as admirable is his mother's wisdom in dealing with the trying situation with which she was confronted. In fact, Augustine ends his account of Monica's marriage by reporting that, as a result of his wife's unceasing efforts, Patricius eventually converted to Christianity and became a much better person. The feminist interpretation is to see Monica as the pathetic victim, whereas Augustine clearly believes that his mother, because of her patience, wisdom, courage, and charity, has brought two recalcitrant male members of her family to the Christian faith.

The *Confessions* (IX, 10) also reports a crucial philosophical interlude between Augustine and his mother at Ostia. The scene occurs soon after his conversion, and not long before Monica's death, when the two are engaged in philosophical conversation together and share a sort of mystical vision of God:

> Higher still we climbed, thinking and speaking all the while in wonder at all that you have made. At length we came to our own souls and passed beyond them to that place of everlasting plenty, where you feed Israel for ever with the food of truth. There life is that Wisdom by which all these things that we know are made, all things that ever have been and all that are yet to be. But that Wisdom is not made: it is as it has always been and as it will be for ever—or, rather, I should not say that it *has been* or *will be*, for it simply *is*, because eternity is not in the past or in the future. And while we spoke of the eternal Wisdom, longing for it and straining for it with all the strength of our hearts, for one fleeting instant we reached out and touched it. Then with a sigh, leaving *our spiritual harvest* [Rom 8:23] bound to it, we returned to the sound of our own speech, in which each word has a beginning and an ending—far, far different from your Word, our Lord, who abides in himself for ever, yet never grows old and gives new life to all things.[25]

This passage is, of course, one of the most famous of the entire work. Among other things, it is used to support the view that Augustine followed the Platonic or Neoplatonic tradition that sees union with the divine as the logical terminus for rational thought. The passage is crucially important for our purposes, however, because it demonstrates quite clearly that in Augustine's view women are capable of achieving the very highest goal attainable in this world. Thus, Augustine's assertion that women, as rational beings, are created in the image of God as surely as men are, is more than an abstract, speculative proposition, for he professes that his mother has gone as far as any earthbound being can go towards union with God.

Augustine's record of Monica's death is likewise very moving. He manages to hold back his tears all through the burial, but finally when he is alone he is unable to restrain himself and weeps unceasingly. This is the image that ends the narrative portion of Augustine's *Confessions* (IX, 13)—this father of western civilization weeping at his mother's death. The section concludes with the author asking that we who read his *Confessions* should pray for her.

It is very difficult to read what Augustine has to say about his mother and think of him as a misogynist. Rather than treating his mother, and the other women in his life, in the way that the feminists seem to see them, as having no other identity than as members of an oppressed group,[26] Augustine treats them as individuals. In the final analysis, Augustine's "philosophy of women," as it were, is radically individualistic and egalitarian in the sense that what counts—all that counts, ultimately—is that each of us is made in God's image. We are all at the same distance from God, that is, He is infinitely superior to any finite being. And we will each have to stand before Him alone. Nations and empires and even academic fashions will perish, but we are to endure forever, and that is what ought to be our principal concern.

NOTES

1. The lecture was generously sponsored by the Intercollegiate Studies Institute and by St. Michael's Institute of Gonzaga University. Unless otherwise noted, the translations used in the essay are by the author.
2. For analysis of this modern myth and its anti-Catholic origins, see Jeffrey Burton Russell, *Inventing the Flat Earth: Columbus and Modern Historians* (New York, 1991).
3. For some discussion of and citation to further literature on the attempt to psychoanalyze Augustine, see Robert J. O'Connell, S.J., "Sexuality in Saint Augustine," in *Augustine Today*, ed. Richard John Neuhaus (Grand Rapids, Michigan, 1993), 60–87.
4. Kim Power's *Veiled Desire: Augustine on Women* (New York, 1996) is an example of the genre. Power consistently theorizes well beyond what the text will allow, stating in her Introduction that, ". . . I believe that the text can convey more meaning than the author consciously intended" (p.11). For example, when Augustine uses the word *ancilla* (female slave) in Monica's description of the relationship of a wife to a husband (*Confessions* IX, 9), Power takes this to be a far-reaching endorsement of a new position entailing an even more degraded situation for the wife than would have been common in the society, that of a slave. This is a thesis which runs through her book, but is impossible to square with the rest of what Augustine has to say about men and women and marriage. Perhaps Monica was speaking somewhat ironically (the text says that her tone was light though her meaning was serious), perhaps she was simply describing the actual situation which the Roman wife had to deal with. At any rate, the evidence is far too slender to support the accusation.
5. Power (p. 13) candidly admits that "no more than Augustine's can my research be entirely value-free. In all my research I am informed by a feminist perspective, . . ."
6. Kari Elisabeth Børresen, "Patristic 'Feminism': The Case of Augustine" *Augustinian Studies* 25 (1994): 139–52 and Rosemary Ruether, "Misogynism and Virginal Feminism in the Fathers of the Church," in *Religion and Sexism*, ed. Rosemary Ruether (New York, 1974), 150–83.
7. The idea that the human being is to be identified with the human soul is key to Cartesian dualism which argues (following Avicenna) that because one is essentially a thinking thing (soul) one can know that one exists, even while doubting that one has a body. This is a common enough view in our time, at least in some circles, and all sorts of practical moral consequences can be derived from it. For example, if it is the thinking part which identifies a human being or a "person," then a human being does not become a full member

of the moral community until such time as the nascent person is actually capable of conscious thought. A number of philosophers advance this argument as a justification of abortion and infanticide. Moreover, if one's body is a mere epiphenomenon of one's true self, then perhaps it is not of major moral significance how that body is to be treated.

8. In Book XIV, Chapter 5, Augustine points out that while the Platonists are not as extreme in their censure of the body as the Manicheans, they nonetheless tend to blame all vice on bodily passions, and this results in a fundamental contradiction at the heart of their analysis of the human condition because they believe that the reason the eternal soul becomes embodied is that the soul itself desires the body.

9. Indeed, Augustine points out that even now some people exhibit remarkable control over their bodies. For example, he knows of a man who can swallow different things and then bring each different thing back up on command, and he has heard of people with other, equally remarkable talents, some of which perhaps ought not be discussed in polite company (*City of God*, XIV, 24). He says in the *City of God* that he could go on about the nature of prelapsarian sex but will not because, being fallen, the reader might take it the wrong way (XIV, 26).

10. He holds to this view in the *City of God* (XIV, 18,) of which the relevant books were written two decades after *On the Good of Marriage*. It is interesting to note, though, that the later work may indicate a more positive attitude towards sex. In the earlier work (Chapter 2) Augustine leaves it an open question whether or not Adam and Eve would have procreated sexually had they never sinned. By the time of the *City of God* he has decided that sexual intercourse would have been a part of life in the Garden of Eden.

11. For a prime example, see the entry on Tolstoy in Paul Johnson's *Intellectuals* (London: Weidenfeld & Nicolson, 1988).

12. Trans. Michael W. Tkacz and Douglas Kries in *Augustine: Political Writings* (Indianapolis, 1994).

13. It is striking that feminist detractors of Augustine often ignore the fact that much of his work is exegetical. Power, for example, complains of the church's tradition of male authority and locates a significant portion of the blame with Augustine. However, she steers entirely clear of what ought to be, for her as a Christian (p.13), a foremost concern: Augustine is working with a text which he believes to be divinely inspired and literally (in a very extended sense) true. It would take almost superhuman ingenuity to read this Pauline text in any way that could square with a feminist account. Presumably the Christian feminist does not feel the same commitment to the biblical text that Augustine does. (Or perhaps she will hold that the text, while important, only "says" what we, the reader, bring to it.) Still, it is interesting that some scholars seem to prefer to blame Augustine, rather than his source. Perhaps they believe that, though he was born a millennium and a half before the advent of deconstructionism, he should have *known* that he need not pay attention to the apparent import of the text.

14. Ruether ("Misogynism," 164) writes, "As wife, woman is also essentially body, but now the image of that totally submissive body, obedient to her 'head,' which serves the male without a murmur even under harsh and unjust treatment." Her citation is to Augustine's praise of Monica in the *Confessions*.

15. The more fundamental problem was that she had decided to become celibate against her husband's will. Neither husband nor wife have the right to do this, Augustine says.

16. See Jean A. Truax, "Augustine of Hippo: Defender of Women's Equality?" *Journal of Medieval History* 16 (1990): 279–99, esp. 289–90.

17. Rosemary Ruether ("Misogynism," 162) writes that in Augustine's view women are there to be "used" by men, either as "baby-making machines" or for the satisfaction of lust. This is not a fair characterization given that the husband is equally under the dual marital obligations to father children and to satisfy his wife's libido. If the husband "uses" the wife, the wife equally "uses" the husband. ("Uses" has a negative connotation, but here husband and wife engage in an activity together with shared goals. Do friends "use" each other for companionship?) Perhaps Ruether, in treating the marriage relationship as one-sided, is operating on the assumption that women in general do not want babies and are not subject to sexual desires. Augustine, who often comes across as much more conversant with the real world than his twentieth-century critics, would clearly reject this premise.

18. See J. Kevin Coyle, O.S.A., "In Praise of Monica: A Note on the Ostia Experience of Confessions IX," *Augustinian Studies* 13 (1982): 87–96, esp. 91–94.

19. Truax, "Augustine," 285–86. Truax's article is extremely informative and insightful, and my criticisms of "contemporary scholars" with respect to this issue are not aimed at her.

20. An example of such abuse was mentioned above (note 17). Ruether says that Augustine promotes a husband's "using" his wife, when in fact he insists (in a way quite radical in his own time) on equality of obligations with respect to the shared goals of children and sexual satisfaction. Another example of what seems to be a deliberate distortion of the text in this same article is when she quotes Augustine as saying that a man should love his wife as God's creature, but, ". . . hate in her the corruptible and mortal conjugal connection, sexual intercourse and all that pertains to her as a wife." Augustine, says Ruether, is exhorting the man to love, "in a way that totally despises her in all her bodily functions as a woman and identifies all depraved psychic characteristics with femininity" ("Misogynism," 161). Other feminist critics of Augustine have borrowed this point from Ruether, see for example Børresen ("Patristic 'Feminism,'" 141–42), Power (*Veiled Desire*, 160). What Ruether does not mention is that this passage is taken from a sermon in which Augustine is trying to explain what Christ could possibly mean when he says (Matt. 5: 31–2) that in order to follow him one must, "hate father and mother, and wife and children." Augustine holds that the Lord is exhorting people to "hate, not persons themselves, but those temporal relationships through which the present life is sustained. . . ." Jean Laporte and F. Ellen Weaver note this in "Augustine and Women: Relationships and Teachings," *Augustinian Studies* 12 (1981): 115–31, see esp. 116.

21. See Truax, "Augustine," 290–92.

22. Catherine Conybeare, "Women's Letters and Lettered Women: The Evidence from St. Augustine," paper presented at the Twelfth International Conference on Patristic Studies, Oxford, August 24, 1995.

23. Augustine never gives us the concubine's name. Truax ("Augustine," 282) suggests that he may have been protecting her.

24. Ruether, "Misogynism," 164.

25. Saint Augustine, *Confessions*, tr. R.S. Pine-Coffin (Penguin, 1961), 197–98. Italics his.

26. Power (*Veiled Desire*, 71) represents an egregious example of this. She begins her discussion of Monica, "It will be argued here that Monica's portrait in the *Confessiones* is based on the template of the ideal Roman mother, which Augustine modifies to incorporate his Christian and philosophic values." (p.71). Her chapters on the Virgin Mary begin, "In the previous chapters the impact of Augustine's culture, life experience and his doctrinal exposition have [sic] delineated three specific stereotypes of women." But these stereotypes are inadequate, being based on real women. "What was needed was a feminine 'meta-symbol,'" the Virgin Mary. But it is the contemporary interpreter, not Augustine, who views all these women as "symbols." On the unimpeachable principle that it is greater to exist in reality than in the mind alone, for Power to turn Monica and Eve and Ecdicia and Mary into theoretical constructs, symbolic characters in a one-note morality play, is to demean them.

Desert Ammas: Midwives of Wisdom

Mary Forman, O.S.B.
Sacred Heart Monastery, North Dakota

The women who came to be known as mothers of the early ascetical-monastic tradition represent the rich diversity of cultural backgrounds and regions in which they are found. Early twentieth-century scholarship on the origins of monasticism tended to hold a monolithic view of the movement of the monastic impulse beginning in the East, particularly Egypt, and making its way via translations of the *Life of Antony* and the stories of the heroes of the Egyptian desert to the West, that is, Italy and Southern Gaul. This approach all but ignored the contributions of the female leaders of households of Christian women in the West, who made pilgrimage to the East; supported whole colonies of male monastic communities in Egypt, Palestine and surrounding areas; and established monasteries for both men and women. In studying the recent translations of the lives of these women and their exploits on behalf of what came to be known as the monastic endeavor, one becomes aware of the unique role in history these women played in the actual foundations of monasticism. The following essay will serve only as an introduction to a few of these women, by addressing the meaning of each of the words in the title, "Desert Ammas: Midwives of Wisdom."[1]

I. Amma

Amma is the term designated for a "spiritual mother," an equivalent term to *abba* given to a "spiritual father." *Amma* derives from the semitic *Em(ma)* related to the Coptic *mau*, whereas *abba* is a transcription of the Hebrew. *Amma* refers to the *ability* one had to become a spiritual guide for another and is not explicitly associated with the role of abbess or superior.[2]

An understanding of *amma* as spiritual guide can be gained from reading a wonderful story told of the monk Zossima and his encounter with Mary of Egypt, a reformed prostitute, who lived as a wandering *amma* in the desert. The story opens with Zossima living a pious and blameless monastic life in the monastery in Palestine, where he had been since he was a weaned child. In his mid-life (at age 53) he began to be tormented by a temptation to think he had attained perfection in everything and needed no further teaching. Once while he was wondering if there were any other monk who exceeded him in virtue, an angel appeared to him, who informed him that he had "done as well as any man could" in the monastic life, but that more was in store for him. He was bidden to leave his native land, like Abraham, and to "go to the monastery which lies near the river Jordan."[3]

So Zossima left his home-monastery and followed the Jordan River until he found the monastery to which the angel directed him. The abbot of the place extended him the usual greetings of hospitality of prostration and prayer, and then asked Zossima from where and why he had come to such a humble place. Zossima responded that the where was not important, but the reason was in order to make spiritual progress; besides, he had heard that the abbot was one who "could draw a soul to intimate familiarity with Christ." The abbot replied that God alone was healer of human infirmity, but that if Zossima were moved by the love of God, he was welcome to stay and be fed by the grace of the Spirit of the Good Shepherd.[4]

Zossima stayed in that monastery and became very edified by the fervor of life he found there. On the first Sunday of Lent, all the monks met in the church to pray for each other, to receive a blessing and then went beyond the gates of the monastery out into the desert with a few provisions to fast and pray. The rule they solemnly kept was to enter into solitude and not to know how the others lived and fasted during Lent. On the twentieth day of his walking in solitude, Zossima came across what at first he thought was an apparition; on coming closer he found it was "a woman and she was naked, her body black as if scorched by the fierce heat of the sun, the hair on her head was white as wool and short, coming down only to the neck."[5]

> [Zossima] knelt down and asked her to give him the customary blessing. She also knelt down. So they both remained on the ground asking one another for a blessing. After a long time the woman said to Zossima, "*Father* Zossima, it is proper for you to give the blessing and say the prayer, for you have the dignity of the office of a priest, and for many years you have stood at the holy table and offered the sacrifice of Christ." These words threw Zossima into greater dread, he trembled and was covered with a sweat of death. But at last, breathing with difficulty, he said to her, "O *Mother* in the spirit, it is plain from this insight that all your life you have dwelt with God and have nearly died to the world. It is plain above all that grace is given you since you called me by my name and recognized me as a priest although you have never seen me before. But since grace is recognized not by office but by gifts of the Spirit, bless me, for God's sake, and pray for me out of the kindness of your heart." So the woman gave way to the wish of the old man, and said, "Blessed is God who cares for the salvation of souls." Zossima answered "Amen", and they both rose from their knees.[6]

The woman is puzzled as to why Zossima has come to her, thinking that the Holy Spirit has sent him to perform a service for her in due time. She inquires about the Christian leadership in the empire and how the church is faring. He responds:

"By your holy prayers, *Mother*, Christ has given lasting peace everywhere. But hear the request of an unworthy monk and pray to the Lord for the whole world and for me, a sinner, that my wandering through the desert should not be without fruit." She answered him, "It is only right, *Father* Zossima, that you who have the office of a priest should pray for me and for all; but we must be obedient so I shall willingly do what you bid me." With these words, she turned to the East and raising her eyes to heaven and stretching up her hands she began to pray moving her lips in silence, so that almost nothing intelligible could be heard. So Zossima could not understand anything of her prayer.[7]

As she continues in prayer, even to the point of levitation, he becomes terrified and cries out within himself, "Lord, have mercy!"

Twice in this account Zossima the priest "father" calls Mary "mother," that is, *amma*, because she is a "Mother in the spirit." Of significance in the story is the fact that the normal cultural expectation that a Christian woman seek a blessing of a priest is reversed; instead Zossima the "father" asks a blessing of the "mother." When later he petitions her to pray for him, she is at first reluctant: "It is only right, Father Zossima, that you who have the office of a priest should pray for me and for all." Her hesitation to extend a blessing, the cultural prerogative of the priest, is transformed into awareness of their mutuality in Christ, "but *we* must be obedient so I shall willingly do what you bid me."

In the rest of the narrative, Mary ministers to Zossima by telling the story of her past sin and call to repentance. As a consequence of her confession, a friendship of hearts develops. In the process, Zossima learns about one who exceeded him in virtue because she allowed the grace of the Holy Spirit to work redemption in her.

This capacity to cooperate with the grace of the Spirit, making of woman a channel of that grace to others, is the reason Mary and other women of spiritual strength were called *ammas*. Three women—Sarah, Theodora and Syncletica—are specifically designated *ammas* and their apophthegms or wise sayings are found in the alphabetical collection of *The Sayings of the Desert Fathers*.[8] The very fact that their sayings appear in the collection indicates their teaching has "doctrinal value." This means that the compilers of the sayings did not discriminate on the basis of gender in their selection of sayings. Even further, these women exercised a spiritual maternity on a par with the spiritual paternity of the *abbas*; thus they could transmit spiritual doctrine with the same right as the monks. The only thing they could not do was absolve sins sacramentally.[9] We encounter the distinction between teaching of spiritual matters and the priestly functions of preaching in the story of St. Pachomius' sister Mary, *amma* and superior of the women's community in the Thebaid, Upper Egypt.

In keeping with the gospel directive to forsake family for the sake of Christ, Pachomius makes no effort to greet his blood sister Mary physically. However, sensing that her purpose might be to follow Christ in the monastic way of life, he provides the means to foster that vocation by having the brothers build her a monastery not far from his own. The story about Mary occurs in "The Bohairic Life of Pachomius," ch. 27, which further relates:

> Later on many heard about her and came to live with her. They practised *ascesis* eagerly with her, and she was their *mother* and their worthy *elder* until her death.
>
> When our *father* Pachomius saw that the number of [these women] was increasing somewhat, he appointed an old man called Apa Peter, whose "speech was seasoned with salt" to be their *father* and to preach frequently to them on the Scriptures for their souls' salvation. [Pachomius] also wrote down in a book the rules of the brothers and sent them to them through [Peter], so that they might learn them.
>
> If ever any of the brothers who had not yet attained perfection wanted to visit one of his relatives among [the sisters], [Pachomius] sent him through his house-master's direction to the holy old man Apa Peter who in turn sent word to their *mother* to come out with her and another sister. They sat down together with great propriety until the visit came to an end; then they got up, prayed and withdrew. When one of [the sisters] died, they brought her to the oratory and first their *mother* covered her with a shroud. Then the old man Apa Peter sent word to our *father* Pachomius who chose experienced brothers and sent them to the monastery with [Apa Peter]. They proceeded to the assembly room and stood in the entry-way chanting psalms with gravity until [the deceased] was prepared for burial. Then she was placed on a bier and carried to the mountain. The virgin sisters followed behind the bier while their *father* walked after them and their *mother* before them. When the deceased was buried, they prayed for her and returned with great sorrow to their dwelling.[10]

Concerning this passage, the monastic scholar Irénée Hausherr writes that the function of the abba took nothing away from the authority of the spiritual mother. Mary was still "the mother of virgins" and she continued in her capacity of "elder until the day of her death." Abba Peter's role was to devote himself to talking to the Sisters about the Scriptures, that is, he was to be a preacher and lecturer of doctrine. In addition, he was in charge of supplies for the manual labor done by the community. But beyond that, the *amma* had full responsibility of her community.[11]

Thus our two sample stories reveal the esteem with which female Christian elders were held and the recognition of their authority as spiritual leaders.

II. Desert

Many of the *ammas* dwelt either in the desert directly or on its edge. The word "desert" for this time period and its many cultures connoted a rather ambivalent term, according to the scholar of early monasticism Antoine Guillaumont.[12] Already in the Bible, there is an idealism or mystique of the desert, because it was the place where the Israelites spent so many years, where God made covenant with them. To the Hebrew prophets a return to the desert was the sign of reconciliation with Yahweh. Another connotation is more realistic: all peoples of the ancient Near East viewed the desert as the complete opposite of inhabited and cultivated land; the desert was a deserted and sterile land, often associated with the devastations of war, or in the case of the Israelites, the curse of Yahweh, for it was there all manner of savage beasts lived. Moreover, in the Egyptian mind, the desert was the dwelling place of demons.

In the literature of the first century before Christ and continuing into the first centuries of the Christian era, there was a Hellenistic notion which provided a romantic nuance to desert, as a place of solitude to which the weary person of the city could retire in order to regain peace and involve oneself in philosophy or meditation. The close association of the Greek words *heremos* [ἔρημος] and *heremia* [ἐρημία] meaning "desert" with *hēremia* [ἠρεμία] meaning "calm" probably accounts for this notion. Accordingly, Origen refers to John the Baptist's enjoyment of the calm life and solitude of the desert.[13] This sense of solitude and retirement is used by Basil of Caesarea in his letter 14 (ca. 360) to his friend Gregory of Nazianzen, the former trying to persuade the latter to join him in his monastic project at Annesi.

Jerome, too, in his early days of solitude in the desert of Chalcis, Syria, will write enthusiastically of the desert to Heliodorus:

> O desert, bright with the flowers of Christ! O solitude whence come the stones of which, in the Apocalypse, the city of the great king is built! O wilderness, gladdened with God's especial presence! What keeps you in the world, my brother, you who are above the world? How long shall gloomy roofs oppress you? How long shall smoky cities immure you? Believe me, I have more light than you. Sweet it is to lay aside the weight of the body and soar into the pure bright ether.[14]

In fact, though, Jerome could only stand the Chalcis desert a couple of years. For his health failed from harsh fasting; he became embroiled in the disputes over the triune Godhead which were raging around the East; and his was a very difficult personality, described by J.N.D. Kelly as "self-willed and sharp-tongued, irascible...inordinately proud of his Roman links," which would only have heightened the uneasy relations he had with his uncultivated, less educated Syriac-speaking neighbors.[15] Although he had the companionship of a team of copyists and a vast circle of correspondents, nevertheless, he craved his former life in Rome.[16]

Later on, Jerome wrote the *Life of Paul*, supposedly the story of the first hermit of the Egyptian desert, but, in fact, a fictitious story told in competition for the attention given to the *Life of Antony*, from which it borrowed a good deal.[17] In this work, the desert was portrayed as a place inhabited by strange and sympathetic animals, as well as a place of miracles. This kind of writing would generate an enduring literary picture of the desert as the place where God dwells, as the scene of battles of heroic monks with the demons of human passions, and as the paradise regained where humans and beasts dwell in idyllic harmony.

Besides the literary desert of monks, there was the real desert of the anchorites in Egypt. Egyptian *fellahs* or peasants, who predominantly lived in the villages along the Nile or in the Delta region, considered the desert a place of terror. Their lives in the oases were boundaried by the great deserts around them: the Libyan Desert to the west and the more mountainous Arabic Desert to the east. The Nile area was called *kémi* or "black land," dedicated to the god of life Osiris and his son Horus, who was posed against Seth, the god of the sterile desert, of the "red land," who was hostile and malevolent.[18]

The desert was not only sterile, but also "the region of the tombs, the domain of the dead, where the Egyptian never ventured without fear."[19] It was the area of bands of nomads—Libyans, Mazic, Blemmyes, who were often hostile to strangers. Moreover, the desert was home to dangerous animals: serpents, hyenas, snakes and jackals, who inhabited its abandoned temples and ruins of the desert. No better description of this desert exists than that of the *Life of Antony* (chapters 12, 50–52), as a wilderness of wild beasts, creeping things and the demons.

Soon so many monks and a few virgins came to dwell in the desert, that it became a veritable city. The term *desertum ciuitas* (the desert a city) acquired two meanings. Literally, the deserts became peopled with hundreds of monks, many of them living in lauras or associations of huts and cells. Eventually, monasteries arose to accommodate the growing numbers and gardens were planted to provide food for the many guests.[20] Finally, in a spiritual sense, the desert was the place of ascetical combat, where the devil had come to tempt Christ. As Antoine Guillaumont has pointed out:

> This scene points to the victory of Christ over Satan, which inaugurates a redemptive work. In this perspective, the monk, by going to the desert to do battle against the devil and to triumph over him, reproduces, continues in a certain manner, the redemptive action. Thus [s/]he is an "athlete", who goes to the desert in order to confront the demons, in order to battle with them...in the open and eye to eye.[21]

While a few ascetics may have gone to the desert to battle the demons, far more sought to find God there. In the desert, the monastic sought to unify one's life, that is, to renounce whatever was the source of division. To do so meant abandoning the pursuit of land, the life of the village and the accumulation of possessions. The desert represented a rupture from the "world," a place far from the attachment to the cares and goods of the world. Thus "flight into the desert" became flight from the responsibilities toward the land, daily contacts with people, especially the opposite gender, in order to pursue *hesychia*: solitude, tranquillity, the practice of continual remembrance of God. It was the attraction of this pursuit that drew so many to the desert and made of it eventually a city.

However, solitude did not mean an immediate freedom from all temptations and distractions. In the desert, the monastic person strove in a battle of his/her heart against the *logismoi*—the passions of gluttony, avarice, lust, pride, vainglory, etc., which manifested themselves in nostalgic memories of past luxuries and relationships; solitude meant facing the daily assaults of discouragement, lethargy and other subtle underminings of one's ascesis and commitment. Over years, the heart became quieted and stilled to welcome pure prayer and the experience of the divine.[22]

Thus, we see that there is a whole range of meanings for the desert. The women who lived this life, the "desert ammas," reflect this range, from the true dwellers of the uninhabited desert regions, like Mary of Egypt, to virgins, who lived "hidden" in households and pondered the philosophy of the scriptures, that is, in a pursuit of the love of wisdom. In this latter category belongs Macrina, Gregory of Nyssa's eldest sister, who founded a Christian household community in Cappadocia.[23] In between are women like Syncletica, who, although she experienced a time of solitude in the tombs, later became an *amma* and superior of a community of virgins in Alexandria.[24] Other women, like Paula and Melania the Elder, would begin by forming households of virgins and widows comprised mainly of relatives and servants, but then would leave their homeland in Rome to co-found double monasteries of men and women in the Holy Land. Jerome and Paula founded monasteries in Bethlehem; Rufinus, a childhood friend of Jerome, along with the wealthy benefactress Melania the Elder, founded monasteries at the Mount of Olives in Jerusalem.[25] Egeria, a holy woman ascetic and member of a community of virgins, purported to be situated in Spain or Gaul,[26] enjoyed several pilgrimages to the sacred biblical sites in the Holy Land. She represented a kind of *amma*, who nurtured her own faith and curiosity by touring the famous desert places where she prayed and worshipped. The vivid account of the many monasteries and shrines which she visited, as well as the monks and virgins inhabiting them, Egeria wrote up and sent to her sisters back home.

III. Midwives

The third term associated with the desert *ammas* is "midwives." By this expression is intended the capacity of these *ammas* to be *pneumataphores* or bearers of the spirit.[27] These women, in their spiritual direction and in their generous sharing either of physical wealth or the wealth of their experience and giftedness, were able to mid-wife Christ's birth in those whom they served. Quite often their direction was a very indirect but specific treatment of an ailment. One such example is that of Melania the Elder's detection of the illness of Evagrius, who had been forced to leave Cappadocia because of an indiscreet relationship with a government official's wife. Palladius' *Lausiac History* records the account, as summarized below.

Evagrius boarded a ship for Jerusalem. Upon landing he met the Roman lady, the blessed Melania, to whom he said nothing about his past indiscretion. While staying at her monastery he developed a fever, which lasted six months and caused a wasting away of his flesh. Doctors were summoned but could not find the cause of his illness. Finally, Melania went to him and said:

> "Son, I am not pleased with your long sickness. Tell me what is in your mind, for your sickness is not beyond God's aid." Then he confessed the whole story. She told him: "Promise me by the Lord that you mean to aim at the monastic life, and even though I am a sinner, I will pray that you be given a lease on life." He agreed, and was well again in a matter of days. He got up, received a change of clothing at her hands, then left and took himself to the mountain of Nitria in Egypt.[28]

Melania detected with her spiritual sight what the doctors were unable to find, namely, that Evagrius had made a promise to God to become a monk and had reneged on that promise once he had left Cappadocia. Moreover, she trusted in the God of her prayer, mindful that she herself was a sinner. Her *surety* contrasted with Evagrius' uncertainty. Her detection of the source of the illness and her prayer brought about the healing of this young man, who would eventually become the first systematician of the monastic life and whose writings would exert a profound influence on Cassian, one of Benedict's predecessors. One wonders how the course of western monasticisms would have been changed had it not been for Melania's intervention. While the midwife has often been neglected by church historians, the child of her intercessory prayer has been remembered for centuries.

She undertook to be responsible with respect to Evagrius' salvation, as well as his physical well-being. Her care for Evagrius represents the ancient practice of being *custos animi*, that is, a relationship implying the three elements of "1) responsiblity for another person's well-being and ultimate salvation, 2) a knowledge of his or her inner life, [and] 3) a spiritual dimension."[29] Her listening intently to Evagrius' dream, revelatory of his inner chaos, became the medicine he needed to become well. Other accounts of her reveal her profound knowledge of the scriptures, from which she drew spiritual nourishment, not only for herself, but also for others.

Moreover, she was a formidable advocate of Christian asceticism, persuading her nephew-in-law Apronianus and his wife Avita to embrace the life.[30] Later on, her granddaughter Melania the Younger, along with her husband Pinian, would settle in Thagaste, first home of Augustine, where they financed many charitable and monastic projects from their vast wealth.[31] Another distant relative of the older Melania, Paulinus of Nola, and his wife Therasia embraced the ascetical life and established a site of pilgrimage, a hostel and monastery at Nola (near Naples) in honor of St. Felix.[32] From this one matriarch of living faith sprang a whole legacy of spiritual children, who were dedicated to the pursuit of holiness.

A different example of midwifery can be seen in a story told by Amma Theodora.

> Amma Theodora also said, "There was a monk, who, because of the great number of temptations said, 'I will go away from here.' As he was putting on his sandals,

he saw another man who was also putting on his sandals and this other monk said to him, 'Is it on my account that you are going away? Because I go before you wherever you are going.'"[33]

The scene was likely a conversation between Amma Theodora and a monk, struggling with the temptation to leave his vocation or desirous to go somewhere else where temptations were less severe. Theodora did not give direct advice, nor say who the second monk was in her story. Rather, like a good teacher, she posed a kind of parable or story, in which the monk was to see himself and then "draw the inescapable conclusion: we each take ourselves wherever we go."[34] Her method of spiritual direction was a form of "indirection," under which lie three assumptions, according to Roberta Bondi:

> The restless monk who undoubtedly [1] could not hear direct advice about running away, [2] *could* hear the story and draw the conclusion, and [3] he was able to hear it because the amma did not stand between him and what she was trying to get him to see.[35]

The capacity to distinguish spirits lying behind behaviors was another of the valuable gifts of midwives of the spirit. Amma Syncletica, a fifth-century spiritual elder, said:

> There is a grief that is useful, and there is a grief that is destructive. The first sort consists in weeping over one's own faults and weeping over the weakness of one's neighbours, in order not to destroy one's purpose, and attach oneself to the perfect good. But there is also a grief that comes from the enemy, full of mockery, which some call *accidie*. This spirit must be cast out, mainly by prayer and psalmody.[36]

A sadness that is beneficial has a far different quality to it than one that leads to depression, guilt or the subtle temptation of *acedia*, that state of mind which, because it is so reliant on self-efforts, encourages giving up the pursuit of holiness altogether. In distinguishing the two kinds of grief, Syncletica reflects the teaching of Cassian.[37] Her unique addition to Cassian's teaching is the notion of the beneficial grief of weeping over one's neighbors. Not only does Syncletica discern the difference between the spirits behind the grief, she is able to recommend the remedies of prayer and psalmody. The dejection that leads to abandonment of the monastic vocation is one which tempts the monastic to give up prayer and psalmody. Thus the very practices one is tempted to cast aside provide the means of healing.

In our final example of spiritual midwifery, Amma Theodora gives an explanation of how one recognizes a true spiritual master.

> The same amma said that a teacher ought to be a stranger to the desire for domination, vain-glory, and pride; one should not be able to fool him by flattery, nor blind him by gifts, nor conquer him by the stomach, nor dominate him by

anger; but he should be patient, gentle and humble as far as possible; he must be tested and without partisanship, full of concern, and a lover of souls.[38]

Theodora teaches that the virtues of true mid-wives of people's spiritual lives are patience, gentleness and humility—the complete opposites to domination, vainglory and pride. The qualities[39] of such a discerning pneumataphore are testings, which have determined the fruit; a lack of partisanship, that is, freedom from an ardent or militant support of a cause, person, party or idea; and being a lover of souls. It is noteworthy that Theodora recommends all these qualities together. In other words, it is not enough to love people in order to be a good spiritual director. One must also be discerning, that is, subject to the testings of the spirit, and reveal a certain detachment from any sole part of things, which takes away from the whole.

IV. Wisdom

Finally, "wisdom" was the gift that allowed these ammas to distinguish one spirit from another. Discernment, the most important of all virtues, is intimately linked with wisdom, at least in the Latin verb. *Sapere*, which initially meant "to taste," eventually came to mean "to discern" and "to be wise."[40]

Apart from the etymology of words, wisdom, or *Hagia Sophia* as she came to be known in the wisdom books of the Jewish scriptures, refers to the divine Word and Wisdom, who "was associated with creation—either as the master craftsman at God's side, fashioning all things well, or as the wide-eyed child who took delight in God's inhabited earth (Prov. 8:30)."[41] In the book of Wisdom 7:22, 25–27, Wisdom became the image of God and queen consort, the partner of God and bestower of every good:

> For within her is a spirit intelligent, holy, unique, manifold, subtle....She is a breath of the power of God, pure emanation of the glory of the Almighty; hence nothing impure can find a way into her. She is a reflection of the eternal light, untarnished mirror of God's active power, image of his goodness. Although she is one, she can do all; herself unchanging, she makes all things new.[42]

In the Christian scriptures, Sophia became associated with Christ, particularly in the writings of Paul, who asserts Christ as "the power and the wisdom of God" (1 Cor 1:24). He addressed his words to some Corinthian Christians who

> had adopted a charismatic spirituality that laid great stress on "wisdom" and "gnosis," visions and revelations, eloquent preaching, ecstatic trances, speaking in tongues, and similar phenomena...he tried to make their religion more christocentric by proclaiming that in Christ alone they could find everything they sought through the cultivation of exotic mystical experience. Above all, Christ alone was the true Sophia, the "secret and hidden wisdom of God...decreed before the ages for our glorification" (1 Cor 2:7).[43]

The pursuit of philosophy (the Greek word *philosophia* means "love of wisdom") in early Hellenistic Christianity was strongly associated with living a deeply committed Christian life. This connection is shown in an excerpt from the *Life of Macrina* by her brother Gregory of Nyssa, in which he related of her the following:

> Our narrative was not based on hearsay, but we talked with detailed knowledge of things our own experience has taught us, without appealing to any outside testimony; for the maiden we spoke of was no stranger to my family so that I had to learn from others the marvels of her life. No, we had the same parents and she was, so to speak, a votive offering of the fruits to come, the first offshoot of our mother's womb. And so, since you were convinced that the story of her good deeds would be of some use because you thought that a life of this quality should not be forgotten for the future and that she who had raised herself through philosophy to the highest limit of human virtue should not pass along this way veiled and in silence, I thought it good to obey you and tell her story, as briefly as I could, in a simple unaffected narrative.[44]

One pauses on the words, "she who had raised herself through philosophy to the highest limit of human virtue should not pass this way veiled and in silence." Kevin Corrigan, translator of this work and himself a professor of philosophy, states that this *vita* and its parallel text, *On the Soul and Resurrection*—a long dialogue between Macrina and her brother Gregory, were intended to portray Macrina as a second Socrates, who searched "for a living wisdom which involved the conversion of the whole person to the Good." Such is the spirit of Gregory's use of the term "philosophy."[45] But the food for Macrina's philosophy is the teachings of the scriptures. Her wisdom

> embraces the whole of human life: prayer, manual work, hospitality, care of the sick, of the poor and the dying. It is a life entirely given to God, a life lived "on the boundaries" of human nature. It includes a vibrant intellectuality, life-long study and a spirit of true inquiry, and it culminates in the divine love of a *person*, Christ.[46]

In this *vita* Macrina is portrayed with all the manifestations of the title of this paper. First of all, she lived a life hidden at Annisa by the Iris River, that was in some ways a form of desert; she was far from the arenas of controversies and theological preoccupations of her three brother bishops. Secondly, she was an *amma*, who even as a young teen served as "father, teacher, guide, mother, counsellor in every good" to her youngest brother Peter, the last of ten children. She never left her own mother, whom she persuaded to join in the ascetic life of their household community, where Macrina eventually became superior of the whole community, comprised of men and virgins, each living in separate dwellings. Thirdly, she was midwife in the sense that Gregory looked upon her as "my teacher in everything." It was Macrina, who, when her brother Basil came home from rhetorical school all puffed up with his new knowledge, took him to task and won him over to the pursuit of Christian philosophy. Finally, the solemn pursuit of her life was philosophy, the love of wisdom, who, in the person of Christ her Beloved, occupied her last dying thoughts.[47]

V. Conclusion

All of the ammas mentioned above were women who experienced a deep love of Christ, nurtured by their dwelling on the scriptures which became Word made flesh in the reality of their lives. In turn, many, like Paula and both Melanias, encouraged the pursuit of scriptural study, dialogues with the commentators on scripture, but most importantly the living out of the wisdom of the scriptures by their works of charity on behalf of others. Others, like Mary of Egypt, Syncletica and Theodora, became living icons of Christ to those who came to them in need of a healing word. From the Word pondered in their hearts, all these women became wise in the ways of Christ and thus were able to serve as mid-wives to the birthing of full Christ-life in others.

NOTES

1. This essay was presented as part of a lecture series at Gonzaga University on "Women in the Early Church," sponsored by St. Michael's Institute of Gonzaga University and the Intercollegiate Studies Institute, February 20, 1997.

2. Irénée Hausherr, *Spiritual Direction in the Early Christian East*, Cistercian Studies 116, tr. Anthony P. Gythiel (Kalamazoo, MI, 1990), 277.

3. Benedicta Ward, "St Mary of Egypt; the Liturgical Icon of Repentance," in *Harlots of the Desert: A Study in Repentance in Early Monastic Sources* (London & Oxford, 1987), ch. 2, pp. 37–38.

4. Ward, "St Mary of Egypt," ch. 3, p. 38.

5. Ward, "St Mary of Egypt," ch. 7, p. 41.

6. Ward, "St Mary of Egypt," chs. 9–10, p. 42. Italics indicates my emphasis.

7. Ward, "St Mary of Egypt," ch. 9–10, pp. 42–43. Italics indicates my emphasis.

8. *The Sayings of the Desert Fathers: The Alphabetical Collection*, Cistercian Studies 59, tr. Benedicta Ward (London & Oxford, 1975): Theodora, pp. 82–84; Sarah, pp. 229–30; Syncletica, pp. 230–35.

9. Josep M. Soler, "Les Mères du désert et la maternité spirituelle," *Collectanea Cisterciensia* 48 (1986): 239.

10. "The Bohairic Life of Pachomius," ch. 27: 'Pachomius' sister founds a monastery for women,' *Pachomian Koinonia I: The Life of Saint Pachomius, Cistercian Studies* 45, tr. Armand Veilleux (Kalamazoo, MI, 1980), 49–51. Italics indicates my emphasis.

11. Hausherr, 285–86.

12. Antoine Guillaumont, *Aux origenes du monachisme chrétien: Pour une phénoménologie du monachisme*, Spiritualité orientale, 30 (Maine & Loire, 1979), 69. This section of my essay (on the desert) draws much from Guillaumont, 69–86.

13. Guillaumont, 73–74, citing Origen, *Homélies sur Luc* XI and X (Ed. Crouzel, Fournier and Périchon, Paris, 1962); cf. *Homélies sur l'Exode*, III.3 (trad. Fortier et de Lubac, Paris, 1947).

14. Jerome, *Ep.* 14.10, *St. Jerome: Letters and Select Works*, tr. W. H. Fremantle, NPNF 2.6, 17.

15. J. N. D. Kelly, *Jerome: His Life, Writings and Controversies* (New York, 1975), pp. 48 and 52 on his fasting; pp. 52–53 on the Trinitarian controversies; and p. 55 on aspects of his personality.

16. Kelly, *Jerome*, 52; see *Ep.* 22.7, NPNF 2.6, 24–25.

17. This is the position taken by Manfred Fuhrmann, "Die Mönchsgeschichten des Hieronymus Form-experimente in erzählender Literatur,"in *Christianisme et formes littéraires de l'antiquité tardive en occident*, Fondation Hardt pour l'étude de l'antiquité classique entretiens, 23 (Geneva, 1977), 41–99.

18. Guillaumont, 77.

19. Guillaumont, 77–78.

20. Guillaumont, 80–81.

21. Guillaumont, 81.

22. Guillaumont, 85–86. For a helpful explanation of the development of the *logismoi*, i.e., impure thoughts (*logismoi akatharoi*) or those leading to the passions, from a beginning suggestion all the way to formation of a vicious habit, see Tomaŝ Ŝpidlík, *The Spirituality of the Christian East: A Systematic Handbook, Cistercian Studies* 79, translated by Anthony P. Gythiel (Kalamazoo, MI, 1986), 238–41.

23. Her *vita* is available in the English translation, Gregory, Bishop of Nyssa, *The Life of Saint Macrina*, Peregrina Translation Series 10 (*Matrologia Graeca*), translated by Kevin Corrigan (Toronto, 1987).

24. See in English translation, Pseudo-Athanasius, *The Life of Blessed Syncletica*, Peregrina Translations Series 21, translated by Elizabeth Bryson Bongie (Toronto, 1995).

25. Jerome documents the founding of monasteries for men and women by Paula, to whom he served as spiritual advisor, in his letter 108.20. Palladius' *Lausiac History* 46.5–6 records the founding of a women's monastery by Melania the Elder in Jerusalem and the fact that Rufinus of Aquileia dwelt close by. J. N. D. Kelly, *Jerome*, writes of the latter pair as starting ascetic foundations in the Holy Land (see p. 121).

26. While the English translator of the travels of Egeria, George E. Gingras, *Egeria: Diary of a Pilgrimage*, ACW 38 (NY/Ramsey, NJ, 1970), p. 11 maintains that Egeria was from Galicia, a province of Spain; and John Wilkinson, translator, *Egeria's Travels* (London, 1971), p. 3, states the following: "She may have been a Gaul from Aquitaine,or a Spaniard from Galicia....[or] some other western province of the Roman Empire"; Hagith Sivan believes that the most likely homeland for Egeria was the Gallic port of Arles (p. 65). The latter argues that the belief that Egeria came from Spain is due to a seventh-century

letter from the Spanish monk Valerius to members of a Galician (Spanish) monastery, which exhorts the community to follow Egeria's untiring devotion to God (p. 59), but in fact, Valerius never tells his readers where Egeria is from (pp. 61–62). See Hagith Sivan, "Who Was Egeria? Piety and Pilgrimage in the Age of Gratian," *Harvard Theological Review* 81:1 (1988): 59–72.

27. Irénée Hausherr, *Spiritual Direction in the Early Christian East*, p. 341, gives the following definition in his glossary: "*Pneumataphore*, a bearer (*pherein*) of the Spirit (*pneuma*), a synonym of *pneumatikos*, 'one who is spiritual.' Refers to the person who bears the Spirit or is borne by the Spirit, depending on tonic accent. Hence, inspired, prophetic. [Bilaniuk, P. B., 'The Monk as Pneumataphor in the Writings of Basil the Great,' in *Diakonia* 15 (1980): 49–63]." Because *ammas* are "spiritual mothers" (Hausherr, pp. 26 and 277), they are no less *pneumataphores* than their male counterparts, the "spiritual fathers."

28. "Evagrius #7–9," pp. 112–113, in *Palladius: The Lausiac History*, tr. Robert T. Meyer, ACW 34, edd. J. Quasten, Walter J. Burghardt and T. C. Lawler (Westminster, MD, and London, 1965).

29. Brian Patrick McGuire, *Friendship and Community: The Monastic Experience 350–1250*, *Cistercian Studies* 95 (Kalamazoo, MI, 1988), p. xvi.

30. See "More About Melania the Elder," 54.4, p. 135 in *Palladius: The Lausiac History*. This English translation by Meyer indicates that Palladius calls "Abita" a cousin to Melania, whereas the edition by Cuthbert Butler (p. 147) calls her "niece." In his stemma for Melania's family tree, Francis X. Murphy indicates that Avita was the daughter of Melania's sister Antonia; see his "Melania the Elder: A Biographical Note," *Traditio* 5 (1947): 63.

31. See *Palladius: Lausiac History* 54.4 for Melania the Elder's influence on her granddaughter. See the following concerning Melania the Younger and Pinian settling at Thagaste: Augustine's "Epistula CXXIV," CSEL 44, Pars III: Ep. 124–184, pp. 1–2, edited by Al. Goldbacher (Vienna and Leipzig, 1904); and Gerontius, *The Life of Melania the Younger*, Studies in Women and Religion 14, translated by Elizabeth A. Clark (Lewiston, NY, 1984), chs. 21–22, p. 44.

32. Joseph T. Lienhard, *Paulinus of Nola and Early Western Monasticism With a Study of the Chronology of His Works and Annotated Bibliography, 1879–1976*, Theophaneia Beitrage zur Religions- und Kirchengeschichte des Altertums 28 (Cologne-Bonn, 1977), 68, 70–72, documents the establishment of this monastery-shrine under the patronage of the martyr Felix. References to details of the patron's life are recorded by Paulinus in his *Carmina* 15, 16, 18, 21, 23, 24 and 26–29. Paulinus is one of our sources for information concerning Melania the Elder, in his letter 29.5–14. In chapter 12 of this letter, he tells of her visit to Nola, where she was welcomed by her children and grandchildren. The English translation can be found in *Letters of St. Paulinus of Nola*, vol. 2, ACW 36, translated by P. G. Walsh (Westminster, MD, and London, 1967), ep. 29.5–14: pp. 105–18; ch. 12: pp. 114–15.

33. "Theodora #7," 84, in *The Sayings of the Desert Fathers*.

34. Roberta C. Bondi, "The Abba and Amma in Early Monasticism: The First Pastoral Counselors?" *Journal of Pastoral Care* 40:4 (December 1986), 320.

35. Bondi, 320.

36. "Syncletica # 27," 235, in *The Sayings of the Desert Fathers*.

37. Cassian, "Inst. 9.1," in Jean Cassien, *Institutions Cénobitiques*, SC 109, edited by Jean-Claude Guy (Paris, 1965), 370; "Inst. 10.1," SC 109.384: "There is a sixth contest for us that the Greeks call *acedia*, which we can name weariness or anxiety of heart. This is related to sadness, as is better known by experience to solitaries and is a frequent and more hostile enemy to those dwelling in the desert"; "Inst. 9.9–10," SC 109.376, distinguishes a dejection or sadness producing despair of salvation from one which leads to penitence for sin.

38. "Theodora #5," 83–4, in *The Sayings of the Desert Fathers*.

39. For a fuller elaboration of these qualities, see the article by Soler, "Les Mères du désert et la maternité spirituelle," 245–7.

40. See Mary Forman, "*Sapere*—Tasting the Wisdom of the Monastic Tradition: The Biblical and Patristic Roots of Discerning," *Benedictines* XLIX:1 (1996: Summer): 33.

41. Barbara Newman, "The Pilgrimage of Christ-Sophia," *Vox Benedictina* 9:1 (Winter 1992): 11. For a study of the development of the Christ-Sophia motif, read the whole of Newman's article, pp. 9–37.

42. Newman, 13.

43. Newman, 16.

44. Gregory, Bishop of Nyssa, *The Life of Saint Macrina*, translated by Kevin Corrigan, 26–7. Hereafter this work will be referred to as Corrigan, *Saint Macrina*.

45. Corrigan, *Saint Macrina*, footnote 2, pp. 63–4.

46. Corrigan, Introduction to *Saint Macrina*, 23.

47. For the events mentioned in this paragraph, see Corrigan, *Saint Macrina*, 37, 41, 43, 32, and 47.

Christian or Secular?
The Tetraconch in the
So-called Library of Hadrian
at Athens

W. Eugene Kleinbauer
Indiana University

The tetraconch building inside the imposing monument commonly called the Library of Hadrian at Athens is today widely believed to offer a linchpin in our understanding of the rise of Christianity in that city (Fig. 1, p. 204).[1] Current scholarship holds that the tetraconch was the first public church building in late antique Athens and possibly the only Christian church in the city for at least half a century. The building is said to date from either 408–410 or sometime in the first half of the fifth century. While such a dating has been advanced for some time, the identification of the function of the tetraconch as a secular or ecclesiastical building was debated until 1980 when John Travlos uncovered the remains of a forecourt or atrium attached to its west end. This discovery convinced Travlos and specialists after him to maintain that the tetraconch was originally planned as a church building. Thus Travlos rejected the secular function he had proposed earlier.[2] But does the forecourt prove that the building was ecclesiastical? More important, how likely is it for a sizeable church of distinctive layout to have been erected in Athens in the first half of the fifth century, if that is in fact when it was built? And what were the actual functions of the enclosing Hadrianic structure at that time? These questions are the focus of the remarks of this tribute to Fredric W. Schlatter.

The tetraconch and its forecourt were laid out exactly on the longitudinal axis of the second-century complex traditionally called the Library of Hadrian, constructed in 131/132 A.D. in the heart of Athens (Fig. 2, p. 205). The tetraconch measured 27.10 m. in overall width and along with its courtyard may have extended to a total length of 65.20 m., just about the length of a long Hadrianic water pool that had preceded the tetraconch on the very same axis. The tetraconch was laid out with a center square space 15.42 m. on a side. To the east projected a semicircular apse 8.63 m. in diameter, while from each of the other three sides projected a semicircular exedra (each 7.49 m. in diameter) in each of which stood four columns. Ambulatories 3.75 m. in width surround the central core on all but the eastern sides, and they gave access to the central core through the columnar exedrae as well as doorways in each of the L-shaped pier-walls at the corners of the center bay. The perimeter walls to the north and south are concentric with the

Figure 1: Tetraconch building in Athens, view to west
(A. Frantz, courtesy American School of Classical Studies at Athens)

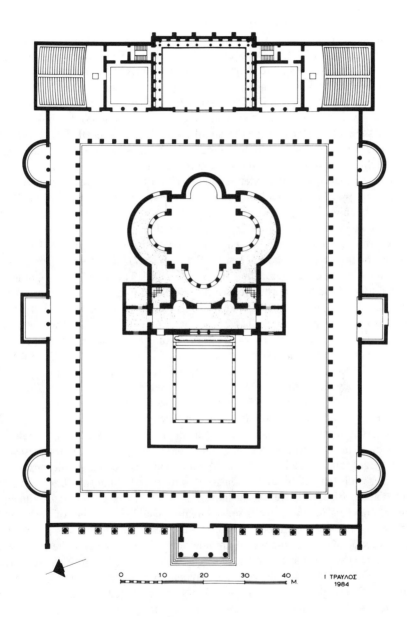

Figure 2: Forum of Hadrian with tetraconch building, site plan
(J. Travlos, courtesy Ernst Wasmuth Verlag)

columnar exedrae of the central core of the edifice. A doorway was positioned at the eastern ends of these two perimeter walls, and provided easy access to the suite of chambers at the eastern end of the "Library of Hadrian."

From the western wall of the west ambulatory three doorways gave access to a rectangular hall 25.12 m. long and 5.42 m. wide. The eastern wall of this anteroom led into small square chambers in which survive the remains of the stone blocks of ascending stairs. Slightly larger square chambers are situated to the north and south ends of the long hall, to the east of both of which were similarly shaped chambers. Although not marked in the plan and reconstruction of the building by Travlos, the more easterly of the two small chambers on the north side featured a door in its north wall.[3] The masonry of these chambers is not bonded into the main tetraconch core, though it is of the same construction.

The excavation of 1980 extended to the west of the narthex and covered an area of 7 m. by 18 m. It established the existence of a western forecourt 26.10 m. in width, but how far the forecourt extended to the west could not be determined. Travlos conjectured that it was 26.7 m. in length and was entered by a single doorway in the center of its west wall on axis with the tetraconch and Hadrianic entry to the huge rectangular enclosure (Fig. 3, p. 207).[4] The forecourt is coeval with the main tetraconch since their walls are bonded. The foundations of at least one peristyle of the forecourt were found some 5.3 m. inside the outer north wall of the forecourt; Travlos believes that peristyles stood on all but its eastern sides, where a sizeable foundation wall (1.2 m. in height, 1.8 m. in width, by 15.2 m. in length) was brought to light. Travlos restores a water fountain on this foundation, such as occurs, he points out, in the church known as Basilica B at Nikopolis in Epirus in Greece, erected prior to 518.[5] A triple-light window featuring small colonnettes carrying capitals pierced the wall above the fountain of the Athenian building and provided illumination for the long hall of its narthex.

The walls of the tetraconch were constructed of two different kinds of masonry. The walls of its square core (0.96 cm. in thickness) were built of reused blocks of Pentelic marble on the inner face, laid in regular horizontal courses of equal height, and reused poros on the outer face. By contrast, the apse and perimeter walls (ca. 1.0 m. thick) consisted of mortared rough rubble with two or three courses of bricks irregularly laid out. Yet the latter are bonded with the former, and thus all these walls are contemporary. The remains of stairs, the thickness of the walls, and remnants of carved architectural elements permit the reconstruction of galleries above the ambulatories.[6] The character of the walls also suggests that the center space and the galleries were covered by timber trusses.[7] By contrast, the exedrae and the apse, we may suppose, were covered by masonry semidomes, though no trace of them has been recorded at the site. Marble pavement slabs may have been laid in the center space, while polychromatic tessellated pavements, portions of which survive, embellished the ambulatories and at least one chamber of the vestibule complex.

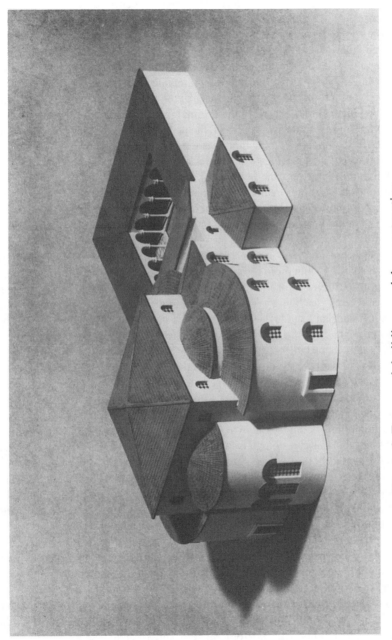

Figure 3: Tetraconch building, model reconstruction (J. Travlos, courtesy Ernst Wasmuth Verlag)

Ringing the inner surface of the eastern apse is a bench preserved to a height of 1.25 m. and 1.42 m. in width. It was covered with marble revetment. In 1950 Travlos attributed its construction to the rebuilding of the tetraconch after a fire presumably destroyed it in the late sixth or seventh century and an aisled basilica retaining the apse of the tetraconch replaced it.[8] In 1986, however, Travlos identified this bench as a synthronon and maintained that it belongs to the original tetraconch because its marble facing was affixed to its surface with a red mortar said to be identical to that used in the original mosaic pavements of the building. Red mortar, however, does not appear in the perimeter walls of the tetraconch, and no scientific examination of the mortar is reported to have been undertaken.

A number of factors indicate that the tetraconch was erected sometime between the later fourth century and the first fifty or sixty years of the following century. At the present time a more precise dating cannot be established on archaeological grounds. No coins or inscriptions were uncovered in the fill immediately below the structure. A terminus post quem might seem to be provided by ceramic sherds that were part of the fill of the long water pool above which the tetraconch was constructed. When first reported in 1950 these sherds were dated "up to the end of the fourth century,"[9] but more recent studies of Athenian pottery show margins of error of 30 to 50 years for the fourth century, and the fifth century poses even greater problems (see below). The marble architectural sculpture recorded at the Library of Hadrian is today widely dispersed and remains unexamined.[10] The various designs of the polychromed mosaic pavements suggest a date approximately in the late fourth or the first fifty to sixty years of the fifth century.[11] The method of wall construction resembles that of the so-called Palace of Giants in Athens which is known to have been erected ca. 410 to 425.[12] But resemblances with other monuments in the city obtain and too few of these related monuments are dated with any exactitude. Numerous archaeological remains are said to attest to a major building boom in Athens at the end of the fourth and the first half of the fifth century, but this chronology is far from archaeologically secure. This activity may have started before Alaric's pillage in the province of Achaea in 396 (see below). Likewise the assertion that evidence supports little extensive building activity in the city in the second half of the fifth century should be re-examined.

Questions of the dating and identification of the function of the tetraconch are often connected with an inscription placed high on an anta on the left side of the west-facing tetrastyle propylon of the "Library of Hadrian." Positioned above a statue of very considerable size now lost, this inscription mentions Herculius and Plutarchus: "Plutarchus, the treasurer (and dispenser) of speech(es) and sophist, set up (the statue of) Herculius, the treasurer of laws, the upright prefect."[13]

Herculius is to be identified with the man who served as the praetorian prefect of Illyricum from 408 to 410 (and possibly from 407 to 412).[14] He is recorded in two other inscriptions. One is from Megara and is dedicated to him for his rebuilding of city walls there and construction of an aqueduct.[15] Herculius may in fact have possibly been responsible for overseeing a broadly conceived defensive strategy throughout Achaea, including Athens.[16] The second inscription mentioning Herculius is carved on a reused rectangular statue base (1.055 m. in height) originally erected beside a statue of Athena Promachus on the Acropolis of Athens and is reported to have been discovered in the early 1870s in front of what was then called the "Stoa of Hadrian," that is, the Library of Hadrian. It records a dedication by Apronianus: "Apronianus, the skillful sophist at Athens, put up (a statue of) you. Herculius, the defender of laws and equitable to all, you, who sit above the highest seats (of office), beside (the statue of) Pallas, the defender of Athens."[17] This Apronianus was a sophist residing in Athens; that is all we really know about him. Whether he held the sophistic chair in the city is possible but cannot be verified.

The name Plutarchus is mentioned in another inscription from late antique Athens. This inscription was carved on a rectangular statue base found in Athens and offers honors to Plutarchus: "The people of Erectheus dedicated (this statue of) Plutarchus, the king of words, the mainstay of firm prudence, who rowed the Sacred Ship three times in all near to the temple of Athena, spending all his wealth."[18] This text informs us that the people of Athens erected a statue in honor of Plutarchus for his generosity involving the Panathenaic procession. Dating in the last decade of the fourth or the first or second decade of the fifth century, it proves that the venerable Panathenaic procession was taking place at that time, but whether it was regularly celebrated as the urban festival without interruption from before 267/68 or was revived after that date cannot be confirmed.[19] The teacher and orator Himerius (born 300–310; died after 380), who spent most of his life in Athens, confirms that it was being publicly celebrated in the fourth century.[20] Its celebration attests to late antique Athens as a veritable stronghold of paganism, a point deserving emphasis.[21]

Whether the two epigraphically attested persons named Plutarchus were one and same man is unclear. There is a strong likelihood that one of these persons is the scholarch and priest of Asclepios (ca. 350–431/434) who is identical with the founder of the Neoplatonic School at Athens. If there were two men named Plutarchus, the other was a contemporary sophist of the same name.[22] In any event the Plutarchus who erected the statue of Herculius was surely a person of substantial means and highly civic minded. Whether one or two persons, the Plutarchus erecting the statue of Herculius must have been pagan, and thus it seems unlikely that he served as a benefactor of Christians who financed public church building.

The inscription attesting to a large-scale statue of Herculius at the single entrance to the Library of Hadrian does not indicate or even allude to the restoration of the complex or the construction of the tetraconch. Nevertheless, Miss Frantz and John Travlos believe that the inscription of Plutarchus on the facade of the Library establishes that the interior elements of the complex were restored by Herculius.[23] The peristyles inside the Library of Hadrian and the suite of chambers at its east end had been destroyed or severely damaged either during the Herulian invasion of 267/68 or as a result of Alaric's pillage in 396. The extent of damage inflicted by the Visigoths in Athens in general and to the Library of Hadrian, if any, however, cannot be archaeologically or historically established. The pagan historian Zosimus (5.6) writes (perhaps ca. 501) that Alaric wrecked no havoc on Athens. If we can trust Zosimus, then the interior elements of the Library of Hadrian were probably damaged by the Herulians, who also seem to have inflicted severe damage on the Parthenon and other Athenian monuments.[24] If this is true, then the Library of Hadrian could have been restored as early as the late third or the fourth century, long before Herculius was appointed to the post of praetorian prefect.

Whenever the Library of Hadrian was damaged, its outer walls survived well enough intact because they were incorporated into the new defensive walls of late antique Athens—the so-called post-Herulian walls—becoming the central section of its north flank (Fig. 4, p. 211).[25] None of the 100 columns or square column bases of the four Hadrianic peristyles inside the Library have been identified at the site. They all were replaced during the restoration of the building with columns standing on pedestals, and six of these pedestals have been recorded on the east side and three embedded in the retaining wall on the south.[26] Less clear is the extent of Herulian destruction to the suite of chambers at the east end of the Library. Archaeological evidence does not suggest that the design of these rooms was changed during the restoration, with the important possible exception of the northernmost chamber. Completely excavated, this chamber (16.20 by 14.55 m.) preserves the rubble remains of three sloping foundations for an auditorium of eighteen rows of seats.[27] M.A. Sisson thought that the inferiority of the construction of these rubble foundation walls indicates that they represent an addition of later date to the Hadrianic chamber.[28] Whether or not the northernmost chamber was provided with tiers of seats in the second century, it served as an auditorium when the Library was restored, and these seats provide evidence of the function of the restored Library whatever the date of the restoration—later third or fourth century. To this important point I will return.

If we cannot establish that Herculius restored the interior of the Library of Hadrian, can we at least accept the attribution of the construction of the tetraconch inside it to him, as Frantz and Travlos have done?[29] The material cited above confirms that while the building could have been erected during his prefecture, it can just as likely have been put up before or after it. No secure evidence permits a more precise date of construction or identity of patronage.

In recent years some specialists have attributed the planning of the tetraconch as a church to the initiative of the empress Eudocia. But does available evidence bear out this identification of patronage?

Although the tetraconch was redesigned as a basilican church in a second building period, not antedating the sixth or seventh century, nothing found in the original construction suggests an ecclesiastical foundation.[30] No Christian remains were uncovered in the debris immediately beneath the pavement of the tetraconch

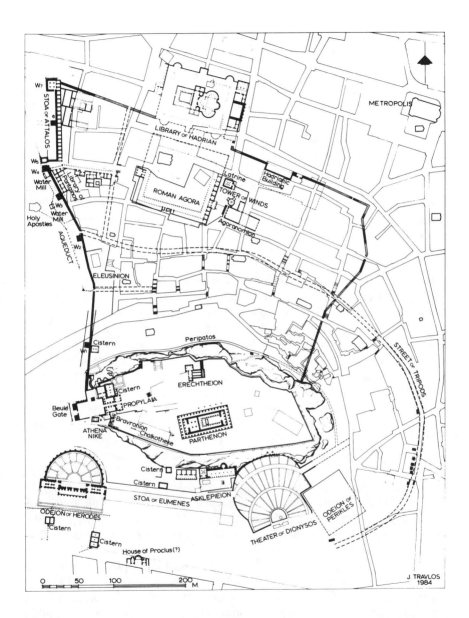

Figure 4: Plan of Athens north of Acropolis in third to fifth century
(J. Travlos, courtesy Ernst Wasmuth Verlag)

that belong to its initial phase. Nothing distinctly Christian occurs in the preserved pavement mosaics. A cross inscribed on the Pentelic wall of the center space dates from the second period of the monument. Graves found beneath the pavement of the west ambulatory stem from the Middle Byzantine period. No trace of a baptistery, a common feature of church buildings of the fifth century, has been detected in the tetraconch or anywhere insider the courtyard of the Library of Hadrian. Nor has any baptismal equipment been found in the main core of the tetraconch or any of the rooms off its vestibule.[31] Nor does the typology of the monument—a double-shell tetraconch—prove Christian usage. While virtually all known tetraconchs were certainly erected as church buildings, including San Lorenzo at Milan which dates from the second half of the fourth century, the aisled tetraconch at Perge in Pamphylia which may date in the fourth century seems to have been constructed as a secular monument.[32] And it has been theorized that this distinctive type of central-plan building originated in pre-Constantinian imperial palace architecture, such as audience halls.[33]

The colonnaded forecourt in front of the tetraconch convinced Travlos and subsequently other scholars that the monument was initially erected as a church building. It is true that atria are common features of church buildings in the fourth through sixth centuries, but they are not exclusive to them. In fact the atrium of the late antique church building is thought to derive from the colonnaded forecourts of Roman buildings known at various localities throughout the Empire.[34] These Roman buildings included imperial and non-imperial monuments. In the fourth-century villa at Piazza Armerina in Sicily, now thought to have been built for a millionaire businessman rather than an emperor, there are two major components that are pertinent in this context. In the northern section of the villa a rectangular peristyle garden led to a transverse corridor and a large apsidal audience hall, while in the southern area a trilobed triclinium was preceded by an oval porticoed forecourt.[35] The audience hall of this villa is very similar in layout to the early fourth-century Basilica of Constantine at Trier which was flanked by porticoed courtyards and preceded by a transverse forehall or narthex, and a larger courtyard beyond the forehall, with peristyles along the sides.[36] Still well preserved, the Basilica was constructed as the imperial audience hall of Constantine around 309 before his fateful encounter with Christianity in 312. These and other examples demonstrate that we cannot single out the forecourt of the Athenian tetraconch as proof of an ecclesiastical function.

Scholars wishing to see the Athenian tetraconch as a church neglect to ask themselves about the intended audience of the church. Did the size of the Christian community in Athens warrant such a large edifice? Were the Christians sufficiently numerous and prominent to warrant an imposing public church in the center of the late antique city? While Christianity is recorded in Athens as early as the first century, available evidence indicates that its growth was remarkably slow until the end of the fifth century or even the early sixth century.[37] For a long time Athens lacked martyrs, and relatively few Athenian bishops are recorded in late antiquity.[38]

Indeed evidence of large-scale Christian building elsewhere in Greece—with the possible exceptions of Philippi and Thessaloniki in northern Greece—dates only from the fifth century. Archaeology has uncovered a number of impressive residential structures in late antique Athens, but not one domus ecclesiae or public church building constructed *de novo*. The first archaeologically documented public churches at Athens were erected in its suburbs. The earliest is sometimes thought to be the basilican church on the Ilissos Island outside the city walls of Athens; it is dated anywhere between 400 and 500, but its time of construction is as uncertain as its original layout.[39] Athenian pagan temples were converted into churches, but at the present time the earliest conversions are not dated before the end of the fifth century at the earliest.[40] Carved architectural sculpture thought to come from late antique church buildings in Athens is preserved in the Agora and the courtyard of the Byzantine Museum at Athens, but its original provenance cannot generally be ascertained. It is known that terra cotta lamps with Christian motifs found in Athens begin to be produced only in the first half of the fifth century, and possibly it is only in the second half of the fifth century that Christian symbols begin to proliferate in the town.[41] Some Christian grave stones ascribed to the fifth century are semiliterate, so evidently they marked the burials of an undistinguished and presumably impoverished group of Christians. This material evidence provides the most reliable index of a Christian community in fourth- and fifth-century Athens, and it suggests a small community which grew slowly in the fifth century.[42] It does not warrant the assumption of the construction of a monumental centralized church building in the heart of the pagan city in the fourth or fifth century. Let us also observe that when the tetraconch was rebuilt in the sixth or seventh century, a time when central-plan buildings were increasing in popularity, its layout was transformed into a basilica. If the tetraconch had originally functioned as a church, why was it then found necessary to convert its layout into a type fading in popularity in Greece?

The discovery of a marble statue base inscribed in honor of the empress Aelia Eudocia has given rise to speculation that she was responsible for the construction of the tetraconch.[43] Although Holum believes she was born in Antioch in Syria, as is reported by Evagrius, it is reasonable to assume that she was born in Athens, certainly the daughter of the pagan sophist Leontius who was appointed to the sophistic chair at Athens in 415 or 416.[44] The statue base was found not near the so-called Library of Hadrian but in the area of the Stoa of Attalus and north of the so-called Palace of Giants. It has been suggested that the statue was erected soon after Eudocia's marriage of Theodosius II in the year 421, but the occasion of its erection remains altogether unknown. One possibility is that it was set up by her brother Gessius who was appointed praetorian prefect of Illyricum after his sister married Theodosius II and obtained honors for her brother.[45] Since the tetraconch may have been built before or even after the erection of this imperial statue, associating Eudocia or any other imperial person with the tetraconch amounts in the last analysis to no more than a speculative hypothesis. The only recorded statue that can reasonably associated with the tetraconch is the abovementioned lost statue of the prefect Herculius (see also *infra*).

Attempts to identify the function of the tetraconch have not taken sufficiently into account what purpose the so-called Library enclosing it served at the time it was planned and erected. The purpose of the original Library of Hadrian has been clarified in recent years: while it accommodated the storage of books, it was more than a library. The site is mentioned by Pausanias who does not specifically identify it by name: "But most splendid of all are the one hundred columns: walls and colonnades alike are made of Phrygian marble. Here, too, is a building adorned with a gilded roof and alabaster, and also with statues and paintings: books are stored in it (I.18.9)."[46] Recently T. Leslie Shear, Jr., has presented arguments why Hadrian laid out the complex as an imperial forum which was modeled on the Templum Pacis at Rome, built by the emperor Vespasian.[47] In Athens Hadrian provided for a huge garden enclosure with a long water pool running down its center and surrounded by statuary and works of art, much like the Templum Pacis. According to Shear, the suite of chambers at the eastern end of Hadrian's Athenian forum included lecture halls and a library in the center hall. The central archives of the whole province of Achaea may have been stored in one or more of the halls in this eastern suite. Shear's identification of the Athenian complex is highly attractive but requires emendation. Pausanias establishes that books were stored somewhere in the complex, but were they shelved in the central hall at the eastern end, as Shear (and Sisson) supposes? Opening onto the eastern colonnade of the quadriporticus, this hall featured sizeable aediculae in three stories, and these aediculae seem more suitable for the display of statuary than for the shelving of rotuli.[48] Thus the central hall may have served as a "Hall of Honor" for Hadrian and perhaps members of his family, statues of whom may have set up in the aediculae, perhaps along with statues of various deities. Not the Athenian site of the imperial cult of Hadrian (which seems to have been the Temple of Olympian Zeus, construction of which was finally brought to completion by Hadrian), the Hall of Honor in the imperial forum would have witnessed sacrifices to the emperor at permanent or temporary altars placed before the presumed imperial statue. In other words, this hall may have served as a shrine for the Imperial cult, a *Kaisersaal* or *kaisereion*.[49]

Numerous parallels for such an "imperial hall" can be found in Asia Minor. An instructive parallel is provided by "Building M" at Side, erected a generation later than the Library of Hadrian. A. M. Mansel, the excavator of this edifice, has identified Building M as the state agora.[50] Specifically calling to mind the Hadrianic structure at Athens, this complex is a large rectangular complex with a row of three halls on the east side. The central hall is open to an eastern peristyle, and its walls were lined with aedicular facades in two stories, raised over the marble pavement by a podium. In the niches of the back wall stood an array of over-lifesized statues of deities, athletes, and in the central niche, it seems, Antoninus Pius. Mansel identifies this chamber as a *Kaisersaal* (*Imperator*

Salonu). The function of the flanking halls is uncertain, but they may have been libraries. Since the Roman *Kaisersaal* not infrequently stored books, books belonging to the provincial archives of Achaea could have been stored in the small rooms located against the eastern wall of the Hadrianic complex at Athens.[51] By contrast, the northernmost chamber and perhaps also its counterpart in the eastern suite served as auditoria.

What remains undocumented by literary sources is the function or functions of Hadrian's complex after its interior elements had been damaged or destroyed by the Herulians. The Herulians seem to have severely damaged at least some of the one hundred columns of the quadriporticus and inflicted damage on the eastern suite of chambers. The columns of the quadriporticus were replaced by new columns, and the east end was restored. How soon after the Herulian destruction the site was rebuilt is unknown, but the location of the site in the center of what became the administrative heart of post-Herulian Athens raises the possibility that the various original functions of the Hadrianic forum continued after the site was rebuilt in the later third or the fourth century. Whether the provincial archival records in the Hadrianic complex were destroyed during the Herulian invasion or were removed from it before their arrival and then redeposited after the complex was restored goes unrecorded in any source. Once the complex was restored, replenishment of the books would have become a pressing necessity.[52] But perhaps books in addition to those containing the provincial archives found their way into the restored complex.

As noted above, the statue of Herculius at the propylon was set up by a sophist named Plutarchus. If Plutarchus extended this honor to the prefect, was his motivation somehow specifically connected to the Hadrianic complex? Unfortunately, the dedicatory inscription does not indicate this. If the eastern end of the complex was restored under the authorization of the prefect and intended for use, say, by the Neoplatonic school in Athens, the gratitude of the sophist is unveiled. On archaeological grounds construction of the tetraconch might also date to the prefecture of Herculius, and if this building was intended as a lecture hall by the Neoplatonists, another explanation of the honor extended by the sophist offers itself. We cannot exclude the possibility that while the tetraconch was being constructed books for use by the Neoplatonists were shelved in the chambers at the eastern end of the Hadrianic site and the whole site became a new location for their philosophic school.

Although it is widely held that the Neoplatonists in Athens taught in their homes, this need not have always been the case. Indeed at an earlier date a philosophic school seems to have existed along the Panathenaic Way just south of the Stoa of Attalos in the Agora of Athens.[53] Between 98 and 102 A.D. a local citizen named Titus Flavius Pantainos made additions to the philosophic school headed by his father Flavius Menander. These additions consisted of three stoas, a peristyle courtyard, and a collection of books, all cited in the dedicatory inscription carved on the lintel of a major doorway leading from the western stoa into the peristyle courtyard behind. This courtyard (20 by 13.5 m.) gave access through a colonnade to a large square room paved with marble slabs like the courtyard. These paving slabs replaced earlier marble-chip floors, suggesting a remodeling of Flavius Menander's establishment. A smaller chamber lay along the northwestern wall of the large square room, and a large rectangular chamber was situated to the northwest of the peristyle courtyard. Chambers identified as shops were situated behind the three colonnades defining the outer perimeter of the complex. Pantainos dedicated his benefaction not to his father but to Athena, the Athenians, and the emperor Trajan. The emperor may actually have been worshiped in the complex since parts of a statue of him along with the base for a second statue dedicated by his priest Herodes Atticus Marathonios were found at the site. It therefore seems reasonable to believe that an unusually designed philosophic school stood near the heart of Athens in the later first century A.D.[54]

A late antique philosophic school situated in direct proximity to an imperial cult site is recorded at Aphrodisias (modern Geyre) in Caria in Asia Minor. Known as the Sebasteion, the imperial sanctuary at Aphrodisias was devoted to the cult of Augustus, his Julio-Claudian successors and to the goddess Aphrodite (Venus).[55] The Sebasteion lies off a main street that ran north-south from the Temple of Aphrodite to the theater and was oriented east-west. It consisted of two parallel porticoes of three superposed stories with half-columns facing one another, and the porticoes were separated by a broad paved processional way. A two-storied aedicular propylon with columnar niches gave access at the west end, and opposite it a Corinthian cult temple rested on a podium and dominated the entire complex. Directly behind the north portico lay a sprawling complex of private residential character. Built and remodeled over a period of time from the early Empire to the fifth century, this complex consisted of a private wing and a more public area with separate access from the Sebasteion sanctuary. This residence featured a large apsidal peristyle building directly behind the Augustan portico, and a smaller but richly appointed smaller apsidal chamber to the north of the peristyle unit which was erected atop an earlier atrium house of considerable opulence.[56] In the fourth or fifth century the larger apsed wall was provided with a tall pedimented aedicular facade which was furnished, it is believed, with a series of marble shield portraits of ancient philosophers and contemporary (fifth-century) thinkers that was found buried just behind this apsidal wall. The discovery of these philosopher portraits has led to the identification of the sprawling residence as the site of a Neoplatonic school, possibly that of Asklepiodotos of Alexandria, a highly successful active master teaching at Aphrodisias in the middle and later fifth century.[57] Asklepiodotos had studied at Athens under the renowned Proclus and was a thorough pagan who defended the old cults and revived pagan worship at Aphrodisias. If this site adjoining the Sebasteion was the town mansion of Asklepiodotos, he would have taught in it. Clearly at Athens sophists had private lecture halls in their private residences.[58]

While the Sebasteion and adjoining residence at Aphrodisias offer points of comparison to the Hadrianic complex at Athens, the latter lacks private residential character altogether and could not have served as the town mansion of a local Neoplatonist. The residences of the late antique philosophers of Athens are widely thought to have to been situated on the south side of the Acropolis and on the Areopagus.[59] But this does not exclude the possibility that the tetraconch was built to serve as a lecture hall by the Neoplatonists. Not all the philosophers in late antique Athens necessarily lectured in their private homes. At the end of the first century B.C. Agrippa built the Odeion as an addition to the Agora of Athens to serve as a concert hall. When the Odeion was rebuilt about 160 A.D. by Herodes Atticus, it seated about 500 persons and is believed to have been used largely as a lecture hall by philosophers and sophists.[60] It was destroyed in the Herulian invasion and never rebuilt.[61]

If the Plutarchus who dedicated the statue of Herculius happened to have been a member of the city council (*boule*) of Athens, his benefaction can be explained differently. Although no evidence has come down to us to suggest that Plutarchus held membership in the *boule*, he was clearly a person of substantial means and thus a candidate for such membership. Proclus, the celebrated early fifth-century Neoplatonist philosopher at Athens, is known to have taken part in civic assemblies and may also have belonged to the *boule*.[62] Traditionally the *boule* of Athens assumed responsibility for the care of public buildings and certain State cults and sacrifices as well as the preservation of all State archives.

The Herulian devastation in Athens resulted in the extensive or total destruction of the Bouleuterion and the Metroön in the Roman Agora.[63] The Bouleuterion, the traditional meeting house of the Athenian *boule*, was not rebuilt, but the Metroön which had served as the repository of the official archives of the city, witnessed soon after the Herulian damage a shabby restoration which included an eating hall and later in the fourth century transformation into a basilica which served a different purpose—both a synagogue and a lawcourt have been suggested.[64] It cannot be shown to have continued its original function as a city archive, "where all the documents of the Athenians used to be kept."[65] Thus two questions may be posed: where were the city and provincial archives relocated after 267/68, and where did the *boule* meet? Given the original functions of the forum of Hadrian, as suggested above, is it not reasonable to postulate that at least the provincial archives were transferred to its east end when the complex was restored following the Herulian invasion? And did the elected civic bodies meet in this complex after 267?

The continuation of both the Council of Areopagus and the *boule* in Athens soon after the Herulian invasion and during the fourth century is attested in inscriptions and literary sources. In a public inscription dated around 270 A.D. or later the Council of Areopagus, the Council of the 750 members, and the people of Athens offer honors to the rhetor and historian Publius Herennius Dexippus for his literary achievements and eloquence.[66] The Council of 750 Members is the traditional *boule* of Athens which earlier is recorded as having 500 members. The increase in the Council's membership may perhaps reflect a shortage of members sufficiently affluent to fulfill the necessary financial civic responsibilities.[67] In the fourth century membership declined to 300. An inscription dating after 372 A.D. records that the Council of Areopagus, the Council of the 300 members, and the people of Athens erected a statue of Rufius Festus, the proconsul of Achaea and member of the Council of Areopagus.[68] Why the number of the members of the *boule* had dropped to 300 from the 750 recorded a century earlier remains unknown. The continuation of the Council of Areopagus and the other Council to this late date is also confirmed by literary sources.[69]

Where the Council of the Areopagus and the Council of 300 members held their meetings after the Herulian invasion goes unmentioned in inscriptions and literary sources. Does archeology offer clues? Was the forum of Hadrian restored after the year 267 to continue to pay homage to the cult of Hadrian and to preserve provincial archives? Did one or both of the city councils meet in the auditoria at the northern and southern ends of the eastern suite of chambers in the forum of Hadrian? Would not the complex honoring the first great imperial person connected with Roman Athens and providing storage for the archives of Achaea and even perhaps the city after 267 have offered an eminently appropriate meeting site for the *boule*? If the councils continued to exist to the very end of the fourth and even into the fifth century, did they find it necessary to erect a larger building for their meetings? Could that building have been the aisled tetraconch inside the forum of Hadrian? The location of the forum in the administrative center of late antique Athens would seem to have offered a natural site for their meetings.

In the light of this context for late antique Athens and the forum of Hadrian, a secular function of the Athenian tetraconch emerges as the most plausible explanation for its construction. Arguments have been put forth to suggest that this monument served either the Neoplatonic schools or, more likely, as the *bouleuterion* of late antique Athens when it was built in the late fourth century or first fifty to sixty years of the following century. Thus this building, along with the aisled tetraconch at Perge in Pamphylia, possibly a fourth-century foundation and, significantly, placed in the center of the Palaestra of Cornutus (which is known to have been dedicated to the emperor Claudius, and possibly a private Claudianum[70]), represent two examples of aisled tetraconch structures serving non-ecclesiastical functions in late antiquity. Church architecture enjoyed no monopoly on the tetraconch plan.

NOTES

1. For excavations and surveys of the monument, see M. A. Sisson, "The Stoa of Hadrian at Athens," *Papers of the British School at Rome* 11 (1929): 50ff.; J. Travlos, "Anaskaphai en tē Bibliothēkē tou Adrianou, " *Praktika tēs en Athēnais Archaiologikēs Hetaireias* (Athens, 1950), 41ff.; G. Knithakes and E. Symboulidou, "Nea stoicheia dia tēn Bibliothēkēn tou Adrianou," *Archaiologikon Deltion* 24 (1969 [publ. 1971]): 107ff.; A. Kokkou, "Adrianeia erga eis tas Athēnas," *Archaiologikon Deltion,* 25 (1970 [publ. 1971]): 150ff.; J. Travlos, "To tetrakogcho oikodomēma tēs Bibliothēkēs tou Adrianou," in *Philia epē eis Geōrgion E. Mylōnan dia ta 60 etē tou anaskaphikou tou ergou* (Athens, 1986), I: 343ff.; A. Karivieri, "The So-Called Library of Hadrian and the Tetraconch Church in Athens," in *Post-Herulian Athens: Aspects of Life and Culture in Athens A.D. 267–529,* ed. P. Castrén, Papers and Monographs of the Finnish Institute at Athens, vol. 1 (Helsinki, 1994), 89ff.

2. Travlos, *Pictorial Dictionary of Ancient Athens* (New York, 1971), 244.

3. As pointed out by G. Fowden, "Late Roman Achaea: Identity and Defence," *Journal of Roman Archaeology* 8 (1995): 561, n. 68.

4. This model was first published in Travlos, "Tetrakogcho oikodomēma," (1986) and republished by him in his *Bildlexikon zur Topographie des antiken Attika* (Tübingen, 1988), figs. 50–51. It is interesting to observe that this model does not include his proposed water fountain at the east end of the forecourt of the tetraconch.

5. A. K. Orlandos, *Hē xylostegos palaiochristianikē basilikē tēs mesogeiakēs lekanēs* (Athens, 1952), 1: 139f., fig. 99; E. Kitzinger, "Studies on late Antique and Early Byzantine Floor Mosaics: 1. Mosaics at Nikopolis," *Dumbarton Oaks Papers* 6 (1951): 81ff.

6. Sisson, "Stoa of Hadrian," 69 and pl. 25; Travlos, "Anaskaphai," 48.

7. As restored by Sisson, "Stoa of Hadrian," pl. XXV; Travlos, "Anaskaphai," 46.

8. Travlos, "Anaskaphai," 49.

9. *Ibid.*

10. K. Kourouniotēs and G. A. Sotēriou, eds., *Euretērion tōn mnēmeiōn tēs Hellados,* vol. 1: *Euretērion tōn mesaiōnikōn mnēmeiōn* (Athens, 1927), 89; D. Pallas, "To tetrakogchon tēs Bibliothēkēs tou Hadrianou: Deuterai skepseis, " *Epeteris Hetereias Byzantinōn Spoudōn* 47 (1987–89): 421.

11. P. Asēmakopoulou-Atzaka and E. Pelekanidēs, *Syntagma tōn palaiochristianikōn psēphidotōn dapedōn tēs Hellados,* vol. 2: *Peloponnēsos-Sterea Hellada.* Byzantina mnēmia, 7 (Thessaloniki, 1987), p. 120, n. 122. Alison Frantz reports that Ruth Kolarik will be showing in a forthcoming study that the mosaics in the tetraconch can be attributed to the second quarter of the fifth century, presumably on the basis of comparison with floor mosaics found at Stobi in Macedonia (*Late Antiquity: A.D. 267–700* [Series: *The Athenian Agora. Results of Excavations conducted by the American School of Classical Studies at Athens,* vol. 24][Princeton, 1988], 44, n. 179). Although we must await the publication of Kolarik, I question whether we can date Athenian mosaics on the basis of stylistic comparisons with monuments as far away as Stobi or even in Achaea itself. I find it perilous to do so because of the presumed assumption that mosaicists working at sites so far removed were operating in tandem according to some implied overarching "principle" of stylistic development. It is true that a number of other late antique pavement mosaics survive in

Athens (see, e.g., Frantz, *Late Antiquity*, 45), but they have not been dated on external evidence. In short, the date of the tetraconch cannot be established with any certainty on the evidence of its mosaics.

12. H. Thompson, in Frantz, *Late Antiquity*, 95ff.

13. *IG* II/III², no. 4224. The inscription is cut on a block 0.57 m. high, 1.53 m. wide. For the epigram and the English translation, see E. Sironen, "Life and Administration of Late Roman Attica in the Light of Public Inscription," in *Post-Herulian Athens*, 50, no. 32. The statue of Herculius was not the first to decorate the facade of the Library of Hadrian. Scholars agree that the original Hadrianic facade of the complex featured statues above its columns (see, for example, Sisson, "Stoa of Hadrian," 54). But these earlier statues may have been destroyed in the later third century when that of Herculius was set up.

14. J. R. Martindale, *The Prosopography of the Later Roman Empire*, vol. 2 (Cambridge, 1980), s.v. Herculius 2. His term of office is fixed for 408–410.

15. *IG* VII, no. 93; L. Robert, *Hellenica; recueil d'épigraphie, de numismatique et d'antiquités grecques* (Limoges and Paris, 1940) 4:60.

16. As argued by Fowden, "Late Roman Achaea," 554ff.

17. *IG* II/III², no. 4225. For the Greek of the inscription and an English translation, as well as commentary, see Sironen, "Life and Administration," 51, no. 32. For Apronianus, see Martindale, *Prosopography*, vol. 2, s.v Apronianus 1.

18. *IG* II/III², no. 3818; Sironen, "Life and Administration," p. 46, no. 29.

19. On the regeneration of the Panathenaic Festival in late antique Athens, see Frantz, *Late Antiquity*, 24.

20. *Orationes* XLVII, 12, ed. A. Colonna (Rome, 1961), 194.

21. In general, consult T. E. Gregory, "The Survival of Paganism in Christian Greece: A Critical Essay," *American Journal of Philology* 107 (1986): 229ff.; A. Frantz, "Athen II (stadtgeschichtlich)," *RAC* Supplemental vol. 1 (1992), cols. 668ff., esp. 676ff.

22. Sironen, "Life and Administration," 47f., for a critical examination of the evidence.

23. A. Frantz, "Honors to a Librarian," *Hesperia* 35 (1966): 379f.; Travlos, *Pictorial Dictionary*, 244.

24. A. Frantz has argued that Julian restored the Parthenon ("Did Julian the Apostate Rebuild the Parthenon?" *American Journal of Archaeology* 83 [1979]: 393ff.), but this has been disputed by M. Korres, in P. Tournikiotis, ed., *Ho Parthenōnas kai hē aktinobolia tou sta veōtera chronia* (Athens, 1994), 143.

25. J. Travlos, "The Post-Herulian Wall," in Frantz, *Late Antiquity*, 125ff., esp. 136f.

26. Sisson, "Stoa of Hadrian," 57. The intercolumniations of these pedestals indicates that the rebuilt peristyles comprised as many as 120 rather than the 100 columns of the Hadrianic structure, and these elements consist partly of spolia (*ibid.*). Sisson dated them to no earlier than the beginning of the fourth century. In 1986 a reinforcement wall immediately behind the west facade of the Library was discovered, and while the excavators attribute its construction to the emperor Justinian I (compare Procopius, *De aed* IV.2.23–25), no archaeological evidence had come to light by the spring of 1995 to buttress this attribution, leaving the date of its construction in abeyance: see Y. Knithakis and Y. Tighinaga, in *Archaiologikon Deltion* 41 (1986 [1990]), *Chronika*, pp. 10f.; and the instructive commentary of Fowden, "Late Roman Achaea," 556 and n. 40.

27. Knithakis and Symboulidou, "Nea stoicheia,"107ff.; Kokkou, 162ff.; Travlos, *Pictorial Dictionary*, 579.

28. Sisson, "Stoa of Hadrian," 62. One block of marble paving survives about one foot above the lowest level of this chamber. The southernmost chamber has not been excavated, but it is widely assumed to have been designed exactly like the northernmost chamber. Yet Sisson's plan of the actual state of the Library in the 1920s (pl. XVII) discloses two parallel spur walls extending to the south of the far south wall of the chamber flanking the central hall at the east end of the complex.

29. Frantz, *Late Antiquity*, 73, jettisons her earlier attribution of the tetraconch to Herculius on the basis of the study of its pavement mosaics by Kolarik and Kitzinger and ascribes the building to the second quarter of the fifth century.

30. Travlos dated the demise of the tetraconch without evidence to ca. 500 or ca. 600: Travlos, "Anaskaphai," 56, 60; Travlos, "Tetrakogcho oikodoméma," 347. It was replaced by a three-aisled basilica in the sixth or seventh century, and in the eleventh or twelfth century by the Megale Panagia which survived until 1885 when the first excavations were undertaken at the site.

31. D. Pallas, "Le baptistère dans l'Illyricum oriental," in *Actes du XIe Congrès international d'archéologie chrétienne* (Rome, 1989), 2485f., proposed that the "Tower of the Winds" served as the baptistery of the Athenian tetraconch church, but the date of conversion of this monument to Christian use remains an unsettled issue, and it is physically too far removed from the tetraconch to have functioned in tandem with it. Fowden, "Late Roman Achaea," 560, assumes that there was a baptistery which was a dependent structure yet to be uncovered just to the north of the tetraconch. In 1967 a church of later date was discovered in this area: G. Dontas, *Archaiologikon Deltion* 25 (1970 [1972]), B'1, pp. 28ff., pl. 41.

32. W. Eugene Kleinbauer, "The Double-Shell Tetraconch Building at Perge in Pamphylia and the Origin of the Architectural Genus," *Dumbarton Oaks Papers* 41 (1987): 277ff. Also see the conclusion of the present essay.

33. Most notably by R. Krautheimer, *Early Christian and Byzantine Architecture*, 4th ed. rev. (Harmondsworth, 1986), 77f.

34. C. Delvoye, "Atrium," *Reallexikon zur byzantinischen Kunst* 1 (1966), cols. 421ff.; S. S. Alexander, "Studies in Constantinian Church Architecture," *Rivista di archeologia cristiana* 47 (1971): 281ff., which examines literary and archaeological evidence of church atria of the early fourth century and shows that they were not a Constantinian innovation. For secular parallels and antecedents, consult R. Stapleford, "Constantinian Politics and the Atrium Church," in *Art and Architecture in the Service of Politics*, ed. H. A. Millon and L. Nochlin (Cambridge, Mass., 1978), 2ff., esp. 12ff.

35. A. Boëthius and J. B. Ward-Perkins, *Etruscan and Roman Architecture* (Harmondsworth, 1970), 529ff. and fig. 202; R. J. A. Wilson, *Piazza Armerina* (Austin, 1983), for discussion of the presumed non-imperial owner of the villa.

36. See the reconstruction in *Frühchristliche Zeugnisse im Einzugsbebiet von Rhein und Mosel*, ed. W. Reusch (Trier, 1965), pp. 144ff., fig. on p. 146 and pl. 114.

37. At present the earliest church buildings in Athens and Attica are dated no earlier than the end of the fifth century: D. Pallas, "Hē palaiochristianikē notioanatolikē Attikē," *Praktika B' Epistēmonikēs Sunantēsēs NA. Attikēs* (1985) (Kalyvia, 1986), 43ff. See also R. Janin, *Les églises et les monastères des grands centres byzantins* (Paris, 1975), 298ff., for a catalog of information on the late antique and Byzantine churches of the city.

38. A. Frantz, "From Paganism to Christianity in the Temples of Athens," *Dumbarton Oaks Papers* 19 (1965): 69.

39. First published by G. A. Soteriou, "Palaia christianikē basilikē Isisou," *Archaiologikē ephēmeris*, (1919): 1ff. L. K. Skontzos, "Hē palaiochristianikē basilikē tou Ilissou," *Archaiologia* (title in modern Greek) 29 (Athens, 1988): 50, attributes this basilican church to the empress Eudocia, without conviction.

40. A. Karivieri, "The Christianization of an Ancient Pilgrimage Site: A Case Study of the Athenian Asklepieion," *Akten des XII. Internationalen Kongresses für christliche Archäologie, Bonn 22.–28. September 1991=Jahrbuch für Antike und Christentum*, Ergänzungsband 20, 2 *Studi di antichità cristiana*, 52 (Münster, 1995) 2: 898ff., thinks it is possible that the first Christian basilica inside the Temple of Asklepeios was constructed at the end of the fifth century, but there is no secure archaeological evidence for this attribution. That this temple was deconsecrated at that time is, however, suggested by Marinus, *Vita Procli*, 15 and 23 (written before the year 485); construction of the Christian basilica occurred later at an unspecified date. Recently Cyril Mango has interpreted a text to suggest that the Parthenon was converted into a church in the second half of the fifth century: "The Conversion of the Parthenon into a Church: The Tübingen Theosophy," *Deltion tēs Christianikēs Archaiologikēs Hetaireias*, 4th ser. vol. 18 (1995), pp. 201ff.. Earlier, however, the transformation of the pagan sanctuaries into functioning Christian edifices was assigned to the seventh century: Frantz, "From Paganism to Christianity," 187ff.

41. J. Perlzweig, *Lamps from the Roman Period*, The Athenian Agora, Results of the Excavations conducted by the American School of Classical Studies at Athens, vol. 7 (Princeton, 1961). Now she dates the lamps to the fifth century: *idem, Miscellanea Graeca* 5, Studies in South Attica I (1982), 139. The dating of Athenian lamps has a margin of error up to seventy-five years: K. W. Slane, *The Sanctuary of Demeter and Kore: the Roman Pottery and Lamps*, Corinth, vol. 18, 2 (Princeton, 1990); J. W. Hayes, *A Supplement to the Late Roman Pottery* (London, 1980). In an announced forthcoming study on Athenian terracotta lamps A. Karivieri reports that he dates the first lamps with Christian motifs in the first half of the fifth century and only in the second half of that century did Christian symbols begin to predominate (Karivieri, "Christianization," 899).

42. Thus I take issue with an essentially opposite interpretation of the rise of Christianity in Athens that is offered by G. Fowden, "The Athenian Agora and the Progress of Christianity," *Journal of Roman Archaeology* 3 (1990): 494ff.

43. See, most recently, Karivieri, "Tetraconch Church," 111ff., with the earlier bibliography.

44. K. Holum, *Theodosian Empresses: Women and Imperial Dominion in Late Antiquity* (Berkeley, 1982), 118f. On Aelia Eudocia, originally called Athenais, see Martindale, *Prosopography*, 2: 408f.; and J. Burman, "The Athenian Empress Eudocia," 63ff. Aelia Eudocia was raised in Athens where she was educated under her father's supervision. She went to Constantinople as a pagan and converted to Christianity upon her marriage to Theodosius II in the year 421 and was proclaimed augusta two years later. Then she founded the original church of St. Polyeuktos in Constantinople (according to the *Palatine Anthology* I.10) and went to Jerusalem in 443. She was buried in the church of St. Stephen in that city in 460. When she visited Antioch in Syria in 438 she donated gold for the restoration of the Bath of Valens which had been previously burned: G. Downey, *A*

History of Antioch in Syria from Seleucus to the Arab Conquest (Princeton, 1961), 451 (cf. 453). For her father see Martindale, *Prosopography*, 2: 668f., s.v. Leontius 6.

45. Martindale, *Prosopography*, 2: 510f (s.v. Gessius 2). Whether Gessius continued to hold the post of prefect after his sister departed for Jerusalem in 443 remains unknown.

46. For recent interpretations of this key text by Pausanias, see Karivieri, "Tetraconch Church" (cited in n. 1 *supra*), 90ff.

47. T. L. Shear, Jr., "Athens: From City-State to Provincial Town," *Hesperia* 50 (1981): 374ff. Earlier J. B. Ward-Perkins (in Boëthius and Ward-Perkins, 383) had observed that the Library of Hadrian was a "very close copy of the Templum Pacis in Rome."

48. The upper tracts of masonry of the central hall are lost. For a plausible reconstruction of this hall, see Sisson, "Stoa of Hadrian," 58ff. and pls. XXI–XXIV.

49. For Roman kaisereia, consult the fundamental study by F. K. Yegül, "A Study in Architectural Iconography: Kaisersaal and the Imperial Cult," *Art Bulletin* 64 (1982): 7ff. The Traianeum in Italica in Spain was probably built by Hadrian and in its design, sculptural program, and function is strikingly close to the Library of Hadrian at Athens: M.T. Boatwright, "The Traianeum in Italica (Spain) and the Library of Hadrian in Athens," in *The Interpretation of Architectural Sculpture in Greece and Rome*, ed. D. Buitron-Oliver [Series: Studies in the History of Art, vol. 49] (Hanover and London, 1997), 193ff.

50. A. M. Mansel, *Die Ruinen von Side* (Berlin, 1963), 109ff.; *idem, Side* (Ankara, 1978), 169ff., figs. 184–204; Yegül, "Architectural Iconography," 19, n. 63 and figs. 20–21.

51. As suggested by Karivieri, "Tetraconch Church," 102.

52. Frantz, *Late Antiquity*, 66, briefly discusses the restoration of books in Athens in the year 416/17 and the possibility of a large scale reorganization of libraries in Athens at that time.

53. J. M. Camp, *The Athenian Agora; Excavations in the Heart of Classical Athens* (London, 1986), 187ff. and figs.157–161; Travlos, *Pictorial Dictionary*, 432ff.; Frantz, *Late Antiquity*, 49, on the destruction of the Library by the Herulians and the incorporation of what remained of the complex in the Post-Herulian Wall. The dedicatory inscription is translated in full by Camp, *Athenian Agora*, on p. 190 and illustrated in fig. 160.

54. T. L. Shear, Jr., "The Athenian Agora: Excavations of 1972," *Hesperia* 42 (1973): 359ff., shows that the Library of Pantainos was rebuilt in the first quarter of the fifth century with spolia. He believes that the site became the residence of a proconsul or praetorian prefect and included an apsidal structure serving as that person's audience hall. Cf. Frantz, *Late Antiquity*, p. 67, pls. 48b, 49, 50b.

55. For a summary of the archaeology of the site and its carved sculpture, see R. R. R. Smith, "Late Roman Philosopher Portraits from Aphrodisias" *Journal of Roman Studies* 80 (1990): 127ff.; K. T. Erim, *Aphrodisias: A Guide to the Site and its Museum* (Istanbul, 1989), 52ff., with reconstruction drawings of the Sebasteion and illustrations in color of its carvings. See also R. R. R. Smith and C. Ratté, "Archaeological Research at Aphrodisias in Caria, 1966," *American Journal of Archaeology* 102 (1998): 226, fig. 1, for the most recent plan of the city. For a restored isometric view of the upper two stories of the south facade of the Sebasteion, see Smith and Ratté, in *American Journal of Archaeology* 101 (1997): p. 19, fig 15. For the imperial cult in Asia Minor, consult the fundamental study of S. R. F. Price, *Rituals and Power; The Roman Imperial Cult in Asia Minor* (Cambridge, 1984).

56. For the "atrium house" and its possible functions (religious, semi-religious, or official activities), see K. T. Erim, "Recent Work at Aphrodisias 1986–1988," in *Aphrodisias Papers: Recent Work on Architecture and Sculpture*, ed. C. Roueché and K. T. Erim, Journal of Roman Archaeology, Supplementary Series Number 1 (Ann Arbor, 1990), 15ff.

57. As suggested by Smith, "Late Roman Philosopher Portraits," 153ff. The life of Asklepiodotus is also discussed by Smith. See also Martindale, *Prosopography*, 2:161ff., Asclepiodotus 3 (161ff.).

58. Eunapius, *Vitae Sophistarum*. 483 (ed. Loeb, p. 467).

59. For a survey of these residences, including the "House of Proclus," see Frantz, *Late Antiquity*, 42ff.; A Karivieri, "The 'House of Proclus' on the Southern Slope of the Acropolis: A Contribution," in *Post-Herulian Athens*, 115ff.

60. Camp, *Athenian Agora*, 184, 194ff.

61. Frantz, *Late Antiquity*, 4.

62. Martindale, *Prosopography*, IIA, s.v. Proclus 4. Proclus was born at Constantinople and grew up in Xanthus in Lycia before being schooled in Alexandria and then, beginning in 430 or 432, in Athens.

63. Frantz, *Late Antiquity*, 4, believes the Metroön was totally destroyed in the year 267, but on p. 25 states that it was badly damaged.

64. Consult the basic study of the Metroön by H. A. Thompson, "Buildings on the West Side of the Agora," *Hesperia* 6 (1937): 195–202, who documents and attributes the transformation of the site into a basilica ca. 400, a date that I think requires re-examination. Thompson suggested that the building was transformed into a synagogue because of a carved menorah on a marble revetment found during his excavations, but D. Pallas, in *Theologia*, 31 (1960): 348, suggests the remodeled Metroön became a lawcourt.

65. Julian, *Oratio* VIII (V), 159B, as cited by Frantz, *Late Antiquity*, 25, n. 84.

66. IG II/III², no. 3669. See Sironen, "Life and Administration," 17. no. 1. This inscription also mentions the Panathenaic games.

67. J. Day, *An Economic History of Athens under Roman Domination* (New York, 1942), 277f. Cf. Sironen, "Life and Administration," 17, no. 1.

68. IG II/III² , no. 4222. See Sironen, "Life and Administration," 29, no. 13.

69. Himerius, *Oratio* VII, addresses the Council of Areopagus, while Julian, *Oratio* V (ed. Bidez [1932]), refers to the *boule*.

70. Yegül, "Architectural Iconography," 19, n. 63. The function of the aisled tetraconch at Perge cannot be ascertained on the basis of present evidence (Kleinbauer, "Double-Shell Tetraconch Building at Perge"). For other examples of Late Antique central-plan buildings situated within walled enclosures, cf. S. Ćurčić, "From the Temple of the Sun to the Temple of the Lord: Monotheistic Contribution to Architectural Iconography in Late Antiquity," in *Architectural Studies in Memory of Richard Krautheimer*, ed. C. L. Striker (Mainz, 1996), 55ff.

History, Community, and Suffering
in Victor of Vita

William Edmund Fahey
Catholic University of America

The story of the Vandal persecution in Africa is fragmentary, preserved largely in three sources, all written from the orthodox Catholic perspective.[1] The most substantial record is that penned by Victor of Vita, a cleric—later to become bishop—and eye-witness to the events.[2] Though Victor dedicates his history to a single individual, it is clear from the petitions which close the work that Victor wrote for a wide audience, both in Africa and abroad. Courtois has already suggested that one objective of Victor was to seek Byzantine intervention on behalf of beleagured African Catholics.[3] While accepting Courtois's proposal as one aim, I hope to show the ways in which Victor addressed his contemporary African audience. More immediately Victor, through his history, attempted to make sense of that suffering which had befallen the Catholics of North Africa at the hands of the Arian Vandals. Through the provision of role models and the establishment of symbolic emblems Victor sought to comfort and inspire his community to remain steadfast in their faith and understand their suffering as having a sublime and redemptive quality.[4] As one who aspires to emulate the interdisciplinary research Fredric W. Schlatter, S.J., has pursued, bringing the careful scrutiny of texts and cultural contexts into the study of art history, I am pleased to offer this essay as a tribute to him.

Victor addresses his prologue to an unnamed senior cleric or official to whom, in fact, the history is ostensibly dedicated. The identity of the individual is unknown. He has been seen, on the one hand, as a Greek member of the emperor Zeno's diplomatic staff, or, alternatively, as the exiled bishop Eugenius of Carthage.[5] For the present paper's purpose it is of little consequence which, if either, of the two is correct. Turning to the preface itself we may, nevertheless, discern several important features of Victor's historiographic assumptions. First, Victor evokes the classical tradition of studying the past to obtain practical wisdom.[6] He then compliments previous historians for their determination that no event remain unknown or hidden.[7] The idea that hidden events must be revealed is one to which Victor will return again in his history.

In the second chapter of the prologue Victor notes that his own work will provide his addressee with material for the composition of a more comprehensive history. In complimenting the addressee Victor further proceeds to establish his own intentions. Unlike pagan historians, "puffed up with the arrogance of worldly love,"[8] Victor's associate takes his inspiration from a "different love": that he might "be seen as radiant in the world to come."[9] In subsequent compliments Victor compares his associate with St. Paul's friend Timothy and with the Evangelist Luke, and in so doing reveals essential points of his own aspirations. "I see another Timothy, instructed from his earliest childhood in the sacred writings, as well as a Luke, sublime and alert among men...."[10] The allusion to Timothy is appropriate to Victor's situation. Both the first and second epistle to Timothy treat the subject of ecclesial leadership during times of persecution. "Therefore I endure all things," wrote St. Paul,

> for the sake of the elect, that they may obtain the salvation, which is in Christ Jesus, with heavenly glory. A faithful saying: for if we be dead with Him, we shall also live with Him, *If we suffer, we shall also reign with Him*. If we deny Him, He will also deny us...[11]

The Pauline redemptive nature of suffering, a suffering with Christ, would have given hope to the distressed African community that their troubles had meaning. The notion that the victim's suffering united him with Christ was well established in the genre of martyr literature from the earliest times and enjoyed continued development under the Fathers.[12] Victor and his compatriots may have seen in First and Second Timothy a prophecy of their own travails: "And all that will live godly in Christ Jesus, shall suffer persecution."[13] It is quite possible that Victor also had in mind Paul's letter to the Colossians (1:23–4), which again addressed the issue of false teaching and persecution, and in which Timothy is mentioned—though not addressed—and the notion of the redemptive and *shared* nature of suffering receives great impetus: ". . . I, Paul, am made a minister. Who now rejoice in my sufferings for you, and fill up those things that are wanting of the sufferings of Christ, in my flesh, for his body, which is the Church." The orthodox understanding of what was "wanting of the sufferings of Christ," was that man had a price to *re*pay for the sins that Christ ransomed, not, of course, that anything was lacking in the suffering of Jesus Christ.[14] This idea of suffering for the body of Christ, understood in the above passage as the Church, allowed Christians a part in paying their debt to Christ, and thus a role in salvation.[15] Such a conception will be readdressed by Victor in the conclusion of his history. In regards to the prologue, Victor clearly viewed the receiver of his work as a leader who, like Timothy, could labor for sound doctrine against violent and false teachers.

It is doubtful that Victor intended to compare himself with St. Paul in addressing his associate as a new Timothy; the allusion to Luke is more helpful in establishing the relationship between the historians. In the opening of the Gospel according to Luke (1:1–4), the evangelist writes

> For as much as many have taken in hand to set forth in order a narration of the things that have been accomplished among us; according *as they have delivered them unto to us, who from the beginning were eyewitnesses and ministers of the word*, it seemed good to me ...to write... that thou mayest know the truth...

Like those ministers of the word who provided Luke with information for his great *historia*, Victor envisions himself as a suitable candidate—being both an eyewitness and a minister—for passing on the history of his day. In concluding his prologue Victor betrays a fear that knowledge of the persecution in Africa might remain unknown. He shall attempt "to reveal" (*indicare*) matters in brief, like a "rural labourer with weary arms" uncovering "gold from hidden caves."[16] The image of the toiling rustic and the hidden gold are not the romantic or pastoral images modern readers may initially assume. As Victor narrates throughout the history, the fate of many loyal African Catholics was to be banished to state plantations and mines or to seek precarious cavern hideaways in the hinterland far away from the fleeting security of the city. The real "gold" of the African Catholics were priests such as the exiled Cresconius of Mizeita, whose rotting body was found in a cave of Mount Ziquense.[17] What the comments of the prologue disclose is the author's concern that a record of the Vandal persecution be preserved and circulated. His allusion to hard labor and obscure exile, and his references to the "hidden" nature of history underline possible anxiety that Catholic depravations would not only continue under the Vandals, but perhaps even be forgotten in time. Victor, as cleric and participant, sees himself as an appropriate chronicler of the persecution of African Catholics. What is more, through a Pauline allusion, he suggests that the suffering of the Roman community can have an important function to play if Catholics maintain their loyalty to orthodox doctrine. As the conclusion to the history shows, Victor does not limit himself solely to the addressee of the prologue, but the relationship which he has sketched reveals the author's concerns. Moving to specific themes allows a fuller appreciation of the manner in which Victor envisions his history being used as both a sort of verbal icon and a form of petition to the Church.[18]

Throughout most of the western Mediterranean Catholics enjoyed relative peace under their Arian barbarian overlords.[19] The Vandal kings of Africa, in an effort at imposing a unified ideology on their subjects—perhaps in imitation of the Byzantine conception of one empire, one church—introduced, in the words of Gibbon, a number of "intolerant laws and arbitrary punishments." Roman Catholic resistance, at least amongst the hierarchy, was true to the feisty African spirit, and under both Geiseric and Huneric, Catholic resistance was met by Arian brutality. In the face of sustained and sometimes brutal persecution, works such as Victor's were essential to the cohesion of the Catholic community.

Victor reassures his audience, time and again, that the details of the persecution which he presents are just that—details; he is not providing a comprehensive report of every single case of abuse. In fact, early in the narrative he admits that he shall speak "only of the most noteworthy things."[20] The apparent magnitude of the subject is such that, by the third book of the history, Victor claims that the task of further chronicling the persecution would daunt Cicero, Sallust, Eusebius, Ambrose, Jerome, even Augustine.[21] If these authors with their eloquence and historiographic experience are insufficient, how then, Victor ponders, can he continue? Such is the author's stylistic departure, but throughout the whole text Victor uses stock phrases for the sake of brevity and discrimination. Locutions such as "I am unable to recount the number," "who will be able to declare how many and how numerous," "why say many things," "I shall mention one thing which happened," "it is known that many others were killed," "who could tell the story," "who would have the ability to set forth...," "who could describe in fitting language or confine himself to just a brief account" indicate that more could be said,[22] but space and decency compel Victor to focus his thoughts about suffering around succinct, but evocative, episodes. Such episodes have lead more sceptical historians to discount most of Victor's record, but as we shall see, it is precisely through such a dramatic narrative that Victor discloses his past to us.[23]

To Victor's local audience, the foremost interest in his history would have been the provision of a *raison d'être* for their suffering. After all, late fifth-century African Catholics were in a curious position. Almost two centuries had elapsed since the state had persecuted Christians, and since that time only groups such as the Donatists and the Circumcellions had encountered organized harassment. With an Arian political hegemony increasing in the Western Mediterranean, however, Catholics found themselves exposed to the ideological whims of the new masters of Africa. First and foremost, Victor wished to explain that such suffering was because of the loyalty of the Romans to the true faith. As subordinationists, the Vandals denied the triple anointing and triple invocation in the name of the Father, Son, and Holy Spirit, and thus desired to see Catholics rebaptized under the Arian formula. Consequently, the issue of baptism provides Victor with one symbol for the Catholics cause, a sign of loyalty. As he details in his third book, extreme steps were taken to rebaptize Catholics during the reign of Huneric.[24] The Vandals aspersed individuals under restraint or while sleeping; Arian priests were sent into the markets to douse the unwary.

Earlier in the narrative Victor suggests baptismal purity as an issue which defines the loyal Catholic. In the process of torturing a man referred to as "our Armogas," the Vandals gouge into the forehead, on which, Victor indicates, "Christ had fixed the standard (*vexillum*) of his cross."[25] This use of the military term *vexillum* is repeated later when bishop Eugenius restores the vision of a man through baptism into the Catholic Church: "he signed his eyes with the standard (*vexillum*) of the cross, and immediately the blind man received his faith..."[26] Such conflation of a reference to a military standards with the Catholic baptismal anointing is an important example of the sort of symbol Victor offers to his reader.[27] Victor enriches with communal meaning what otherwise may have seemed a burdensome ritual to the faint at heart. At other points, Victor refers to the loyal Catholic people as an "army" (*exercitus*)[28] and the exiled clergy as the "crack troops of God's army" (*dei exercitu comitantes*),[29] while an old woman is described to be eager "to associate with the army of Christ" (*exercitui Christi sociari*).[30] Like the "standard" of Christ image, such a description, however brief, explains to persecuted Catholics that what may seem unwarranted causes for their suffering are the very sureties of their faith. Resisting the Arians, even under torture, signifies that an individual is moving along "the right path;"[31] and in a further military image, Victor encourages Romans to maintain their Catholicism as "the wall of faith" against Arian assaults.[32] The imagery is interesting given that the Romans in Africa had long been stripped of opportunities to act in a military capacity. Victor restores a little of the lost martial pride, channeling communal energies towards a new and spirtualized combat.[33]

While ethnic and cultural distinctions would have been easy to discern in the opposing parties in the persecution, Victor heightens the degree to which the Catholic struggle could be seen as a test of loyalty by depicting Vandals as subjects of the devil, or by characterizing, on the one hand, the Vandal king as a Pharaoh and, on the other hand, the Romans as the people of God. The Arian church in Africa is, at one point, described as a building (*aedificium*) which the Devil toiled to erect, but which Christ decrees to demolish.[34] As with the aforementioned military imagery, Victor's imaging of Christ destroying an Arian church reverses the sad reality of contemporary society where it was instead the Catholic community that suffered confiscation and arson. While this is the only explicit conjuring of the devil, Victor has other means of defining and characterizing the struggle. Later, in book two, we read that, "The enemy was perhaps already saying 'I shall divide the spoils, I shall fill my soul, I shall kill with my sword, my hand shall have dominion . . .'"[35] The passage, referring to the thoughts of Huneric, is a direct quotation from Exodus 15.9 and it is likely that Victor's audience was to understand the allusion to Pharaoh as applying to their current master. That he never explicitly makes the comparison between one of the Vandal kings and Pharaoh is not surprising, for earlier Victor had mentioned that exile awaited those clergy who had previously spoken, even in passing, of Pharaoh, Nabuchodonosor, Holofernes, or any other Old Testament overlord.[36]

Christians had long understood themselves to be the new Israelites,[37] but the appropriation of the Exodus story in Africa would have resonated even more dramatically with the oppressed Catholic community. Thus it is to be expected that we discover Victor commonly employing the expression "the people of God" (*populus dei*) for his fellow Catholics.[38] In such passages Victor uses the more dignified and more inclusive word *populus* and never the baser *plebs*.[39] Although *plebs* does appear in a speech of the bishop Eugenius which Victor preserves, this limited occurrence only strengthens the case for the careful and selective use of author's own vocabulary.[40] It may be that Victor is, consciously on unconsciously, keeping to the range of meaning for *populus* delineated by St. Augustine, especially in his *City of God*, in particular books 2 and 19.[41] Other commendatory titles which Victor gives to the Catholics include "servants of Christ" (*famuli dei*), "church of God" (*dei ecclesia*), and "church of Christ" (*Christi ecclesia*); while he reserves for the Arians epithets such as "brood of vipers" (*serpentina proles*), "robbers of souls" (*animarum praedones*), "lackeys" (*satellis*), "servants of falsehood" (*ministri erroris*), and other choice sobriquets.[42] It is interesting to note, in fact, the sensitivity of the Arian Vandals to titles. They, in contrast, referred to the Catholics as *homousians*,[43] seeing themselves as the orthodox faith. Victor claims that upon hearing Eugenius read his treatise *The Book of the Catholic Faith*, the Vandals went wild: "their blind eyes found it impossible to endure the light of the truth; they raved with intolerable shouts taking it amiss. . . ."[44] Clearly, crafting emotive communal titles played an essential part in the rhetoric of the day.

In a manner as careful and as vivid as his denominations of the sides in the crisis,[45] Victor provides numerous concrete examples of how the faithful should behave with an eye to *why* they should behave.[46] Often Victor makes use of phrases such as *pro Deo*, or *pro Christo* to remove suffering from a temporal or political context. His inclusion of oppressed Vandal Catholics and individuals from all conceivable social classes underlines his rigor in treating the persecution only in spiritual terms.[47] Apart from the many expected references to bishops, priests, and monks, we find the office of lector (*lector*) and archdeacon (*archidiaconus*) represented.[48] Various degrees of the nobility are mentioned including the *illustris*, *clari*, senators, *honorati*, and a count (*comes*).[49] The lower class receive lesser attention by the scattered appearances of slaves (*servi*) and handmaidens (*ancillae*).[50] A surprising number of specialized vocations appear: a pantomime (*archimimus*), a notary (*notarius*), merchants (*negotiatores*), the superintendent of the royal household (*procurator domus*), the superintendent of the kingdom (*praepositus regni*), a proconsul, and a butler (*cellarita*).[51] Finally the largest group is simply "the people," most frequently referred to as *populus*, but once as "the laity" (*laici*).[52] Within the *populus*, however, Victor directs his attention to stories about families, specifically episodes which involve children or struggles between husbands and wives over the adaptation of a course of resistance—and often martyrdom.[53]

The inclusion so many levels of Romano-African society opens the struggle to all social ranks, but as we have seen Victor also intends to limit the political shadings of persecution. One story, in fact, elevates personal or political grievance to the level of the spiritual.[54] Beaten with rods, stretched on the rack, dragged through the streets until all the skin tore from his torso, Servus of Tuburitana endured great agonies for Christ (*pro Christo*). In answering the question of why this aristocrat (*generosus et nobilis*) maintained his resistance, Victor reveals that Servus held an old grievance against the Vandal establishment, but deftly turns this into an opportunity for praise:[55]

He had already suffered things quite like these in the time of Geiseric, for not making public the secrets of a particular friend: *how much more would he suffer now, when he was safeguarding the mysteries of his faith (fidei)?* And if he faithfully (*fideliter*) displayed his faith (*fidem*) for the sake of a man, and for no gain, how much more must he have done so for the sake of the one who will render him for his faith (*fide*) a reward.

The accumulation of the various forms of *fides* audibly drums the message that this is a religious war in which Catholics must defend their precious faith at all costs. The final word of the episode points to the end of loyalty—a reward (*mercedem*).[56] Victor gives some substance to the concept of *merces* two chapters later when he speaks of the martyrial crown (*martyrialem coronam*) that the murdered proconsul Victorianus received.[57] But this achievement is a rare commodity in the *History*. It cannot be that Victor thinks his compatriots unworthy; it is not because he discounts the many bloody sacrifices made by the Romano-Africans. It is simply that Victor aims neither to limit the category of martyr to those who perish,[58] nor does he feel it is within the bounds of orthodox theology to applaud and encourage *only* those few who resist apostasy to the point of death.

Victor's argument for resistance is not merely a negative one based on opposition to Arian heresy, but a positive defense for a theological point: the fullness of the Catholic sacrament of baptism. For this defense Victor reserves his most powerful image, that of the wedding garment, or baptismal robe. Several gripping vignettes set forth this imagery in such a way that Victor's intent that they should rally the Catholic community is evident.

During the persecution of King Geiseric public torture and humiliation intensified and, if we accept Victor, the Arian provocateurs increasingly targeted women, especially women of the nobility.[59] One case concerned a woman named Dionysia. As with other female victims she was stripped *contra iura naturae*, as Victor objects,[60] in preparation for clubbing. "Torture me however you like," Dionysia exclaimed, "but do not uncover those parts which would cause me shame."[61] This cry only encouraged her tormentors who forced her naked into a "prominent place, making a spectacle in front of everyone."[62] The results of her humiliation worked against the Arians. Dionysia, armed with a "full knowledge of divine scriptures" inspired others to resist; "by her holy example she set nearly the whole country free," Victor concludes.[63] At one point Victor gives us the speech Dionysia makes to her young and frightened son. After "casting wounding glances and reproving with her motherly authority" she emboldens him:[64]

"Remember, my son, that we have been baptized in the Catholic mother in the name of the Trinity. Let us not lose that garment of our salvation, in case the host when He comes, does not find the wedding garment and says to His servants: 'Cast him into the outer darkness, where there will be weeping and gnashing of teeth' (Mt. 22.13). The punishment to be feared is the one that will never end, and the life to be desired is the one which will be enjoyed forever."

It is interesting to speculate on the levels of meaning possible in this story. First, there is the woman's name, Dionysia. Literally this Greek name would refer to a woman devoted to the god Dionysus. Dionysus, it should be noted, was most often compared with Christ. This is a minor observation, but the woman's Greek name is rare in the late antique Christian west, even in Carthage with its old Hellenistic community, and hence offers itself for a deeper reading. Second, we should mark the careful parallelism between Dionysia with her maternal authority (*auctoritate materna*) and the Catholic Church, the mother, as Victor says, in whom the Romans have been baptized (*in catholica matre*). Victor seems to be impressing a personified Church onto a historical figure. This interpretation is supported by the language that Victor employs in describing her admonishment. Dionysia begins by "casting wounding glances" as translator John Moorhead renders it. But the Latin means more than this. *Verberans eum nutibus oculorum*: the crucial word is *nutibus*. *Nutus* does not refer to a glance, but "nod as a symbol of absolute power."[65] *Nutus* was the motion of the head which Jupiter, or a Roman consul made in giving assent or denial, as in "he nodded assent and with that nod made all Olympus tremble."[66] Such an authoritative gesture from a female figure in possession of the "full knowledge of scripture" should certainly be considered as representing more than an historical mother, heroic though Dionysia undoubtedly was. Dionysia does not mince her words—or rather, the words of Christ—when it comes to the fate of apostates: eternal damnation. Such wrathful exclamation may have come from the lips of an individual mother concerned for her individual son, but the passage is in no way distorted if we read Dionysia as Victor's universal mother and the son as anyone of an imperiled Catholic community. The words which Victor attributes to her deliver a message consistent and evident throughout his narrative: defend the Trinitarian baptism and orthodox faith through all trials. The final symbol in Dionysia's speech, the symbol which links her words with other episodes, concerns the image of the garment. Initiates into the Christian faith in the fifth century continued to wear baptismal robes while receiving the sacrament. The evocation and connection of the robe to the wedding garment spoken of by Christ allows Victor to exploit a powerful emblem for the Catholic cause.

The potency of this image of the baptismal garment is brought to bear most forcefully in subsequent speeches. At some point during his reign, Huneric initiated a second wave of pogroms and exiles. The five hundred remaining clergy were rounded up for public humiliations and torture. Among these was a venerable old deacon (*venerabilis diaconus*) named Murrita. One of the chief ministers of interrogation was Elpidoforus, a former Catholic who had been baptized by Murrita in the presence of Victor himself. Elpidoforus, we are told, was responsible for mangling the limbs of the prisoners during torture (*cui fuerat delegatum membra confessorum Christi suppliciis grassantibus laniare*). When Murrita was brought forth to be racked he produced from a concealed spot the linen towels in which had wrapped the young Elpidoforus after his baptism. Brandishing these before the crowd, he addressed his tormentor, according to Victor, with the following:[67]

"These are the linen cloths, Elpidoforus, you servant of falsehood, which will accuse you when the Judge comes in his majesty. I shall be careful to keep them as a testimony of your perdition, so that you will be sunk in the abyss of the sulphurous pit. They clad you when you rose spotless from the font, and they will follow after you the more bitterly when you begin to possess a flaming gehenna, because you have 'put on a curse like a garment' [Ps. 108.18], breaking asunder and letting go of the sacrament of true baptism and faith. What are you going to do, you miserable man, when the servants of the head of the family begin to bring together the people invited to the king's supper? Then the king, with frightened indignation, will see that you, a person who was at one time invited, have taken off the wedding garment, and he will say to you: 'Friend, how have you come hither without a wedding garment? [Mt. 22.12] I do not see that which I conferred on you; I do not recognize what I gave. You have lost the cloak worn by my soldiery, which I wove on the loom of virgin limbs for ten months, stretched out on the fuller's stretcher of the cross, cleansed with water, and beautified with the purple dye of my blood, I do not discern the adornment of my sign; I do not see the branding mark of the Trinity. Such a man will not be able to take part in my banquet. Bind him hand and foot with his cords, because of his own free will he had desired to separate himself from the Catholics who were formerly his brothers."

The crowd wept upon hearing his speech, while Elpidoforus, Victor relates, "was speechless, roasted by the fire of his conscience before he experienced the fire which is eternal."[68] In this discourse the symbol of resistance is made concrete; no longer merely *symbolic*, but now *physical* garments are introduced into the narrative. Of course, the towels still signify the sacrament, and the speech stays primarily on a spiritual level, but Muritta's use of the linen towels allows Victor to hint at a sacramental weapon. Not only do the Romans possess the correct liturgical rites and theology, but they have tangible objects to prove it. Victor, again, displays his adeptness for turning the tables in the Catholic community's favor. Muritta, the prisoner, is the one producing evidence against Elpidoforus, the "testimony of your damnation" (*testimonium tuae perditionis*) as he exclaims; it is the jailer who will be bound and cast into a dark pit; and it is the disarmed Catholics who wear the soldiers' cloak (*militiae clamidem*). Furthermore, the Catholic claim is given ultimate authority by the words of Christ. These words, as with Dionysia's speech, are taken in part from the parable of the wedding feast found in the gospel of Matthew (22:1–14).

But Victor adds to them words which make the validity of the sacrament exclusive to the Catholic Church. The Christ of Muritta's harangue develops an extended (and mixed) metaphor of the Catholic Church as the dispenser of the wedding garment. The loom of the virginal limbs is a reference to Mary, but most references to Mary were understood as applying to the Church herself.[69] That the robe was "stretched out on the fuller's stretcher of the cross" could be taken in a limited sense as a reference to the individual suffering of Christ on the cross, but given Victor's Pauline leanings and given that the catechumen himself wears this robe, a notion of shared suffering can be understood. The mention of water and blood, long a symbol of the institution of the Church, assures the reader of the metaphor. But the element which most narrowly limits the description to the Catholic community is the comment "I do not discern the adornment of my seal (*cultum signaculi mei*); I do not see the branding mark of the Trinity (*caracterem trinitatis*)." The reference to the Trinitarian seal is, of course, the most obvious rebuff to Arianism. The word *cultus*, however, is also significant. *Cultus* can, of course mean simply adornment, as in the Moorhead translation, but more typical is the sense of behavior, religious devotion and lifestyle.[70] The single Latin word renders a rich meaning to Victor's narrative. Here, the Christ of the narrative implies that His whole manner of living is lacking in the Arians.

Is there any evidence that this emblematic stature of the robe was known more widely among the North African community? During Huneric's second campaign against the Catholics, Arian clergy were dispatched with military escort to force Arian baptism upon all by trickery or force. While the wiser knew that such compulsions had no validity, the "less intelligent and the ignorant thought that because of this they were guilty of defilement and sacrilege."[71] In reaction to this liturgical violation many Catholics—we cannot tell whether they were the learned, the simple, or a mixture of both—reacted in such a way as to demonstrate the emblematic stature of the baptismal robe:

> Many straightway scattered ashes on their heads, and others in sorrow at what had happened, clad themselves in hair shirts. Some plastered themselves with filthy mud and tore into shreds the linen cloths which had been put on them by force, and with the hand of faith they threw them into cesspits and foul places.[72]

Ashes, hairshirts, even mud—all these elements seem to be applied as a symbolic repellent against the Arian baptismal rites, while the people clearly view the robes themselves with great vitriol. The fact that the linen clothes are not simply removed, but cast into latrines underscores the suggestion that such items as robes took on a symbolic quality. The positive and negative treatment of these objects express the communal sentiment and loyalty.

In his long conclusion (3.61–70), Victor employs the language of the Psalms and Lamentations to call upon various communities to rescue the Romano-Africans. After appealing to earthly, heavenly, and ecclesiastical powers, Victor ends by addressing Peter and finally Paul "to recognize what the Arian Vandals are doing."[73] The placement of Paul after Peter may seem a bit odd given Victor's emphasis on Peter's importance in the evocation (*praecipue tu, Petre beate...*), until one reads the following words in the concluding chapter:

We know that we are unworthy of your prayers, because these torments which have taken place to try us were the deserts, not of the holy, but of those who deserve ill. . . . May these things which have been justly imposed on us suffice for our rectification. . . . Who can fail to understand that our sinful and shameful acts brought these things upon us . . . ?[74]

We have returned to the same notion of suffering evoked in the prologue of the work. Unless this passage is understood in terms of St. Paul's belief that our temporal suffering is the completion of Christ's suffering, that is, repayment for sinfulness, the passage makes little sense and undermines the entire concluding plea, and indeed, the whole of Victor's history. Victor is humbly recognizing that earthly suffering is never unjust, rather it is a necessary part of the way of salvation. The events of the Vandal persecution have occurred *ad probationem* of the Catholic community—that is for its reform, edification, warranted castigation, and proof of worthiness.[75] Suffering is then, for Victor, the natural result of man's sinfulness, which comes to all who are members of the true faith. The centrality of baptism to the Catholic community is a necessary focus for Victor's explication of suffering. Again, the notion is Pauline:

Know you not that all we, who are baptized in Christ Jesus, are baptized in His death? For we are buried together with Him by baptism into death; that as Christ is risen from the dead by the glory of the Father, so we may walk in the newness of life. For if we have been planted together in the likeness of His death, we shall also be in the likeness of His resurrection. Knowing this: that the old man is crucified with him, that the body of sin may be destroyed, to the end that we may serve sin no longer.[76]

Victor had Paul's letter to the Romans in mind, when he alluded to Paul as the "teacher of the gentiles, who preached the gospel of God 'from Jerusalem as far as Illyricum.'"[77] In Romans, Victor found the identification between baptism and Christ's passion which assisted in his sublimation of suffering. Through the acceptance of their suffering, the members of the community share in Christ's Passion and witness the end of their sinfulness. It was baptism that initiated the communion which Christians share with Christ. Suffering is a worthy continuation of that communion, perhaps even an essential expression of the Church's sacramental life."[78]

   In reading Victor, as elsewhere, it is essential to distinguish between suffering and injustice. Injustice may be decried and worked against, hence the litany of quotations from Lamentations and the Psalms in the conclusion of book three. Yet, Victor, as a beneficiary of St. Augustine, knew too well that injustice could never be entirely eradicated from an earthly community, and indeed that all such communities are constrained by sin.[79] Suffering, however, is a natural result of the Fall, transformed only through the Incarnation, Passion, and Resurrection of Christ. It is not suffering, *per se*, against which Victor railed, but the historical particulars involved: the efforts of the Arian Vandals to extirpate Catholicism in North Africa. In his narration Victor provided models for his community and strove to explain the nature of anguish and grief. The figures in Victor's history come from all levels of African society; they have names and they come from the great and small towns of the North African province. By so concentrating his stories on individuals and daily commonplaces, Victor gives suffering a human face. His history is not merely the bald chronicle of events that he suggests in the prologue, but a study in the nature of suffering—both its perennial and redemptive nature—and as such is worthy to be read for more than historical research alone.[80]

NOTES

1. On the history of late Roman Africa generally see B.H. Warmington, *The North African Provinces from Diocletian to the Vandal Conquest* (Cambridge, 1954); C. Courtois, *Les Vandales et L'Afrique* (Paris, 1955); and S. Raven, *Rome in Africa* (London and New York, 1993). In addition to the chief three—Victor of Vita's *Historia*, the *Vita S. Fulgentii episcopi Ruspensis* (PL 65.117–50) and the *Bellum Vandalicum* of Procopius—also extant are the anonymous *Passio septem monachorum* and the *Notitia Provinciarum et civitatum Africae* found with Victor's *Historia Persecutionis Africanae Provinciae* in CSEL 7 (1881) edited by M. Petschenig.

2. The Latin text used throught this chapter is that of M. Petschenig, CSEL 7 (1881); I have used, with occasional modification, the translation of J. Moorhead, *Victor of Vita: History of the Vandal Persecution* (Liverpool, 1992). On the little biographical information that can be assembled regarding Victor see C. Courtois, *Victor de Vita et son oeuvre* (Algiers, 1954), 5–10.

3. C. Courtois, *Les Vandales*, 51.

4. This paper has throughout been influenced by the notions of drama and communal participation found in Monique Clavel-Léveque, *L'Empire en Jeux Espace Symbolique et Pratique dans Le Monde Romain* (Paris, 1984) and Hans urs von Balthasar, *Theo-Drama: Theological Dramatic Theory.* 4 vols., trans. G. Harrison (San Francisco, 1988), esp. vol. 1, 89–155.

5. Courtois argues in favour of the former in *Victor de Vita*, 21ff., while Moorhead, *Victor*, 2, n. 3 (following H.-I. Marrou, "Diadoque de Photiké et Victor de Vita," *Revue des études anciennes* 44 [1943]: 225–32), insists on the bishop of Carthage.

6. Victor, prologue 1: *Quondam veteres ob studium sapientiae enucleare atque sciscitari assiduae minime disistebant, quae forte vel qualia prospere vel secus provinciis, locis aut regionibus evenissent . . .*

7. Victor, prologue 1: *...dabantque operam ut nequaquam lateret in totum, quod in parte forte fuerat gestum.*

8. Victor, prologue 2: *...illi fastu mundialis amoris inflati . . .*

9. Victor, prologue 2: *...dispari tamen amore;... ut praeclarus appareas in futuro...*

10. Victor, prologue 3: *Alium video Timotheum ab incunabulis infantiae sacris litteris eruditum, nec non inter alios sublimem atque expeditum magisteri genitum Lucam. . . .* Petschenig notes that the comparison to Timothy quotes from II Tim 3:15.

11. II Tim. 2:10–12; cf., Col. 1:24. The emphasis here, as in all other quotations in this chapter, is mine own.

12. R.L. Fox, *Pagans and Christians* (New York, 1987), 441; T. Spidlik, *The Spirituality of the East* trans. A.P. Gythiel (Kalamazoo, 1986), 137–39; V. Guroian, *Life's Living toward Dying* (Grand Rapids, 1996), 35–40 and 93–96.

13. II Tim. 3:12, one of a plethora of verses which could be evoked to describe the north African situation at the end of the fifth century.

14. Cf. the note of R. Knox in his translation of *The Holy Bible* (New York, 1950) 208: "...St. Paul only represents himself as taking a *share* in the afflictions here referred to; and probably the metaphor is that of a poor man *contributing* to pay off a sum which a richer man has paid in advance. Thus the obvious meaning of Christ's sufferings, although fully satisfactory on behalf of our sins, leaves us a debt of honour, as it were, to repay them by sufferings of our own."

15. Irenaeus was to give the ransom theory one of its earliest elaborations, but the tradition would be continued by many of the Fathers, see J.N.D. Kelly, *Early Christian Doctrine* (New York, 1978), 175f. *inter alia.*

16. Victor, prologue 4: *...quasi rusticanus operarius defatigatis ulnis aurum colligam de antris occultis...*

17. Victor, 3.52.

18. On the creation of such verbal icons in early Christian literature see A. Cameron, *Christianity and the Rhetoric of Empire: the Development of Discourse* (Berkeley, 1991), 47–68.

19. On the persecution in general see C. Courtois, *Les Vandales*, 277f. and 297–8.

20. Victor, 1.9: *... de necessariis loquar....* This statement is particularly in reference to which buildings were destroyed or confiscated in the persecution, but exemplifies Victor's selective tone.

21. Victor, 3.61: *Sed quid ego iam iam inmoror in hoc, quod explicare non queo? Nam si nunc superessent vel eis fari de talibus rebus licuisset, et Tullianae eloquentiae fluvius siccaretur et Sallustius elinguis omnimodis remaneret. Et ut alienos indignos rei tanta praeteream, si Caesariensis surgeret Eusebius ad hoc opus idoneus, aut eius translator Graecae facundiae Latinisque gloribus Rufinus ornatus—et quid multa—non Ambrosius, non Hieronimus, nec ipse noster sufficeret Augustinus.*

22. Victor, 1.7; 1.10; 1.12, 2.23; 1.19; 1.42; 3.25; 3.28; 3.31, *inter alia.*, respectively.

23. Edward Gibbon, if he noted such disclaimers, still found Victor passionate and utterly unreliable as an witness, for him the *Historia* hid the truth behind a "veil of fiction and declamation." Gibbon prefered the seemingly rational account of Procopius; towards Victor he maintained a pointed scepticism:"the stubborn mind of an infidel is guarded by secret incurable suspicion;" see his 38th chapter of *The History of the Decline and Fall of the Roman Empire.* I have found helpful the observation of John Lukacs that "re-presentation is neither mere substituition, nor is it purely symbolic abstraction. The symbol

must represent something real;" see his *Historical Consciousness: The Remembered Past* (New Brunswick, 1992), 243 *inter alia.*

24. On Huneric's religious policy see C. Courtois, 293–99.

25. Victor, 1.43: *Christus vexillum suae fixerat crucis.*

26. Victor, 2.50: *Simulque vexillo crucis consignans oculos eius, statim caecus visum domino reddente recepit.*

27. Such use of military imagery in times of crisis was not new to Victor, see of course, A. Harnack, *Militia Christi: Die christliche Religion und der Soldatenstand in den ersten drei Jahrhunderten* (Tübingen, 1905); followed with greater reference to North African authors by E.L. Hummel, *The Concept of Martyrdom According to St. Cyprian of Carthage* (Washington, 1946), 56–90.

28. Victor 1.13; 2.31; and 3.60 *inter alia.*

29. Translation is my own; Moorhead render this expression as "the company of the army of God," but Victor, in describing his heroic clergy in exile, clearly means something robust and distinctive.

30. Victor, 2.30.

31. Victor, 2.9: *...a recto intinere...*

32. Victor, 2.10: *At ubi isto modo fidei infringere non valuit murum.*

33. Feelings of military virtue had long been at the centre of classical performances of suffering and struggle, especially in the arena, see R. Auget, *Cruelty and Civilization* (London and New York, 1972), 182–83.

34. Victor, 2.24: *Sed hoc aedificium ubi construere nisus est diabolus, statim illud destruere dignatus est Christus.*

35. Victor, 2.31: *Sed ubi adversarius, qui iam forte dicebat partibo spolia, replebo animam meam, interficiam gladio meo,dominabitur manus mea...*

36. Victor, 2.22: *Ut si forsitan quispiam, ut moris est, dum dei populum ammoneret, Pharaonem, Nabuchodonosor, Holofernem aut aliquem similem nominasset, obiciebatur illi, quod in persona regis ista dixisset, et statim exilio trudebatur.*

37. Augustine had already established such terminology in north African ecclesiastical circles; see J. Adams, *The Populus of Augustine and Jerome: A Study in the Patristic Sense of Community* (New Haven, 1971), 34–53 and 79–80.

38. Victor, 1.17; 1.22; 1.23; 1.41; 1.42; 2.8 *inter alia.* This does not include references to "men of God," "virgins of God," "slaves of God," etc.

39. J. Ratzinger, *Volk und Haus Gottes in Augustins Lehre von der Kirche.* Müncher Theologische Studien, 2 (Systematische) Abteilung, vol. 7 (Munich, 1954), 159–69.

40. Eugenius' usc of *plebs* may be found at Victor, 2.41. On the general connotations of *populus* and *plebs* among late antique Christians see J. Adams, Populus *of Augustine and Jerome,* esp. 109–120.

41. On which, see J.D. Adams, *The* Populus *of Augustine and Jerome,* especially 17–69; also note the cautionary observations of E.L. Fortin, "The Patristic Sense of Community," *Collected Essays,* vol. 1, ed. J.B. Benestad (Lanham, MD, 1996). That Victor read St. Augustine scarcely requires argument. He refers to him proudly as *omni laude dignus beatus Augustinus* (1.10) and *noster Augustinus* (3.61).

42. See, e.g., Victor, 1.37; 2.25; 3.63; 3.48; 2.53; 3.36.

43. See Huneric's edict preserved in Victor, 2.39–42 at 39.

44. Victor, 3.1: *...veritatis lumen nequaquam sufferre caecis oculis potuerunt, insanientes vocibus inferendis graviterque ferentes...*

45. It is important to note that Victor's work defines both Catholic and Vandal behavior, and thus would have 'created' a Catholic way of perceiving the Vandals; on depicting the 'opposition' in such literature, compare Victor's history with later works such as Reformation trial plays, cf., J.E.A. Dawson, "The Scottish Reformation and the Theatre of Martyrdom," in *Martyrs and Martyrologies*, ed. D. Wood (Oxford, 1993), 259–70.

46. On the tradition of giving the audience a role, by association, with the "people" in a story, see A. Cameron, *Christianity and the Rhetoric of Empire*, 74ff.; cf. M. Harris, *The Dialogical Theatre: Dramatizers of the Conquest of Mexico and the Question of the Other* (New York, 1993).

47. On the persecution of Vandal Catholics see Victor, 2.10; 2.12; and 2.14–16.

48. Victor, 1.41 and 3.35.

49. Victor, *inlustris* 1.7 and 2.3; *clari* 1.14; senators and *honorati* 1.15; and Count Sebastianus 1.19.

50. Victor, 1.30 and 1.48, *inter alia.*

51. Victor, 1.47; 2.41; 3.41; 1.48; 2.15; 3.27; and 3.33, respectively.

52. Victor, 1.14.

53. Victor, 1.35; 1.48ff.; 2.14; 2.29; 2.30; 2.34; 3.22ff.; 3.26; 3.34; 3.49; and 3.50ff.

54. An example of the tendency, among Christian authors, to shift the emphasis in such grim issues from the mundane to the sacred; see A.J. Droge and J.D. Tabor, *A Noble Death: Suicide and Martyrdom Among Christians and Jews in Antiquity* (San Francisco, 1992), 158.

55. Victor, 3.25: *Iste iam temporibus Geiserici non valde dissimilia pertulerat, ne amici cuiusdam sui secreta nudaret; quanto magis nunc, ut suae fidei sacramenta muniret? Et si homini gratis fideliter exhibuit fidem, quantum debet illi, qui redditurus est pro fide mercedem.*

56. Faith (*fides*), which had, to the Romans, been the virtue of slaves, was elevated to the level of *devotio*, a concept which embraced the highest ideals of duty towards one's community, see A.J.L. van Hoof, *From Autothanasia to Suicide. Self-killing in Classical Antiquity* (London and New York, 1990), 127ff.

57. Victor, 3.27.

58. For the application of the title to the living see Victor, 3.28.

59. Victor, 3.21: *Mulieres et praecipue nobiles... in facie publica cruciabant.*

60. Although the sufferings of women had long been a subject of fascination for the ancients, Christianity showed a dramatic degree of admiration for the travails of woman, and usually depicted them as triumphant over the oppression of their enemies, see C. Jones, "Women, Death, and the Law During the Christian Persecutions," in *Martyrs and Martyrologies*, ed. D. Wood (Oxford, 1993), 23–34 and 32–4.

61. Victor, 3.22: ... *'qualiter libet cruciate, verecunda tamen membra nolite nudare'...*

62. ibid,: ... *amplius illi magis furentes celsiori loci vestimentis exutam consistunt, spectaculum eam omnibus facientes...*

63. ibid, : ... *Et quia est scripturarum divinarum scientia plena, artata poenis et ipsa iam martyr alios ad martyrium confortabat; quae suo sancto exemplo paene universam suam patriam liberavit.*

64. ibid,: ... *verberans eum nutibus oculorum et increpans auctoritate materna ita confortavit...* 'memento, fili mi, quia in nomine trinitatis in matre catholica baptizati sumus. *Non perdamus indumentum nostrae salutis, ne veniens invitator vestem non inveniat nuptialem et dicat ministris: mittite in tenebras exteriores, ubi erit fletus oculorum et stridor dentium. Illa poena timenda est quae numquam finitur, illa desideranda vita quae semper habetur.* 'Moorhead's translation begins "casting wounding glances and threatening with her motherly authority..." I have slightly modified the Moorhead translation here.

65. *OLD, Nutus*: entries 1, and especially 2b.

66. Virgil, *Aneid*, 9.105: ... *adnuit et totum nutu tremefecit Olympum.* Cf., *OLD* for similar citations.

67. Victor, 3.36–7: ... *'haec sunt linteamina, Elpidofore minister erroris, quae te accusabunt, dum maiestas venerit iudicantis; custodientur diligentia mea ad testimonium tuae perditionis, ad demergendum te in abysso putei sulphurantis: haec te inmaculatum cinxerant de fonte surgentem, haec te arcius persequentur, flammantem gehennam cum coeperis possidere, quia induisti te maledictionem sicut vestimentum, scindens atque amittens veri baptismatis et fidei sacramentum. Quid facturus es, miser, cum servi patris familias ad cenam regiam congregare coeperint invitatos? Tunc te aliquando regiam congregare coeperint invitatos? Tunc te aliquando vocatum terribiliter indignatus exutum stolam rex conspiciet nuptialem dicebitque tibi: amice, quomodo huc venisti vestem non habens nuptialem? non video quod contuli, non cognosco quod dedi. Perdidisti militiae clamidem, quam in tela virgineorum membrorum decem mensibus texui et tendiculae crucis extendens aqua mundavi et purpura mei sanguinis decoravi. Non conspicio cultum signaculi mei, caracterem non video trinitatis: talis interesse non poterit epulis meis. Ligate eum pedibus et manibus funiculis suis, quia se ipse voluntarie separare voluit a catholicis dudum fratribus suis....*

68. Victor, 3.37: ...*igne conscientiae ante ignem aeternum obmutescens Elpifodorus torrebatur.*

69. C. Dillenschneider, *Le Mystère de la Corédemption Mariale* (Paris, 1951) and H. de Lubac, *The Splendor of the Church*, trans. M. Mason (New York, 1963), 198–235.

70. See *OLD, cultus*, definitions 3 and 8–12.

71. Victor, 3.48: *In quo minus capaces et ignavi impletum in se pollutionis sacrilegium imputabant, prudentiores vero nihil sibi, quod nolentimus atque dormientibus ingestum est, obesse gaudebant.*

72. Victor, *ibid*: *Nam et multi eadem hora cinerem capitibus suis iniecerunt, alii sese, vel quia factum, cilicio lugubri texerunt, nonnulli caeno fetido linierunt et linteamina violenter inposita per fila consciderunt atque in latrinis fetidisque locis manu fidei proiecerunt.*

73. Victor, 3.69: ... *cognosce quid Vandali faciunt Arriani.*

74. Victor, 3.70: *Sed scimus quia indignum est vobis pro nobis orare, quia ista, quae venerunt nobis ad probationem, non quomodo sanctis, sed malis meritis supplicia debeantur.... Sufficiant castigationi quae iuste inlata sunt nobis.... Quis ignoret haec nobis probrorum nostrorum scelera procurasse...?*

75. See the various shadings of meaning for *probatio* in the *OLD*.

76. Rom. 6:3–6; see also Col. 2:12.

77. Victor, 3.69: *Tu, sancte Paule, gentium magister, qui ab Hierusalem usque ad Illyrcium praedicasti evangelium dei...* The allusion is taken from Rom. 15:19.

78. To diminish the centrality of sacramental expression could lead modern readers to extract a secular and pluralistic message from Victor, as has been done with St. Augustine; see G. Bonner's critique of R.A. Markus and others in *"Quid imperatori cum ecclesia?* St. Augustine on history and society," *Augustinian Studies* 2 (1971): 231–51, especially 244ff.

79. E.L. Fortin makes this point of Augustinian realism clear, "The Patristic Sense of Community," 71–72; as does R.A. Markus, *Saeculum: History and society in the theology of St. Augustine* (Cambridge, 1970), 173.

80. This essay is offered not only as a tribute to Fredric W. Schlatter, S.J., but also to the memory of Robert Bryan Eno, S.S. (†1997) in whose seminar on post-Augustinian North Africa a version of this paper was first given: *sed certe mihi nulla dabatur copia sciscitandi quae cupiebam de tam sancto oraculo tuo, pectore illius....*

Toward a Pragmatics of
Archaic and Paleochristian Greek
Inscriptions

Joseph W. Day
Wabash College

Most of us read ancient inscriptions as sources of specific verbal information, and this colors our understanding of how they functioned in their own contexts.[1] We view inscriptions as political, legal, or social-historical records, or as tags naming owners, occupants of graves, and donors of dedications, in other words, as conduits of verbal messages from writers to readers. Epigraphers, with their knowledge of graffiti, magical amulets, curse tablets, and other less "grand" genres, have never wholly accepted such a view. Recently, several classical scholars, combining evidence for the functioning of inscriptions in ancient cultures with ethnographic parallels and modern theories of communication, have begun developing a "pragmatics" of inscriptions. The idea is to reconstruct the force of making or receiving inscriptions, that is, to determine how the writing or reading of an inscription can be understood as a significant act in itself, something more than the transfer of a message, something comparable to John Austin's "illocutionary act."[2] The difficulty inherent in such an approach is our inability to construct more than a rough picture of ancient writings and readings; but the attempt is worth making.[3]

My previous contributions to this project have concerned archaic Greek metrical inscriptions.[4] However, emboldened by the example of Fr. Schlatter, whose fine studies of Christian *Spätantike* are built on a foundation of *Altertumswissenschaft*, I take in this essay a first step toward extending my approach from archaic to paleochristian Greek inscriptions. A study corpus of Christian texts that seemed both typical and conducive to an approach based on pragmatics was assembled from four well-annotated regional corpora.[5] This material was expanded with parallel inscriptions from six other publications;[6] and for section 3 below, a fuller list of inscribed Trisagia was made (see Appendix). Three kinds of inscription were chosen for study, curses in conditional grammatical form, epitaphs concerned with the status of the deceased, and ritual utterances (especially the Trisagion troparion). What follows are three *sondages* to determine whether my pragmatics of archaic epigrams might suggest ways of reconstructing the force of writing and reading these paleochristian inscriptions in their very different cultural context.

I. How to do Things by Inscribing Conditionals

If inscriptions are to be understood as means of doing things with words, this "doing" must be viewed from two perspectives, writing and reception (reading or hearing someone read). For the ancient Greeks and others, the act of writing on an object, especially one with high symbolic value like a gift, magical talisman, grave marker, or dedication, was a significant, even ritual act, completing as well as perpetuating the force of oral, often ritualized utterances.[7] Uses of conditional curses illustrate how the mentality persisted in Christian times.

Whoever wrote or caused to be written the following very early inscription (ca. 735–20 B.C.) clearly felt that, by means of the act of inscribing, the force associated with a special utterance could be locked permanently into the object on which it was written:[8]

Νέστορός : ε[ἰμ]ι : εὔποτ[ον] : ποτέριον.
| hὸς δ' ἄν τόδε πίεσι : ποτερί[ο] : αὐτίκα κένον
| hίμερος hαιρέσει : καλλιστε[φά]νο : 'Αφροδίτες.

I am Nestor's good-for-drinking drinking cup. Whoever drinks from this drinking cup, immediately the desire of beautiful-crowned Aphrodite will seize him.

The conditional logic of the second sentence appears in many early Christian epitaphs threatening reprisals against anyone disturbing the tomb. The protasis may be a relative clause as above, a participial phrase, or a true conditional as in this fourth- or fifth-century example from Philippi:[9]

†Κυμητήριον Παύλου | πρεσβοιτέρου τῆς Φιλιππισίων ἁγίας τοῦ |
Θεοῦ ἐκλησίας· ἤ τις δὲ | μετὰ τὴν ἐμὴν κατάθε|σιν ἐπιχειρήσει ἐνθάδε
ἔτε|ρον θεῖναι νεκρόν, λόγον δώ|σει τῷ Θεῷ · ἔστιν γὰρ μονό|σωμον
πρωτοπρεσβοιτέρου.†

The resting-place of Paul, priest of the Philippians' holy church of God. If anyone, after my burial, attempts to place another body here, he shall render an account to God. For it is the one-place (tomb) of a first-priest.

The punishment invoked varies from generalities like this, to the curses of Judas or Anna and Kaiaphas, explicit punishments to be endured by violators, and payment of an amount of money.[10]

One might initially interpret these two inscriptions from the viewpoint of their reception. The former can be taken as a witty addition to a proprietary inscription intended for reading aloud and light-hearted fun in a symposium.[11] The latter can be read as a sign warning off potential violators of sepulchral space. Indeed, those threatening monetary damage do look like "no-trespassing" signs. While such readings are possible, an understanding of ancient concepts of the power of language suggests the intended and perceived force of the words lay in their being written more than in their being read.

Those epigraphic conditionals would be associated in the ancient mentality with a powerful class of performatives, utterances believed to cause an action by saying it or, in our case, writing it. C.A. Faraone locates the epigram on Nestor's cup in such a cultural context, arguing that it echoes a grammar of oaths, curses, and magical incantations stretching from archaic times to late antiquity. He concludes that "the two hexametrical lines are precisely what they claim to be—a magical spell designed to work as an aphrodisiac."[12] Speakers of such incantations expected to do something with words, but so did writers. Writing the words on the cup was part of the magical act, locking their force into the object, turning it into a talisman designed to overwhelm the drinker with sexual desire. Despite hierarchical hostility, pagan mentalities and forms persisted among Christians, as in prophylactic inscriptions such as the amulets, house entrances, and tombs inscribed with Psalm 90.[13] Likewise, writing a conditional threat on a Christian grave locked into it the utterance's power to affect reality; it would protect the tomb or, failing that, bring about the violator's punishment. The force of these words was generated in the act of writing: anyone who drank from Nestor's cup or violated Paul's tomb would suffer the consequences. Reading the inscription was not necessary.

II. The Force of Reading Inscribed Epitaphs

Force is also generated in the reception of inscriptions. We may conceive of it as symbolic, evoked, not by reading, but by viewing an object endowed with the authority of public presentation and high economic or cultural value.[14] My concern, however, is the force of the words being read— a visual act but also an aural one, as most reading would have been aloud, and often a communal act involving several people.[15] Epitaphs will again provide my paradigm. Tombstone curses conjured up force in being written, but other aspects of epitaphs generated their intended force in being read. The key point is this: whoever read out an archaic or paleochristian epitaph would assert, affirm, create, or request a certain status for the deceased.[16]

I cite one archaic example, on a *kouros* base from Attica dated approximately 540–30 B.C.:[17]

στέθι : καὶ οἴκτιρον : Κροίσο | παρὰ σέμα θανόντος :
hόν | ποτ᾽ ἐνὶ προμάχοις : ὄλεσε | θôρος : ῎Αρες.

Stop and pity by the marker of Kroisos having died, whom once in the front ranks raging Ares destroyed.

Whether the dominant tone is praise or lament, and whether the words echo funerals or not,[18] reading this epitaph would conjure up in archaic hearers' minds a familiar, culturally defined *persona* and assign a name to it: Kroisos, the heroic warrior, dead before his time. Reading would affirm, indeed each reading would re-create, the status of the deceased in the minds of the living human community. Moreover, besides ensuring the survival of one person's memory, such a reading would reinforce the social bases on which that *persona* was constructed, affirming that certain behaviors were ideal or certain deaths especially lamentable. Whoever read the inscription to willing listeners performed such constitutive speech acts, a fact explicitly built into the grammar of many early inscriptions such as this one: every reader speaks *in propria persona* to anyone in earshot.[19]

If reading an archaic epitaph affected the status of the deceased in the community of the living, the force of reading a paleochristian one concerned his or her salvation. Readers would assert their faith in that salvation, pray for it on behalf of the deceased, or do both. The simplest assertion of faith appears in a common name for the grave, *koimêtêrion,* sleeping place.[20] As passers-by read out even the simplest formula (*koimêtêrion* with the name of the deceased in the genitive), they asserted that the dead only slept, awaiting salvation or bodily resurrection. Various brief, formulaic additions make this hope explicit, as in the following sixth- century example from Corinth:[21]

[κοιμητήριον . . .] | πληρω[θὲν σώματι] | ἕως ἀ[ναστάσεως | ἐ]ωνί[ας] . . . .

[Sleeping place of ?], filled [with the body] until eternal resurrection . . . .

Occasionally readers would pronounce a more elaborate assertion, as in speaking a fourth-century epigram from Crete that begins:[22]

ἡμετέρης κάλλιστον ἔχεις, Λόγε Χ(ριστ)έ, χορίης
Μάγνον ἐν εὐσεβίεσσι{ν} πανηγυρίεσσι δικέων . . .

You, Christ the Word, have Magnos, the finest of our congregation, in the pious assemblies of the just . . .

Though salvation is asserted, the epitaph is phrased as an address to Christ and its praise of Magnos' piety suggests the reader would, at some level, be persuading Christ that Magnos deserved to be saved. Many epitaphs make the prayer for salvation explicit, and we should take these as serious prayers; the intent was to insure that passers-by directed a perpetual flow of prayers to God.

The commonest prayers are requests that God remember or help the deceased (e.g., Κύριε μνήσθητι, Κύριε βοήθει), but there are many common formulas.[23] Some prayers are utterances of the deceased, such as the following fifth- or sixth-century example from Edessa in Macedonia:[24]

μημ † [όριον] | 'Αθαν[ασίου] | κ(αὶ) Χρυσ[έρωτο]|ς. ⳨ Χ(ριστ)έ, [σῶσον] | κ(αὶ) πάλ[ιν ἀνά]|στησ[ον ἡμᾶς].

Memorial of Athanasios and Chryserôs. Christ, [save us] and make [us] rise up again.

Readers might also utter the prayer *in propria persona*:[25]

[Name] | [ἐνθά]δε [κῖτε·] | ΙΧΘΥΣ, σῷ[σον] |τὴν ψυχὴ[ν] | αὐτῆς.

[Name] lies here. J(esus) Ch(rist) G(od's) S(on) S(avior), save her soul.

Most interesting are epitaphs construed entirely as such prayers, as is this one from Thessalonika, probably of the fifth century:[26]

·'Ι·(ησο)·ῦ· Χρ(ιστ)ὲ · ὁ | ποιήσας | ἐνὶ λόγου | τὰ πάντα, | δὸς ἄνεσ|ιν καὶ ἄφε|σιν ἁ[μ]ᾳ[ρτιῶν] <το> | τῷ δούλῳ | σου Φορτου|νάτῳ.

Jesus Christ, (who) made with one word all things, grant remission and forgiveness of sins to your servant Phortounatos.

Finally, we find features that, while neither explicitly asserting salvation nor praying, seem to support such an assertive or supplicatory force. These include eulogistic statements about the deceased, which at their simplest state that he or she was faithful, a servant of God, or just "Christian," but they can be quite elaborate.[27] I also include here acclamations, some of which are addressed to the deceased, like ζήσαις ἐν Θεῷ, "may you live in God."[28] Others seem to be addressed to God, for instance, a fifth- or sixth-century Macedonian epitaph beginning, ΙΧΘΥΣ ΧΜΓ † Α † Ω †.[29] Especially in the East, many epitaphs contain the acclamation εἷς Θεός, "God (is) one" or "(There is) one God."[30] I suspect eulogies and acclamations could be read either as statements of faith in the salvation of the deceased or as attempts to persuade God that he or she deserved salvation, or both.

In the jargon of pragmatics, a context emerged as an archaic or paleochristian reader spoke an epitaph aloud, a hearer agreed to listen, and the two negotiated the character of the context on the basis of previously encountered speech situations.[31] As a context emerged, speech acts would be performed affecting the status of the deceased. Insofar as the hearers (including the reader[32]) were human, the utterance would be instantly effective, establishing in the hearer's mind a certain status for the deceased. Insofar as the intended audience was divine, it would seem that the inscription's author could only hope for a friendly reception. However, as regards the reading itself, anthropologists of religion recognize that invocations of deity and prayers have performative force if uttered by believers within an appropriate cultural context, that is, such utterances are felt to bring about what they describe, invoke, or request. Believers who apostrophize a deity, for example, experience the presence of that deity at the level of discourse, if not in some deeper spiritual sense.[33] Performative religious speech has been studied mostly as it occurs in ritual contexts, where music, dance or other gestures, and special objects or physical surroundings enhance the power of spoken words. Arguably, for pious readers of inscriptions who were conversant with the significant rituals of their culture, a reading was experienced at some level as ritual. The emergent context would be ritual of a certain kind.

III. Reading Inscriptions as Activation of Ritual

Archaic and paleochristian inscriptions often echo the phraseology of ritual, the former that of funerals or festivals, the latter that of Christian liturgy. Was this language read as mere allusion, or did it affect the force of readings?[34] Ritual words only exert their full force in ritual contexts; but "reading" acts of the sort described above were often parallel to acts performed in common kinds of ritual, though on a greatly reduced scale of elaboration. For example, a reader praying for the salvation of the deceased did something comparable to what was done in funerary liturgy. In that case, ritual epigraphic language would reinforce a hearer's sense that a ritual act was being done, and the words would acquire something of the power they had when embedded in full ritual. Reading would become activation of ritual. Illustrative examples can be drawn from epigraphic uses of ritual song or chant.

Let us set the stage with an archaic dedicatory epigram I have discussed elsewhere.[35] The following pair of hexameters is incised on the front of a small bronze statue, probably representing Apollo (ca. 700–675 B.C.):[36]

Μάντικλός μ᾽ ἀνέθεκε Ϝεκαβόλοι ἀργυροτόξσοι
τᾶς {δ}δ|εκάτας· τὺ δέ, Φοῖβε, δίδοι χαρίϜετταν ἀμοιβ[άν].

Mantiklos set me up for the far-shooting, silver-bowed (god), out of a tithe. May you, Phoibos, grant a *charis*-filled return.

The epigram reflects the phraseology of ritual hymns. The divine epithets are abbreviations of the portions of hymns that narrate a god's exploits, as the *Homeric Hymn* glorifies Apollo as archer. The prayer reflects a major hymnic theme known from literary hymns and ritual hymns inscribed and set up in sanctuaries. Such hymns invite the god to enjoy the festivity and song, that is, to experience the *charis* or pleasure of the occasion; and they include the prayer that, in return, the god grant *charis* to the worshippers and make the festivity *charis*-filled.[37] I give examples, from literary and inscribed hymns, of both sides of this request for a reciprocal exchange of *charis*. On the one side, as *Homeric Hymns* often conclude with a request that the god enjoy the song (e.g., χαῖρε . . . ἀοιδῇ), so the refrain of an inscribed hymn from Palaikastro asks the god to enjoy the performers and be happy with the song (χαῖρέ μοι . . . γέγαθι μολπᾶ<ι >).³⁸ On the other side, as a dithyramb of Pindar opens with a prayer for the gods to "send famous *charis* to the chorus" (δεῦτ' ἐν χορόν . . . ἐπί τε κλυτὰν πέμπετε χάριν), so an inscribed paean from Erythrai prays that the god give *charis* to the participants for the *charis* they give him (χαῖρέ μοι . . . δὸς δ' ἡμᾶς χαίροντας).³⁹

When a visitor to Apollo's sanctuary read Mantiklos' epigram out loud, a speech act would be performed, one that did something like what festive ritual would do with its hymn-singing. The echoes of hymnic language would deepen this effect; for all who were familiar with it and accepted the possibility of ritual interaction with the god, the words would appear to activate such a ritual precisely by bringing about the kind of reciprocal exchange of *charis* invited and similarly activated in the performance of hymns. In apostrophizing the god, pious readers would conjure up the god's actual presence (supported visually by the statue), calling his attention to the offering and the offerant's name. In reading the epithets, they would offer the god the *charis* of praise for his feats of archery, pleasing him and winning his favor. Just as the singing of a hymn would do, uttering the epithets would affirm Phoibos' place in the pantheon as archer god.⁴⁰ The first half of the hymnic reciprocity, "experience *charis*, oh god," is not present in this epigram; but it is in others, where readers would describe the effects of their own reading. In the archaic mentality, the aesthetic experience of *charis* in a gift automatically provokes from the receiver an ethical response of *charis*, a feeling of favor and a reciprocally pleasurable counter-gift. In rituals, the participants would feel the god's counter-gift of *charis* reified in their sense of the god's epiphany and more concretely in the joyous festivities, sometimes accompanied by images of the god or actors playing the god's part. Similarly, readers of Mantiklos' epigram would feel the *charis* of the god's presence reified in their own aesthetic response to the beautiful and valuable statue. As they said aloud, "grant a *charis*-filled return," they would describe precisely what they were activating in their own acts of reading and viewing, the god present with a feeling *charis*. Every time someone read out the inscription while viewing the statue, a context of ritual *charis* would be generated in Apollo's sanctuary. In this way, a reader would successfully mediate between Mantiklos and Apollo (and any other human in earshot), just as the performers of a paean offered by Mantiklos would. A methodologically parallel case can be made for the ritual force of reading many paleochristian inscriptions.

Despite difficulties in establishing the forms and language of paleochristian liturgies, it is evident that many epigraphic expressions echo the liturgies of their place and date. A notable example is provided by the troparion commonly called the Trisagion.⁴¹ The simplest, oldest form heads a Justinianic inscription mounted on a gate at Miletos and recording its construction in 538:⁴²

ἅγιος [ὁ Θ]εός, | ἅγιος ἰσχυρός, | ἅγιος ἀθ[ά]νατος, | ἐλέησον ἡμᾶς.

Holy (is) God, holy (and) strong, holy (and) immortal, have mercy on us.

Tradition reports the Trisagion was first chanted in a *litê* in Constantinople in 438/9, though an ostrakon from Egypt may attest to its liturgical use there in the fourth century. Tradition also holds that Monophysites, beginning in and around Antioch in the 470s and thereafter, added a phrase between the last two conventional ones. Epigraphical evidence supports this tradition in that Syria has produced many inscribed Trisagia with this addition, as on a door lintel from a fifth- or sixth-century church near Antioch:[43] ... [σ]τα<υ>ρ<ω>θ<εὶ>ς δι' ἡμᾶς. . . . , "(who) was crucified for us." These words supported the Christological interpretation always given the Trisagion in Syria, Egypt, and some other places, but they added an explicitly theopaschite challenge. In response, the Orthodox either omitted the addition and retained the Trinitarian interpretation always given in Constantinople and elsewhere; or they accepted the Christological interpretation, but deflected the controversy through a series of additions constituting a Trisagion-hymn. In any case, the Trisagion was so well known that abbreviated versions appear as acclamations or invocations, perhaps meant to invite a reader to utter the whole thing from memory, as in the following example on a fifth- or sixth-century gravestone from Stobi:[44]

ἐνθά[δε]|| κῖτε Θε |όφιλος Z[ω]|πύρου | ἀρχιδ(ιάκονος). | ἅγ(ιος) ὠ Θ(εό)ς.

Here lies Theophilos, son of Zôpyros, archdeacon. Holy (is) God.

One could reconstruct the reading of inscribed Trisagia in the way reading Mantiklos' epigram was reconstructed above. Whoever read one aloud mediated between God and those who put up the inscription, or the deceased, or simply those present at the reading, just as those who chanted the Trisagion in liturgies mediated between God and congregation or other objects of their prayers. In the basic form, God's or Christ's holiness, strength, and immortality would be asserted and praised. In the context of the doctrinal controversies, depending on which version was read and who was reading or listening, the unity of Christ's nature or the Trinity would be affirmed. The public praise and affirmation of the deity's acts or nature would invoke His presence and beneficence, thereby justifying the request for divine assistance and motivating a divine response.[45] Expressing the request in the words of a prominent liturgical refrain would strengthen the force of reading the inscription by generating a sense of participation in liturgy.

Specific epigraphic uses of the Trisagion support the suggestion that its liturgical force continued to be felt by those who wrote it and presumably those who read it. Readings of inscriptions on ritual equipment, and perhaps those on ostraka and column capitals from inside churches, might have occurred during liturgies. The Trisagion in epitaphs may suggest it was incorporated into funerary liturgy.[46] Here, however, let us examine in greater detail the Trisagion inscribed on entrances like the gate at Miletos noted above. A marble cross from Crete, apparently from a church, had a Trisagion with a version of the theopaschite addition on one side, and on the other Psalm 117:20, "this is the gate of the Lord."[47] Since that verse was regularly inscribed over entrances, our Cretan cross probably stood by a door or gate. Indeed, of the sixteen Trisagia on architectural elements from Syria, thirteen are from lintels, gates, or arches associated with the entrances of churches, houses, or other structures, such as the one from near Antioch quoted above. Finally, the Trisagion can appear on a processional cross. This association with entrances and processions is not fortuitous.

In Constantinople and perhaps generally, the Trisagion was first chanted liturgically in stational processions, a function that was perpetuated as the refrain became fixed in Eucharistic liturgies as part of the Little Entrance.[48] Whoever read those inscriptions as they entered a church or other structure, therefore, would physically, as well as verbally and pragmatically, imitate those who chanted the Trisagion in Eucharistic entrances and other processions. Like those who, according to John of Damascus, first chanted this refrain in a *litê,* they would call on God's strength to protect those within against evil, an utterance with prophylactic force especially suitable to a lintel or gate.[49] Processions were also sites for doctrinal declarations, and the Trisagion chanted in *litai* in the fifth and sixth centuries became a doctrinal manifesto. Readers of the inscriptions would likewise utter such a manifesto.

To reduce my argument to a perhaps minimally functionalist level: reading aloud the Trisagion from a paleochristian inscription or a prayer for *charis* from an archaic dedicatory epigram would accomplish, within their respective cultural contexts, the same kind of thing. Readings would establish a relationship with divinity comparable to that established by a kind of ritual, a relationship in which the reader would mediate between human and divine. The use of phraseology widely recognized as belonging to that kind of ritual would enhance a sense that such ritual was being activated. To read Mantiklos' epigram aloud in Apollo's sanctuary was at some level to engage in ritual of the sort accompanied by hymns sung there; to read the Trisagion aloud while entering a church, gate, or house was to engage in a familiar form of processional liturgy.

IV. Conclusion

Despite Christians' identification of themselves as people of the Book, orality played a vital role in their early communities. We catch a glimpse of the continuing power of the spoken word and an example of the written word's subordination to it by adopting a pragmatics-based approach to paleochristian inscriptions. To a degree, such texts can be viewed as a continuation of ancient epigraphic traditions and the broader cultural traditions behind them, some of which can be traced back to the eighth century B.C., as in the case of conditional curses. However, my goal has not been to trace continuities, but something more limited: by pairing a series of archaic and paleochristian inscriptions, I have illustrated some of the ways inscribed writing could function similarly in two cultural environments still predominantly oral.

In both periods, writing a powerful, even performative utterance on an object could be conceived of as part of a speech act, the permanent fixing of its force. This explains the power of written curses, threats, and oaths. More interestingly, reading an inscription aloud can be reconstructed as itself a speech act, an interaction between reader and hearer in which something was actually done.[50] One who reads aloud an epitaph publicly asserts or prays for a certain status for the deceased and at some level is felt to reify that status. But what if such assertion or prayer were a major function of funerary ritual, and what if the epitaph's words echoed the language of such ritual? In that case, reading would at some level activate funerary ritual; a minimal funeral would take place every time the inscription was read. This is how, as we have seen with Mantiklos' dedication and epigraphic Trisagia, well-known hymnic or liturgical language could generate the force of religious ritual when read. Those who erected such inscriptions ensured that readers would perform a never-ending stream of ritual acts.

APPENDIX:
A PRELIMINARY LIST OF INSCRIBED TRISAGIA[51]

1. Lintels, gates, arches, and other objects associated with entrances:

   A. C. Bandy, *The Greek Christian Inscriptions of Crete*, Χριστιανικαὶ
   'Επιγραφαὶ τῆς 'Ελλάδος, vol. 10.1 (Athens, 1970), no. 53. (T)

   H. Grégoire, *Recueil des inscriptions grecques-chrétiennes d'Asie Mineure*,
   fasc. 1 (Paris, 1922), no. 219 (see my note 42).

   H. Grégoire, "Voyage dans le Pont et en Cappadoce," *Bulletin de
   correspondance hellénique* 33 (1909): 69, no. 49.

   IGLS, nos. 289, 357, ?358, 633, 1726, 1847, 1861 (all T).

   IGLS, nos. 317A, 338, 637, 1775, 2529, 2606.

   IGSK 14, no. 1369.

   R. Mouterde and A. Poidebard, *Le limes de Chalcis*, Text vol. (Paris, 1945),
   192, no. 19.

2. Other architectural inscriptions:

   Grégoire, *Inscriptions d'Asie Mineure*, no. 114[6] = *IGSK* 14, no. 1359 (perhaps
   a street entrance).

   IG 7.2187.

   IGLS, nos. 482, 747 (T), 1474.

   G. Laminger-Pascher, *Die kaiserzeitlichen Inschriften Lykaoniens* = *Tituli
   Asiae Minoris*, 15.1 (Vienna, 1992), no. 157.

   Monumenta Asiae Minoris Antiqua 4, no. 110.

3. Liturgical equipment:

   M. M. Mango, *Silver from Early Byzantium* (Baltimore, 1986), no. 42; cf. 67.

   C. Metzger, "Croix à inscription votive," *Revue du Louvre* 22 (1972): 32–34.

   F. Preisigke, *Sammelbuch griechischer Urkunden aus Ägypten,* vol 1
   (Strassburg, 1915), no. 3940.

   I. Ševčenko, in S. A. Boyd and M. M. Mango, eds., *Ecclesiastical Silver Plate
   in Sixth-Century Byzantium* (Washington, D. C., 1992), 43–44.

   E. Sironen, *Late Roman and Early Byzantine Inscriptions of Athens and Attica*
   (Helsinki, 1997), no. 343.

   G. A. Soteriou, "Αἱ παλαιοχριστιανικαὶ βασιλικαί," *Ἀρχαιολογικὴ
   ἐφημερὶς* 1929, 232–3, fig. 65.

4. Graves:

D. Feissel, *Recueil des inscriptions chrétiennes de Macédoine du IIIe au VIe siècle, Bulletin de correspondance hellénique*, Supplement vol. 8, (Paris, 1983), no. 281.

D. Feissel, "Notes d'épigraphie chrétienne (vi)," *Bulletin de correspondance hellénique* 107 (1983): 615–17.

J. Kulakowsky, "Eine altchristliche Grabkammer," *Römische Quartalschrift für christliche Altertumskunde und für Kirchengeschichte* 8 (1894): 60.

Monumenta Asiae Minoris Antiqua 7, no. 309 (?a lintel for a grave); 10, no. 22.

Supplementum Epigraphicum Graecum 8.660. (T)

5. For ostraka with Trisagion-hymns, see L. Koenen (cited in note 41).

6. Uncertain function and other:

Bandy, *The Greek Christian Inscriptions of Crete*, nos. 24B, 52.

R. Demangel, *Contribution à la topographie de l'Hebdomon* (Paris, 1945), 51–53.

Grégoire, *Inscriptions d'Asie Mineure*, no. 230.

IGLS, nos. 2528, 2543.

IGSK 29, no. 119 (see my note 49).

G. Lefebvre, *Recueil des inscriptions grecques-chrétiennes d'Égypte* (Cairo, 1907), no. 777.

E. Popescu, *Inscriptiones intra fines Dacoromaniae repertae* (Bucharest, 1976), no. 383.

?*Supplementum Epigraphicum Graecum* 36.1267.

G. A. Soteriou, "Αἱ χριστιανικαὶ Θῆβαι τῆς Θεσσαλίας," *Ἀρχαιολογικὴ ἐφημερις* 1929, 107, no. 2.

G. Tchalenko, *Villages antiques de la Syrie du Nord,* vol. 3 (Paris, 1958), 28, no. 27a.

V. W. Yorke, "Inscriptions from Eastern Asia Minor," *Journal of Hellenic Studies* 18 (1898): 309–10, no. 6. (T)

NOTES

1. This article could not have been written without the assistance of friends who know far more than I about early Christian Greek culture and epigraphy; I thank especially C. S. Snively, D. R. Jordan, and T. E. Gregory. I am grateful to R. F. Taft, S.J., for advice on the Trisagion. For retrieving the bibliography they recommended, I thank Deborah Polley, Interlibrary Loan Librarian at Wabash College. A debt of gratitude of a different order is owed Fr. Schlatter: without his teaching, my career would never have come into existence at all.

2. See J. L. Austin, *How to Do Things with Words* (Cambridge, Mass., 1962).

3. Compare C. Sourvinou-Inwood, *'Reading' Greek Death* (Oxford, 1995) 1–9.

4. J. W. Day, "Rituals in Stone," *Journal of Hellenic Studies* 109 (1989): 16–28; "Interactive Offerings," *Harvard Studies in Classical Philology* 96 (1994): 37–74; "Epigram and Reader," in M. Depew and D. Obbink, eds., *Matrices of Genre* (Cambridge, Mass., forthcoming). A monograph, *Epigram and Reader, Dedication and Viewer,* is nearing completion.

5. The four collections are: A. C. Bandy, *The Greek Christian Inscriptions of Crete,* Χριστιανικαὶ Ἐπιγραφαὶ τῆς Ἑλλάδος, vol. 10.1 (Athens, 1970); N. A. Bees, *Corpus der griechisch christlichen Inschriften von Hellas,* vol. 1 (Reprint: Chicago, 1978); J. S. Creaghan, S.J., and A. E. Raubitschek, "Early Christian Epitaphs from Athens," *Hesperia* 16 (1947): 1–54, Plates I–X; D. Feissel, *Recueil des inscriptions chrétiennes de Macédoine du IIIᵉ au Vᵉ siècle, Bulletin de correspondance hellénique,* Supplement vol. 8, (Paris, 1983).

6. I. Barnea, "L'épigraphie chrétienne de l'Illyricum oriental," *Actes du Xᵉ congrès international d'archéologie chrétienne,* vol. 1, Hellênika, vol. 26 (Thessalonika, 1984), 631–678; H. Grégoire, *Recueil des inscriptions grecques-chrétiennes d'Asie Mineure,* fasc. 1 (Paris, 1922); M. Guarducci, *Epigrafia greca,* vol. 4 (Rome, 1978), 301–556; C. M. Kaufmann, *Handbuch der altchristlichen Epigraphik* (Freiburg im Breisgau, 1917); G. Lefebvre, *Recueil des inscriptions grecques-chrétiennes d'Égypte* (Cairo, 1907); C. Wessel, *Inscriptiones graecae christianae veteres occidentis,* Inscriptiones christianae Italiae, Subsidia 1 (Bari, 1989).

7. Compare D. T. Steiner, *The Tyrant's Writ* (Princeton, 1994), ch. 2, esp. 61–75; J. B. Wilkins, "Urban Ritual Language," in *ibid.,* ed., *Approaches to the Study of Ritual,* Accordia Specialist Studies 2 (London, 1996), 123–41.

8. Skyphos, Pithecusae, *Carmina Epigraphica Graeca,* ed. P.A. Hansen, vol. 1 (Berlin, 1983), 1.454.

9. Feissel, *Inscriptions de Macédoine,* no. 238.

10. Bees, *Inschriften von Hellas,* nos. 15–29; Creaghan and Raubitschek, "Epitaphs from Athens," 9–11, nos. 15, ix, xii, xvi, xix, xx; Feissel, *Inscriptions de Macédoine,* nos. 32, 62, 123, 197, 218, 219, 231, also 59, 215. Compare D. Feissel, "Malédictions funéraires en Attique," *Bulletin de correspondance hellénique* 104 (1980): 459–472; S. P. Ntantis, Ἀπειλητικαὶ ἐκφράσεις εἰς τὰς ἑλληνικὰς ἐπιτυμβίους παλαιοχριστιανικὰς ἐπιγραφάς (Athens, 1983); J. H. M. Strubbe, "'Cursed be he that moves my bones,'" in C. A. Faraone and D. Obbink, eds., *Magika Hiera* (Oxford, 1991), 33–59.

11. See C. A. Faraone, "Taking the 'Nestor's Cup Inscription' Seriously," *ClAnt* 15 (1996): 78; K. Robb, *Literacy and Paideia in Ancient Greece* (New York, 1994), 45–48.

12. *Ibid.* 77–112; the quotation is from 79.

13. For amulets, see *ODB* s.v. (G. Vikan); for Psalm 90, D. Feissel, "Notes d'épigraphie chrétienne (vii)," *Bulletin de correspondance hellénique* 108 (1984): 572–579, and "La Bible dans les inscriptions grecques," in C. Mondésert, *Le monde grec ancien et la Bible* (Paris, 1984), 227, 229.

14. See R. Thomas, *Literacy and Orality in Ancient Greece* (Cambridge Univ., 1992), and "Literacy and the City-State in Archaic and Classical Greece," in A. K. Bowman and G. Woolf, eds., *Literacy and Power in the Ancient World* (Cambridge Univ., 1994), 33–50; also Steiner, *Tyrant's Writ*, ch. 2.

15. Cf. Day, "Epigram and Reader," Sourvinou-Inwood, *'Reading' Greek Death.*

16. Other actions would also be done (e.g, affirming the status of the deceased's family and consoling its living members), but these do not concern me here.

17. *Carmina Epigraphica Graeca* 1.27.

18. Contrast Day, "Rituals in Stone," to Sourvinou-Inwood, *'Reading' Greek Death,* ch. 3.

19. Sourvinou-Inwood, ibid., 279–284, J. Svenbro, *Phrasikleia: An Anthropology of Reading in Ancient Greece,* trans. J. Lloyd (Ithaca, 1993), chs. 1–3, 9.

20. Creaghan and Raubitschek, "Epitaphs from Athens," 5–6; Guarducci, *Epigrafia greca,* 306.

21. Bees, *Inschriften von Hellas,* no. 26. Compare Feissel, *Inscriptions de Macédoine,* no. 119. See also, for example: the deceased rests or lives in peace, or in God, the Lord, or Christ (Wessel, *Inscriptiones occidentis,* nos. 803–12).

22. Bandy, *Inscriptions of Crete,* no. 80. Compare Guarducci, *Epigrafia greca,* 412–4.

23. Compare Lefebvre, *Inscriptions d'Égypte,* xxx; Kaufmann, *Handbuch,* ch. 5.

24. Feissel, *Inscriptions de Macédoine,* no. 35.

25. Bandy, *Inscriptions of Crete,* no. 99; fourth-century.

26. Feissel, *Inscriptions de Macédoine,* no. 180.

27. Compare Feissel, *Inscriptions de Macédoine,* nos. 271–2 (a funerary eulogy with no surviving prayer) with no. 267 (containing a prayer).

28. See Feissel, *Inscriptions de Macédoine,* nos. 8–11.

29. Feissel, *Inscriptions de Macédoine,* no. 25. On XMΓ, see also Bandy, *Inscriptions of Crete,* 10–11; Barnea, "Epigraphie de l'Illyricum," 676; Guarducci, *Epigrafia greca,* 460–461; Kaufmann, *Handbuch,* 72; *Supplementum Epigraphicum Graecum,* 1992.1828. Readers may have verbalized such abbreviations.

30. *ODB* s.v. acclamations, apotropaic (G. Vikan); E. Peterson, Εἷς Θεός (Göttingen, 1926).

31. See also Day, "Epigram and Reader," citing A. Duranti and C. Goodwin, eds., *Rethinking Context,* Studies in the Social and Cultural Foundations of Language, vol. 11 (Cambridge Univ., 1992).

32. Compare Svenbro, *Phrasikleia,* ch. 9.

33. Sourvinou-Inwood, *'Reading' Greek Death,* 280, 404–5. Compare R. H. Sinos, "Divine Selection," in C. Dougherty and L. Kurke, eds., *Cultural Poetics in Archaic Greece* (Cambridge Univ., 1993), 73–91, esp. 84–5 on Orthodox liturgy.

34. For the parallel question of biblical quotations, see Feissel, "La Bible," and L. Malunowicz, "Citations bibliques dans l'épigraphie grecque," *Studia Evangelica* 7 (1982): 333–37.

35. Day, "Interactive Offerings" and "Epigram and Reader"; compare M. Depew, "Representing Genre in the Texts of Greek Prayer and Hymns," *Classical Antiquity*, forthcoming.

36. *Carmina Epigraphica Graeca* 1.326; ?Thebes.

37. The only exact literary parallel for Mantiklos' prayer accompanies a sacrifice at *Odyssey* 3.58.

38. See, for the former, *h.Di.* 9.7 = *h.Mat.d.* 14.6; for the latter, M. Guarducci, *Inscriptiones Creticae*, vol. 3 (Rome, 1942), no. 2.

39. See, for the former, Pindar, fr. 75.1–2 SM; for the latter, H. Engelmann and R. Merkelback, *Die Inschriften von Erythrai und Klazomenai*, vol. 2 = *IGSK* 2 (Bonn, 1973), no. 205, l. 24.

40. J. S. Clay, *The Politics of Olympus* (Princeton, 1989); W. D. Furley, "Praise and Persuasion in Greek Hymns," *Journal of Hellenic Studies* 115 (1995): 40–41; compare H. S. Versnel, "Religious Mentality in Ancient Prayer," in Versnel, ed., *Faith, Hope, and Worship*, Studies in Greek and Roman Religion, vol. 2 (Leiden, 1981), 47–56.

41. See Appendix. For the Trisagion's history, see S. Brock, "The Thrice-Holy Hymn in the Liturgy," *Sobornost* 7.2 (1985): 24–34; L. Koenen, "Ein Christlicher Prosahymnus des 4.Jhdts.," in E. Boswinkel, B. A. van Groningen, and P. W. Pestman, eds., *Antidoron Martino David*, Papyrologica Lugduno-Batavia, vol. 17 (Leiden, 1968), 31–52, and "Der erweiterte Trishagion-Hymnus des Ms. Insinger und des P.Berl. Inv. 16389," *Zeitschrift für Papyrologie und Epigraphik* 31 (1978): 71–76; W. K. Prentice, "Fragments of an Early Christian Liturgy in Syrian Inscriptions," *Transactions of the American Philological Association* 33 (1902): 81–100, esp. 82–83; H.-J. Schulz, *The Byzantine Liturgy* (Baltimore, 1986), 21–25, 161–163; R. F. Taft, S.J., *ODB* ss.vv. Lite, Liturgy, and Trisagion, and *Liturgy in Byzantium and Beyond*, Collected Studies Series 493 (Brookfield, 1995), II.111–114.

42. Grégoire, *Inscriptions d'Asie Mineure*, no. 219; D. F. McCabe and M. A. Plunkett, *Miletos Inscriptions* (Princeton, 1984), no. 627.

43. *IGLS* 2, no. 633. The addition usually begins with the article, ὁ. Other variations occur (e.g., Bandy, *Inscriptions of Crete*, no. 53), including placement after the last phrase (*IGLS* 4, no. 1861).

44. Feissel, *Inscriptions de Macédoine*, no. 281.

45. I have not emphasized—but could—the social aspects of the function of readings, e.g., the construction of a community of faith along certain lines. Reading would be socially constitutive in ways outlined in section 2 above with Kroisos' epitaph.

46. Feissel, *Inscriptions de Macédoine*, no. 281.

47. Bandy, *Inscriptions of Crete*, no. 53, dated vi/viii; but the condemnation of the theopaschite addition in 691 (*ODB* s.v. Trisagion [R. F. Taft, S.J.]) makes an eighth-century date unlikely.

48. F. E. Brightman, *Liturgies, Eastern and Western*, vol. 1 (Oxford, 1896), 35, 118, 255, 369, 527, 535; see also 77, 155, 218, 250, 313, 353, 399, 423, 481, 530.

49. *Expos. fidei,* 3.10 (section 54, Kotter). Such force is explicit in the expanded Trisagion at T. Corsten, *Die Inschriften von Kios = IGSK* 29 (Bonn, 1985), no. 119, but the inscription's function is unknown. Of course, one could argue that, as in section 1 above, the force was in the writing rather than reading; but see below, n. 50.

50. The distinction between the two sites of epigraphic force (writing and reading) is more fluid than my words may imply. A threatening Christian epitaph can replace the apodosis of the condition (the curse) with *horkizô,* "I adjure"; see Barnea, "Epigraphie de l'Illyricum," 670, Bees, *Inschriften von Hellas,* no. 23, Grégoire, *Inscriptions d'Asie Mineure,* no. 209, *IGLS* 2, no. 1535, Kaufmann, *Handbuch,* 157–159, Wessel, *Inscriptiones occidentis,* nos. 613, 616–7, and also Feissel, *Inscriptions de Macédoine,* no. 215. Readers would thus play the part of the original speaker, reiterating the force of the oath in their acts of reading.

51. This list was compiled partly through normal library detective work, and partly from a search for ἅγιος in the Packard Humanities Institute, CD ROM # 7 with Pandora 2.5. I hope to extend the list in a future study. Most texts are to be dated to the fifth or sixth centuries, few if any later than the seventh. "T" indicates that a version of the theopaschite addition survives; note that it may have been in many other inscriptions which are now extant only in fragments.

Eastern Monasticism
in South Italy in the
Tenth and Eleventh Centuries

Anthony P. Via, S.J.
Gonzaga University, Florence

Around the year 1570 Gabriele Barrio di Francia, who was called the Herodotus of Calabria, wrote in his *De antiquitate et situ Calabriae* that this region had become in the seventh and eighth centuries the new Thebaide.[1] What is known of south Italian monasticism is very limited and derives principally from the various hagiographies of the more heroic examples of monastic life. In addition to salient features about the lives of the monks themselves, these hagiographies also yield information concerning the cultural, political, and religious life of tenth- and eleventh-century south Italy. More specifically, by drawing upon a range of sources rarely collated, this essay will try to cast some light on Byzantine monasticism in south Italy.

The presence of many monks in Sicily and south Italy is attributed to the mass immigration of hermits, anchorites, and cenobites from Syria, Egypt, and Palestine, a movement stimulated by the Persian invasions of Byzantine territories in the east (611–18). The fact that these monks came from the eastern patriarchates and not from Constantinople has been confirmed by a number of scholars who have traced the origins of the south Italian monks. Giovanni Mercati, for example, has shown that the peculiarities of ritual revealed in the *Euchologion* of the monastery of Santa Maria del Patir in Rossano clearly confirm the eastern Mediterranean origin of the monks.[2] Father A. Vaccari has shown that the New Testament texts used by the monks have an eastern Mediterranean provenance.[3] The most obvious clue to the source of the monastic tradition in south Italy, however, is to be seen in the organization of the cave dwellings which resemble the many lauras of Egypt and Syria. Perhaps the best direct proof of the eastern origins of the monasticism in Sicily and south Italy is the letter of Maximus the Confessor (ca. 580–662) who, between the years 646 and 648, sent a long and anti-monothelite letter in Greek to the "*hegoumenos*, monks, and orthodox population of Sicily."[4] This area had become so thoroughly identified with Byzantine political and religious life that in 731 Emperor Leo III (717–41) removed this area from the jurisdiction of the western church and placed it under the control of the Byzantine patriarch.[5]

Perhaps it should be pointed out here that the iconoclastic controversy did not provide a stimulus for Byzantine migration to Sicily and south Italy—the iconoclastic legislation prevailed in Byzantine Sicily and south Italy just as much as it prevailed in other parts of the Empire.[6] There is reason to believe, however, that the iconodules did flee to those parts of Italy not under the direct control of Byzantine authorities such as those areas north of Byzantine south Italy and especially in the area around Rome and Naples.[7] St. Theodore the Studite in a letter to the Sicilian Theophanes laments the penetration of the iconoclastic heresy in Sicily;[8] he remembers "our brothers" who are incarcerated on the island of Lipari for resisting the iconoclasts.[9] We know further of St. Gregory the Decapolite who fell into the hands of an iconoclastic bishop in the city of Taranto.[10]

In the ninth century the Arab invasion of Sicily which began with the conquest of Mazara in 827 caused another migration of eastern monks; this time from Sicily into Calabria and other areas of Italy. By the year 902 with the fall of Taormina, the conquest of the island was complete and Calabria thus became the great haven for eastern monks. The Arabs did not cease their attacks, however, with the conquest of Sicily. Even while the conquest of Sicily was going on and especially afterwards, Arabs raided the coasts of Italy especially the areas around Reggio, Tauriano, Nicotera, Tropea, Vibona, and Santa Eufemia. This resulted in further migrations of monks toward the northern part of Calabria and into Lucania. By the mid-tenth century, besides the famous monastic eparchy of the Mercurion in the upper Lao Valley, the monks had established themselves in various other monastic centers in Calabria: the Saline just north of Reggio, the region of Mesiano, the area of Mount Mula near Cassano, the Latinianon along the middle of the Sinni River, and the centers of Carbone, Teana, Chiaramonte, Noepoli (Medieval Noa), Kir Zosimo, the valley of the Cilento River all the way to the gates of Salerno, the region of the Volturno River, and the area of Tricarico with its Théotokos del Rifiugio.[11]

Many questions can be raised concerning the nature of this monasticism but whatever answers are given must find confirmation first and foremost in the lives of the monks, the most important source for the monastic history of this period and region.

I. St. Elias of Enna (823–903)

Saint Elias the Younger was born in 823 at Enna in Sicily.[12] He is called "the younger" to distinguish him from St. Elias, the Old Testament prophet. Confusion is probably more apt to occur, however, with Saint Elias Spelaiotes (ca. 865–960) of whom more will be said later. St. Elias the Younger of Enna, then, according to our biographer, was born of devout and illustrious parents who belonged to the noble family of the Rachiti. His biographer and closest disciple, Daniel of Taormina, tells us that at the age of twelve years, Elias, who had been baptized John, was captured by Arab raiders (ca. 837). The ship, which made its way to

North Africa, was intercepted by a Byzantine ship from Syracuse and Elias and the other prisoners were liberated. Elias returned to his parents and remained with them for three years. During this period his father died. In 839 (*ca.*) another Arab raid resulted in Elias' capture once again. This time he was brought to Africa as a slave and was sold to a Christian who used him as a general manager of his many business affairs. Because Elias refused to succumb to the temptations of his master's wife, she falsely accused him of taking advantage of her. Although Elias was submitted to torture, his innocence was not proven until the husband discovered his wife in an adulterous act with her lover. Elias was then freed and was able to make his way in pilgrimage to Palestine. It is difficult to determine the historicity of this episode—it parallels too closely the story of Joseph and Pharaoh's wife.

At this time Elias was confirmed in the possession of thaumaturgic powers and he performed many miracles. Because of his teachings, he ran afoul of Moslem leaders and was imprisoned. Elias, continues our biographer, was soon miraculously delivered from jail and he then made his way to Jerusalem (ca. 878) where he was invested with the habit of a monk by Elias III, the patriarch of Jerusalem. Our saint adopted the name of the patriarch at this time.

After visiting all the holy places in Jerusalem, Elias then went to Mount Sinai where he attended for three years to the counsels of the monks who lived there. He then went to Alexandria where, our biographer says, he worked so many miracles that his fame spread far and wide. His popularity induced him to leave Egypt and he traveled on to Persia where he planned to venerate the relics of the three children of the old Testament martyred in the fiery furnace and the relics of the prophet Daniel. A political disturbance forced him to change his plans and he made his way to Antioch. Here a dream persuaded him to return to his home land. He returned by way of North Africa, converting several Moslems along the way.

He arrived in Palermo where he met his mother, who was still alive. At this time the Emir in Palermo was planning an attack on Reggio. The Byzantine Emperor (Basil I, 867–86) sent his admiral, Basil Nazar, with a fleet of 45 ships. Confirming a prophecy of Elias, the Byzantine navy inflicted a stunning defeat on the Saracen fleet (August 1, 880). Elias then moved to Taormina where he received as his disciple the pious and noble monk, Daniel, and conferred upon him the monastic habit. Together they fled the city of Taormina, now under Saracen attack, and went to the Peloponnesus where they settled around the city of Sparta and prayed at the church of Saints Cosmas and Damien. Soon after, both monks left Sparta for Buthrotum (Butrinto), a coastal city in Epirus, where they were taken as spies by the second in command of the army and thrown into prison. Their innocence was proven on the very next day: their accuser was knocked down by his horse and his chest was crushed by the horse's hooves. The prisoners were released and then began to make their way to Rome to pray at the tombs of the apostles.

The two monks disembarked, however, at Reggio Calabria and went to the area called the Saline where Elias founded a monastery. Here he gave himself over to ascetical practices, subjecting his flesh to prayer and fasting. Having been invited in a vision by SS. Peter and Paul, Elias and Daniel made a pilgrimage to Rome (*ca.* 885–86) where they were received with special honor by Pope Stephen V (885–91). They returned to the monastery at the Saline. It was at this time that Elias predicted the fall of the city of Reggio to the Moslems, which took place June 10, 901. The commander of the Byzantine fleet, Michael, approached Elias for advice on how to defeat the Saracens. He was advised to keep his men from dissolution and fornication. Michael's liberation of Reggio took place in the spring of 902.

Meanwhile Elias' fame spread far and wide. Even Emperor Leo VI (879–912) asked him for special prayers. Elias predicted the fall of Taormina which occurred on August 1, 902, after which the Saracens crossed the straits, sacked the territory around Reggio, and made their way to besiege the city of Cosenza. There the leader of the Saracens died of dysentery on October 23, 902. Elias at this time was in Amalfi where he miraculously cured a nephew of the prefect of Amalfi.

Having returned to the Saline, he continued to perform there many miracles. But by this time Elias was very old and burdened with infirmities. Nevertheless he accepted the invitation of Leo VI (879–912), who wanted to visit with Elias in Constantinople. Elias, accompanied by the imperial messenger Cusonio, made his way to Constantinople by way of Epirus, Naupactus, and Illyricum. Elias never made it to Constantinople. He fell ill at Thessalonica and remained at the entrance of the city in a church dedicated to the Holy Apostles. He asked to be brought to the Church of St. Demetrius. There on the north side of the church and immediately adjacent to it, Elias died on August 17, 903. His body was brought back to the Saline where it was buried with all due honors. Leo VI, our biographer assures us, endowed the monastery with many generous gifts so that it became one of the most famous monasteries in Italy.

II. St. Elias Spelaiotes (ca. 860–960)

Saint Elias Spelaiotes was born between 860 and 870 in Reggio Calabria of very wealthy parents.[13] His anonymous biographer tells us that at a very early age he gave himself over to the study of holy scripture. At church one day he was counseled by a monk to give up his rich purple clothes and to invest himself with the habit of a monk. Having thought about this for a long time, he left his parents and with a friend, made his way to Sicily to the church of St. Auxentius on the hill of San Nicone. His friend did not persevere and his biographer asks us to believe that it was on account of this that he was later killed by Saracens. Elias then went to Rome where he put himself under the guidance of a hermit named Ignatius. He returned to Reggio and took up his habitation with a monk by the name of Arsenius at Mindinon, a metochion of the monastery of Santa Lucia. Because this property was claimed by a priest of Reggio, Elias moved to St. Eustrathius at Capo d'Armi. Saracen raids forced him to leave this place and he moved with his companion to Patras. He remained here eight years and then returned to St. Eustrathius and placed himself in close contact with Elias of Enna and Daniel, who were in the vicinity at the Saline. Indeed, Elias of Enna had expressed the wish that upon his death (903) Elias Spelaiotes would govern his monks. He did but not for long; he sought greater peace and solitude for prayer and thus retired to a cave in the territory of Melicucca (south of Seminara) with two companions, Cosmos and Vitalis. Because the fame of Elias had attracted so many monks, Cosmos and Vitalis chose to go elsewhere for greater solitude and peace. Elias, however, remained to govern the monks who placed themselves under his direction. The monastery was enlarged, an altar was constructed, and here Elias remained till his death on September 11, 960, assisted by his many followers and in the presence of the Bishop of Taureana. The remainder of his biography is concerned with the miracles performed through the intercession of Elias after his death.

III. St. Nilus (910–1004)

Without a doubt, the most famous of the Italo-Greek monks is Saint Nilus of Rossano (910–1004).[14] Several reasons make his life significant. First of all his memory is kept alive by the monastic foundations which he established, one of which exists to this very day, Grottaferrata. Secondly, St. Nilus became deeply involved with several political figures and was himself an important personage of his day. St. Nilus was also fortunate enough to have as his biographer St. Bartholomew the Younger who died around 1065. He has provided us with so many rich details and concrete facts that his biography is an excellent source for the social, economic, and political conditions of the time.

Nilus was born of a wealthy and pious family in Rossano in the year 910. While still a boy (ca. 925) Nilus lost both of his parents and was brought up by a married older sister who was very devoted and pious. Nilus married a girl from Rossano who is described as having a rare beauty but of humble origin. Nilus had a daughter by her.

At around the age of 30, Nilus was moved by God to embrace the monastic life. In conformity with Byzantine civil and ecclesiastical law, Nilus left his home and family and went to the celebrated monastic eparchy, the Mercurion. Because the governor of Rossano was unwilling to allow Nilus to leave his city, the *hegoumenos* was prohibited from accepting and tonsuring him. For this reason Nilus betook himself to the monastery of St. Nazario which was located where the Lombards held control. Here he made his monastic profession. After living this cenobitic life for about three years, he withdrew to a cave in the same region dedicated to St. Michael the Archangel in order to lead the life of a solitary. Here he gave himself over to extraordinary penances and long prayers and fasting. Also at this time he began the work of copying manuscripts, a labor which he would continue for the rest of his life.

At this time Nilus was joined by two disiples, Steven and George, also from the city of Rossano. Around the year 953, approximately ten years after St. Nilus had first moved to his cave-oratory, he was required to move again. Severe raids by the Moslems, who by this time had gotten as far as the regions of the Mercurion and Latinianon, forced Nilus to move to a new location. At the foot of the Sila highlands he took over an old church, turned it into a monastery, and dedicated it to the holy martyrs, SS. Adrian and Natalia (S. Adriano a S. Demetrio Corone). Again he attracted followers who imitated his severe poverty and dedication to prayer. Nilus remained here for twenty-five years and his fame spread throughout the area. It was during this period of Nilus' life (*ca.* 976) that there took place his celebrated intervention on behalf of the citizens of Rossano who rebelled against the Magistros Nicephorus.

More Saracen raids, even in the remote and inacessible area inhabited by Nilus and his monks, compelled him to leave his monastery and move northward to territory controlled by the Lombards. He first stopped at Capua where he was received with honor by Pandulf Ironhead (961–81), who wanted to name him archbishop of Capua. Pandulf's death put an end to that plan. Nilus then benefited from the hospitality of Aligern, Abbot of Monte Cassino, by accepting the monastery of Valleluce near Monte Cassino. Here Nilus remained with his followers who by this time numbered 60. The relationship between the monks of Monte Cassino and the monks of St. Nilus were excellent and Nilus remained here for about fifteen years. During this time St. Adalbert, Archbishop of Prague, sought admission to Nilus' monastery, but realizing that God had special plans for him (Adalbert was martyred in East Prussia), Nilus recommended that he enter the monastery of Saints Alexius and Boniface in Rome.

In the meantime Abara (or Alvara), the widow of Pandulf Ironhead, was stung with remorse because of her planning and executing of the murder of her cousin, a high and very popular functionary of the count of Capua. She wanted very much to have a visit with Nilus in order that he might intercede on her behalf for the remission of her sin. We do not know the nature of the penance he imposed upon her but since she was unwilling to perform it, he left the city after having prophesized that she and her family would soon lose power. As it happened, a younger son of Alvara assassinated his older brother and in revenge the German Emperor, Otto III (996–1002), had him imprisoned and the family disappears from history.

In 994 Aligern, the Abbot of Monte Cassino who held Nilus in such great esteem, died and was succeeded by Manso, cousin of Pandulf. Since Nilus judged this man to be worldly, he did not want his monks to be corrupted by the new abbot's bad example. Nilus, now at the age of 85, abandoned the monasteryValleluce and led his monks to a new monastery he founded at Serperi near the city of Gaeta.

In March of 998 Nilus was drawn into imperial-ecclesiastical politics: In September of 996 the family of the Crescentii had taken advantage of Emperor Otto III's absence from Italy and deposed the German pope, Gregory V, who had been selected by the Emperor. He was replaced by John Philagathos, a Calabrian monk from Rossano, who was a friend of Nilus. Philagathos had taken the name John XVI. In February of 998 Otto III returned to Rome, deposed the anti-pope, mutilated him, and had him imprisoned. Nilus, in spite of his advanced age—he was now close to 90—betook himself to Rome to plead with Otto III for the life of his friend and compatriot. He was very well received by Otto who gave Nilus the monastery of SS. Vincent and Anastaius (Tre Fontane), but the purpose of his trip to Rome was not fulfilled. Having failed to secure the freedom of John Philagathos, Nilus returned to Serperi at Gaeta.

Nilus learned that the Duke of Gaeta was preparing for him a monumental sepulcher. Because this was repugnant to Nilus' sense of humility, he left Serperi with a couple of companions in the middle of the night (July, 1004) and made his way to Rome where he founded his last monastery. As Nilus and his companions were making plans for the church and monastery at "Cryptoferrata," just outside the ancient city of Tusculum, Nilus fell ill and was brought to the monastery of St. Agatha near Tusculum, where he died on September 26, 1004.

IV. Monastic Organization

The peculiar conditions in which Italo-Greek monasticism developed in the ninth and tenth centuries in south Italy make it very difficult to categorize this monasticism according to the classical or traditional divisions: heremitic, cenobitic, or laureatic. The lives of the Italo-Greek monks we have described make it eminently clear that during the tenth and eleventh centuries our monks were relatively independent hermits. They did not seem to live a community life because, as the biographers themselves assert, the monks wished to live a life of solitude and contemplation sustained by severe ascetical practices and in the company of a very few others who shared these objectives. Only gradually, as Agostino Pertusi asserts, does Italo-Greek monasticism begin to conform itself to the regulated cenobitic way of life.[15] Pertusi makes the further point that just as Byzantine monasticism was reformed in the direction of cenobitism by St. Theodore the Studite, so too did Italo-Greek monasticism experience its reform in the same direction by St. Bartholomew of Simeri (or of Rossano) (d.1130).[16]

Although the possibility of leading a heremitic way of life in practice was never seen to be absolutely contradictory to the cenobitic life, in south Italy the frequent Arab attacks quite clearly made it very difficult to practice a cenobitic life in its complete perfection. This is known on the testimony of St. Nilus himself.[17] The Italo-Greek *typika* are not necessarily helpful in this discussion because the redactions that have come to us date from the Norman period.[18] As many monks migrated into Calabria from Sicily in the face of the Arab invasions and because of the unsettled conditions in Calabria that further Arab raids created, the lives that we have examined seem to reveal a monasticism that moved from a type of anchoritism or hesychastic heremitism to a type of community life that could be cenobitic or laureatic.[19]

The lives also make clear that the monks did not seem to observe precise regulations regarding the age in which a young man could enter a monastery nor when he could be invested with the monastic habit; nor did they observe precise rules regarding the passage from the heremitic way of life to the life in a monastery or vice versa. It seems that the ideal of the south Italian monk may not have been the cenobitic life but *hesycheia*, that is, contemplation in tranquility and in silence; not the *hypomoné*, the life of obedience required by the cenobitic life, but simply the *apotagé*, the life of renunciation of the world and a consequent acceptance of *hypotagé*, the submission to a spiritual father.

The monasteries which are mentioned in the sources, however, follow the patterns that were established in the classical period of monastic foundation: at the head of a monastery was the *hegoumenos* or abbot. If he were ordained a deacon or priest, he held the title of cathegumenus. The abbot was usually selected by his predecessor and was chosen from among those monks who best exemplified the ideals of monastic discipline and spirituality. But the abbot did not always make the selection. Mention has been made of monasteries that were founded by lay persons who, even though they did not themselves take up the monastic life, nevertheless continued to exercise control over it. The most important of the founder-owner's privileges was the right to select the abbot.[20] He could control also the possessions of the monastery, using them, if he wished, for his own advantage. Examples of this *ktetorika dikaion* are found in south Italy, but the sources for them are late (mid-eleventh century at the earliest)[21] and are not found in our biographies. The bishop, the patriarch, or the emperor could grant the rights over monastic property to a layman. This is called the *charistikia* and was granted as a means of recompensing a faithful subject either out of gratitude or as a way of insuring his loyalty. Ostensibly the purpose of the grant was to restore to their former splendor monasteries that had fallen into disrepair. The *charistikia* was not a formal donation of land; it granted to a layman for life or for one or two generations the right to administer the temporal affairs of the monastery. He assumed, however, all the responsibilities for maintaining the monks as well as the monastery. An example of this can be found in south Italy in the year 999 but, again, no description of it is found in the hagiographies.[22]

An institution often referred to in the lives of the south Italian monks is that of the *metochion*, that is, a small monastic dependency erected by the mother house and subject to its control. Although these might be erected for purposes of managing a distant property or estate, in south Italy a *metochion* was a place of hermitage.[23] These *metochia* did not have their own *hegoumenos* but were directed by a monk placed in charge by the *hegoumenos* of the mother house.

Although each monastic foundation was independent of the other and although each was governed by its own *typicon*, the idea of a congregation of monasteries was not unknown in south Italy. In this case the head of the congregation is called the archimandrite. It is usually thought that examples of this are not seen in south Italy until the twelfth century and came either as a result of the increasing influence of Theodore the Studite as more normal conditions began to prevail in south Italy or from pressures brought to bear upon the Italo-Greeks by the Normans (St. Bartholomew of Simeri).[24] Although both factors account for the development of the large Byzantine monastic houses of south Italy in the twelfth, thirteenth, and fourteenth centuries, still the idea of a congregation was not foreign to the experience of our Italo-Greek monks. Not only is the title archimandrite found in the life of St. Nilus,[25] but the life of St. Saba and the lives of SS. Christopher and Macarius recount that Saba was the head of all the monks who lived in the region of the Latinianon and Mercurion. That he took the role of archimandrite is testified to by the fact that he often went to visit the various monks, a function which passed to his brother, Macarius, when he took over after Saba's death. St. Luke of Armento also seems to have acted as the head of several monasteries when, during a serious epidemic, he visited all the monks subject to him.[26] In fact he died shortly after his return from one such visit to his monasteries.[27]

Theoretically no monastic house could be established without the approval of a local bishop, the exarch. Although our sources several times affirm explicitly the dependence of the Italo-Greek monasteries on the local bishop, still the moral authority of the monks was so great among the populace that for all practical purposes the monks were independent of local ecclesiastical authority. Indeed, on the few occasions when bishops are explicitly named in connection with the monasteries, they are usually in the position of a client asking for some kind of assistance.

In the Byzantine empire the more important monastic foundations all sought to withdraw themselves from the local bishops and from some financial obligations by placing themselves directly under the control of the patriarch or Emperor. It seems that the biographer of St. Elias of Enna wanted to confirm the imperial status of the Saline monastery when he described the gifts given by the Emperor Leo VI upon the death of St. Elias.[28] Another later example can be found in the description of the monastery of S. Pietro di Taranto: it is described explicitly as imperial in a charter of 1033[29] and in another of 1035.[30] Vera von Falkenhausen, however, believes that in south Italy, as for all the monasteries in the provincial periphery, it was more advantageous to be under episcopal jurisdiction.[31]

V. South Italian Cenobitism and the Studite Reforms

It is clear from the lives of the ninth- and tenth-century saints that we have reviewed, namely, St. Elias of Enna, St. Elias Spelaiotes, and St. Nilus, that the cenobitic and community life, a life regulated in the practical and spiritual details of daily life in a monastery, are not yet found in the completeness that we might recognize and identify as cenobitic monasticism. Indeed, the disciple of St. Nilus, St. Stephen, frankly admitted that he was acquainted with the monastaries but he preferred to live as a hermit.[32] It is clear, however, that even toward the end of the tenth century a transition toward a more complete cenobitic life can be witnessed in the monastic eparchy of the Mercurion. The area of the Mercurion is located in the upper valley of the Lao River in northern Calabria. From the lives especially of St. Christopher (d. 990–91) and his two sons, SS. Sabas (d. 990) and Macarius (d. 1000), we learn that here in the Mercurion the *regula mixta* was observed and the virtue of obedience was practiced. Their biographer, Orestes, Patriarch of Jerusalem from 986 to 1006, describes a life of relative cenobitism which permitted the practice of some heremitism. And even though St. Nilus may have had reservations about cenobitic life for himself, he was certainly moving in that direction with the establishment of his monastic houses, the descriptions of which betray a movement toward and a favoring of a more regulated cenobitism.

It is in the eleventh century that more explicit testimony can be found which reveals the triumph of the cenobitic life over the heremitic. The lives of St. John Teristes of Stilo (d. *ca.* 1050) and of St. Bartholomew of Simeri (d. *ca.* 1130) exemplify this. We are told that the monks observed "the rules and the ascesis of Basil the Great," "the rules of Basil the Great and of St. Theodore the Studite and of all the Fathers," as well as the "divinely inspired" rules and "the sacred canons."[33] Although the monks seem to have lived a normal community life behind monastic walls, they could leave to lead a more ascetic or heremitic life, but only with the permission of the superior whom the monks elected "according to the traditions of our holy father," St. Theodore of Studios.[34]

That this movement toward a complete cenobitism is the result of a conscious effort to put into effect some of the reforms of St. Theodore or St. Athanasius the Athonite, is shown by the presence in south Italian monasteries of Greek manuscripts from the east which reveal a Studite origin. For example, in the monastery of Santa Maria Odigitria, the Patir, at Rossano, founded by St. Bartholomew of Simeri, and in the monastery of Grottaferrata founded by St. Nilus, Robert Devresse has identified certain codices as having a Studite origin: there are several *Menologies*, the *Homilies* of St. Gregory of Nazianzen, and the *catechesis* of St. Cyril of Jerusalem.[35] Other texts of the tenth and eleventh centuries show traces of Studite influence in their writing. Other manuscripts of the tenth, eleventh, and twelfth centuries found in the archives of the Escurial, the Vatican, Naples, Paris, and Messina contain the ascetical works of St. Theodore the Studite transcribed by Italo-Greek monks. Another twelve or thirteen copies were to be found in various Calabrian monasteries. Old inventories inform us of even more manuscripts of St. Theodore in various Sicilian and Calabrian monasteries. The mere presence of these manuscripts does not necessarily mean that the monks made use of them, but explicit testimony is available: In the *Typikon* of the monastery of Santa Maria del Mile (Vat. gr. 1877, a. 1292), one of the Calabro-Sicilian *typica*, we read the following instruction for the first Sunday of Lent, the feast of orthodoxy:

When the monks hear the sound of the *simandra* [in English, semantron, a wooden bar struck by a mallet], all the monks, those who are laboring or who are doing any work, great or small, should immediately leave it and betake themselves as quickly as possible to the church to listen to the *Catechesis* of the Studite; and after having listened to it, they should genuflect, and return quickly to their work; and this is what should be done throughout all of Lent.[36]

Another very significant source which reveals a relationship not only to St. Theodore but also to the Athonite monasteries is contained in the *Typikon* provided by St. Bartholomew of Simeri for the monastery of Patir at Rossano. Although this document is listed as being preserved in the Univeritätsbibliothek of Jena, it seems to be lost. A faithful copy of it, however, was made for the monastery of Grottaferrata and is preserved in the archives there. Although the text has not yet been edited completely, it reveals that Mount Athos is the inspiration for St. Bartholomew's *Typikon* for his monastery of Santa Maria Odigitria.

The Italo-Greek manuscript tradition of the works of St. Theodore is not only great in the number of texts involved but it is also the oldest. Indeed, only by means of the Italo-Greek manuscripts do we have the primitive redactions of the *hypotyposis* (disciplinary regulations) of St. Theodore, the very one that inspired St. Athanasius the Athonite in the composition of his. Although it can, indeed, be found in various eastern manuscripts, these documents all date back only to the thirteenth century; the Italo-Greek copies go back to the tenth and eleventh centuries.

VI. Cultural Contributions

The life of St. Nilus is especially rich in offering us details of the cultural life of the Italo-Greek monks and of the general cultural level that prevailed in these parts. At the beginning of the tenth century the youths of the city of Rossano would gather in the shadow of the cathedral to be instructed or they might go to the monasteries where they would not only obtain an introduction to the profane sciences but they would also learn something of the sacred sciences, namely, scripture, sacred music, and calligraphy. We learn further that at the Mercurion there existed those houses which were well furnished not only with liturgical books but books of secular learning.[37] In the life of St. Nilus we are told that St. Fantinus, anticipating destructive Arab raids, wept at the inevitable ruin of the libraries and the destruction of the books.[38]

Perhaps a more practical proof of the cultural achievements of the Italo-Greek culture is to be found in the men it produced. The unfortunate John Philagathos, the anti-pope John XVI (997–98), was regarded as a luminary of his time. A native of the city of Rossano, he was a friend of St. Nilus, whose biographer describes for us in some detail the extent to which that friendship constrained Nilus to intercede on his behalf when the anti-pope's fortunes were reversed. To have been selected by Theophano, the wife of Otto II (973–83), as her adviser and the godfather and teacher of her son more than suggests that John was a well-educated man. St. Nilus himself, as his biographer affirms, was capable of transforming ploughmen into theologians and literati. His successor as *hegoumenos* at the monastery of St. Adriano, Proclus of Bisignano, because of his remarkable learning, was called a "walking archive."[39]

The biography of St. Nilus gives us the names of the authors and the titles of the works that were familiar to him. The references force us to conclude that at some time in his life he must have been exposed to these works in more than a casual way. The list includes above all the great fathers of the eastern church: Athanasius, Basil, Gregory Nazianzen, John Chrysostom, Ephraim the Syrian, John Damascene, and Theodore the Studite.[40] References are also made to the *Apocolypse* of Simon the Stylite, the younger, and to the *Religiosa Historia* of Theodoret, and to the lives of SS. Anthony, Saba, Hilarion, Arsenius, John Calibita, and to the Greek translation of the *Dialogues* of St. Gregory the Great.[41]

The biography of St. Nilus tells us that he spent a considerable amount of time copying manuscripts. It may be of interest to list here the titles of those manuscripts which he and his monks brought with them to Grottaferrata in 1004, the date of the founding of the monastery. Several of these are actual autographs of St. Nilus and are still located in the Abbey:

B.α.20: *The Doctrines* of Dorotheus, copied by Nilus, 965.

B.α.19: The ascetical *Works* of Mark the Monk and Diadocus, the discourses of Basil of Seleucia, copied by Nilus, 965.

Δ.γ.12: Tropologium, copied in 970.

B.α.1: The Letters of Isidore Pelusius, written at the request of Nilus in 985.

B.α.4: A collection of works of St. Maximus the Confessor, copied before 992; the last fascicule was copied by Nilus.[42]

The Italo-Greek monks of the eleventh century possessed an impressive patrimony indeed and it was off of this rich endowment that the Italo-Greek monks would have to draw their inspiration because after the Norman conquest and after the schism, the monks of south Italy would be cut off from the East.

VII. Economic Life

The lives of the Italo-Greek monks provide us with numerous details which yield considerable information about the economic life of south Italy during the tenth century.

First of all there was no question that the monks were expected to give themselves over to labor which was in conformity with their state of life. St. Basil, who clearly expected the monks to engage in some manual labor, specified, furthermore, that work in the fields seemed to him to be more appropriate to the monastic life. The prescription of manual labor was confirmed by St. Theodore the Studite.

How did the monks of south Italy implement these prescriptions? At the very beginning of the tenth century, we learn that St. Elias Spelaiotes had his men cut down huge trees in order to clear the land.[43] In the mid-tenth century St. Christopher of Collesano, the father of SS. Sabas and Macarius, cleared the area around Agira (Ctisma, Tisima) in Sicily in order to build the church of St. Michael and his oratory. Around this same time Jonas, a monk of the monastery of Theotokos del Rifugio, south of Tricarico in Lucania, is described as clearing for cultivation a large amount of land close to his monastery. His work, furthermore, is seen as a continuation of work that his predecessors had done before him. SS. Sabas and Macarius put under cultivation a large amount of land in the Mercurion (the upper Lao River valley) and later in the area called the Latinianon, an area located northeast of mount Pollino and in the mid-Sinni River valley. This too was seen as a continuation of the work of monks who had preceded them in the area. Our biographer sees these two monks coming to the Latinianon and concluded that it would be a good place to build a monastery, the monastery of San Lorenzo. They cut down the trees and drained the swamps and thus prepared the soil for cultivation.[44] There can be no doubt that the monks built very simple structures, but because they were self-sufficient we must conclude that they possessed the tools needed for their labor. The life of St. Elias Spelaiotes tells us of one of Elias' monks, Cosmos, who built a mill for milling grain and who also prepared a salt bed. As St. Nilus observed a few years later, the monks must take care of their own needs.

Monasteries were in a position to receive lands already cultivated. We learn that the monastery of Theotokos del Rifugio, upon the death of one of its monks, was the beneficiary of a large expanse of farm land located near the monastery. Too much for the monks to cultivate, the abbot Cosmos calls in free citizens who are burdened with fiscal obligations to cultivate the land and pay off their debts. After fifteen years the property is placed on the tax rolls and the administrative representative provides a formal document for the monastery recognizing the monastery's ownership of the property.[45]

Even tenth century monasticism in Italy could be endowed with great benefactions as we learn from the life of St. Elias of Enna. Leo VI (879–912) some time between the years 904 and 912 granted to the monastery established by St. Elias in the Saline certain incomes. As a result, the biographer says, it became the most famous of all the monasteries in Italy.[46]

An interesting episode in the life of St. Nilus is particularly revealing in so far as it tells us something of the extent to which viticulture flourished in south Italy. Besides the various saints' lives, other sources inform us that vines grew on the hillsides and could be found at an altitude even higher than 2700 feet. The following episode is provided by our biographer:

"Fathers, we planted many vines, which for us are a surplus because we have more than what we need. Let us cut some of them and keep only what we need."

When he saw that they all agreed to his words, he slung a hatchet over his shoulder and went to the most flourishing part of the vineyard, and they all followed behind him without saying a word . . . and, after saying a prayer, they cut from the morning until the third hour. . . .The event became widely know even on the Holy Mountain [Mt. Athos] and in Sicily, and nobody was able to understand the reason for it: some people said the monks were drunk, others that they owned too many vines and could not cope with the work. This is not surprising, for even the people who cut them [the vines] did not know why they did it, except for those to whom the great man revealed the mystery.[47]

The incident shows that the monastery obviously produced more wine than was needed. From the comment of the biographer we learn further that the cutting of the vines was considered an extraordinary and drastic way of providing a means of mortification if not of temperance. André Guillou deduces from this incident that a surplus, therefore, existed, and he concludes that wine production must have formed a significant part of the economic picture of south Italy.[48]

VIII. Political Involvements:
Monks and the Secular World

One of the more interesting encounters that St. Nilus had with persons of this world who occupied high places in society was the episode (described at some length by his biographer) involving Alvara, the widow of the Lombard prince of Capua, Pandulf I Ironhead (961–81). With the support of Otto I and Otto II, this prince, Pandulf I, had been able to unite under his control the Duchies of Langobardia (Benevento, Capua, and Salemo) as well as the Marches of Spoleto and Camerino. After Pandulf I died in 981, Alvara along with her son Landenulf (982–93) was able to maintain this political unity, but in doing so both were ruthlessly unscrupulous to the point where they were implicated in the murders of many rivals, even relatives. Alvara, at one point, was overcome with remorse and asked St. Nilus, who was still at Valleluce, to come to Capua to console her. When Nilus confronted her, he discerned that she was unwilling to make restitution for the damage she had caused and he pronounced the prophecy predicting the extinction of her house. Shortly after in 992 she died. So unpopular had Alvara been, however, that she and her son, Landenulf, were murdered in the church of St. Marcellus in Capua. Her other son, Laidulf, who was implicated in the murder, succeeded to the principality.

The prophecy of St. Nilus was to be fulfilled by no less an agent than the Emperor himself, Otto III (996–1002), who had succeeded his father in 996. After these events in Capua had transpired, he sent his trusted minister, Adhemar, recently named margrave of Spoleto, to bring order in these parts. He placed Laidulf under arrest for fratricide and had him brought in chains to Germany.

Adhemar took over control of Capua, thus bringing to an end the rule of the family of Pandulf Ironhead and his wife Alvara.

St. Nilus was also involved in the tragic story of John Philagathos, the anti-pope John XVI (997–98). John Philagathos was a native of Rossano in Calabria and thus a compatriot of Nilus. At an early age he entered one of the monasteries of that region and it is probable that at this time he became a disciple or at least a friend of Nilus. The next thing we know of Philagathos is that he was selected by Theophano to be the teacher of her son, Otto III. We can presume, therefore, that Philagathos must have been a very learned man and one who had won the confidence of the queen Theophano. That he was an intimate of the imperial family is demonstrated by the fact that he was selected to be the godfather not only of Otto III but also of the young Otto's first cousin, the man who was to become Pope Gregory V (996–99). He may have attracted the attention of the imperial family on the occasion of Otto II's campaign against the Arabs in south Italy, which ended in the disastrous battle of Stilo (982). During this expedition Otto II was accompanied by his wife Theophano and their son Otto III as well as Otto II's sister Luitgard and her son, Bruno (Gregory V). While Otto II was conducting his campaign, his family remained in Rossano under the protection of the Bishop of Metz. Having ingratiated himself with Otto II and the members of the imperial family, therefore, Philagathos accompanied them to Rome where he took up his duties as instructor of the future emperor. In 996 he was entrusted along with the Bishop of Wurzburg to lead an embassy to the court of Constantinople to seek a wife for Otto III. Although this mission did not have immediate results, nevertheless, the ground was laid for the success which the follow-up mission secured. The early death of Otto III (1002) brought these negotiations to an end.

Philagathos now occupied a very high place in the imperial circle and moved from honor to honor. He became the bishop of Piacenza, which was immediately raised to an archbishopric for his benefit. He was also made abbot of the very rich monastery of Nonantola. These honors that were heaped upon Philagathos came to him because he was, indeed, a truly sincere and good man and not some sort of an ecclesiastical adventurer. Otto II himself testifies to his character in the document granting him the monastery of Nonantola.

> The archimandrite John [Philagathos] is a serious, reserved man of good habits, instructed in Greek letters who has a splendid reputation for prudence and sanctity. On the advice of wise and Godfearing persons he [Otto] agreeing to deprive himself of the very useful counsels of this venerable personage concedes to him the abbey [of Nonantola].[49]

What, then, brought about his downfall? The biographer of St. Nilus, contrasting the humility and self-effacement of Nilus with that of Philagathos, tells us that it was an overriding ambition that blinded Philagathos and brought about his disgrace. The following chain of events chronicle this sad episode in the history of the church.

In the year 985 the Roman Patrician Crescentius, the leader of the anti-imperial and pro-Byzantine factions in Rome, found himself—in the absence of the Emperor—master of Rome and of the papacy. He deposed the legitimate Pope John XIV (983–84) and had him imprisoned in Castel Sant' Angelo where he starved to death. Crescentius then put on the papal throne his own candidate, Franco, who took the name Boniface VII (984–85). The Romans, outraged at these actions, deposed Boniface VII and had him killed. His successor, John XV (985–96), found himself completely under the control of Crescentius and the pro-Byzantine faction. Upon his death in 996, however, Otto III's cousin Bruno was made pope as Gregory V (996–99). Crescentius, unhappy with this selection, offered the papal throne to Philagathos who had just returned from Constantinople where he had been negotiating for a Byzantine bride for Otto III. The ambition of Philagathos compelled him to accept this offer and this brought about his downfall. In May of 996 Otto III had come to Rome to receive the imperial crown from his cousin the Pope. It was on his way back to Germany that he received word of the revolt of Crescentius and the acceptance by Philagathos of the papal throne with the name John XVI. Gregory V had fled to Pavia, held a council there in 997, and excommunicated Crescentius and Philagathos. In February of 998 Otto III returned to Rome accompanied by Gregory V and had Crescentius beheaded along with his accomplices. Philagathos, by the this time repentant, fled southward toward Campania where he was caught up by the supporters of Gregory V and Otto. He was then blinded, his tongue and nose were cut off, and he was eventually imprisoned in a monastery, probably Fulda, where he lived another fifteen years. He died in 1013.

The biographer of St. Nilus wants us to believe that Nilus had a premonition of what was to happen and had sent word to Philagathos that he should step down from the papal throne. Philagathos instead remained obdurate. When Nilus heard of the events that had transpired, he wasted no time in making his way to Rome to intercede on behalf of his compatriot. Arriving in Rome, he learned of what had happened, and even though he was well received by the Emperor Otto III and by Pope Gregory V, he chastised them for treating Philagathos so severely. After all, he told them, they should not have blinded the man who, as their godfather, had been responsible for their spiritual light. Although we are told that the Emperor was moved to tears by Nilus' remarks, the Pope, on the other hand, who was of cruel character, took Philagathos from prison, had him dressed up in priestly robes, and had him led throughout the city of Rome as an object of derision. When word of this came to Nilus by means of a messenger sent to him by Otto for the purpose of explaining away this action, Nilus exclaimed to the messenger that just as the Pope and Emperor had not shown any mercy toward Philagathos, so too God would have no mercy on them. Shortly after, Gregory V met a violent death on February 18, 999, at the hands of rebellious Romans. He was 30 years old. Just two years later, in February of 1001, Otto III had to flee Rome because of another uprising of

Romans. Making his way northward, he died at Paterno near Città Castellana on January 23/24, 1002, at the age of 22.

IX. Religious Tensions

Religious tensions between Greek and Latin practices in the area were a reality throughout this period of the ninth, tenth, and eleventh centuries. They became especially acute in the eleventh century as several examples from the *Life of St. Luke*, Bishop of Isola Capo Rizzuto (d. 1114), testify.[50]

The anonymous biographer of the life of St. Luke informs us that on one occasion, toward the end of the eleventh century, St. Luke undertook a missionary trip to Sicily. Sicily at the time was completely under the control of the Normans. The biographer describes the excursion to Sicily as an example of Luke's missionary zeal. Sicily is in the hands of "inimical atheists" and Luke, therefore, goes about preaching the word of God and stopping in various cities to ordain priests. Questions have been raised as to the identity of these inimical atheists. Several scholars have asserted that these must be Moslems still remaining in Sicily after the Norman conquest.[51] (The conquest was completed with the capture of Palermo in 1072.) Giuseppe Schiro argues most convincingly that they were not Moslems but were rather Latins, Norman or otherwise. Luke undertook his missionary journey to Sicily with the apostolic purpose, therefore, of strengthening in the true faith the Greeks, who must be encouraged to withstand Latin aggression. He did this by preaching the word of God to them and by ordaining priests who could administer the sacraments for them.

It is interesting to note that the biographer, immediately after describing Luke's missionary journey to Sicily, tells us that he returned to his see of Isola Capo Rizzuto and shortly after embarked on a trip to Constantinople. Because of a difficulty of which we are not informed, Luke's trip was interrupted at Taranto and he returned to Isola. Can anything be made of the fact that Luke was on his way to Constantinople? If he were going for ecclesiastical business, would not Rome have done just as well? Obviously Luke still regarded (at the end of the eleventh or the beginning of the twelfth century) Constantinople as the source of his authority and looked to the Patriarch for guidance.

On another occasion and within his own diocese, St. Luke engaged in a controversy with some Latin rite Christians in which he was constrained to defend the use by Eastern rite Christians of leavened bread in the celebration of the Eucharist. In the course of the argument, St. Luke quotes the relevant texts from the gospels and then in very strong language asserts: "You Latins, interpreting the scriptures in the manner of the Pharisees, use unleavened bread in the manner of the Jews; besides, you administer baptism at any time; and not thinking clearly you fall into innumerable heresies."[52] Because of the severity of these words, we might be inclined to regard them as expressing the feelings of the biographer rather than those of the saint. But by the end of the eleventh century, this kind of language had entered into the mutual exchanges of the highest ecclesiastics.

Regarding the administration of baptism, St. Luke defended the ancient practice of the church in administering this sacrament only at Easter time and at Epiphany time. So angered were Luke's Latin adversaries that they captured him and prepared a cabin in which he was to be burned alive. Before being placed in the cabin, Luke obtained permission to offer the liturgy there. When St. Luke was finished, the cabin or house was set on fire but the saint remained unharmed. Clearly this incident offers us a very convincing example of the deep antipathy between the two rites.

One more incident associated with St. Luke witnesses to the antagonism between Greek and Latin. This event occurs some time after his death. A Norman from the city of Briatico (in the diocese of Mileto) was accustomed to treat the "priests of God," i.e., the priests of the Eastern rite, in an insolent and insulting fashion. Furthermore, since he held some sort of official capacity, he was in a position to impose on the priests taxes or dues that were higher than those which others paid. Even while still alive, St. Luke admonished the Norman official against this practice but to no avail. The Norman official one day fell ill almost to the point of dying, and remembering the admonition of St. Luke, he went to his tomb and there swore that he would not mistreat the "priests of God" again. The Norman was cured and was even given many other blessings. But after a certain amount of time, the Norman forgot his many promises and began again to mistreat the priests. His illness returned and he became so paralyzed that he resembled a cadaver, unable to speak, abandoned by God and by St. Luke. So much for those people who abuse the "priests of God."

One thing emerges from the conflicts exemplified in the life of St. Luke: even though the differences between the two traditions have little or nothing to do with anything touching the essentials of dogma, still it is evident that one would be hard pressed to convince anyone of the contemporaries of this. Furthermore, the animus behind the disagreements described in the life of St. Luke suggests that anti-Latin and anti-Greek attitudes were of long standing duration and did not come about with the Cerularian schism of 1054.

Greek-Latin conflicts, however, would soon be determined by the changing political order in the south. It was inevitable, therefore, that with the passage of time the kind of monasticism described here would disappear from south Italy. As this area was brought more and more within the orbit of Rome and western Europe and with the decline of Constantinople and the Byzantine Empire, Italo-Greek monasticism, always somewhat fragile and now unsponsored, disintegrated, leaving only a few traces of its otherwise rich legacy.

NOTES

1. T. Aceti, ed. *De Antiquitate et situ Calabriae*. Rome, 1737. Cited in Francesco Russo, "Il monachismo calabro-greco e la cultura bizantina in occidente," *Bollettino della badia greca di Grottaferrata*, 5 (1951), 5. This has been repeated by Ferdinando Ughelli, *Italia sacra*, 2nd ed. N. Coleti (Venice: S. Coleti, 1721), vol. 9, col. 175; and by Pietro P. Rodotà, *Dell' origine, progresso, e stato presente del rito greco in Italia* (Rome: G. Salomoni, 1758), "Prefazione," Jules Gay, *L'Italie meridionale et l'empire byzantin depuis l'avènement de Basile Ier jusqù à la prise de Bari par les Normands (857–1071)*, Paris, 1904), 254.

2. Giovanni Mercati, "L'Eucologio di S. Maria del Patire con un frammento di anafora greca inedita, "*Opere Minori*, vol. 4 [Studi e testi, 79] (Vatican City, 1937), p. 485 ff. This article is reprinted from *Revue Bénédictine* 46 (1934), 224–240. See also H.W. Codrington, "The Anaphoral Fragment in the Rossano Euchologion," *Revue Bénédictine* 48 (1936): 182 ff.

3. A. Vaccari, "La Grecía nell' Italia meridionale," *Orientalia Christiana* 3 (1925): 284–303.

4. P. Sherwood, *An Annotated Date List of the Works of Maximus the Confessor* [Studia Anselmiana Philosophica Theologica, 30] (Rome, 1952), 55.

5. F. Dölger, *Regesten der Kaiserkunden des Oströmischen Reiches von 565–1453* [Corpus der Griechischen Urkunden des Mittelalters und der Neueren Zeit, Reihe A, Abeilung 1]. (Munich and Berlin, 1924), 1 Teil, p. 36, no. 301.

6. *Vita s.Junioris, Junioris*, PG 100, cols. 1117, 1120.

7. *Ibid.*

8. *Theodori praepositi studitarum epistolae, Liber secundus, Theophani monacho*, PG 99, col. 1577–1581.

9. *Theodori praepositi studitarum epistolae, Liber primus, Athanasio filio*, PG 99, col. 1072.

10. A.A. Vasiliev, *History of the Byzantine Empire, 324–1453* (Madison, 1952), 263. See also F. Dvornik, *La vie de saint Gregoire le Décapolite et les slaves macédoniens au IXe siècle* (Paris, 1926), 41, 58.

11. Mario Scaduto, *Il monachismo basiliano nella Sicilia medievale. Rinascita e decadenza, sec. XI–XIV* (Rome, 1947), pp. xxv–xxxii; Silvano Borsari, *Il monachismo bizantino nella Sicilia e nell' Italia meridionale prenormanne* (Naples, 1963), 23–76; Biagio Cappelli, *Il monachismo basiliano ai confini Calabro-Lucani* [Deputazione di Storia Patria per la Calabria, Collana Storico, III] (Naples, pp. 13–33); Jules Gay, *L'Italie meridionale*, 254–86.

12. Giuseppe Rossi Taibbi, ed. *Vita di sant' Elia il giovane* [Istituto Siciliano di studi bizantini e neoellenici, Testi e monumenti 7, Vite dei santi siciliani III]. Palermo, 1962; G. da Costa-Louillet, "Saints de Sicile et d'Italie méridionale aux VIIIe, IXe, Xe siècles," *Byzantion* 29–30 (1959–60): 95–109; *AASS*, August, vol. 3, 479–509: Commentary and Latin text (Rome and Paris, 1867); *Bibliotheca hagiographica graeca*, 178.

13. G. da Costa-Louillet, *op. cit.*, 113–24; *AASS*, September, vol. 3, 843–88; G. Minasi, *Lo speleota ovvero S. Elia di Reggio di Calabria, monaco basiliano net 9 e 10 secolo* (Naples, 1983).

14. Germano Giovanelli, ed. [Life of Saint Nilus] (Grottaferrata, 1972); Germano Giovanelli, ed. and trans. *Vita di S. Nilo fondatore e patrono di Grottaferrata* (Grottaferrata, 1966); *AASS*, September, vol. 7, 282–342; PG 120, cols. 15–165; G. Minasi, *S. Nilo di Calabria, monaco basiliano nel decimo secolo con annotazioni storiche* (Naples, 1892).

15. Agostino Pertusi, "Aspetti organizzativi e culturali dell' ambienti monacale greco dell' Italia meridionale, *"L 'Eremetismo in occidente nei secoli XI e XII* [Pubblicazioni dall' Università Cattolica del Sacro Cuore, Miscellanea del centro di Studi Medioevali, IV] (Milan, 1965), 393–94.

16. *Ibid.*

17. Germano Giovanelli, ed., *Vita di S. Nilo, fondatore e patrono di Grottaferrata* (Grottaferrata, 1966), 46–48; Teodoro Minisci, "Riflessi studitani nel monachismo italo-greco, *"Il monachismo orientale* [Orientalia christiana analecta, 153] (Rome, 1958), 219.

18. Placide de Meester, " Les typiques de fondation," *Atti del V congresso internazionale di studi bizantini* [Studi bizantini e neoellenici, 6], (Rome, 1940), vol. 2, 506–508; Agostino Pertusi, "Rapporti tra il monachismo italo-greco ed il monachismo bizantino nell' alto medio evo," *La chiesa greca in Italia dall' VIII al XVI secolo* [Atti del convegno storico interecclesiale] (Padua, 1972), 482–91; Teodoro Minisci, " I Typika liturgici dell' Italia bizantina, *"Bollettino della badia greca di Grottaferrata* 7 (1953): 97–104.

19. Agostino Pertusi, "Aspetti organizzativi....," p. 392: "Ed in fondo e questa la situazione che troviamo agli inizi del monachesimo italo-greco: e un continuo altalenare fra un tipo di anacoretismo o di eremitismo esicastico e un tipo di comunità lavriotica o cenobitica; e tutto ciò nella più assoluta libertà." Enrico Morini, "Eremo e cenobio nel monachismo greco dell' Italia meridionale nei secoli IX e X, " *Rivista di storia della chiesa in Italia* 31 (1977): 1–39; 354–390. On p. 374 the author summarizes: ". . . alcuni conducono una vita completamente et assolutamente solitaria, in colloquio con Dio solo . . . ; altri rimangono in piccole dimore adatte a practicarvi l'hesycheia . . . ed altri obbediscono ad una 'regola mista' e si esercitano nella lotta dell' obbedienza. . . . ."

20. Silvano Borsari, *Il monachismo bizantino nella Sicilia e nell' Italia meridonale prenormanne* (Naples, 1963), 98.

21. Gertrude Robinson, *History and Cartulary of the Greek Monastery of St. Elias and St. Anastasius of Carbone* [Orientalia Christiana, vol 15, num. 53, June–July, 1929], 138.

22. Placide de Meester, *De monachico statu iuxta disciplinam bizantinam.* Sacra Congregazione per la Chiesa Orientale. Codificazione Canonica Orientale. Fonti. Serie II, fasc. X. (Vatican City, 1942), 109; E. Hermann, "Ricerche sulle istituzioni monastiche bizantine. Typika, ktetorika, caristicari, e monasteri 'liberi,'" *Orientalia Christiana Periodica* 6 (1940), 316–47; J.M. Hussey, "Byzantine Monasticism" *The Cambridge Medieval History*, vol. 4: *The Byzantine Empire*, part II: *Government, Church, and Civilization* (Cambridge, 1967), 161–84. J.M. Hussey, *Church and Learning in the Byzantine Empire,867–1185* (London, 1937), 175–77.

23. *Vita Sancti Eliae, AASS*, September, vol. 3, p. 853, (par. 14).

24. Francesco Russo, "Il monachismo calabro-greco e la cultura bizantina in occidente," *Bollettino della badia greca di Grottaferrata* 5 (1951): 17: "Quando poi vogliano restaurare la disciplina religiosa, non sanno far di meglio che ricorrere a quei monaci calabro-greci, che erano luminari di scienza e di santità. Principale strumento di

questa loro politica ricostruttiva fu S. Bartolomeo di Simeri." See also Pierre Batiffol, *L'Abbaye de Rossano, contribution à l'histoire de la Vaticane* (Paris, 1891), 9.

25. Germano Giovanelli, ed., *Vita di S. Nilo*, par. 55, p. 71.

26. *Vita S. Lucae Abbatis, AASS*, October, vol. 6, 340–41, par. 12.

27. *Ibid.*, 341, par. 16.

28. Giuseppe Rossi Taibbi, ed., *Vita di sant' Elia il giovane* [Istituto siciliano di studi bizantini e neoellenici, Testi 7, Vite dei santi Siciliani 3] (Palermo, 1962), 120, par. 75.

29. Francesco Trinchero, ed., *Syllabus Graecarum Membranarum*, (Naples, 1865), no. 27, 31–32.

30. *Ibid.*, no. 30, 35–36.

31. Vera von Falkenhausen, "Aspetti economici dei monasteri bizantini in Calabria (sec. X–XI)," *Calabria bizantina, aspetti sociali ed economici*, [Atti del terzo incontro di studi bizantini] (Reggio, Calabria, 1978), 50.

32. Germano Giovanelli, ed., *Vita di s. Nilo* (Grottaferrata, 1966), par. 26, 44.

33. Silvano Borsari, "Vita di san Giovanni Terista (Testi)," *Archivio Storico per la Calabria e la Lucania* 22 (1953): 142–45.

34. Agostino Pertusi, "Rapporti tra il monachismo italo-greco et il monachismo bizantino nell' alto medio evo," *La chiesa greca in Italia dall' VIII al XVI secolo* [Atti del convegno storico interecclesiale, Bari, 30 Apr.–4 Maggio. 1969] (Padua, 1972), vol. 2, 479.

35. Robert Devreesse, *Les manuscrits grecs de l'Italie méridionale* (Vatican City, 1955), p. 19, n. 12, p. 36, n. 4.

36. Pertusi, "Rapporti," 481–82.

37. Francesco Russo, "Relazioni culturali tra la Calabria e l'oriente bizantino nel M.E.," Thessalonika, 12–19 April, 1953 (Athens, 1956) vol. 2, 597. See also Francesco Russo "Il monachismo calabro-greco e la cultura bizantina in occidente," *Bollettino della badia greca di Grottaferrata* 5 (1951): 13.

38. Germano Giovanelli, *Vita di S. Nilo* (Grottaferrata, 1966), 41–42, par. 24.

39. *Ibid.*, 57, par. 40.

40. *Ibid.*, 64, par. 47; 94, par. 77; 26–27, par. 11; 32–33, par. 16; 65–66, par. 49; Biagio Capelli, *Il monachesimo basiliano ai confini calabro-lucani* (Naples, 1961), 119–43.

41. *Ibid.*, 64, par. 47; 32–33, par. 16; 14–15, par. 2; 60–61, par. 44; 94, par. 77.

42. Robert Devreesse, *Les manuscrits grecs de l'Italie méridionale* (Vatican City, 1955), 27–28.

43. *Vitasancti Eliae Spelaeotae, AASS*, September, vol. 3, par. 68, p. 875.

44. *Vita et conversatio sancti patris nostri Sabae junioris in Historia et laudes ss. Sabae etMacarii iuniorem e Sicilia*, ed. Joseph Cozza-Luzi (Rome, 1893) par. 9, pp. 17–18; André Guillou, "Inchiesta sulla popolazione greca della Sicilia e della Calabria nel medio evo," *Rivista storica italiana*, 75 (1963), 61– 63; André Guillou, *Les actes grecs de s. Maria di Messina, enquet sur les populations grecques d'Italie du sud et de Sicile (XIe–XIVe s.)* [Istituto siciliano di studi bizantini e neoellenici, Testi e monumenti, Testi 8] (Palermo, 1963), 25–27.

45. André Guillou and Walter Holtzmann, "Zwei Katepansurkunden aus Tricarico," *Quellen und Forschungen aus italienischen Archiven und Bibliotheken* 41 (1961): 26–28.

46. Giuseppe Rossi Taibbi, ed., *Vita di sant' Elia il giovane* [Istituto siciliano di studi bizantini e neoellenici, Testi e monumenti, Testi 7, Vite dei santi siciliani III] (Palermo, 1962), 120.

47. Germano Giovanelli, ed., *Vita di S. Nilo di Rossano* (Grottaferrata, 1966), par. 45, pp. 61–62. Translation is that of André Guillou, "Production and Profits in the Byzantine Province of Italy (Tenth to Eleventh Centuries): an Expanding Society," *Dumbarton Oaks Papers* 28 (1974): 92.

48. Guillou, *ibid.*

49. *Monumenta Germaniae Historica, Diplomatum regum et imperatorum Germaniae* (Hannover and Lepzig, 1888), vol. 2, part 1, no. 283, p. 330.

50. Giuseppe Schirò, ed. *Vita di s. Luca, vescovo di Isola Capo Rizzuto* [Istituto siciliano di studi bizantini e neogreci, Testi e monumenti, Testi 2, Vite dei santi siciliani, 1] (Palermo, 1954).

51. Domenico Martire Cosentino, *La Calabria sacra e profana*, lib. I, (Cosenza, 1887), quoted by G. Schirò, *op. cit.*, 46.

52. G. Schirò, *op. cit.*, 106.

FREDRIC WILLIAM SCHLATTER, S.J. BIBLIOGRAPHY OF SCHOLARLY PUBLICATIONS

"The Problem of Jn 1:3b–4a," *Catholic Biblical Quarterly* 34 (1972):54–8.

"Isocrates *Against the Sophists*, 16," *American Journal of Philology* 93 (1972):591–97.

"The Early Church: Liberator or Oppressor of Women?" *Charter* (1976):28–34.

"The Return of Peace to Ignatius' Antioch," *Journal of Theological Studies* 35 (1984): 465–69.

"The *Opus Imperfectum in Matthaeum* and the *Fragmenta in Lucam*," *Vigiliae Christianae* 39 (1985):384–92.

"The Pelagianism of the *Opus Imperfectum in Matthaeum*," *Vigiliae Christianae* 41 (1987):267–85.

"The Author of the *Opus Imperfectum in Matthaeum*," *Vigiliae Christianae* 42 (1988):364–75.

"The Text in the Mosaic of Santa Pudenziana," *Vigiliae Christianae* 43 (1989):155–65.

"Interpreting the Mosaic of Santa Pudenziana," *Vigiliae Christianae* 46 (1992):276–95.

"John Hammond Taylor," *Dictionary of North American Classicists* (Westport, 1994), 633–5.

"A Mosaic Interpretation of Jerome, *In Hiezechielem*," *Vigiliae Christianae* 49 (1995):64–81.

"The Two Women in the Mosaic of Santa Pudenziana," *Journal of Early Christian Studies* 3 (1995):1–24.

[Review of] T. F. Matthews, *The Clash of Gods*, in *Heythrop Journal* 37 (1996):110–1.

"Gerard Manley Hopkins: The Dublin Notes on Homer: Part II," *The Hopkins Quarterly* 24 (1997): 95–127.

CONTRIBUTORS

Andrew James Carriker is a doctoral candidate in history at Columbia University, where he teaches in the Core Curriculum. A former student of Fredric Schlatter, S.J., and a recipient of the Jacob K. Javits Fellowship, he is currently doing research on the library of Eusebius Pamphili.

Anne Patricia Carriker is a doctoral candidate in classical studies at Columbia University. She is a contributor to *St. Augustine through the Ages: an Encyclopedia* and a former student of Fredric Schlatter, S.J. She is presently researching the poetry of Gregory Nazianzen.

Joseph W. Day is associate professor of classical studies at Wabash College. A former student of Fredric Schlatter, S.J., he did his graduate study at Stanford University. He is the author of *The Glory of Athens: The Popular Tradition in Aelius Aristides* and articles in *Harvard Studies in Classical Philology*, *The Journal of Hellenic Studies*, and elsewhere.

William Edmund Fahey is a doctoral candidate in early Christian studies at The Catholic University of America and instructor of Greek and humanities at Brookfield Academy in Wisconsin. He is currently writing on the late antique community of Saint Maximus of Turin. His reviews and essays have appeared in *Classical Bulletin, Classical World, The Journal of the American Academy of Religion*, and *The University Bookman*.

Mary Forman, O.S.B. is scholar-in-residence at the Benedictine Spirituality Center at Sacred Heart Monastery in Richardton, North Dakota. She did her doctoral studies at the University of Toronto. Her scholarly articles have appeared in the *American Benedictine Review, Vox Benedictina, Benedictines*, and elsewhere.

William H. C. Frend is professor emeritus of eccesiastical history at the University of Glascow and bi-fellow at Gonville and Caius Colleges, Cambridge. Educated at Oxford, he is the author of many books and articles, including *The Donatist Church, Martyrdom and Persecution in the Early Church, The Rise of the Monophysite Movement, Saints and Sinners in the Early Church*, and *The Archaeology of Early Christianity*.

Charles Kannengiesser is professor emeritus of theology at Concordia University in Montréal and former fellow of the Institut Catholique. His many publications include *Sur l'incarnation du Verbe par Athanase d'Alexandrie, Politique et theologie chez Athanase d'Alexandrie*, and *Early Christian Spirituality*.

W. Eugene Kleinbauer is professor of fine arts and Near Eastern langauges and cultures at Indiana University and has recently served as Frederic Lindley Morgan Visiting Professor of Architectural Design at the University of Louisville. He took his doctorate at Princeton University. Among his book publications are *Early Christian and Byzantine Architecture: An Annotated Bibliography and Historiography, Research Guide to the History of Western Art*, and *Modern Perspectives in Western Art History: An Anthology of Twentieth Century Writings on the Visual Arts*. His many articles have appeared in *Cahiers archéologiques, Dumbarton Oaks Papers, Gesta, American Journal of Archaeology*, and elsewhere.

Douglas Kries is associate professor of philosophy at Gonzaga University. He did his doctoral studies at Boston College. He is coeditor and cotranslator, with Ernest L. Fortin and Michael W. Tkacz, of *Augustine: Political Writings*, and editor of *Piety and Humility: Essays on Religion and Early Modern Political Philosophy*. His articles have appeared in *The Thomist, The Review of Politics*, and elsewhere.

Daniel J. Nodes is director and professor of graduate liberal studies at Hamline University. He did his doctoral study at the University of Toronto and is the author of *Doctrine and Exegesis in Biblical Latin Poetry, The Fall of Man (Avitus, Books 1-3)*, and articles in *Vigiliae Christianae, American Benedictine Review, Recherches de théologie ancienne et médiévale*, and elsewhere.

Katherin A. Rogers is assistant professor of philosophy at the University of Delaware. She did her graduate study at the University of Notre Dame. She is the author of *The Neoplatonic Metaphysics and Epistemology of Anselm of Canterbury, The Anselmian Approach to God and Creation*, and articles appearing in the *American Catholic Philosophical Quarterly, International Philosophical Quarterly, The Journal of Value Inquiry*, and elsewhere.

Edward A. Synan is late professor of philosophy at the University of Toronto and senior fellow and president emeritus of the Pontifical Institute for Mediaeval Studies. He did graduate study at The Catholic University of Louvain and The Catholic University of America. Among his many publications are *The Popes and the Jews in the Middle Ages, The Works of Richard of Campsall, Adam Burley's Questiones on the De anima of Aristotle* as well as numerous articles in *Mediaeval Studies, American Catholic Philosophical Quarterly*, and elsewhere.

Robert F. Taft, S.J. is Professor of Oriental Liturgy at the Pontifical Oriental Institute in Rome. Educated there and at the Catholic University of Louvain, he is the author of many books and articles, including the multi-volume *History of the Liturgy of St. John Chrysostom* and *Beyond East and West: Problems in Liturgical Understanding*.

Roland J. Teske, S.J. is professor of philosophy at Marquette University. He did his doctoral study at the University of Toronto. Among his many publications are translations of St. Augustine's works as well as the works of William of Auvergne and Henry of Ghent. His numerous articles have appeared in *Traditio, Augustinianum, American Catholic Philosophical Quarterly, The Modern Schoolman, Augustinian Studies, International Philosophical Quarterly*, and elsewhere.

Catherine Brown Tkacz is formerly assistant editor and project manager for the *Oxford Dictionary of Byzantium*. An independent scholar, she is currently a Pew Fellow (1997-98). She did her doctoral studies at the University of Notre Dame. She is the author of *The Key to the Brescia Casket: Typology in Early Christian Art*, as well as articles in *Traditio, Revue des Études Augustiniennes, Vigiliae Christianae*, and elsewhere.

Anthony P. Via, S.J. is director of the Gonzaga-in-Florence Program and professor of history at Gonzaga University. He did his doctoral studies at the University of Wisconsin and is the editor of *Liberal Studies and Career Education* and the author of articles and reviews in the *Catholic Historical Review* and elsewhere.

INDEX